everything

(A BOOK ABOUT MANIC STREET PREACHERS)

SIMON PRICE

Virgin

First published in Great Britain in 1999 by Virgin Books
an imprint of Virgin Publishing
Thames Wharf Studios
Rainville Road
London W6 9HT

A catalogue record for this book is available from the British Library.

ISBN 0 7535 0139 2

Book design: Roger Kohn Designs

Typeset by TW Typesetting, Plymouth, Devon

Printed and bound by Creative Print and Design, Wales

This book is dedicated to Richey Edwards, wherever he may be

Our romance is having total power because we know we have nothing to lose. We're secure in the knowledge that we already lost a long time ago

CONTENTS

ACKNOWLEDGMENTS

The author would like to thank: Ian, Rob, Carolyn, Roz, Guy, Kefi, all at Virgin and Graham Smith (for patience beyond the call of duty); Martin, Terri, Caffy, Karen, Julian, Lizzie and all at Hall Or Nothing (not merely for permission, but for active encouragement); and Lucy Madison for the mother of all research jobs (and putting up with me).

For advice, assistance and inspiration: Erol Alkan, Gill Allen, Jeff Barrett, David Bennun, Fiona Bond, Daniel Booth, Darren Broome, Martin Carr, Ceri and Greg at Big Noise Studios, Carol Clerk, DI Michael Cole, Mike Connolly, Hannah Corr, Ben Daniels, Gwen Davey, Louis Eliot, Rhian Evans, OCU Foley, 'Welsh' Emma Gillingham, DI Tom Gorringe, Jane Graham, Karen Gray, Andy Gritton, Tammy Hoyle, Mitch Ikeda and his electronic baby, 'The Other' Aled Jones (master of the Internet), Patrick Jones, Clive Kelly, Dr Desmond Kelly, Martin Kelly, Steve Lamacq, Sarah LeClaire, Traci Lords, Tony Maggs, Timothy Mark, Ben Marshall, Paul Mathur, Adam Mattera and his Margot Kidder anecdote, David Mearns, Kylie Minogue, Caitlin Moran, PC Stephen Moray, Andrew Mueller, Tessa Norton, Peter Paphides, Alan Parker, Taylor Parkes, Kevin Pearce, Gillian Porter, Pricey Senior and June, John Robb, Erika Sage, Tom Sheehan, Martin Smith (Manics archivist *par excellence*), Mat Smith, Rhiannon Smith, Neil Sparnon and his Oxford history degree, Rockin' Bob Stanley, Bodyguard Steve, Chris and Rob Summers, Jody Thompson, Pete Wiggs, Sophie Woodforde, fanzine editors of the world, the MSP Nation . . .

. . . and Nicky, James, Sean and Richey.

REVOLUTION
REVOLUTION
REVOLUTION

author's introduction

'ROCK AND ROLL ADOLESCENTS STORM INTO THE STREETS OF ALL NATIONS. THEY RUSH INTO THE LOUVRE AND THROW ACID IN THE MONA LISA'S FACE, THEY OPEN ZOOS, INSANE ASYLUMS, PRISONS, BURST WATER MAINS WITH AIR HAMMERS, CHOP THE FLOOR OUT OF PASSENGER PLANE LAVATORIES, SHOOT OUT LIGHTHOUSES, TURN SEWERS INTO THE WATER SUPPLY, ADMINISTER INJECTIONS WITH BICYCLE PUMPS, THEY SHIT ON THE FLOOR OF THE UNITED NATIONS AND WIPE THEIR ASS WITH TREATIES, PACTS, ALLIANCES' – William Burroughs

The needle hit the plastic.

'. . . revolution–revolutioN–revolutiON–revolutION–revoluTION–revolUTION–revoLUTION –revOLUTION–reVOLUTION–rEVOLUTION–REVOLUTION–REVOLUTION!–REVOLUTION!!– REVOLUTION!!!'

The crudely looped Public Enemy sample whispered from the speakers. Then it got louder . . . and louder . . . until it filled the room, only to be disrupted by the static crackle and clunk of a jack plug being jammed into a cheap amp, its dial turned to eleven.

A rash of slashed Clash powerchords tore the air apart. I checked my watch. Then I checked my calendar. What year was this? Wait – what *decade* was this?

In 1991, the music scene offered a dispiriting choice between *lumpenproletarian* Madchester yobbery and neo-psychedelic Home Counties apathy; between getting blissed or blitzed on expensive weed or cheap Es. The legacy of punk, such as it was, meant bastardised Buzzcocksian happy-happy boy-girl banality made by nice bourgeois boys slumming it in Transit vans.

And yet, here was this record, cheap and tinny, incensed, incendiary, raining down alienation on the Second Summer of Love, jamming together the politics of Paris 68 and the music of London 77. How could anyone really be allowed to do this? *What the Holy Fuck was going on?*

I checked the sleeve, with that famous photograph of a broken watch, stopped at the moment of the atomic blast on Hiroshima. I remembered what the man from *NME* had said: 'How can it be retro if you're eighteen and you've never heard it before?' I remembered what the pretty one in the lacy blouse had said: 'When we jump around onstage it's not a rock 'n' roll cliché, but the geometry of contempt.' Things were starting to make sense.

The singer was hurtling, breathless now, headlong towards the end, as if afraid someone was suddenly going to inform the band that, no, they weren't really allowed to do this – before pulling the plugs. Too many words for each line, too many big ideas for one little song; I couldn't make out more than a phrase or two here and there. I thought I caught something about 'All you slut heroes offer is a fear of the future' (you what?!). I checked the sleeve again.

'Motown Junk a lifetime of slavery/Songs of love echo underclass betrayal/Stops your heart beating for 168 seconds/Stops your brain thinking for 168 seconds . . .'

Then, as the song imploded around him, the voice howled one final declaration into the void – 'WE LIVE IN URBAN HELL . . . WE DESTROY ROCK AND ROLL' – while the track slowed and skipped to a halt like a broken record player, as if someone had, indeed, pulled the power.

'Every generation has its one defining moment. We are yours' – Nicky Wire

Rock 'n' roll, at the twilight of the twentieth century, doesn't matter any more. Once upon a time, pop music *was* modern culture – devoured it, defined it, emblemised it, could stop wars and start revolutions (or at least, so it narcissistically believed). As the new millennium approaches, however, it has become merely one of the geometrically expanding abundance of leisure options available to the modern human (examine that phrase, 'leisure options', and savour the taste of death in the very words). Sure, the big sellers will continue to break sales records, beneficiaries of a *Which CD?* culture which says 'If you only buy one album this year . . .' in the knowledge that most consumers will do exactly that. Sure, the sorry circus of recycled trends will continue, like an endless *Groundhog Day*, in ever-narrowing spirals. And sure, there'll never be a shortage of willing vulture-sluts with guitars round their necks, forever shuffling the cards, raking through the embers one more time, squabbling over the chattels of the dead. But even they, in their heart of hearts, know that no one is listening. *It's over.*

Manic Street Preachers are a rock 'n' roll band from south Wales. It is, to no small degree, their point-blank denial/ingenuous ignorance of the immutable truths above, their naïve raging against the dying of the light, which makes them so compelling; which, against all odds, commands absolute attention and seizes the imagination. From day one, these Angry Young Men, these *enragés*, were an anachronism, 'a speed band in an E generation' (in Steven Wells of *NME*'s wonderfully succinct phrase), a band that thought like Chomsky and rocked like the Pistols. It is one reason why, although Manic Street Preachers are not quite, at the time of writing at least, the biggest band in the country (although they are getting there with terrifying speed), they are easily the most important.

Of course, there is literally one *Hell* of a story to tell here. So I have tried to tell it. (A lot of the time, I was there or thereabouts. If I wasn't, I have spoken to the people who were.) This is the easy part. In any case, it is a story that tells itself: a tale so intrinsically dramatic it hardly needs embroidering or sensationalising, and which can only be demeaned by sentimental clichés such as 'triumph in the face of adversity'.

But the meaning of Manic Street Preachers goes far beyond anything that mere chronology and biography, dates and diary entries, can explain. This is why I have included ten analytical essays on various aspects of the band: their sexuality, Nicky's over-zealous domestic habits, Richey's self-harm, their relationship with Wales (and America), and the fan culture they catalysed (and which now exists almost in isolation from the band itself). This is not, however, a work of uncritical hagiography; nor is it the Official Version. I have always taken the Manics to task where necessary; I have continually raised – and occasionally answered – the awkward but essential questions (a prerogative which, to their credit, the band members have always respected). This is *my* truth.*

To many, the Manics' story divides cleanly into two separate parts: the Richey Years and the Success Years; to some, the Manics are actually two separate bands. I disagree with both opinions. The same currents, the same tension between insurrectionary fervour and melancholy inertia, the same restless intelligence, run in an unbroken flow from 'Motown Junk' to 'If You Tolerate This . . .', just as they will do to whatever the band does next. If this book achieves one thing, I hope it will encourage the Manics' ever-growing legion of 'New Fans' to investigate the old stuff, and encourage their hardcore army of 'Old Fans' not to give up on them now. This is the same band. It's a soul thing. *It's not over yet*.

Manic Street Preachers always were, and still remain, more than a rock 'n' roll band, because the Manics are about more than rock 'n' roll. (As Nicky Wire once told BBC Radio Wales: 'It wasn't a band, it was a manifesto for life.') In an era when most bands were about nothing, the Manics were about *everything*: an eloquent scream, a *j'accuse* to the entire moribund millennium.

As Neil Kulkarni of *Melody Maker* perceptively put it, the Manics are '. . . the last honest white band. Seething with questions, doubling back on themselves, changing their minds every which way, thinking things through to a complexity that bewilders and paralyses.' Schizophrenia, contradiction, paradox and uncertainty: these are the only valid responses to the fragmentary chaos of the modern world. The Manics still leave me uncertain. Which means they leave me *thinking*. This is their ultimate triumph.

The needle hit the run-out groove, clicked and stopped. After 237 seconds, I was left reeling, stunned, thrilled, confused. In an instant, Manic Street Preachers were the only band in the world.

They were *everything*.

Simon Price, 1999

*Nicky Wire originally agreed to write a foreword to this book, on the condition that I would allow him to check my manuscript for factual errors before publication. In the event, however, he told me that he found the task of reading about his own history a little too difficult and emotionally painful (understandably enough), and regrettably had to bow out of the deal. Having read around one-third of the book, he told me that, although he respected my subjectivity (he signed off with 'It is YOUR truth – and that's cool'), there were also 'a lot of mistakes, some minor, some major'. Frustratingly, tantalisingly, we may never know what they are . . . until Nicky Wire tells *his* truth.

1. IN THE BEGINNING

'If you built a museum to represent Blackwood, all you could put in it would be shit. Rubble and shit' – RICHEY

THE LOCALS CALLED HIM SHIRLEY.

With his moussed-up mop of peroxide hair, testicle-restricting stretch jeans, inexpertly applied kohl and fondness for wearing (and, it must be said, *resembling*) a big girl's blouse, Nick Jones was not exactly the average bloke on Blackwood High Street.

One of those Gwent mining villages that looks like a row of Lego bricks which has been dropped, randomly and incongruously, halfway up a hillside by a careless God, Blackwood (pop. 7,300) lies off the A472 between Newbridge and Ystrad Mynach on the side of the Sirhowy Valley, deep inside an isolated pocket of the United Kingdom where a number-one crop and a bushy moustache are unambiguous talismans of *hetero*sexuality, and where every fourteen-year-old eagerly cultivates upper-lip bumfluff as soon as hormones allow. Dressing the way he did, Nick Jones was cruising for a serious queerbashing but, at nearer 7ft than 6, the lads tended to leave him alone – just in case.

Born on 20 January 1969 into a 'lower-middle-class' family, Nicholas Allen Jones was always tall for his age. With his gangling, wiry frame, Nick was quickly able to compete at football on equal terms with his brother Patrick, four years his senior, and invariably forced Patrick to keep goal. Throughout the long cricketing summers, Patrick had his revenge: Nick always had to bowl (until Patrick discovered girls and left cricket behind). Although he took rudimentary guitar lessons at school, sport, rather than pop, was Nick's childhood obsession. While most of his friends were plastering their walls with images of Debbie Harry and Adam Ant, Nick's first pin-ups were golfer Seve Ballesteros, athlete Steve Ovett and Tottenham Hotspur FC. Patrick remembers Nick – a gifted, speedy attacker and winger – as 'the temperamental, George Best type'. Always able to dance rings around the older boys in park matches, by the age of fourteen Nick had been made captain of Wales Schoolboys, and was invited to take part in trials at Arsenal. Only a failed medical test at Highbury (thanks to a dodgy back which ran in the Jones family) stood between him and a potential future as the next Ian Rush.

Nick's closest friend, one of the older participants in the park kickabouts, lived just two hundred yards down the road, but in a relatively 'posher' area than Jones's 'scummier' (his description) district. Richard James Edwards was born on 22 December 1967, at the height of the festive season, and narrowly avoided being named Christmas – a fate which later befell one of his cousins. His mother Sherry and father Graham ran the high street's sole hair salon (Graham had previously spent four years in the parachute regiment).

To the other children, Richard Edwards was 'Richey'; to Nick Jones, he was 'Teddy Edwards' ('because he was so cuddly'). A shy, polite kid, who kept himself to himself, he got on better with his dog Snoopy than with any human. As is not uncommon in valley communities, Richey grew up in a house which had been in the family for eight generations (his earliest memory was seeing his father put coal on the open fire), together with his grandfather and ailing grandmother, and his mother, father and younger sister Rachel. When Richey was ten, his grandmother died, and the family left the ancestral home for a modern bungalow at the bottom of a cul-de-sac.

The valleys of south Wales have always been a stronghold of non-conformist religion: Methodism, Baptism and various other sub-denominations. Like many Blackwood families, the Edwards were devout Methodists, and, from the age of seven, the reluctant Richey was dragged to the local tin-shack chapel three times a week. By the age of thirteen, he could recite huge chunks of Isaiah and Luke, parrot-fashion.

'I never saw the point of organised religion,' he would later bitterly attest, '– some fat eighty-year-old cunt on stage, screaming at you, naming you, humiliating you.' As soon as he was old enough to refuse, he stopped going to church altogether, and did not set foot inside one again until the day his grandfather died.

'You don't make any true friends beyond the age of seventeen' – JAMES

One mile down the road in neighbouring Pontllanfraith, James Dean Bradfield, like his friend Richey Edwards, also had a near-miss with Christian-name hell. Monty Bradfield, a carpenter by trade, and his wife Sue, who worked in a betting shop, spent months arguing over what to christen their offspring. Right up until the day of his birth, 21 February 1969 (also the day of Malcolm X's assassination), Monty was set on calling his son Clint Eastwood. Luckily for the baby, the common sense of Sue – who argued that if the infant *had* to be named after a film star, at least let it be one who wouldn't get him beaten up at school – prevailed.

James was one of those kids who acquires nicknames like other kids acquire scabs on their knees. Along with the obvious (and enduring) 'Bradders', he suffered 'Beaker', 'Prof', 'Crossfire', 'Terence McCann' and 'Radar', mostly deriving from his cross-eyes or the glasses he wore to correct them. By his own admission, he was 'a Woody Allen-esque little nerd' although, even if the other boys enjoyed calling him names, they weren't so quick to pick a fight with him. He may have sung with the school choir but, like his dad before him, James was tough despite being short (another of his nicknames was 'He-Man'). During the Falklands War of 1982, he briefly became obsessed with joining the army, and, despite the fact that he showed no signs of approaching the minimum height requirement, started running and lifting weights in preparation.

After reading George Orwell's *Animal Farm* James snapped out of his militaristic fantasies, but he still kept up the physical training, enduring the loneliness of the long-distance runner to become a promising marathon competitor, and entertaining visions of becoming a world-famous athlete. 'Nick and I had this dream that I was going to bring glamour to the steeplechase,' he later told *Select*. 'I mean, no fucker's interested in the steeplechase. The angle was sort of the illustrious, industrious Welsh mountain goat. The thing is, down at the local sports ground, there was this 400m track, but it only had two steeplechase hurdles. Nick would just stand there and watch me. I don't know, perhaps he was taking the piss – I mean, 5ft 5, I was never going to win a steeplechase, was I?'

James's first true loves were football (in particular Brian Clough's glamorous Nottingham Forest team of the late 70s/early 80s) and rock music, in that order. The first record he bought, however, was 'My Old Piano' by Diana Ross, a prime slice of Motown junk, which earned him the mockery of the local metal kids for the next six months when one of them, a certain 'Dids', caught him sneaking it out of Woolworths. 'For the next month, I was a poof,' he later winced. James rapidly learnt to keep his eclectic tastes a secret.

James's cousin Sean was also small for his age. Born on 30 July 1970, he was, then as now, 'the quiet one'. When, at the age of ten, Sean had to watch his parents going through a painful divorce, his mother, Jenny Moore, decided that the best thing for him would be to live with her sister, Sue Bradfield, who lived nearby. Although Jenny visited regularly, Sean was made to feel part of the Bradfield family, and he and James – already close friends – grew inseparable, and more like brothers than cousins. The Bradfields happily made room for the new arrival, putting up a bunk bed for Sean to share with his cousin James. This same historic bunk bed, in which James would later lose his virginity (one trusts that poor Sean was not trying to sleep underneath at the time), and in which Sean would later be violently sick after drinking the family whisky, would be kept waiting for the pair's return well into their adulthood; it was finally dismantled in late 1996.

James and Sean discovered music together, and bought their guitars on the same day. It is a little-known fact that Nick Jones actually gave James his first lesson, but pupil fast outstripped tutor, and James set about learning the Rolling Stones' *Exile on Main Street* from beginning to end. Sean's approach to music was rather more formal and classical. He took up the trumpet, studied for an A Level in Music, and joined the South Wales Jazz Orchestra (based in nearby Newbridge), becoming the youngest cornet player in the orchestra's history.

The four all attended the same junior school (Pontllanfraith), comprehensive (Oakdale) and tertiary college (Cross Keys). When they weren't learning together, they would play together. Usually, they'd meet by a man-made lake called Pen-Y-Fan pond, built when the mines closed, '. . . but now the water has turned green and slimy,' Nick ruefully recalled in *Vox*. 'They put two thousand fish in it, but they died. There's a whirlpool in the middle where about two people drown every year.'

Speaking to *Time Out*, Richey would later give a poetical description of the dismal vista. 'They try to put grass over the slagheaps, and every time it rains they turn into muddy slides – the landscape is swallowed by a huge slap of blackness.'

'Everything happened there,' says James. 'Bonfire night, Hallowe'en, a lot of people lost their virginity there. If there was a fight between Pontllanfraith and Springfield (*populated, one imagines, by Matt Groening kids with yellow skin and bulging eyes*), it happened on this slagheap. It's gone now, levelled. When I go back, what strikes me is there's less places for people to hide. Hide and just be innocent. Lose their innocence too.'

'Adrift in cheap dreams, don't stop the rain/Numbed out in piss towns, just wanna dig their graves . . .' – 'MOTOWN JUNK'

Despite the desolate surroundings, the boys' childhoods were happy – even 'magical', according to Richey. 'All I remember is green fields, blue skies and Clarks shoes with the compass in the bottom,' Nick reminisces. The foursome's fondest memories are of unofficial football matches on the pitch owned by the nearby Gossard corset factory, in which the Pontllanfraith end of town (James and Sean) would compete against the Woodfieldside end (Richey and Nick) for a trophy unearthed by Nick's dad on a rubbish tip. The trophy was actually for crown green bowls, '. . . but we ran down the street with it anyway when we won!'

'We generally had a blissful childhood, really,' Nick would later tell *Melody Maker*. '. . . our childhoods were *too* good – we weren't just reading books or watching films, experiencing second-hand culture, we were, y'know, building dams, messing around in dirt, things like that, which, looking back, seemed much more worthwhile.'

Blissful, yes, but – crucially – uneventful. While Blackwood may have been as good or bad a place as any to be a small child, it was no place to be a teenager. There were no clubs, no leisure centres (unless you counted a snooker hall) and, when the boys were about twelve, even the town's single-screen cinema, described by Richey as 'the poorest and most crap in the country', shut down. (Years later, cinema would return to Blackwood, with grim irony, in the hollowed-out shells of former miners' institutes.) Escape was not an option, either: the nearest big town, Newport, was an hour's bus ride away, and the last bus home left at 9 p.m., making nights out near-impossible. Every evening, gangs of youths would hang out in shop doorways on Blackwood's high street, or would congregate at the town's hottest nightspot: the 24-hour garage. There was, literally, nothing else to do – with inevitable results. 'Richey's dad's hair salon has been burgled eight times,' Nick later recalled, 'and there is nothing to steal but shampoo. They just go down to the park and empty the bottles on the grass.'

For Blackwood natives, this pervading, pernicious boredom follows relentlessly through into adulthood (perhaps non-coincidentally, south Wales has more satellite dishes per head than anywhere else in the UK). There is practically nothing to do but get drunk. As early as 1842, Blackwood could claim the highest pub-to-person ratio in Wales, with one drinking establishment for every five inhabitants. To this day, Gwent has the highest alcohol-poisoning rate in the UK; a statistic that bears a chillingly modern echo in the fact that an estimated £1 million worth of heroin is sold on the streets of Mid-Glamorgan each year.

Against this background, the gang of four bided their time and studied hard, first at Oakdale Comprehensive and then at Cross Keys Tertiary College. Nick achieved ten good O Levels in all the usual subjects (plus, unusually, Political Constitution), and two A grades and one B in English, Sociology and Politics at A Level. Richey was even more of a model pupil, eventually leaving with ten O Levels (all straight As) and three A Levels (also perfect A grades).

Sean was a shy, withdrawn student who Richey, for one, considered a 'totally scary' figure. Although 'massively gifted', he wouldn't answer what he considered to be stupid questions from teachers and was intermittently relegated to the CSE stream as a result, although he stayed long enough to achieve his A Level in Music. All four spent most of their time in the top class, the 'Is' (the 'I' standing for Islwyn, the parliamentary constituency in which they lived), and both Nick and Richey were put forward by the school for Oxbridge entry.

What none of their teachers realised, however, was that these star pupils loathed school. As Nick has since confirmed, it was 'the most depressing time for all of us'. By his own admission, he was something of a 'sickly mammy's boy' – he would sometimes sit on his mother Irene's bed for hours, just watching her do her hair and make-up – and was never accepted as one of the 'cool' kids. Some used to call him 'Joey Deacon', after the elderly cerebral palsy sufferer who, in one of the worst miscalculations in television history, was regularly invited on to *Blue Peter* to encourage children to understand the disabled. Others called him 'Gaylord'.

Richey, in particular, found comprehensive life unbearable. From the age of thirteen, his restless mind was numbed by the dull curriculum (with the exception of English, where he discovered Orwell's *1984*), and he was horrified by the school's attempts to coerce all the brighter students into attending career talks by representatives of the local branches of Nat West, Barclays, Midland and Lloyds.

For James, the solution was simple: don't turn up. In his later years at school, a cross would appear more often than a tick next to the name 'Bradfield' on the register (he decided to turned up for the very last day, but found the gates locked: he'd got the date wrong).

For conscientious Richey, such direct action was inconceivable. Instead, he would sometimes faint during assembly just to avoid the soul-destroying day ahead. At around this time, he was also struck by a bad case of acne. 'Six months before that, I'd made my first vain attempt at going out . . . then acne descended, and it was like, bye bye!' And as he commented later: 'Everything was going wrong. I just hit the wall.'

'Where we come from, there is natural melancholy in the air' – RICHEY

Growing up in small-town south Wales in the early 1980s, you never saw your home town on television; never read its name in print. Even if something newsworthy were to happen – then or today – you might never hear about it, as topographical anomalies mean that many households cannot receive local television news (their aerials point to the west of England instead). For all you knew, the place you came from might as well not exist.

In 1984, however, something of note *did* happen in Blackwood. Margaret Thatcher's Conservative Government, hell-bent on converting Britain to 'cheaper, safer' nuclear power and itching to provoke one final war against trade unionism, began shutting down Britain's coal mines with terrifying enthusiasm. The Miners' Strike that ensued was one of the bloodiest, most bitter industrial disputes in British history. In the Blackwood area alone, twelve pits were closed. Suddenly, Blackwood was a mining town with no mines.

South Wales had always had a proud tradition of militant socialism, dating back to the previous pit dispute when Winston Churchill – no hero in south Wales – sent in the troops to crush the miners. One coal community, Maerdy, was christened 'Little Moscow' because its library boasted one of the finest collections of Marxist literature in the country and because its mayoress was a communist.

The Miners' Strike of 1984–5 radicalised anyone growing up at the time. During school lunch-hours, loose change was collected for the National Union of Mineworkers in orange plastic buckets. For Nick, James, Sean and Richey, the conflict between scabs and strikers was a formative experience, as Nick remembers: 'If a man went back to work, his house would be covered in paint. Fair enough. I'm proud that the Welsh miners were the last miners to go back to work. Quite cool.'

The four could not help but be affected. 'When I became old enough to understand anything of it,' Nick would later claim, 'I went into Marxism. Marx and Lenin were as attractive to us as any pop stars.' Sean even played trumpet on NUM marches.

Inevitably, demoralised by police batterings and starved back to work, the miners were eventually defeated. The only mine to remain 'open' was The Big Pit, a poignant museum to a prosperous past. Nick, James, Sean and Richey resolved to heed the lessons of the miners' valiant but doomed defiance. 'We didn't want to rely on "the passion of a true heart",' said James. 'We didn't want to be bludgeoned like our predecessors in history.'

In two short years, the Gwent valleys had become one of the most deprived areas of Britain, with a rate of unemployment approaching 80 per cent. Blackwood attempted to reinvent itself as a centre of manufacturing and light industry. A succession of companies – Aiwa, Pot Noodle, Toshiba, Sony – set up factories in the area, attracted by a desperate, willing (and therefore cheap) workforce, to make electrical toys that the employees could never have afforded to buy for themselves. The companies hired unemployed miners on three-month contracts, rehiring them after that period if required (and therefore avoiding the need to pay redundancy settlements).

Even the area's socialist tradition was compromised. The local MP, Labour leader Neil Kinnock (who lived in the same street as James and Sean), had shunned the miners' cause, to Richey's disgust. 'Everything Neil Kinnock stands for is everything my grandfather would have spat at: desperate craving for power at any cost. Labour were told by a right-wing press that they had to move towards the centre. But they should have gone more extreme. In areas like Blackwood, Labour's always going to win even if a cheese sandwich stands for election.'

For the four teenagers, all this was not a remote, theoretical phenomenon, and the aftermath of the Miners' Strike directly affected their families. For instance, when Nick's dad Alan left the army, he had become a miner; then, when the pits started to close, he had to retrain as a builder. James was moved by the common sight of great, hulking men carrying bags of shopping from Tesco and Somerfield, when once they had carried coal. 'The thing that really affected me,' he remembers, 'was when they closed the mines down and they were sending fifty-year-old men to Restart courses. They were learning to type, and their hands were so big they couldn't even hit the keys.'

'Art is revolt against fate' – ANDRÉ MALRAUX

Disowned by the outside world, politicised by the class struggle on their doorstep and frustrated by their provincial prison, the four friends locked themselves away and manufactured their own parallel universe. In Richey's words: 'Blackwood is a shithole, where the only way to escape was to create your own reality.'

Throughout their teens, Nick, James, Sean and Richey would gather in one or other of their houses (usually James's and Sean's bedroom), and voraciously devour twentieth-century culture. The absolute absence of alternative diversions offered them little choice. This wasn't anything as glamorous as ennui, just sheer hair-tearing tedium. As Richey told me: 'It's just boredom. I don't mean a *Generation X/Less Than Zero* thing, driving around in a white Mercedes and feeling sorry for yourself – but real boredom.' And they endured it together. 'For the first eighteen years of our lives,' said Richey, 'we were living in an environment where there's nothing to do. We'd just go round each others' houses, talk, read and play and that's it, like 24 hours the same every fuckin' day.'

This had a dual effect, the first aspect being to form a solid bond between the four individuals. In addition to the familial closeness of James and Sean, Nick and Richey – both born under the sign of Capricorn ('They have an aura of seriousness and aren't overly jolly; although many have sharp wits and are funny, underneath the laughter one can sense the profundity at their core; they worry a great deal and are often beset by a certain oppressive heaviness which they find difficult to shed') – became more like twins than friends, and, completing the circle, Nick and James were inseparable (as the latter told *Q*, 'I was Baldrick to his Blackadder'). The second consequence of having nothing to do was a crucial sense of apartness from the rest of the town's populace. 'Me and Richey especially were attracted to being clever to prove that we were better than the other . . . plebs, to be nasty about it,' confessed Nick, suggesting that their feelings of class solidarity did not prevent a certain insular snobbishness.

When *NME* published its '100 Best LPs of All Time' in 1985, the foursome set out to own the lot, yet they in no way considered music to be superior to other art forms. In their relativistic man-made pantheon of heroes, all authors, actors, fine-artists, poets, politicians and pop stars were interchangeable, and of equal value. George Orwell's *Homage to Catalonia*, Albert Camus' *L'Etranger*, Tennessee Williams' *A Streetcar Named Desire*, William Burroughs' *Naked Lunch*, J.D. Salinger's *Catcher in the Rye*, Sylvia Plath's *The Bell Jar* and Bret Easton Ellis's *American Psycho*; the paintings of Munch, Bacon and Warhol; the philosophies of Timothy Leary, Valerie Solanas and Guy Debord; the beat verse of Ginsberg and Kerouac; Philip Larkin's *High Windows*, Rimbaud's *Ma Bohème*, Greil Marcus's *Lipstick Traces*; classic albums by Guns N'Roses, Public Enemy, Sex Pistols and The Who; *Apocalypse Now, Rumblefish, A Matter of Life and Death*; biographies on the Rolling Stones and Kiss; *Kes, The Loneliness of the Long Distance Runner*; The Clash's *Rude Boy* on video . . . Crucially, each work was treated with the same intense seriousness: each was dissected, discussed and analysed.

'Everything we discovered,' Nick explained, 'from *Betty Blue* to Malcolm Lowry . . . came fast to us. We are a microcosm. We get bored so easily that we put into three years everything that took the Rolling Stones twenty. It's just the way we are; we are modern people.'

Having assimilated the works of the greatest minds of the modern age, the next logical step was to try their hands at writing. For Nick, this came naturally. A leading light in the school debating society, he had always been highly literate (Patrick Jones remembers catching him writing verse at the age of twelve). Patrick, whose day job in

Blackwood library provided the four with all the books they needed, was already writing avant-garde verse on the alienation and meaninglessness of life in post-industrial Wales. Patrick's influence on his younger friends cannot be measured, although the inspiration flowed both ways. One day Patrick came back from the pub feeling depressed, and saw fifteen-year-old Nick in bed writing a poem. 'I remember thinking: "He's got the right idea." Even though he's my younger brother, he paved the way a bit.'

Drawing on Patrick's cut-up, free-association style (as well as on the influences of Morrissey, the Sex Pistols and Philip Larkin), 'Aftermath 84', Nick's first serious attempt at poetry, was inspired, inevitably, by the Miners' Strike and by the recriminations, betrayal and mistrust that it caused (one line of the poem berated Margaret Thatcher as 'The woman that fatefully sowed this seed'). Nervously, Nick showed it to James. The next day, Bradfield gave it back to him with the scribbled comment: 'These deserve to be the next Morrissey/Marr.' The pair began co-writing verse which they both wincingly remember as being 'dreadful'. Richey, meanwhile, wrote a 24-page poem, 'Another Dead Eleven O'clock', and collaborated with Nick and Sean on a play called *Tearproof*.

This hive of activity caused James to conceive the ambitious idea of an art collective, 'The Blue Generation', loosely based on Andy Warhol's 'Exploding Plastic Inevitable'. The collective consisted of himself, Nick, Richey, Sean and Patrick, together with a couple of James's friends, a dancer and an actor (for a while, James even fancied himself as a thespian), both of whom have since gone on to greater things. Patrick, too, has become a well-respected poet, with several volumes of his verse – *The Eloquence of Screaming* (described by one critic as 'the literary equivalent of *Generation Terrorists*'), *The Guerrilla Tapestry* and *Mute Communion* – reprinted several times; a CD collection, *Commemoration & Amnesia*, on sale; and a play, *Everything Must Go*, in production. Just as he once helped his brother's generation to express themselves, Patrick now runs a young writers' group in Blackwood.

Cocooned in the Bradfield/Moore bedroom, and inspired by the glamour of Duran Duran and Hanoi Rocks, the gang first started experimenting with make-up – for their own private amusement, rather than to shock the locals. Sadly, Richey's parents couldn't provide them with free glam-rock hairdos in their salon (blue rinses for senior citizens being their forte). Instead, the four improvised, hacking at their own hair and spiking it with liquid soap and Coca-Cola in an attempt to look like Sid Vicious.

'We were never particularly victimised,' Nick admits, 'because no one saw us.' When he and Richey did venture outside, their utterly un-Blackwood image drew comments like: 'Look at those fags over there! Go and suck each other's dicks in the corner, you faggots!' Nick was only beaten up once, for wearing a Kylie Minogue T-shirt (when Kylie heard this story a decade later, she exclaimed, 'Bless! Bless him entirely! Oh, God! *Triple* bless!'). Rather than hide from the abuse, Nick almost seemed to relish it. 'I didn't look at those people and think "worthless scum". If they've been working in a factory all week then they've got every right to get smashed out of their brains and take the piss out of my haircut.' In any case, he loved turning heads. 'Dressing up is just the ultimate escape,' he told *Gay Times*. 'Nothing could excite me except attention, so I'd dress up as much as I could.'

When they ventured into the outside world, the quartet became notorious as the village weirdos: Nick bleached and warpainted, James in leather trench coat and big boots, Richey wearing the 80s indie uniform of fluffed-up hair and long overcoat, looking for all the world like a junior member of Echo and the Bunnymen (a big favourite with him, James and Sean, and the first band they ever went to see). They would troop along dutifully whenever one of the big alternative rock bands of the day – The Cult, Gary Numan, Spear of Destiny, Bob Mould, Sonic Youth, The Smiths (Nick's personal favourites) and The Waterboys (whose fan club James once considered joining) – visited Cardiff University. They also frequented the Square Club in Cardiff, where they once saw The Stone Roses play to 24 people. James even ventured as far as the west country for the WOMAD festival, which he found a deeply depressing experience: rain, students, James, veggieburgers, Bunnymen, more students and more rain.

Mostly, however, their social life was limited to a quiet pint at The Red Lion or the Bierkeller or, more often, to an even

Situationist graffiti, Paris, May 1968.

quieter cuppa. Sold on the attractive myth of Parisian left-bank café culture, they would gather around a table in Dorothy's Café, the local working men's greasy-spoon diner, and pose meaningfully, holding copies of Marx's/Engels's *Communist Manifesto* and Debord's *Situationiste Internationale*, making one cup of tea last an hour. There was, they later admitted, something slightly sad about their insular reluctance to participate in the normal teenage pastimes of drinking, dancing and snogging. 'We'd be sitting on the bed on a Friday night discussing politics and music,' remembers James, 'and we'd hear the clip-clop of high heels on the street outside and think, "This *isn't* healthy."'

Not that their interests were purely cerebral. Nick, Richey and Patrick spent as much time playing video games as they did reading novels. On one occasion they acquired a hardcore porn video, which they watched at home every lunch-time for three weeks, until it got boring and they reverted to *Bullseye* and *Pebble Mill*. They were also avid armchair followers of football, golf, cricket and darts (Nick once tried to get an autograph from the obese Scots darts maestro, Jocky Wilson. To his eternal pride, Wilson told him to 'fuck off').

James was always the most outgoing of the gang. In the space of one year, he drank his first pint of beer (not counting a couple of sneaky cans from the offy, down by the railway track), had his first fight and his first snog, all in the same pub. Nick has since claimed, 'Me, Richey and James were retards when it came to girls . . . very, very shy,' and that 'Most people thought we were gay, so they didn't even bother.' Brother Patrick, however, tells a different story, insisting that far from being the 'social cripple' he has portrayed, Nick was always popular at the youth club disco, where he went to the lengths of devising a special dance routine to Billy Joel's 'Uptown Girl' to impress the females. When Nick was sixteen he met Rachel, 'my first love and my last', the girl with whom he lost his virginity two years later. ('It was a reasonably pleasurable experience, actually. It was one of those slipped-in-by-accident things when you know it's going to happen and you pretend you don't know. And I ended up marrying her. So I must have made some impression.') Sean, too, had a steady girlfriend, Rhian. Only Richey showed no apparent interest in the opposite sex (the feeling, perhaps due to Richey's troublesome complexion, appears to have been mutual). As a child, he had been shown a porn magazine by a friend called Brian Summers; after ten minutes he had had to run outside, feeling sick.

One Friday night in 1986, Channel Four screened a documentary, directed by Anthony Wilson, on the tenth anniversary of punk. It was a catalytic conversion: for James, the programme – particularly the vintage film of a Clash concert – was a road-to-Damascus revelation, while Nick preferred the Pistols ('They were more arrogant, more stare-you-in-the-face-and-psyche-you-out'). The foursome had toyed before with the idea of making music, and had even recorded a few rudimentary demo tapes, but this was the real lightbulbs-over-heads moment. The following morning, James and Nick caught their regular bus to Cardiff (for them, as for just about every teenager within a fifty-mile radius, Saturdays meant a one-hour bus ride on a ritual pilgrimage to the relative cosmopolitan glamour of the Welsh capital), but this time they took their guitars. When they

The Manics' very earliest demo recordings, made in two main bursts over the winters of 1985–6 and 1986–7, have recently become available on a Dutch bootleg (James, apparently, was horrified). They are, to be euphemistic, for fans only – but assuming that you are a fan, they do make fascinating listening.

The first handful, from 1985–6, are particularly tinny recordings and the lyrics are frustratingly difficult to make out, but the music is heavily influenced by the jangly indiepop of the then-dominant cutie scene. The next sessions, from 1986–7, possess more recognisable elements of the now-familiar Manics sound. 'Whiskey Psychosis', possibly a eulogy to Bradfield's beloved Jameson's, is a fairly transparent xerox of 'Clash City Rockers' (there is a touching moment at the end when James can be heard to say 'All right, Nick?'). 'England Is a Bitch' features a chord change which would later be resurrected as the intro to 'Enola/Alone'. A sketchy version of 'R.P. McMurphy', the earliest song to survive into the band's 'proper' career, also crops up for the first time.

James's guitar playing is clearly already more than competent. Technically it isn't showy, but neither is it primitive. If anything, it is more complex than the early MSP singles – raising the intriguing theory that they pretended to be less musically proficient than they were (and opposing the accepted wisdom that they 'became more accomplished with time'): they could have made 'Bohemian Rhapsody' if they had wished, but they chose to make 'White Riot' instead.

A number of slightly later demos have been available on bootleg for years

arrived, they headed straight for the city's quaint Victorian shopping arcades, and began bawling out rough-and-ready acoustic versions of punk classics (the thought of James Dean Bradfield, bare-chested and shaven-headed, screaming 'Garageland' at startled old ladies, is enough to make you wish that security video cameras were more common in the mid-1980s). But the performance was never, *never* for money. Anyone who dared to toss coins their way risked a barrage of Bradfield/Jones abuse.

The foursome had found its vocation. Previously, they had considered directing their restless creative energies into authorship. Now, fired and inspired by the DIY ethic of their punk forebears, they decided that their chosen mode of expression would be music. For the first time, the idea of forming a band was seriously discussed. 'Where we came from, pop and football have always been the classic escape routes. We were a group of four friends against the rest of the world . . . We were a band before we even picked up guitars.'

By now Richey Edwards was fifty miles away, studying Political History at the University of Wales in Swansea.

In his very first term, he broke a lifetime vow of temperance and began drinking neat vodka 'for purely practical reasons', just to get himself to sleep amid the usual undergraduate rowdiness in the multi-storey hall of residence where he lived. 'I used to get woken up constantly by pissed-up students coming home thinking it would be really funny to rampage up and down the corridors knocking on everybody's door and decid-ing to have a party in the kitchen at one in the morning. Pathetic!'

Richey led a hermit-like existence –

(look out for 'Lipstick Traces', from Media Slut Productions, and 'Turning Rebellion into Money', on Dalmation Records). Again, the principal value that these tracks hold for the Manics trainspotter is historical: to spy phrases that would crop up on later works, to trace the way the band cannibalised bits of 'Go Buzz Baby Go' and 'Behave Yourself Baby' to create 'Motorcycle Emptiness' and to discover that, contrary to subsequent statements, they did write love songs ('Just Can't Be Happy' being just one example). This time, they were ripping off the Pistols: 'Anti-Love' is highly reminiscent of 'Holidays in the Sun'.

The early demos contain also several themes which would recur throughout the band's career: androgyny ('Love in a Make-up Bag'), self-destructiveness ('Eating Myself from Inside'), anti-establishmentarianism ('England Is a Bitch', not a Welsh nationalist number) and self-prostitution (the line 'I was born to exploit'). Above all, titles like 'Where Have All the Good Things Gone' and 'Dying a Thousand Deaths', and lines like 'I just want to lay down in my bed' show that, even in their adolescent prime – the 'best' years of their lives – the Manics were prematurely prone to morbidity and melancholia.

Derivative they may have been (The Clash, Sex Pistols, the cuties) – but which nascent band isn't? Crucially, the Manics, unlike many of their peers (The Stone Roses, The Charlatans), do not have an embarrassing goth, mod or teddy-boy past. They arrived fully formed, with a well-defined aesthetic and a clear direction.

They knew where they were going.

he actually wore slippers – and rarely socialised: 'There'd be big dub reggae discos, but I'd be in bed after *Minder*.' On one now-legendary occasion, Richey painted himself white and dressed up as a sperm for Rag Week (years later, with beautiful symmetry, an Italian fashion mag would ask him to do exactly that once again for a photo shoot).

Generally, though, he was uninterested in the life of the Students' Union, and found the hedonistic attitude of his fellow students disgraceful. As he later told *NME*: 'I despised those people who sat in the bar going, "Ooh, I was really rebellious today, I didn't go to one lesson!" I thought university would be full of people who wanted to sit around and talk about books and it wasn't like that at all. It was full of people who wanted to sit around and do as little as possible other than have as much fun as they could. But I never equated university with fun. I thought it was about reading and learning, but for most people it was about getting laid.'

Richey, by contrast, arrived and left with his virginity intact.

One year after Richey's arrival at university, in September 1987, it was Nick's turn. His first shot at higher education lasted all of a fortnight. Like Richey, he had been put forward by the school for Oxford and Cambridge, but – as is mysteriously so often the case with pupils from the state system – their applications were not deemed acceptable. By the summer, Nick's A-Level teachers having predicted low grades for him, the best offer on the table was a course at Portsmouth Polytechnic. Jones loathed the place instantly, failed to attend a single class, and went on what he describes as: 'a massive bender, a Club 18–30 holiday'. During this lost weekend, his exam results came through: an A and two Bs. He deserved better than Portsmouth.

Nick's mother, Irene, telephoned the University of Wales (where her other son Patrick had studied), and did some hard bargaining. The following week, Nick had enrolled on a Politics course, and was living in a loft with two sporty jock types. Eventually he moved in with Richey in a flat on King Edward Road, a student district high above the city.

Student life was even less to Nick's liking than it was to Richey's. University was the first time Nick had encountered glaring social differences: '. . . the privileges of other classes and how they treat those privileges very lightly. Someone having a car seemed unbelievable, let alone having a BMW. Those sort of things were an eye-opener.' (Nick, like Richey, was one of the last generations of the 'Educated Poor', a social class in danger of extinction post student grants.) In three years, he didn't visit the Students' Union once (a fact of which he remains proud), virtually never drank, never took drugs, never stole a single shopping trolley or traffic cone, and made just one friend, a certain 'Psycho', who still remains a good friend to this day.

In fact, Nick did only two clichéd student things. The first was becoming a three-year vegetarian and then reverting to meat-eating on the day he left university. The second was finding himself stranded six miles from home at kicking-out time after a rare visit to a pub, making a pathetic attempt to hotwire a car, passing out drunk, and waking up in a police cell. He escaped with a caution.

Nick didn't really want to be a student at all. 'A lot of it was three more years of not knowing what you want to do with your life. I've literally never done a day's work in my life, not even a paper round, so I couldn't handle going to work in an office. And I guess a lot of going to university is to please your parents, and they'd always been pretty good to me.'

He went home every weekend, and wrote to James and Sean three times during the week. Unlike Richey, he couldn't even find solace in the library. 'I wanted to study what I was interested in rather than following a course. And the lecturers were terrible, more interested in writing books than actually teaching.'

A descent into chronic absenteeism ensued. 'By the second year, people thought I'd actually left because I didn't turn up.' When he should have been studying, he skived off to play golf with Richey, and insisted on looking the part, even wearing ill-advised casual Pringle sweaters. A harmless enough pastime, but Nick's other passion was rather more dangerous. When the weather didn't favour golf, he would abscond to the city centre and spend all day in amusement arcades, feeding the fruities. He became something of an expert, yet still found himself £3,000 in the red. Something to do with putting £50 worth of tokens in, to win £4 worth of tokens for buying meals (mathematics never had been his strong point). He made one feeble attempt to rectify the deficit by working for the Post Office at Christmas, but even that was hopeless: 'My dad ended up helping me deliver the letters. The bag was too heavy, and I just didn't know where I was going.'

'Boredom is the only reason we exist' – RICHEY

James and Sean each had the chance to taste the academic life (James to study Philosophy, Sean to attend Music College), but both sacrificed the opportunity for the sake of the proposed band. Sean took a dull desk job in the Civil Service, and James found himself drawing the dole. For a while, it looked as though the rock dreams of 'The Blue Generation' were drifting away.

James, more than the others, kept the flame burning. By night, he served Brains Dark to the ex-miners in the local boozer (kindly dipping into his cash-in-hand wages and posting fivers and tenners to Nick to help with his gambling debts). By day, while his parents were out at work, he shut the living-room curtains and learnt another classic album from beginning to end: Guns N'Roses' *Appetite for Destruction*. Oddly, James now remembers this self-imprisonment as 'an incredibly romantic time'.

Reunited for the summer vacation of 1988, the highlight of the quartet's week was Wednesday morning, the day on which *NME*, *Melody Maker* and *Sounds* arrived in Blackwood (to this day, Nick has an unnerving habit of quoting reviews back to journalists, verbatim). Week after week, they would read the purple prose lavished upon the critics' latest indie darlings and would order the latest Sonic Youth or Primal Scream single from Spiller's in Cardiff, and week after week they would be crushingly disappointed by the reality behind the hype. They often made the eighty-mile round trip to an indie club called Raffles in Port Talbot (it's been written out of history now but, for all their rockist rhetoric, the four were basically indie kids at heart) to see bands like Talulah Gosh, The Soup Dragons, The Primitives and The Close Lobsters at first hand, often missing the last train home and sleeping under railway bridges with the hoboes. Richey once went as far as Nottingham to see The Jesus and Mary Chain.

Yet, without fail, they would arrive home and wonder why they had bothered, as Richey bitterly testified in *Select*: 'Bands were written about in the music press as if they would change your life. You'd go and see them, and there would be twenty people there, and the bands would be fucking shit. Every song, total and utter rubbish. We just found it sad, forlorn. Then we would go home and look at our old videos of The Who and The Clash, and that meant so much more to us.'

The only band with which they felt any affinity was Birdland (briefly popular peroxide-punk upstarts from Tamworth), who played Merthyr Tydfil Town Hall, but even that turned out to be depressingly apolitical. The foursome looked at their record collections (Pistols, Presley, Stones); they looked at the front covers of the indie press (Wonder Stuff, Happy Mondays, Ride). These were second-class times indeed. Something had to be done.

In the absence of a band they could believe in, there was only one course of action: to form one themselves.

At first, the band was very much James Dean Bradfield's baby. Casting himself as lead guitarist, James assembled a line-up consisting of Nick Jones, rechristened 'Nicky Wire' (because of his wiry frame) on Telecaster rhythm guitar; Sean Moore on drums; and a certain 'Flicker' (real name: Miles Woodward), an old-style punk rocker they knew from school, on bass. For a short time, they experimented with a female singer – James had never seen himself as a frontman – but this didn't work, and James reluctantly had to take to the mike himself. He even penned a handful of lyrics ('Jackboot Johnny', a song about the local Oi!/skinhead scene, among them), but quickly and happily surrendered that job to Nicky. There was, however, no place for Richey Edwards, who had shown no discernible signs of musical talent.

Rehearsals took place in the Bradfield family living-room. Recalling this era, James told *Melody Maker* that the sight of his dad lying unconscious 'after a long day's surviving' was a reverse inspiration – a living example of what they never wanted to be. Nicky and Flicker would turn up at around midday with fish and chips, practise a mixture of cover versions and original material (using lyrics rescued from their poetic endeavours), watch videos and argue intensely. From the very beginning, visual presentation was given as much consideration as aural impact, as Nicky later told me: 'We learnt eight songs in James's room perfectly. Jumping up and down was more important than playing properly.'

For a while, they dabbled with the name Betty Blue for the band, after the English title of the 1980s student classic/soft porn Beatrice Dalle vehicle, *37.2° Le Matin*. Thankfully, however, they thought again. The origins of the name Manic Street Preachers are in dispute. One version of events – that Richey nicked the name from a Jasmine Minks album title (*All Good Preachers Go to Heaven*) – is almost certainly false, given that he wasn't even a member of the band at the time. Another legend has it that James got the name during one of his Cardiff busking outings. Someone had dared to throw some loose change his way, and he tore after them down the arcade hurling verbal abuse. A passing elderly gent, witnessing the scene, asked, 'What are you, boyo? Some sort of manic street preacher?' The only certain fact seems to be that James chose the name, though where he got the idea remains a mystery. 'I thought of the name in my sleep,' he now claims. 'It just came to me.'

However it came about, it would prove an inspired choice. Among the blank, monosyllabic band names in vogue during the late 80s/early 90s (Ride, Curve, Blur), it stood as an instant symbol of the Manics' difference; in the context of the blissed-out music scene of the day, the very name Manic Street Preachers was a statement in itself.

As Simon Reynolds wrote in *The Sex Revolts*: '. . . "manic" was their amphetamine-spiked renunciation of dreampop's sleepiness; "street" signified a return to the urban spaces of punk as opposed to inner space – a zone of revolution rather than reverie; "preacher" announced the Manics' intention to "tell it like it is", as opposed to the hazy apolitical ambiguities of the dreampop aesthetic.'

Shortly before Christmas 1988, the Preachers' progress was put on hold in a most unpleasant manner. On 22 December, Richey and James headed into Newport to celebrate Richey's 21st birthday. At around 7 p.m., they were in McDonald's when a group of fifteen lads – presumably not even drunk at that hour – burst in and, taking exception to the pair's dress sense, began attacking them. After having their burgers pushed into their faces, Richey was karate-chopped in the neck and kicked in the face, while James fared worse: his jaw was shattered. 'James couldn't sing for half a year,' Richey later recalled. 'That was the end of our night, really, a very thrilling birthday. We haven't been out since.'

Such random bloodshed is not uncommon in south Wales, as Richey also confirmed: 'On a Friday or Saturday night, mindless violence is just the acceptable thing. Fifty-two weeks of the year, you go to a pub and put a glass in somebody's face.' In retrospect, he was surprisingly forgiving about the whole episode: 'We're getting used to being beaten up.' Many years on, James would go one step further at Newport Centre: 'To the blokes who broke my jaw, I'd just like to say I know why you did it.' Nicky, however, echoing Public Enemy's condemnation of black-on-black violence, wished this Welsh aggression could be channelled in a political direction instead of against one another: 'It's really frustrating – people can't articulate their anger, they just attack each other. If they ran down the high street and smashed up Tesco or the Job Centre, that would be perfect.'

Several months later in the spring of 1989, once James's wired jaw had healed, the quartet was ready for its first public performance. This was a support slot at the Crumlin Railway Hotel, a modest pub venue in Newbridge, populated by black-clad rockers waiting for the headline act (a now-forgotten goth band), and casual drinkers on their regular Saturday night out. To the band's delight, their appearance provoked something akin to The Jesus and Mary Chain's legendary, riotous early gigs. The band walked onstage in poorly applied make-up, nouveau punk apparel and white school shirts bearing the stencilled aerosol slogans 'KILL YOURSELF' and 'TEENAGE BEAT', as the goths stood stony-faced, arms folded. Before the first song had ended, pints of snakebite and blackcurrant began to arc through the air. A Manics tradition was born.

Amid the sound of breaking glass, the set list that night included a number of covers – The Jesus and Mary Chain's 'Just Like Honey', 'Teenage Kicks' by The Undertones and 'God Save the Queen' from the Sex Pistols – along with a handful of original compositions: 'Anti-Social', the *Rumblefish*-inspired 'Colt 45 Rusty James' and 'Love in a Make-Up Bag' (none of which, sadly, have survived), plus 'Suicide Alley', 'Spectators of Suicide' and 'Go Buzz Baby Go' (an embryonic version of 'Motorcycle Emptiness'). Nine songs in just over ten minutes, and broken glass an inch deep on the floor.

Faced with such a negative reaction, many bands would have given up rock 'n' roll as a bad mistake. The Manics – contrary, masochistic bastards from day one – couldn't wait to do it all again. They hired themselves a manager of sorts: Mark Jones, a friend of Richey's who had been a year above him at school and whom Nicky has affectionately described as 'mental' (among other eccentricities, Mark was obsessed with building home-made rockets). It was he who booked the Manics' next show. A well-attended multi-band bill at Blackwood's Little Theatre (a converted Methodist chapel), this occasion was even more violent than the first. A gang of football lads from the infamous Cardiff City hooligan firm The Soul Crew had found their way in, and took immense delight in heckling the Manics right from the start with taunts of 'You're worse than Swansea City!', and, somewhat bizarrely, 'Simple Minds! Simple Minds!' Soon, beer bottles were raining down once again. After a mere ten minutes, the show imploded as the band responded in kind, smashing their equipment in what press releases would later glorify as 'an orgy of nihilistic fury', while the football contingent invaded the stage and fought among themselves.

Amazingly, the Preachers were booked to play two more nights at the Little Theatre, followed by a trip slightly further afield to Pontypridd Rugby Club. This show was disastrous. Faced with a bemused, indifferent crowd, the Manics responded by pulling out all the stops to wind them up. As a finale, Flicker stepped up to the mike and started abusing the audience with a stream of obscenities. The moment the band left the stage, they were told they would never play Ponty again.

Flicker had never quite fitted in; never quite comprehended the Manics' aesthetic. Furthermore, even in the context of the band, he was musically inept: he had removed two strings from his bass, partly because that was what Sid Vicious had done, but mostly because he found four too tricky to handle. Presented with the excuse they had been looking for, James, Nicky and Sean unceremoniously ejected the bassist from the band. He took a job with British Telecom instead, and is now working in a factory in Oakdale.

For the first time (but not the last), the Manics were reduced to a trio, with Nicky moving from rhythm guitar to bass. In June, the threesome managed to scrounge some cheap studio time at Sound Bank Studios (SBS) in Cwmfelinfach; these were run by a local musician called Glen Powell, whose main claim to fame was having once played with Jimi Hendrix.

To save time, only James and Sean, the more musically competent Manics, actually played. In forty minutes – all they could afford, even at 'mates' rates' – they recorded two tracks, produced by Powell and his assistant Tony. 'Suicide Alley' – a compact, simplistic three-chord punk paean to adolescent angst – was, even then, far from being their best song. The B-side, 'Tennessee (I Feel So Low)', was an attack on Bible Belt bigotry, partially inspired by Tennessee Williams.

Unable to afford to pay for the master tapes, they took their own third-generation copy to the pressing plant, which explains the fuzzy, murky sound quality (the band would later fall out with Glen Powell over rights to the original, when he tried to reissue the single at the same time that they were planning to put it on the 'Little Baby Nothing' CD). They had three hundred seven-inch singles made, which they kept in boxes under James's bed. They glued the sleeves themselves as and when required, and began mailing copies to journalists.

Steven Wells of NME made 'Suicide Alley'/'Tennessee (I Feel So Low)' his 'Single of the Week' (or, to borrow his precise Trotskyist-on-speed vernacular, 'White Rock

Rebelboy Single of the Week'). Another recipient of the single, Mark Brennan of *Beat the Street* fanzine, was sufficiently impressed to include both sides on *Underground Rockers Vol 2*, a punk/Oi! compilation on Link Records. When Brennan phoned Sean to ask where he should send the royalties cheques, Moore just laughed: 'Give 'em to charity.'

The three-piece Manics played a handful of local gigs at venues such as TJ's in Newport and the Square Club in Cardiff (attended by just two people: manager Mark Jones and Richey's sister Rachel). As well as being the first appearance of a three-piece Preachers, the show at TJ's – a tiny, friendly dive on the small-time indie circuit – has another historical significance: at Nicky Wire's insistence, the band took the stage kitted out in tight white jeans and white Dunlop Green Flash plimsolls. As visual gimmicks go, it was a stroke of genius. If the colour code of the 80s – the signifier of tired 'alternativeness' – was black (scuffed black denims and lager-soaked black suede boots), the Manics were a clear-out, a farewell, a kiss off/piss off to all that. Clean clean clean, neat neat neat. (The plimsolls, however, arose simply from expediency: they were more comfortable on Nicky's dodgy feet.) As John Robb, who would later write the Manics' first music press front cover for *Sounds*, puts it: 'They looked so out of context. Everyone else was wearing baggy, so they went tight – anything to go against the grain.'

That night, once again, they managed to get themselves banned from a venue, this time for antagonising the ageing leather-clad punk regulars – their idea of fun.

But still, something – *someone* – was missing.

'I am a little man and this is a little town but there must be a spark in a little man that can burst into a flame' – JOHN STEINBECK

Richey Edwards helped out the Manics in every way he could. The only person they knew with a driving licence, he became their chauffeur (a position he would continue to fulfil, in fact, throughout the band's career), ferrying them to gigs and helping to carry their equipment. He also took the cover photo for 'Suicide Alley' – the first known picture of the band.

As well as being driver and official photographer, Richey's role was now becoming something roughly akin to that of Public Enemy's 'Minister of Information', Professor Griff. Richey began sending letters to the press on the Manics' behalf (although it was James, in fact, who drafted the first missive), proclaiming them as 'the best band in the world' and announcing their 'Extreme Sense Of Now'. He also wrote their first press release, a piece of vintage Richey rhetoric which read: 'We are young, beautiful scum, pissed off with the world . . . We are the suicide of the non-generation. We are as far away from anything in the 80s as possible, e.g. 80s' pop automation, the long-running saga of the whimsical pop essay and the intrinsic musical sculptures of post-modernism . . . We are the only young kids in UK Channel Boredom to realise the future is in tight trousers, dyed hair and NOT the baggy loose attitude scum fuck retard zerodom of Madchester.'

Although not yet a full band member, Richey was the mouthpiece, the expert propagandist, and an oracle of wisdom to whom the other, younger Manics clearly looked up. He also had the best cheekbones, looked cool with a guitar around his neck and had a way with words. As James put it: 'We didn't know how, but we knew Richey had to be a part of it.' (And besides, they hated the idea of remaining a three-piece: it reminded them too much of The Jam.) It was James who persuaded Edwards officially to join the band.

Richey had recently bought a second-hand guitar with his student grant, and James promised to teach him the basics. The Manics' next engagement was, as luck would have it, a gig at the University of Wales in Swansea, booked by Richey's friend Dan who was on the Entertainments Committee. For most of the show, Richey watched from the wings. When the band walked out for the encore, 'Sorrow 16', he joined them, played the two chords he had managed to master, threw a selection of practice-perfect Keef/Townshend/Strummer poses and, starting as he meant to go on, trashed the instrument he had purchased only days earlier.

Back at Swansea University, final exam time was approaching for Richey and Nicky. In the Easter holidays before Richey's finals, James visited him, and was shocked to find him dragging the point of a compass across his forearms while revising. He had been doing this, Richey explained, alongside his 'medicinal' drinking, to help him retain control and maintain concentration. More worryingly, his weight had dropped alarmingly (he had been subsisting on a frugal budget meal he'd invented called 'White Noise', involving rice, a jacket potato and corn on the cob). According to Nicky, who saw him more frequently, Richey was not an alcoholic exactly, but he would binge-drink at weekends (on weekdays, he was too busy studying); he hadn't started cutting himself exactly, but was merely 'scratching'; he wasn't anorexic exactly, but was just 'undereating'. By the time of the exams, Richey weighed a little over six stone. He managed a 2:1, but the grade rankled with him: for the first time in his life, his academic achievements were less than perfect. He was just two per cent away from a First, and he was devastated.

Nicky, by contrast, was showing less concern than ever about his education. The Manics had received their first coverage in *NME*, and he was convinced that the big time was around the corner. The night before one of his final exams, the Manics played a gig supporting The Levellers, which offers some indication of how seriously (or otherwise) Nicky took his studies; when he should have been revising hard, he was feeding the fruities. 'I was convinced that we were going to be famous by then, anyway, uncontrollably convinced – it didn't matter how much money we owed or anything. Hence spending it all on fruit machines. It was coming. I knew it was going to be.' One day, directly before an important exam, he visited the local Oxfam shop, bought a job lot of white shirts, and spent an afternoon in his room, nearly choking on aerosol fumes, spraypainting slogans like 'AESTHETIC DEBRIS', 'DEATH SENTENCE HERITAGE', 'CULTURE SLUT', 'PICTURESQUE RIOT', 'RIOT STAR', 'I WILL KILL MYSELF ON VALENTINE'S DAY', 'WE ARE YOUR SACRIFICE' (a title of a Patrick Jones poem) and 'USELESS GENERATION', while Richey cooked Fray Bentos pies. Nicky even got Richey to write two of his final dissertations for him. Miraculously, he scraped a 'Desmond' – a 2:2 – and he was pleased to have done so well.

Freed from education, the Manics faced a stark choice for the future: to go into overdrive with the band, or to accept defeat and fill in an application form for Pot Noodle – which was, of course, no future at all. Pooling what was left of their grant cheques and Christmas double Giros, the band went back into SBS and demoed every song they had written. However, there was only so far they could go with a DIY, mail-order, word-of-mouth, support-slot-scavenging, underground *modus operandi*. It was time to break out.

London was calling.

For a time, the Manics did exactly what every bunch of naïve provincial hopefuls does: they sent demo tapes and self-pressed singles to the A & R departments of London's major record labels, and invited the talent scouts to come and watch them play the local pub.

After one standard rejection letter too many saying 'We'll see you when you get to London', they took the hint. As Richey later put it: 'We saw bands do, like, all the pubs where we lived, do two hundred gigs a year, get really big local followings, and they're all under the illusion that somebody from Sony Music will be driving through the middle of south Wales and go,"Hey, what a good band! Sign here!" And of course, we knew they never would. We knew we had to move to London.'

When this truth dawned, doing the rounds of the local boozers was no longer an option. 'Once we got our minds set on what we were doing,' Richey remembered, 'we didn't play a single gig in Blackwood. It was straight to London and scrounging for money to get on the pay-to-play circuit. Locally, to be in a band you basically had to do R & B covers and play the pub circuit. So for a year we just thought about coming to London with enough money to stay, do all the crap gigs, and find an audience.'

Throughout the summer of 1989, the four rehearsed tirelessly in James's living-room – or, increasingly, in Nicky's front room, which meant a two-mile walk across town for James, carrying his guitar and amp. Every powerchord, star-jump, shout and sneer was choreographed to perfection. On Friday 20 September, the Manic Street Preachers climbed into a hired mini-van and, with Richey Edwards at the wheel, headed down the A472, on to the M4 ('We didn't even know how to get across the Severn Bridge,' Richey later confessed) and due east for their first assault on the citadel of the mainstream music industry.

'London, England, consider yourself . . . WARNED!' – PUBLIC ENEMY, 'REVOLUTIONARY GENERATION'

The venue was far from glamorous. The Horse & Groom, a Victorian pub on Great Portland Street, had an upstairs function room which normally played host to amateur jazz and folk musicians.

The Manics were part of a multiple-band night of underground pop, headlined by mod revivalists The Claim. The gig was organised by Kevin Pearce, editor of the *Esurient Communication* and *Hungry Beat* fanzines (read avidly by one R. Edwards, who occasionally contributed vitriolic Dexys-style rants) and author of the brilliantly obsessional pop iconography *Something Beginning With 'O'*. Pearce had hired the room for a nominal £10 by hoodwinking the proprietors that he was arranging a jazz gig.

There was no dressing-room – the bands had to wait around on the stairs – but that made no difference to the Manics, who hid in their van, too shy to come out. Seconds before their allotted stage time, James, Richey, Sean and Nicky finally trotted out of the vehicle and into the pub, wearing mod-style jackets with prison arrows sewn on, and white shirts adorned with DIY slogans like 'SUICIDE BEAT', 'CLASSIFIED MACHINE' and 'ENGLAND NEEDS REVOLUTION NOW' and resembling cheap market-stall imitations of McLaren's and Westwood's Seditionaries range. The barman, bumping into them on the stairs, said: 'Ah, you must be the jazz band.'

At around 9 p.m., the Manics took to the tiny stage (in front of a rather incongruous backdrop comprising paintings of famous jockeys), announced 'New Art Riot', and clattered into their opening number. There was a polite – if bemused – ripple of clapping. 'Th-thanks,' stammered James. 'That's the most applause we've ever had.'

Bob Stanley, now of Saint Etienne but then a *Melody Maker* freelancer who had been sent to review the night, could only stand and giggle. 'We were laughing, but only because it was so unexpected. The presentation was total Clash. They were wearing old school shirts with slogans stencilled on them – not ones bought in a junk shop, but the actual ones they'd worn at school.'

Sadly, no photographs of this momentous event exist, although a bootleg tape does survive. The set list ran 'New Art Riot', 'Soul Contamination', 'Dead Yankee Drawl', 'Anti-Love', 'Strip it Down', 'Destroy the Dancefloor', 'Sorrow 16', 'Faceless Sense of Void' and lastly, in traditional showbiz style, the latest single, 'Suicide Alley'. As James Dean Bradfield and his cohorts tear through their 100 m.p.h. set, he grows audibly in confidence, making relaxed, self-deprecating quips between songs: 'Every time we have a drink, it isn't rock 'n' roll, we just need one'; then 'Um, we can't sing this one,'; then 'If anyone wants to know how to play this . . .' (he demonstrates the chords); and, finally, rather sweetly: 'This is a single we released a bit ago – we've got a few to give away if you want.'

They made enough of an impression for Kevin Pearce to book them for another night at The Horse & Groom, this time headlining above the Jasmine Minks (the Manics waived their £50 fee to help Kevin put out the next Claim single on his Esurient label), and on 25 October they were doing the M4 run yet again (this time, Richey didn't drive – they clubbed together and hired a pro) for another show in the smoke. At The Rock Garden – a soulless pay-to-play cellar in Covent Garden, more geared towards shifting bottled beer to tourists than to showcasing the future of rock 'n' roll – the band had to scrape together £100 for the privilege of appearing there. Just fifteen people turned up.

a) To show from where I came . . .

(WELSHNESS AND THE WIRE)

'We can trace almost all the disasters of English history to the influence of Wales' – EVELYN WAUGH, *DECLINE AND FALL*

THERE IS A PRECEDENT, a century and a half into the mists of Welsh history, for Manic Street Preachers' transvestite sedition.

In 1838, a wave of uprisings, mutinies and revolts known as the Rebecca Riots swept the Narberth and Pontardulais areas, then the whole of Camarthenshire, and eventually all of west Wales. After a bad harvest had caused mass starvation, gangs of farmers dressed in women's clothes grabbed their shotguns and set fire to English-owned workhouses and tollgates (whose English absentee landlords were charging extortionate fees for use of the roads).

The leader of the riots, a particularly well-built Welshman, had needed a disguise to protect his identity, and borrowed a dress from a large lady called Big Becca – the only person whose clothes would fit him – in a neighbouring parish. He, in turn, became known as Becca, and his acolytes followed suit, borrowing their wives' clothes, ostensibly to evade detection (although they probably just enjoyed it) and hailing Genesis 24:60 as their inspiration and justification: 'They blessed Rebekah, and said unto her: "Our sister, be thou the mother of thousands, of tens of thousands, and let thy seed possess the gates of those which hate them."'

It took five years and all the king's men to suppress the cross-dressing, firestarting, trigger-happy Welsh mob; one hundred and fifty years later, in a field in west Wales, it took one Swansea City fan just one well-aimed wine bottle to suppress another large and rebellious Welshman in a dress. The missile which struck Nicky Wire in Singleton Park failed to knock him unconscious – but was he conscious that the noise of glass against skull bore the echo of history?

. . . And apologies to Greil Marcus for *that* one. There is arguably a closer comparison to be made between the Manics and the slightly earlier Chartists: members of the Gwent-based, manifesto-waving movement which demanded a voice for the disenfranchised (although, as far as anyone knows, the Chartists weren't so keen on wearing their mums' frocks). However, spurious similes about drag dissenters aside, can it ever be said that Manic Street Preachers are, really and truly, a *Welsh* band?

For the first six years of their career, one had to search very hard to detect a single trace of Welsh culture in the Manics' music, lyrics or statements: their reference points were almost entirely British or American. 'If I tried to write a Springsteen-esque lyric about Wales,' Richey Edwards once told me, 'it'd be: "I went to the Pontypool factory/Then drove up Caerphilly mountain/And drank tea from a plastic cup." You can't do it.'

Of all the Preachers, he was the least likely ever to hoist the red dragon. 'Richey was really paranoid about ever coming across as Welsh,' Nicky later confirmed. 'He always called it the Neil Kinnock Factor: "Turn Out The Lights!"' (A reference to the infamous front page of the *Sun*, widely credited with swinging the 1992 election for the Tories, which pictured the Welsh Labour leader's head in the shape of a lightbulb with the headline: 'If This Man Becomes Prime Minister, Will The Last Person to Leave Britain Turn Out The Lights?')

Dylan Thomas, asked about Welsh nationalism, once famously replied: 'The land of my fathers? My fathers can have it.' Richey Edwards, asked about his homeland by Bob Stanley of *Melody Maker* in 1991, described south Wales as: '. . . a soul-destroying place; we'd rather say we're from Europe.' Nor did Nicky feel any stirrings of latent patriotism. In 1992, I asked him if he felt European, British or Welsh. 'Nothing,' he bluntly replied. 'I wish we could feel something – maybe we'd be more rounded people. We've always been too alienated.'

Far from being flag-waving nationalists, the Manics were more apt to be accused of anti-Welshness. Their negative remarks about Blackwood are documented elsewhere but it is worth mentioning here that, after one particularly vitriolic Nicky Wire outburst against the Land of His Fathers in the music press, one local newsagent refused to stock *NME*, and the *South Wales Argus* ran a shock-horror story under the banner headline: 'Local Band Attacks Home Town'.

'There are still parts of Wales where the only concession to gaiety is a striped shroud' – GWYN THOMAS

Having said all this, can a case be made that the Manics were not just Made *in* Wales, but Made *by* Wales? In many ways, the answer must be no. When Richey, in 1991, said, 'Everything we do is shaped by where we come from,' what he really meant was that it was shaped by the *sort* of place they came from. This was why they quickly struck a chord with people in dead-end hellholes, provincial backwaters and forgotten towns all over Britain, not just in the Gwent valleys. While it is not quite accurate to say that the Manics could only have come from south Wales, it is true to say that they could only have come from somewhere *like* south Wales – anywhere in chronic exile from the swing of things. Despite early songtitles like 'England Is a Bitch', there was nothing specifically Welsh about their desire to rise up and dance in the ruins of Buckingham Palace. Cymric nationalism, cottage-burning and 'Ffree Ffred Ffrancis' graffiti were never part of their agenda. This wasn't about country, it was about class: Us Against You.

On the other hand, there *was* a vague, intrinsic, unwitting Welshness to the Manics if you chose to see it. For a start, of course, there was no way they could hide those gorgeous, endearing, rich accents, which made their every utterance resonate with music and poetry (although James didn't see it that way, as he told *Select*: 'People think it's the funniest accent in the world. Nobody finds it sexy. It was so hard to pull girls when I was young. Nobody ever said, "Ooh, say that again!"')

And when John Robb wrote in *Sounds* of their 'delicate, almost Welsh melodies' you felt you knew what he meant. Robb sees 'the sadness in Welsh culture' reflected in the Manics' music, 'the melancholy lilt, the minor key'. This wallowing in sadness is a profoundly Welsh trait. James Dean Bradfield says that, in Blackwood, 'Melancholia comes up from the hills, from the ground,' while Nicky Wire has suggested that this tendency is due to the climate. To reverse-paraphrase The Mamas and The Papas, it always rains in south Wales.

Arguably, too, the Manics' Welshness was behind their militant anti-cool factor. 'The very fact that we were from Wales meant that there was no point trying to be cool,' Nicky later told *Select*. 'People will always call us dull, moronic Taffs whatever we do.'

Dull, moronic Taffs? The Manics have been called that and worse. As *GQ* editor James Brown pointed out in BBC2's *Close-Up* documentary on MSP: 'By the early 90s the Welsh were well on the way to becoming the new Pakistanis, or the new Irish.' Which is why early Manic Street Preachers reviews were littered with anti-Welsh racism: it was the only form of racism that was still tolerated. Nowadays, in educated circles, it is no longer considered acceptable to make Irish jokes; nor would anyone dare to laugh at the Scots, who have a reputation for standing up for themselves. The Welsh, however, are considered a soft touch – sitting ducks. An Englishman recently said to me: 'We like the Irish but we don't respect them. We don't like the Scots, but we respect them. We neither like nor respect the Welsh.' And so the butt of every old-skool racist punchline has merely switched nationalities from Irish to Welsh (or, on occasion, to Belgian). But why should it be any more politically correct to laugh at a nation which has been economically raped by its English masters and whose people have been quietly tossed on to the human scrapheap of unemployment, than it is to poke fun at those who have a noisier and more direct grievance against English colonialism?

These jokes are not confined to bar-rooms or working mens' clubs. In 1997, A.N. Wilson wrote a column in London's *Evening Standard* entitled 'Why We Hate The Welsh'. The supposedly enlightened indie rock scene, too, was perfectly happy to

Those racist Manic headlines in full:

'TO LIVE AND DAI IN L.A.'
'THE WELSH DRAG ON'
'THE RHYL THING'
'THIS IS SPINAL TAFF'
'YOU SEXY MERTHYR FUCKERS'
'THE NEWPORT DOLLS'
'MEEK LEEK MANIFESTO'
'DAI HARDER'
'THE BOYOS ARE BACK IN TOWN'
'MEET THE NAFF TAFFS'
'BOYOS TO MEN'

'Would "Potato-Eating Paddy" ever get a Therapy? cover line?!' (Richey Edwards)

mock the Welsh (as if, growing up with nothing to do, no job to look forward to and few means of escape, those of us born west of Offa's Dyke didn't have enough to contend with). Above a Manics-related letter from a Welsh fan in *Melody Maker*, the headline read 'A Welshman Writes (A First For Medical Science)'. At around the same time, *NME* cheerfully reported the story of the Edinburgh indie shop which refused to stock 'Motown Junk' on the grounds that '[Manic Street Preachers] are crap, they're Welsh and they wear eyeliner' (the Manics responded by sending the shop an autographed copy, which the hypocrites were only too happy to auction).

'We took a lot of racism early on,' Wire told me in 1996, 'and it's not too strong to call it racism. Any other country would have stood up and said so. It's only because we're such non-confident wet bastards . . .' Wire did, indeed, stand up and say so in 1992 when I introduced him to *Melody Maker* colleague Andrew Mueller (having temporarily forgotten that Mueller had described the Manics as 'Welsh fuckwits'). 'I wouldn't spit on you, you racist!' Nicky raged at him, before flouncing away in a huff.

Perhaps understandably, then, the Manics were reluctant to wear their Welsh credentials on their sleeves. At a Cardiff show in 1994, James Dean Bradfield branded rugby player Scott Quinnell (who had switched from union to league) a 'traitor'; there was also a brief reference to bilingual road signs in the single 'P.C.P.' . . . and that was about it. By that time – the era of *The Holy Bible* album – the Manics had abandoned Americana but were still fleeing their Welsh roots, this time for Europe. James, after praising the early Simple Minds for similarly rejecting Scottishness in favour of a European aesthetic, told me: 'I think it's obvious we felt the same way about Wales, until the press went on about it so much that it bred resilience.'

Resilience? Yes. Pride? Not yet. But neither was James prepared to allow shame to be forced upon him. Bradfield had always been adept at brusquely shrugging off any anti-Welsh taunts. When a crowd made 'baa' noises, heckled him with cries of 'sheepshaggers' or even threw stuffed toy sheep onstage, James would retort, 'Yeah, we shag 'em, then you eat 'em,' and get on with the next song. But he, and the band, were starting to tire of all the jokes.

> '"The Welsh," said the Doctor, "are the only nation in the world that has
> produced no graphic or plastic art, no architecture, no drama. They just sing,"
> he said with disgust, "sing and blow down wind instruments of plated silver"' –
> EVELYN WAUGH, *DECLINE AND FALL*

One of the biggest jokes of all was the Welsh music scene. It was a widely held truism that, in forty years of pop culture, all that the alleged Land of Song had given the world was Tom and Shirley, Shaky and Bonnie, and (God preserve us) The Alarm. Although this is slightly unfair (the Welsh language scene, spearheaded by Ankst Records, has always been strong, and mainstream pop is rife with Welsh musicians who had to move to London to make their break), it is certainly true – and I speak from first-hand experience – that during the 80s and early 90s the Cardiff/Newport gig circuit was pub rock/glam metal/cabaret cover band hell.

Welsh alternative/independent music, such as it was, was under the jealously guarded control of Welsh speakers (or 'Gogs', as they are disparagingly known by non-speakers). Like most people in south Wales, the Manics were raised as Anglophones. Unusually, however, Welsh wasn't even taught in Oakdale Comprehensive. 'The Welsh language was never important to us at all,' said Richey Edwards. 'I mean, what's the point of resurrecting something that's just completely dead? Dead culture doesn't interest us.' The Welsh language nearly died out entirely a hundred years ago, until it was artificially revived by a concerted campaign. Although it is admittedly a genuine living tongue in many rural areas, it has also been adopted as something of a middle-class hobby. Among the Cardiff-based media, fluency in Welsh is the equivalent of a freemason's handshake or an old school tie. If you want to get on, replace those pesky English vowels with Ws and Ys, and start doubling those Ls and Ds. The same was true of the music scene.

Even in their local context, the Manics were alienated from other musicians. 'Welsh-speaking bands give us grief for not singing in Welsh,' Richey told me. 'I don't expect roses and petals at our feet, but a bit of respect would be nice.' James, on the other hand, actually complained about Welsh fans who attempted to co-opt the Manics into some sort of Cymric renaissance. 'They think you're trying to do something good and important for Wales,' he told Q. 'Why do they bother? We've never said good things about where we come from. All we've said is, we're from Wales, from a town where there's nothing to do. We've never felt any sense of pride in where we come from.'

In 1995, during the Manics' enforced year-long absence, something happened. A few of the better Welsh-speaking bands (Super Furry Animals, Catatonia, Gorky's Zygotic Mynci) suddenly went bilingual and started releasing records in English. London style gurus, noticing that a handful of half-decent indie bands was emerging from the principality, decided that, in the footsteps of Seattle, Manchester and Camden Town, Wales was suddenly where it's at. Suddenly and improbably, being Welsh was painfully hip. A Welsh actor appeared in *EastEnders* (Ammanford-bred Richard Elis, himself a long-time Manics fan), and this was followed by a soap called *Tiger Bay*, based entirely in Cardiff. There was even a Swansea-based movie, *Twin Town* (hyped as 'The Welsh *Trainspotting*'), which featured MSP's *Motown Junk* on the soundtrack, quickly followed by the Welsh family drama *House Of America* (which featured 'Motorcycle Emptiness'). The Manics, by acting as fall guys/flak fodder for racist critics, had paved the way for the New Welsh Cool and, by gradually accruing critical respect, had helped to create a climate in which the notion of a good Welsh rock band wasn't such a ridiculous concept.

Quickly and fittingly, the Manics became adoptive godfathers of the emergent Taffia, outflanking the misgivings of the Gogs by taking Catatonia, Super Furry Animals, Gorky's and Stereophonics on tour with them (the latter, hitting their own peak of popularity with a huge gig at Cardiff Castle, returned the compliment by dedicating their last song to the Manics). 'When we started,' Sean told *Select*, 'the idea of Welsh music was like the Ivory Coast in the Olympics: one bloke carrying the flag and one walking behind. Now there's more of us and we can carry our banner with pride.'

'An impotent people/Sick with inbreeding/Worrying the carcase of an old song'
– THE WELSH RACE AS DESCRIBED BY R.S. THOMAS

This cultural sea-change was mirrored by a change of attitude in the Manics themselves. Nicky Wire had been reading R.S. Thomas, the formidable poet of rural Wales, and studying the legend of Owain Glyndwr (about which he has considered writing a screenplay), and has since shown philanthropic generosity towards the Welsh arts, donating prizes to a Young Writers' competition in the Valleys and giving funds to Cardiff's Sherman Theatre. He also succumbed to the less highbrow pleasures of Britain's longest-running soap, *Pobol y Cwm* (albeit with English subtitles). The new, all-Welsh Wire became increasingly partisan towards Welsh sportsmen: golfer Ian Woosnam, the Glamorgan cricket team (whose Matthew Maynard received a namecheck on 'Mr Carbohydrate'), the Cardiff Devils, said to be the hardest ice-hockey team in the UK (whose shirt Nicky has often worn onstage and whose player, Jason Stone, he sponsors) and Leeds/Cardiff/Juventus/Wales striker John Charles (about whom he has amassed a video library).

During the recording of the Manics' fifth album (*This Is My Truth Tell Me Yours*) in France, Wire followed Glamorgan's victorious county cricket championship by satellite, and sent a hamper of champagne to the players. The story made the front page of the *Western Mail*. 'It was a nice gesture,' said the Glamorgan chairman, 'but we haven't heard of them.' Nicky has hailed prehistoric Welsh rockers Badfinger and, when in Europe, listens to Tom Jones's 'Green Green Grass of Home' to alleviate – or possibly to exacerbate – his feelings of *hiraeth* (a peculiarly Welsh form of homesickness). When he goes on holiday these days, he even takes Welsh water and beef with him.

James Dean Bradfield, too, has developed an increasingly pro-Welsh stance, which runs much deeper than just wearing a Cardiff RFC shirt on *Later With Jools Holland*. At a Newport gig in April 1996, he performed Andy Williams's 'Can't Take My Eyes Off You', which had been adopted as the anthem of Wales's World Cup campaign, adding the interjection: 'God, I hate the Romanian football team' (a reference to Wales's untimely exit at the hands of Romania). That Christmas, he went one step further and played a snatch of the real national anthem, 'Hen Wlad Fy Nhadu', before 'Motorcycle Emptiness', and at the Royal Albert Hall the following April he publicly berated a journalist from the *Express* for describing Welsh people as 'dimwitted'.

In 1996, I asked Wire what was behind his apparent U-turn. 'I've become more conscious of [Welshness] lately,' he told me. 'I've started to really support the Welsh rugby side. *Vanity Fair* interviewed Sharon Stone recently, and they asked her to name her favourite Irish author, and she said Dylan Thomas! Things like that wouldn't have annoyed me before, but they really do now.' (A poem by Dylan Thomas, 'The Boys of Summer', was projected on to a giant screen on every date of the Manics' 1996/7 tours.) Seemingly trivial slights like these seem to wind up The Wire. 'Wales for most of the south-eastern English media is just a convenient size comparison,' he complained to *Q* magazine. 'Rainforests that burn down are always "the size of Wales".'

However, Nicky's feelings towards Wales are too complex for a term as simple as 'patriotism'. As he himself puts it: '"Patriotic" is not the right word, but . . . I have felt like a second-class citizen for so long about being Welsh, and it's the first time I've actually come to peace with myself about it.' At the Manics' 1997 Royal Albert Hall show, he ended 'Motown Junk' with the perverse taunt: 'We come from a shithole, but it isn't as bad as this!'

During The Big Comeback, Wire conveniently forgot his earlier dismissal of patriotism in 'Repeat' ('dumb flag scum!'), and draped his bass amp and, on occasion, as at the Brit Awards, himself in a Welsh flag. This was quickly imitated by the fans − even English ones. At festivals and the Oasis mega-gigs, the red dragon was semaphore for 'I am here for the Manics' (whether the bearer was Welsh or not).

If the Manics had found a way of loving Wales, the feeling was reciprocated in spades. Although Welsh rock fans had always adored the band − homecoming MSP gigs had always been incredibly atmospheric events − it is not too much of an exaggeration to say that by 1996 the four were becoming symbols of national pride among the broader public, who were rightly gratified that the most important British band of the 90s came from Wales.

Cardiff RFC knew this when they asked the Manics to play as pre-match entertainment at the Arms Park to ensure a capacity crowd for their Heineken European Cup match against Llanelli. And, in May 1998, with the band's approval, the Welsh Tourist Board used the Stealth Sonic Orchestra instrumental of 'A Design for Life' in a TV ad with a voice-over from weather girl Siân Lloyd. 'By using a song which is almost an anthem,' explained the WTB's Robin Gwyn, 'we want to tap into the new feeling that there is about Wales, that it's a happening place, no longer a backwater − if it ever was.' Weirdly, the Manics themselves were even touted as a tourist attraction, eliciting a somewhat surreal comment from Sandra King of the Newport and Gwent Tourist Office: 'It wasn't easy for Manic Street Preachers, because one of their mothers is a hairdresser.'

The first concrete sign of the Manics' change of heart was the Welsh-inspired lyric to 'A Design for Life'. By the time *This Is My Truth Tell Me Yours* arrived, the influence was sufficiently strong for Nicky Wire to call it 'the first true Welsh folk album'. But why had it taken so long? Wire explained it to Darren Broome on BBC Radio Wales: 'With your first album, you just want to escape. When you're young you wanna run away from where you were born, and when you're older you want to understand what made you feel like that.'

There is another historical precedent for Manic Street Preachers. In Welsh culture, there exists a tradition called *ceffyl pren* (literally, 'wooden horse'). It means holding someone up to ridicule by carrying their effigy (or, in cases of exceptional cruelty, their actual person) aloft on a pole.

With their recent, vindicating success and their new, defiant Welshness, Nicky, James and Sean have climbed down from the racist critics' pole and shoved it where the sun don't shine.

2. NEW ART RIOT

'The revolutionary class is every kid that's pissed off. You're just not going to get old people involved, they've got too much to lose. Young people have got no fear. When you've got no fear you can do anything' – NICKY

ANOTHER DECADE, ANOTHER REJECTION LETTER. On 3 January 1990, Richey opened his mail to find a standard thanks-but-no-thanks from WEA's Ben Wardle. Mr Wardle is not believed to be working for WEA any more.

That night, as luck would have it, the Manics, having broken a promise to themselves never to play another pointless local pub gig, were booked to play a depressingly meaningless show at the Lady Owen Arms in Newbridge, Gwent, supporting something called The Desirables. Their next scheduled 'record' release, if you could call it that, was a flexidisc given free with the March issue of *Goldmining* fanzine, featuring a song called 'UK Channel Boredom' (previously titled 'Brighton Hotel Rock' and then 'Dresden Dance', the song would finally reappear as 'Vision of Dead Desire'), which they had recorded at a cost of £25. For a while, the Manics' dreams of world domination seemed to be fading away.

If the majors weren't interested, and this was what the DIY approach had to offer, then any record deal, surely, was a better idea than this stasis, this purgatory. Three weeks later, someone called Ian Ballard got in touch. Ballard, the one-man motor behind the punk/indie label Damaged Goods (home to the likes of The Snivelling Shits), had been alerted to the Preachers' potential by Mark Brennan at Link Records, and had been in the audience at the Horse & Groom the previous autumn. Although Damaged Goods was, as James would later tell *NME*, 'totally divorced from anything we've ever believed in', Ian Ballard did seem, in Nicky's words, to be 'the most honest person we've ever dealt with, and the most efficient'.

On 24 January, the Manics 'signed' to Damaged Goods. No contracts were exchanged, but hands were shaken and a gentlemen's agreement made. For one single, at least, Manic Street Preachers had a record deal. On 15 March, the band checked into Dave Morris's dirt-cheap Workshop studio in the bleak Midlands town of Redditch. In just two days, with the help of producer Mark Tempest, they had recorded a four-track EP at a total cost of £186.

Shortly after this, on 7 April 1991, Bob Stanley interviewed the band for *Melody Maker*'s 'Sidelines' section, in what was the band's first music-press interview. It was one of Stanley's stranger journalistic experiences. 'We did the interview in the pub, and none of them drank. They put all their money into the fruit machines – a kind of nihilistic thing to do. They had to go back to Wales the next day, and we had quite a big flat, so we invited them to crash on our spare mattresses. They said, "No, it's all right, we're going to sleep in the van." It must have been freezing!' Starting as they meant to go on, they lied to Bob about their ages, all claiming to be teenagers except for 'twenty-year-old' James.

After the interview, Nicky wrote a thank-you note to Bob – the first Bob had ever received. Richey sent him a home-made T-shirt stencilled with the slogan 'REVOLUTION FLOWER' and, oddly, glam-rock songtitles like 'Ballroom Blitz' and '48 Crash', and wrote to him regularly for the next eighteen months (he had already joined the Saint Etienne fan club, with a letter reading simply 'Dear Bob, inspire me'). Bob returned the compliment in Saint Etienne's *Clenbuterol* fanzine by writing a hilarious tribute to Edwards in limerick form, rhyming 'Richey' with 'titchy'.

The band gave Bob permission to put out a limited-edition single (five hundred copies only) on his mail-order label, Caff. The single, under the banner 'Feminine is Beautiful', eventually surfaced the following July. It featured the original SBS demo versions of 'New Art Riot' and 'Repeat After Me', copied from a cassette sent by the band to Bob (they had long since lost the master tape), and with a sleeve designed by punk historian Jon Savage.

Meanwhile, the band played any and every gig they could (usually at a net loss of around £50 per night), scavenging one-off local support slots here and there – Mega City Four and Senseless Things in Swansea, Cranes and The Family Cat in Bristol – often procured by writing begging letters to the bands (some of these would later be made into a bootleg T-shirt by a malicious entrepreneur). On one occasion they drove through blizzard conditions, despite weathermen warning motorists to stay at home, to play a thirty-minute set to just fifty people in an Oxford social club, before driving straight back home again.

On 22 June, this grisly winter was pierced by a ray of sunshine: the first 'proper' Manic Street Preachers record release. The 'New Art Riot' EP (the title had been one of their earliest T-shirt mottos) contained the results of the Workshop sessions. Its title track was nothing less than a state-of-the-nation address: a declarative, heroic assault on the stifling, creeping paralysis of British culture ('Vintage aromas and vintage ideals . . .'), blowing open the façade of Thatcherism ('Hospital closure kills more than car bombs ever will') and finding time along the way to spit in the face of Madchester ('Everybody's taking drugs because it makes governing easier'). 'Last Exit', which equated love songs with drug addiction, and the nihilistic 'Teenage 20/20' ('Take a spraycan to my useless vote'), which lurched from a 'Johnny B. Goode' intro into a Sham 69 riff, comprised the B-side. But it was 'Strip It Down' – more or less an unconnected parade of situationist slogans ('Decaying flowers in the playground of the rich') arranged around a wheeling, circular guitar riff – that was singled out as the lead track. A video was made, featuring the band decked out in their whites (James with '1990' on his shirt in huge numerals) and performing in front of a weirdly Summer of Love-friendly psychedelic fractal screen. Of all their very early songs, 'Strip It Down' would survive longest in their live set (well into 1992).

Packaged in a sleeve entitled 'Collapsed European Stars' (a distorted EC flag, designed by Richey's old student mate Dan), each of the original thousand copies came rubber-stamped: 'MADE IN WALES'.

* * *

Philip Hall knew the music business – and, importantly, the music media – inside out. Born in Ealing on 27 August 1959, he had studied at Wimbledon College and the London College of Printing, and had graduated to a job as a journalist at *Record Mirror* before switching sides in the propaganda wars and working in the press offices of EMI and Stiff Records.

In 1985, he quit Stiff to go it alone, and set up the independent PR and management company Hall Or Nothing with his younger brother Martin. The company quickly grew to become arguably the biggest in the business, handling a phenomenally successful series of press campaigns including those of The Pogues, The Waterboys, The Stone Roses, James, The Sundays and The Beautiful South, among many others. Philip Hall was a true gentleman in an industry often populated by sharks, and his relaxed, friendly manner achieved better results, and was much more pleasant to deal with, than any amount of high-pressure wheeler-dealing. He twice won the trade magazine *Music Week*'s Leslie Perrin PR of the Year Award (for The Pogues and The Stone Roses).

By the time Manic Street Preachers approached Philip, he was already aware that something of a buzz was growing around them. Ian Ballard had sent him a copy of 'New Art Riot', and both Kevin Pearce (who had booked the band for the Horse & Groom gigs) and *NME*'s Steve Lamacq had recommended that Philip should check them out. In the summer of 1990, Richey wrote Philip a highly emotive letter, pleading that if he didn't help them to escape they would die of boredom. Hall, strangely moved, wrote back, promising to catch their next London gig. The Manics didn't have a London gig lined up, so Philip and his brother Martin drove all the way to Gwent to meet the band and to watch them rehearse.

It nearly went horribly wrong. By the time the Hall brothers arrived at Newbridge School, where the band was going through its paces, Nicky Wire was covered in blood. He had somehow managed to whack himself in the face with the end of his bass, rupturing a blood vessel in his nose. James, meanwhile, didn't say a word, and after a few minutes walked out of the room. It was, of course, shyness, but could easily have been mistaken for hostility. Martin took one look at the blood-spattered Wire and the brooding Bradfield, and whispered to his brother: 'Let's get out of here.' Fortunately, however, Philip was oddly captivated by this chaotic, intense, driven unit. He wanted to see more.

In mid-August, with Hall's encouragement (and against their better judgement), the band played another showcase at The Rock Garden. On this occasion, thirty people turned up (a 100 per cent improvement on the last time). Two of the audience were Jeff Barrett and Martin Kelly of independent label Heavenly Records, there on the recommendation of Bob Stanley, Kevin Pearce and the Halls (who they knew from various Happy Mondays/Stone Roses gigs). 'They played the most amazing set ever,' Kelly later told *Record Collector*. 'Nicky trashed his bass at the end. It was a Rickenbacker, worth God knows what, and he totally smashed it to pieces. In front of a handful of people! We were completely blown away.'

Kelly and Barrett rushed 'backstage' (again, there was no dressing-room as such – just a corridor). 'We said: "We've got a label, can we sign you?" They went, "Aah, fuck off! Who are you, then? EMI?!" They weren't the slightest bit interested. In fact, they were really abusive . . . but it was a really good attitude.' The pair persisted, telling the band they were from Heavenly, home to Flowered Up and, more importantly, to Saint Etienne, of whom the Manics were major fans (and were now friends). The ice was broken. All four members simultaneously stood up and shook their hands.

The next morning, Barrett and Kelly held a meeting with the Hall brothers, the mutual conclusion being: 'If you're in, so are we.' Philip contacted the band to tell them that not only did he want to be their publicist, he wanted to be their manager as well. Although the Manics had been doing a reasonable job of managing themselves (having parted amicably with amateur rocketeer Mark Jones some time ago), they needed a professional to take them to the next level. As Nicky put it: 'We really had no notion of what Philip really did, or how helpful he could be to us. We just thought he sounded like a person who could help us out.'

Hall would become the Manics' Malcolm McLaren, but in a far quieter, more understated and dignified way. His high-powered status, the respect he commanded in the business and his shrewd management skills all proved invaluable. 'He had to put up with a lot,' Nicky later admitted. 'Even when we smashed up our equipment, he never got pissed off – in fact, he used to encourage it, he used to have a glint in his eye. He loved a good wind-up.'

Hall also passionately believed in the band, sometimes in the face of not-inconsiderable ridicule, and showed a courageous (one might almost say foolish) degree of faith in it. Without a proper record deal, however, the band members were penniless, and had tried in vain to get a bank loan, as Richey would later recall: 'We used to go into Nat West, all the banks, and try to get a loan. We used to go and tell them: "This country is dead musically. There's got to be room for an exciting rock band." We'd show them *NME*: "Look at that, anything good in there? Now look at us, we're really exciting." We told them we were going to be this really exciting rock 'n' roll band. They couldn't see it.'

Philip Hall, amazingly, *could* see it. Within six months – unasked – he had plunged £45,000 of his own money into the band. (Contrary to many versions, he never needed to remortgage his house, but it was nonetheless a hefty and risky investment in what many saw as an untested bunch of hapless chancers.)

Jeff Barrett and Martin Kelly also honoured their side of the bargain. On 30 August, the Manics 'signed' with Heavenly (again, it was a gentlemen's agreement without contracts). Although there was no cash advance, the days of scraping together dole cheques and getting paper cuts from assembling DIY singles sleeves were over. Barrett and Kelly may not have shared the Manics' precise aesthetic, but they could at least empathise with it. Reciprocally, the Manics considered Heavenly 'the most exciting label around at the time'; it was (and is) a label run by music fans, with what could loosely be termed a punk attitude. The 'signing' was, nonetheless, a move which surprised outsiders. Creation Records' supremo Alan McGee phoned up in fits of laughter: 'What the fuck are you doing, signing that dodgy Welsh punk band?!' It seemed a strange marriage from both sides. After all, Heavenly was basically the London wing of the Madchester movement, and Jeff did the PR for The Happy Mondays and Primal Scream. Indeed, as Barrett confirms: 'There was a bit of friendly needle. Our lifestyle was something [Manic Street Preachers] considered frivolous and pointless.' He recalls the Manics' first visit to Heavenly's HQ: 'I'll never forget the look on their faces when they walked into the office and saw all the Mondays memorabilia on the walls.' The sheer incongruity of an ultra-cool London indie-dance label signing an angry situationist rock unit from Gwent appealed enormously to Jeff's sense of perversity.

For a while, life with a record deal wasn't too different from life without one. Much of the autumn was spent driving up to London for profile-raising gigs in sweaty indie pubs (the White Horse, the Bull & Gate), playing sets of barely more than fifteen minutes, going out 'wining and dining' with music biz acquaintances until 4 a.m., then driving back to Blackwood after no sleep and carrying on the next day.

On 25 October, Heavenly sent their new acquisitions into London's Power Plant studios for four days, to record ten songs for two singles (on the condition that the label choose the A-sides). Resident producer Robin Evans was assisted by Dave Eringa, a blond-haired Essex rock kid of Dutch descent who, at just 21 years old, was something of a studio prodigy. Eringa instantly hit it off with the band, and ended up contributing keyboards as well as engineering the sessions.

Once freed from the studio, however, it was back to a familiar ritual: the support slot with the gruesomely inappropriate headline act. On 1 November, the band drove to Salisbury Arts Centre to open once again for crusty folkers The Levellers (another Hall Or Nothing band, and just about the only gig the Halls could get them at the time), and performed to a room of bewildered dreadheads, many of them sitting cross-legged on the floor. Even Nicky throwing soap at them and jeering: 'It's time for you to take your greyhounds for a walk, you scabby lot!' didn't stir a reaction. Maybe he tried the wrong approach: as Richey unforgettably told *Melody Maker*: 'You could go to any Levellers concert and stand in the middle and shout "Jeremy!", and 75 per cent of the audience would turn round.' The sight of all those middle-class kids self-consciously slumming it left an indelible impression on Edwards. 'You can tell they're middle-class poseurs because they wanna dress down like scummy people. The working-class tradition has always been to want to be clean. All my dad's friends want to do when they come home from the pit or whatever is have a wash, have a shave, dress up and go out.'

On 16 November the Manics made an equally doomed attempt to convert a roomful of baggy kids by supporting Flowered Up, Camden Town's answer to The Happy Mondays, at Manchester International. The Joe Bloggs-wearing Mancs were as unresponsive as the crusties and loitered at the back, Boddingtons in hand. James taunted them: 'I'd be scared to come down the front too if I was you.' Nicky, perhaps allergic to the city itself, discovered a number of grotesque boils on his neck after the show, and had to go to a hospital to have them lanced.

In general, however, rubbing shoulders with the Heavenly Mafia meant a better class of support slot. The Flowered Up gig was booked via Jeff Barrett, who was pulling out all the stops to give maximum exposure to his new protégés. He also let the Manics open for Saint Etienne in Birmingham, and arranged a series of similar Heavenly package shows.

Caffy St Luce of Hall Or Nothing was doing Heavenly's regional radio plugging when a wild-eyed Barrett took her off to the pub and enthused about the Welsh punk band he had just signed. One listen to a tape of the next single was enough to convert Caffy, and she made sure of a place at the front for their next show, supporting Teenage Fanclub at

Highbury's T&C2 (now The Garage) on 6 December, a show which was also being filmed by BBC2's *Snub TV*.

As Caffy remembers, the Manics sacrificed accuracy to excitement: 'It was as if the Beatles had taken too much speed at Hamburg. Poetry over a tune. I fell in love. They were dreadful! They were throwing shapes and poses – you could hear the tunes, but they were playing them too fast. The amount of mouths open in the crowd was the main thing. It was the stuff that myths are made of, the only mythical band of the 90s. I'd given up on that ever happening again.'

It wasn't that they couldn't play – they just thought putting on a show was more important. On one occasion, Nicky was so busy jumping around that he forgot to turn on his bass. When he finally noticed, mid-song, and flipped the switch, it caused an earsplitting screech of feedback. Of course, many assumed they were simply incompetent. Even their long-serving soundman, Handsome John, has gone on record as saying: 'They were a fucking shambles to begin with, but they had ambition.' But not everyone was fooled. As The Buzzcocks' Pete Shelley remarked after one early gig: 'Very good, in fact *too* good . . . How do they do all those squiggly guitar bits?'

Other dinosaurs of alternative rock were less keen to dig the new breed. To Steve Hanley of The Fall, they looked like 'someone doing The Clash in a school play'; to William Reid of The Jesus and Mary Chain, they were 'all attitude and no music. I've never been into cabaret. If that's what you want, fine, but fuck off to Las Vegas'.

Image-wise, the Manics weren't even ready to fuck off to Lyme Regis. They were still sufficiently poor to need to attempt glamour on a budget, and it didn't always work. But as Caffy St Luce charitably puts it: 'If they'd done it properly, it wouldn't have been the Manics. You know how there's always a kid at school who looks like they've stepped out of *The Face* magazine and, no matter how hard you try to look like them, you still look like you've just woken up? That's what the Manics are like. They're punks by birth rather than by dress sense.'

Their make-up was the cheapest available (more Boots 17 than Bourjois), and their clothes were invariably second-hand. James sometimes wore a salmon-pink pyjama top which had once belonged to Nicky's auntie, with 'I AM A SLUT' stencilled on it (presumably not by Nicky's auntie), or an old darts shirt bearing the words 'AESTHETIC DEBRIS' (causing Nick to call him 'Jocky Wilson').

On 13 December, the band returned to London to play the Heavenly Christmas Party at the Camden Underworld, alongside Saint Etienne, Flowered Up and Martin Kelly's own band, East Village. Previously, Jeff Barrett had insisted that Heavenly package gigs rotated their running order from show to show, and tonight it was the Manics' turn to open, with East Village next. Kelly protested: 'No way! How are we supposed to follow that?!' In the end the Manics did open, with Nicky Wire announcing to the assembled bizzy bodies: 'The only reason we're on first is because we're the best!'

It was a triumphant but erratic performance, with Wire swigging red wine from a bottle throughout, nearly stumbling offstage and hitting many a bum note. It was also on this night, so legend has it, that Richey finally lost his virginity. After the party, too drunk to know what he was doing, he was dragged into a toilet cubicle by a music-biz press officer, an unprepossessing woman at least a decade Richey's senior. Until that night, he hadn't even kissed a girl. James, so the story goes, was furious, cornering the woman afterwards and hissing at her, 'Do you realise what you've done?'

'The city is the graveyard of the guerrilla' – FIDEL CASTRO

In the New Year of 1991, Philip Hall made another great sacrifice for the Manics. Only a few short months after getting married, he allowed the band to come and live in his house in Shepherd's Bush with himself and new wife Terri.

It was an odd arrangement – Nicky and Richey would share a bed in one room, while Sean and James slept in another, like Morecambe and Wise, or Bert and Ernie from *Sesame Street* (although, contrary to romanticised legend, they never slept on the kitchen floor or in the bath). 'I woke up with the vodka seeping out of Richey's skin,' Nicky later told *Esquire*. But the four, aware of just how far the Halls were putting themselves out, did everything to make it work. Philip described them as 'sweet' house guests. While he was out at work, they'd gather in the kitchen and prepare his tea. Caffy St Luce remembers the unlikely sight of James Dean Bradfield hunched over the sink in his Marigolds on many an occasion. Terri Hall's main memory of the Manics' time on her floor, she told *Q*, was 'Babycham in the fridge and four totally different-sized pairs of white Levis in the washing machine.' Nonetheless, there were tensions. According to Wire, Terri could occasionally be heard shouting at Philip: 'Why don't you go and sleep with those dodgy old Manics?'

MSP mythology has often held that Richey, unaware of what he was doing, would idly cut himself while watching TV *chez* Hall, until someone would cough, and he'd stop and apologise. ('He was subconciously drawing blood the way other people chew nails,' *Select* once wrote.) In fact, Richey was far more considerate. On one occasion he appeared to be about to stub out a cigarette on his arm, but Philip took him to one side and had a quiet word, asking in no uncertain terms that he desist out of respect for Terri, who disapproved of that kind of thing – a request to which Richey happily adhered.

Metropolitan living was, to say the least, a culture shock to the Manics, who had not even been on what they touchingly called 'the big train' until they took the Inter-City 125 to London for band purposes. As a somewhat bewildered Richey told *Top* magazine, 'Up here people seem to put a lot of work into things we never thought about when we were growing up, like being seen to wear Calvin Klein underwear, to be seen to be doing the right thing. I'd never even heard of bottled water before I came to London; back home you've got to really search for your Evian!' James was equally scornful of Londoners who 'never sit down to Sunday dinner' and 'can't even keep pets properly'.

The Manics' next chance to convert the Evian-swilling hordes came on Friday 11 January. Royal Holloway College, at Egham, Surrey, is a palatial green-belt outpost of the University of London (Richey went away afterwards mistakenly believing that it was a public school). As it was a Friday night and a mere £20 black-cab ride from Chelsea, a gaggle of major-label A & R men gathered – like the peculiar lemming/vulture crossbreeds they are – at Royal Holloway to see what Philip Hall had been bending their ears about for the last six months. The Manics set about turning the place upside-down while the men from WEA, EMI, Def Jam and Sony watched stunned, and – with one exception – appalled.

For the time being, in any case, the Manics were still a Heavenly act. Jeff Barrett and Martin Kelly had been scanning the Power Plant tapes for potential singles. The first choice stood out a mile.

> 'The social revolution . . . cannot draw its poetry from the past, but only from the future. It cannot begin with itself before it has stripped itself of all superstitions concerning the past' –
> KARL MARX

Released on 21 January at the height of the Gulf War, 'Motown Junk', a new song, was a tiny cyclone, an apocalypse in miniature. Its frame of reference spanned generations (the intro sampled Public Enemy, the outro sampled The Skids), and yet in essence and spirit it was utterly NOW. *The Face* made a prediction: 'It will be the most awesome and scandalous rock record of 1991.' And, context being everything, it was exactly that: a magnesium-white flare of adrenalin amid a year of dope smoke and little fluffy clouds.

The song was not literally an attack on the Tamla Motown label (of which James is quite a fan), but of its debased late-80s imitators, the blue-eyed soul-sters – Wet Wet Wet, Simply Red, George Michael – whose apoliti-cal love-ballad sludge was satu-

"'Never' ever wanted to be with you
All you ever gave was the boredom I
suffocate in
Adrift in cheap dreams dont stop the rain
Numbed out in piss towns just wanna
dig their graves.'"

'Motown Junk' lyrics, as scrawled by Richey.

rating the airwaves. The chorus hinged upon the jaw-dropping line: 'I laughed when Lennon got shot' – an outrageous act of generation terrorism. This was rock 'n' roll patricide (the Manics had once described themselves as 'four baby Hamlets'): the clearest expression of their impulse to destroy history, both musically and culturally. As they told *NME*: 'By denying ourselves a past we are trying to find a worthwhile present out of this junky wreckage of life.'

The planned B-side tracks for the single were the ballistic, nihilistic 'Sorrow 16' (featuring a rare Nicky Wire backing vocal: 'I feel like falling . . . IN HATE!') and the anti-monarchist 'Ceremonial Rape Machine'. However, there was a problem. The workers at the pressing plant refused to print the latter and, under pressure from Heavenly, the band renamed the song 'We Her Majesty's Prisoners' – a move which still rankles with James. The sleeve was also vetoed. The original version, designed by Paul Cannell, was to feature a photograph of John and Yoko with a gun to their heads. On Jeff Barrett's advice, this was ditched, and was replaced with the picture of the watch stopped at the moment of the Hiroshima blast. The Manics were learning the hard way that working within the music industry invariably entails compromise.

Nonetheless, the single became technically their first chart hit, peaking at No. 92. It also made No. 7 in the indie charts (not that they would have cared). More importantly, it won them their first ever music-press front cover: a John Robb feature in *Sounds* (26 January 1991). And this was where I came in. I had already fallen in love with the interviews, the manifesto, the hype. Then Caffy St Luce sent me a copy of the single.

It stayed glued to my turntable for the next month. But I have already mentioned that . . .

On the night of the single's release, BBC2's *Snub TV* included a feature on the Manics, comprising live footage of 'Motown Junk' from the T&C2 gig, as well as one of the most brilliant (and hilarious) rock 'n' roll interviews ever screened. Their heads dramatically lit, resembling the 'Bohemian Rhapsody' video or some be-maquillaged Mount Rushmore, the four took it in turns to deliver a stuttering but articulate rant, often finishing each other's sentences.

'Youth culture has always been controlled by the same people, selling the same goods at inflated prices . . . If you're told what youth culture is, it's not much use . . . Youth is the ultimate product . . . We just want to mix politics and sex and look brilliant onstage and say brilliant things . . . We're the most original band of the last fifteen years . . . We'll never write a love song, ever, or a ballad, or a trip-out (a line which would be quoted, years later, in the chorus of Saint Etienne's 'Wood Cabin'), we'll be dead before we have to do that . . . We don't even want to reach the music papers, we just want to reach the *Sun*, *Daily Star*, the *Mirror* . . . We'd rather be sensationalised than be just another *NME* band and get critical respect.'

'Demand the impossible' – PARISIAN GRAFFITO, MAY 1968

The Manics had also made a promise which they would repeat in several publications over the next year, but which would haunt them for far longer. They would, so the outrageous claim went, release one double album, shift around sixteen million copies (the exact figure varied from interview to interview) into every home from Bangkok to Senegal, headline Wembley Stadium for three nights, and then split up. 'No one has ever sacrificed themselves,' said Richey. 'If we become huge and just throw it away, that is a big statement.'

For the time being, however, Wembley would have to wait. A mini-tour of the UK's smaller venues – the band's first real campaign – was arranged to support the single, but the first four dates had to be cancelled when Nicky required emergency surgery to have a thyroid cyst removed from his throat; he needed twelve stitches, from which a faint scar is still visible. A wry Hall Or Nothing press statement explained that: 'According to the specialist who treated him, it arose out of "boredom and physical inertia due to a lifestyle of force-fed TV, no sleep, and a diet of Coke and chips".'

Eventually, on 23 January, the foursome piled their gear into a pale blue purpose-built mini-van (its interior decorated with an R. Edwards collage), and, with Richey in the driver's seat, took to the road. From Glasgow down to Brighton, the Manics would roll into town, stride onstage to a tape of Allen Ginsberg's *Howl*, and tear through a set which invariably culminated with instruments being reduced to matchwood *à la* Townshend. Instrument-trashing had long been one of rock's classic pantomime gestures – the epitome of rock 'n' roll's capitalist waste. There was nothing new in the Manics' axe-smashing, nor were they reinterpreting the act in any post-modern, ironic or symbolic way. It was pure end-of-gig adrenalin. As Caffy St Luce saw it: 'Once one of them started, it caught on like a yawn. If Richey smashed his guitar, James smashed his as well. A lot of people were horrified, but Richey always said, "It's a piece of wood and some strings, not a baby!"'

The aggro onstage was often the catalyst for violence in the crowd, and the band was hardly innocent of provocation (when one Scouse punter shouted 'Faggot!' James yelled, 'I'm gonna fuck you so hard up the arse after the show!'). Early MSP audiences tended to be an odd mixture of the curious, the belligerent (the gobbing, bottle-hurling types who come out of the woodwork whenever a 'punk revival' materialises) and small anti-Manics factions, infuriated by something the band had said in the press (or by their general attitude and appearance), who turned up specifically looking for trouble.

The worst incident occurred on 8 March at Glasgow's Gourock Bay Hotel. Throughout the set, beered-up Glaswegians climbed onstage aiming punches at the band, threw glasses and, adding a quaint local touch, fired hypodermics filled with lager (this, at least, was the band's optimistic assessment of the syringes' contents). Someone dived into Sean's drumkit, almost decapitating him with a cymbal, and then a glass smashed into James's mouth, drawing blood. 'Do that once more and I'll bash your face in with my guitar,' he growled, launching into 'Slash 'N' Burn'. Almost inevitably, he was struck seconds later by a flying beer can. Subsequent press reports claimed that he needed eighteen stitches (in fact, he needed none, although this probably says more about James's head than it does about journalistic mendacity).

Sean, James, Nicky and Richey had thus far managed to reach the ages of 20, 22, 22 and 23 respectively without ever having left the UK. When Heavenly arranged a quadruple bill at the Locomotive Club in Paris on 21 March, all four Manics had to buy passports the day before.

Spending such a long time on a bus together exacerbated the culture clash between the Manics and their label-mates (there was simmering antagonism between MSP and Flowered Up, in particular, all the way), but the Manics were too polite to cause a scene. Indeed, when Richey put on a Hanoi Rocks tape, he actually apologised to an incredulous Pete Wiggs of Saint Etienne. Wiggs also commented later: 'I remember one time, when we got off the bus, Nicky Wire actually cleaned up the floor with a dustpan and brush. It was amazing!'

This was a common experience. Despite their firebrand rhetoric, anyone who actually met the Manics was surprised and charmed to find a bunch of sweet, polite Welsh boys who loved their mams – a rock 'n' roll version of *Viz*'s Pathetic Sharks. (Caffy St Luce's first impressions had been 'Oh, bless! They had none of the usual seen-it-all-before London cockiness. Nicky was just a big floppy puppy.')

The Manics may have been out of step with Heavenly's hedonistic post-acieed/baggy clique back in London, but in Paris such considerations were irrelevant. Taking the stage long after midnight, they stormed the joint. Thirty minutes later, during their now-traditional wrecking session, a shirtless James threw his guitar in the air. It hit the neon Locomotive sign and crashed down into Sean's drumkit (much to Sean's displeasure). Seconds later, Wire launched his microphone stand into the delirious crowd. Martin Kelly takes up the story: 'It was one of those ones with a really heavy iron-tripod base, and I remember thinking, "Jesus, that must have really hurt someone!" Anyway, we were all staying in this really cheap hotel that night, and the Manics' room was opposite mine. In the morning, I heard Nicky and Richey leaving their rooms, and Nicky saying: "I wonder what happened to the guy who got hit by my mike stand? I feel really guilty about it now." Then five minutes later, these two Welsh rugby supporters came out of another room (Wales was playing France that day), with one of them saying, "Aargh! My shoulder kills! That bloke who threw the mike stand at me was Welsh an' all!" An incredible coincidence. Of all the hotels in all of Paris . . .'

My own first Manic Street Preachers experience came on a miserable Monday night in Rainy City. On 29 April, for the second time, the Manics were sharing a stage with a baggy band in the indie dance capital, Manchester. After months of alternate nagging and sulking, I had finally been given the chance to review them for *Melody Maker*.

Their co-headliner at the Irn Bru Rock Week night at the Boardwalk was First Offence, a sorry shower of homophobic knuckledraggers in hooded tops, purveying third-rate white-trash hip-hop. A war of words was already underway: F/Off had told the press, 'They wear make-up, they're faggots. We hate faggots. You can put that down.' (If anyone resembled 'a ball of chopped, seasoned liver, served baked', I knew who my money was on.) At the end of a farcical set, they left the stage to a tape of 'Motown Junk' mixed with chicken noises.

At 11.20 p.m., Nicky Wire – an etiolated streak of sex with what *Iconoclastic Glitter* would describe as 'steely, watery blue eyes' and a shark-in-lipstick smile – hobbled onstage and announced: '*Our* first offence is to be beautiful.' The Manics – every bit as much a reaction against their native environment (the art-hating, meat-eating, beer-drinking, rugby-obsessed, ultra-macho hell that is south Wales) as First Offence were a cretinous reflection of theirs – proceeded to treat the queerbashers to one long, slow, glorious wind-up.

In the very first song, Nicky licked James's neck; he then dragged Richey to the floor, straddled him and started dry-humping him, while boring, boring Manchester just stood there in bowlcuts and flares, sexually threatened, speechless.

I remember thinking that Edwards was the most beautiful man I had ever seen – the eyes of Elizabeth Taylor with New York Dolls hair (he was greeted with a 'Johnny Thunders!' heckle); a baby Ronnie Wood with Townshend's scant respect for guitars. As Caitlin Moran of *The Times* would later write, 'Richey has that patented aura of rock star about him. He looks like all the cool members of The Rolling Stones put together.'

I remember being bemused by Nicky Wire: sarcasm-on-stilts, a rock 'n' roll Oscar Wilde, in perfect DIY glamour from head down to ankles – then a battered Green Flash plimsoll on one foot and a mucky plastercast on the other. I also remember thinking, 'That little mod bloke isn't very glamorous, maybe they ought to get rid of him . . .' Then I noticed that the screwed-up ball of intensity behind the mike was playing all the music.

Somehow, the crazy cacophony of tinny, trebly guitars and sexy star-jumps was enough to make me predict that they would become 'the most important reference-point of the decade, a Rock 'n' Roll Suicide (they ARE rock 'n' roll; they wanna DESTROY rock 'n' roll)', in a review littered with phrases like 'ATTITUDE × ARROGANCE × REVOLUTION × SEX' and 'Insurrection as pure pop thrill'.

* * *

Back in the bar of an unglamorous Rusholme boarding house, I was amazed to find myself discussing politics and cultural theory with Sean Moore (the drummer, for Christ's sake – what kind of a band was this?!). Meanwhile, Richey Edwards was gamely attempting to discuss politics and cultural theory with two local rock chicks, before eventually capitulating and ushering them upstairs to give them what they really wanted.

These were the Manics' decadence days; it was their era of Byzantine excess-all-areas and Hammer of the Gods hedonism (albeit on a pitiful budget of £5 a day each). Sex was becoming plentiful, and Nicky would often shag a groupie while room-mate Richey read books in the other bed, or vice versa. Sometimes – presumably if the book were a little dull – they would both get involved.

The *NME*'s James Brown once reported a lurid tale about Nicky and Richey sharing something called a 'downhill skier'. 'It's when two of you lie naked on either side of a woman,' they supposedly boasted, 'and she grabs your dick and wanks you both off at the same time . . . downhill skiing. We had a competition to see who'd come first.' The band have since denied the story (it remains unclear whether they invented it to impress Brown, or Brown invented it to entertain his readers, or they cooked it up between them). Brown *was* present, though, when Wire, having spent his daily fiver on an expensive cocktail, threw up, chewed some gum to freshen his breath, and started snogging some poor girl.

Nicky knew deep down, however, that he wasn't cut out for this sort of thing. One night in May, he had a Road To Damascus (well, Warrington) revelation. 'We were driving to Warrington for a gig and we stopped at this pub and I just thought: "I wanna go home to my mum and stop drinking." I saw the light.'

He drank that night, though, downing an irresponsibly lengthy succession of Smirnoff/Babycham cocktails before puking on Richey's bed and making a doomed attempt to have sex with a lucky Cheshire lass. The next morning, they awoke to a knock on the door. James Brown, no mean hedonist himself, was there to do an interview. 'Oooooh, my cock!' were Wire's words of greeting. 'I've had herpes since I was fifteen,' he lied (his mother didn't see the funny side: when she read this, she wouldn't speak to him). Richey, curled up in the bed opposite, had no sympathy. '"Sorry babe, wait till morning, I've had too much to drink" – that's what you were telling her! I'm never embarrassed by his behaviour, because it's never long enough to get embarrassed about it! His chat-up lines are the worst.' Nicky sportingly re-enacted a prize example. '"When I look into your eyes, I'm lost . . ." I was between her legs when I said that.'

At the end of the tour, Nicky was hospitalised with a liver-threatening dose of hepatitis (a possible legacy of the condition is that, to this day, Wire needs to urinate four times before going onstage, much to James's exasperation: 'The intro's running and he's just pissing on and on! The last thing I do is pull his zipper up!'). Nicky was later diagnosed as suffering from a liver disease called Gilbert's Syndrome, brought on by drinking. Put simply, a missing enzyme means that he is in danger of going yellow with jaundice if he drinks too much alcohol.

Six months of ultra-decadent behaviour ended that night. No more drink, no more screwing around. Nicky Wire's days of sex, booze and rock 'n' roll excess were over. Since

he only went into pubs for the fruities, he didn't really miss the drink: 'I was never a pub person anyway. I'd only drink in nightclubs, or before the band went onstage. I needed it to be a bit more showbiz glitzy.' The girls had lost their fascination, too, and before long Nicky was reunited with his childhood sweetheart, Rachel.

From now on, Richey Edwards would have to conduct his pursuit of pleasure alone.

'Camus said that "If God does not exist, then I am God." That was our philosophy' – RICHEY ON *VIVID TV*

The Manics' next single could scarcely have been more anthemic without morphing into 'La Marseillaise'. Released on 7 May, 'You Love Us' was Heavenly's second selection from the Power Plant sessions.

Beginning with a sustained squall of scraped strings, sampled from Penderecki's 'Threnody to the Victims of Hiroshima', it kicks into an us-against-the-world fusillade – a fanfare for the uncommon man which echoes the defiant spirit of Millwall's 'No one likes us, we don't care' chant, and inverted both the Stones' 'We Love You' and the Pistols' 'I Love You'. The fade-out samples Iggy Pop's 'Lust for Life' (a Wire favourite, itself named after a 1956 biopic of Vincent Van Gogh, who crops up more than once in the Manics' story). A brilliant video was made in which a Marilyn Monroe lookalike tears off her wig, smears lipstick across her face and turns into Nicky Wire (a direct steal from David Bowie's 'Boys Keep Swinging'), and a fabulously apt promotional item was sent to journalists: a Rimmel powder compact with the band's name scrawled lipstick-style (a parody of the New York Dolls logo) across the mirror.

As well as a live version of 'Strip It Down' recorded at Bath Moles, and 'Starlover', a frankly hypocritical attack on groupies (although the line 'Leper cult disciples of a stillborn Christ' was apparently dedicated to Ian Brown and Shaun Ryder), the EP includes what was probably the band's most accomplished work yet. According to Wire, 'Spectators of Suicide' incorporated ideas stolen from the Dada, situationist and futurist manifestos. Specifically, in title and content, it is a clear reference to Guy Debord's 1967 situationist text *The Society of the Spectacle*. The theories of the situationists had had a formative fascination for the Manics. An anti-ideology which flourished in the Paris uprising of 1968, situationism was all about demanding a more real life – passionate, participative – as opposed to the futile living-death subsistence offered by capitalism, which could only be jolted by creating 'revolutionary situations' or 'disruptive events' (which, on a good night, might suffice to describe a Manics concert). Debord believed that people do not experience the reality of capitalism, but the 'spectacle' which hides the awful reality and the contradictions (MSP, in a similar spirit, longed to explode the sorry 'spectacle' of early 90s pop culture). He also noted the way in which revolution is always appropriated by the mainstream and resold as fashion (this was why the Angry Brigade blew up the Kensington boutique Biba) . . . ironically, exactly what the Manics' detractors accused them of doing.

The 'You Love Us' sleeve was intended to be a shot of Chris Eubank, an appropriately unapologetic love/hate figure, until threats of legal action forced its withdrawal. Instead, Richey made a collage featuring a gallery of MSP icons: Monroe, De Niro, The Clash, Marley, Crowley, Townshend and Dalle (prompting a minor fuss that the images had been used without permission). Richey's fondness for collage, which he was by now applying to the walls of hotel rooms, tour buses and studios, was no accident. The cut-and-paste aesthetic was intrinsically symbolic: Picasso had used collage as a badge of his anarchist sympathies, using 'low' materials such as newsprint as a slap in the face to the oil-on-canvas 'high' art of the status quo (compare this to Richey's comments on high/low forms of music in the 'Condemned to Rock 'n' Roll' chapter).

'You Love Us' made No. 64 in the Gallup charts and also, for what it was worth, reached the Indie No. 1.

Then something happened.

b) Condemned to rock 'n' roll?

(THE MANICS AND THE ROCK)

Fanzine: 'Are the Manics the future of rock 'n' roll?'
Nicky Wire: 'Rock 'n' roll has no future'

I N THE EARLY 1980S, when the junior Manic Street Preachers were first discovering the music press, the pages of *New Musical Express* provided the battleground for a war between the rival factions known as Rockists (discophobes who clung to punk values of 'authenticity' and 'realness') and Soul Boys (post-modern types in love with surface glamour and the fast-moving trends of black music).

The Manics, in musical terms at least, were Rockists to the core. One early live number, 'Destroy the Dancefloor', blatantly echoed the clarion call of The Smiths to 'burn down the disco'. James Dean Bradfield and Richey Edwards were both to be seen wearing T-shirts reading, respectively, 'I LOVE SLASH, WE HATE DANCE' and 'DEATH BY DISCO', with no apparent irony – an uncomfortable throwback to the 'Disco Sucks' campaign (the covertly racist/homophobic offensive launched by American redneck DJs in the late 70s, and stupidly adopted by punks).

'We started at a time when rock 'n' roll was dead,' said Richey in his defence. 'The UK was in the grip of dance, rap and the acid house thing. We were consciously reacting against all that. Our friends laughed at us because they said there was no audience for us. But we felt we had to do something to bring back rock 'n' roll.' An inglorious motive, it must be said – on a par with trying to save morris dancing, the pound note or the British banger. Eventually, the Manics would screech into a handbrake U-turn away from their Luddite, Morrissey-esque anti-dance stance: since the techno reworkings of 'Faster', no MSP single has been complete without a selection of remixes by the most droppable names of the moment (although Nicky couldn't help showing his true colours, making disparaging remarks about 'the fucking Chemical Brothers' in the press).

The band's relationship to hip-hop and funk was more complex. Richey was in love with Public Enemy ('like Aretha Franklin on smack,' he commented approvingly), and once expressed a disturbing fondness for Jamiroquai. James was well into old skoolers like Ultramagnetic MCs and NWA (and remains a knowledgeable rap-fiend); even Nicky, who will freely admit that his musical tastes are the most traditional within the band, once said, 'The only way for a white band to assimilate hip-hop is through the bass,' and studied Trouble Funk twelve-inchers for ideas. The Manics' twin inspirations, they regularly proclaimed, were Guns N'Roses and Public Enemy. So why didn't they *sound* as though that were true? (Richey's and Nicky's lyrics may have been Chuck D, but James's and Sean's music was pure Slash.) After all, at exactly the time that MSP were claiming to be a fantasy meeting of Public Enemy and Guns N'Roses, other bands – Rage Against the Machine, Senser, Anthrax, Red Hot Chili Peppers, Fishbone, Beastie Boys and Faith No More – were, to varying degrees, already putting the theory into practice. 'Our first idea was to become a rap band,' explained Richey, 'but it would've been so fucking shit, so typical of a lot of white English bands at the time which suddenly changed from playing guitars to sampling and going, "Yeah!" We can only really make basic, straightforward white rock music, cos we're not patronising people to pretend we understand "the street", or we understand New York City. You know, we live in a crap little town in Britain.'

'Rock 'n' roll is dead. But it's our only culture' – RICHEY, PRIVATE LETTER, JANUARY 1991

That 'crap little town' was responsible not only for the Manics' message, but for the very material of their discourse. The valleys of south Wales are, and have always been, solid Heavy Metal country. Richey once noted that 'In the provinces, rock music never dies at all', and this was certainly true of Blackwood, where 'Thou Shalt Dig Motley Crüe' is still the Eleventh Commandment. 'Our friends at school were faced with a choice between Hanoi Rocks and The Smiths,' said Nicky, 'and they chose Hanoi Rocks every time.' The Manics were no different (the first record that Nicky Wire ever bought was 'Neon Knights' by Black Sabbath). This is why they utilised what one writer called 'the sort of arrogant power chords which British indie groups are far too namby-pamby, fey and self-conscious to use'. Most alternative rock acts, at some point in their ascendancy, record a Peel Session; the Manics went straight for the Tommy Vance show.

Heavy Metal is, in many ways, comparable to movie genres such as horror, action and sci-fi: frowned upon as 'trashy' by highbrow cinéastes, governed by formula, cliché and convention, but able to provide undeniable visceral thrills. The Manics understood the 'low' kicks that rock could give. 'Literature is dead in the twentieth century,' claimed Richey in 1991. 'It has been made bankrupt, and rock 'n' roll is the only culture the masses have got left. Books have gone, graffiti is all we've got left. We're into low forms of art that people can understand.' Some critics considered the Manics' beloved HM to be intrinsically reactionary (one writer referred to 'their usual formula of Left Bank sensibilities and right-wing guitar music'). This was a line of attack the band didn't take lying down. An *NME* questionnaire once posed the question 'Glam: Laughable or Seminal?' to Richey. 'Hanoi Rocks gave us Guns N'Roses,' he replied, 'the Byrds gave us critically acclaimed lumps of static shit. T. Rex = Hanoi Rocks = Guns N'Roses = Glamour/ Seminal, The Byrds = Velvet Underground = Orange Juice = Primal Scream =

Laughable.' Nicky, asked to justify Guns N'Roses, was more direct: 'If you're gonna rock, then really fucking rock.'

'Originality is so boring and safe' – RICHEY

Personal taste and social environment were not the only factors behind Manic Street Preachers' metallic KO. They knew exactly what they were doing.

The Manics had no time whatsoever for what they termed 'the empty statement of art-school dissension' ('Soul Contamination'). 'There's a tendency in this country for people to demand really dry, avant-garde originality,' complained Richey, 'which we don't have much respect for.' At a time when many music hacks were particularly hung up on notions of art-rock experimentalism, the Manics were on a one-way ticket to the critical abattoir, but they refused to bow to the indie conceit of what Richey called 'white middle-class kids playing at being artists when all they ever wanted to do was have a few beers and have a laugh'. They showed no mercy to the press darlings of the day. 'My Bloody Valentine, for example, are just atrocious,' said Nicky. 'I'd rather listen to my mother's vacuum cleaner.' (To be fair to MBV, Wire would probably prefer the sound of his mother's vacuum cleaner to any band you cared to mention.)

And so, at a time when The Stone Roses were bizarrely being hailed as messiahs for their quaint Herman's Hermits/Freddie & The Dreamers impressions, Manic Street Preachers were condemned for being 'retro' (James Brown called them 'The time capsule that fought back'), and were mocked for their apparent 'punk revivalism'. Richey resented the punk tag, insisting that 'We see ourselves carrying on in the fine tradition of British guitar rock: The Who, Stones, T. Rex.' Indeed, James's guitar sound – a Les Paul through a Marshall amp with no effects pedals whatsoever – could barely have been more classic, but the lyrics to 'Motown Junk' and the T-shirt slogan 'BOMB THE PAST' should have dropped the hint that there was more than mere reverence at work in the Manics' magpie-like thievery of rock's crown jewels. Apparently sharing the anarchist idea that originality is a myth, the Manics nakedly appropriated the biggest (and only the biggest) rock heroes: Who, Stones, Pistols, Guns N'Roses – the ones Warhol would have bothered with.

'Our only icons were the obvious ones,' said Richey. 'Not the 13th Floor Elevators.' And, as Nicky once told me, 'The Sex Pistols were the best band in the world, but they were followed by shit like Wire and Television: the critically acclaimed avant-garde. So we knew we had to be massive, and obvious.' This was a tactic known as *entryism*: using already popular forms of music as a vehicle for subversive Big Ideas. 'Imagine a band with the stance of Big Flame and the commercial success of Kylie Minogue,' said Richey, dreaming of mixing politics with pop(ulism). Their eventual choice of Rock-Music-as-Trojan-Horse had as much to do with pragmatism as with love of the form. 'Ultimately,' said Richey in 1992, 'we just think that rock is the only musical backdrop we can have, 'cos it's the most popular.' The decision resulted from a historic band debate – the Guns N'Roses versus McCarthy argument – which smouldered for a whole summer. As James later told me, 'We were discussing whether it was more important to be like Guns

N'Roses and use it as a vehicle, or be like McCarthy, Big Flame and Gang of Four [determinedly obscure politicised indie bands of the mid-80s]. That crystallised us. We realised it was the saddest thing in the world to glorify the indie ethic when you're saying important things.'

At first, the tactic failed. Despite their desire to be as populist as possible, the Manics were always too difficult, too insoluble to reach Oasis-size; the Bon Jovi-esque pop-metal riffs jarred uncomfortably with the inscrutable Fall-style syntax. Sometimes, though, entryism can work in mysterious ways. In my case, for instance, the Trojan horse went backwards. Initially, I loved almost everything about the Manics except their music. 'Great,' I thought, 'a glamorous Marxist pop group . . . but they sound a bit heavy metal.' Slowly, however, the message made me swallow the medium. While they were trying to make the rest of the world believe what it did not believe, they succeeded in making me love what I did not love.

In 1996, of course, the Manics' entryism *did* work: a gigantic pop/rock anthem, half-Steinman, half-Spector, sung in student bedrooms *and* prole pubs across the nation, carrying a lyric about the defeat/defeatism of the working class, and selling a quarter of a million. The song, 'A Design for Life', stole shamelessly from several eras and didn't sound remotely modern. On the sleeve, there were quotes from Antonio Gaudi: 'Man does not create . . . He discovers,' and 'Originality consists in returning to the origin.' Wire, Bradfield and Moore were not ashamed of plagiarism, nor of being retro or traditional. They were *proud*.

Manic Street Preachers had finally mainlined their message into the veins of the mainstream – the old-fashioned way.

3.4 REAL

'We are not your sinners, our voices are for real' – 'YOU LOVE US'

STEVE LAMACQ WAS INTRIGUED by Manic Street Preachers from the moment the package landed in his pigeonhole.

Along with a copy of the 'Suicide Alley' single and a demo tape of the forthcoming 'New Art Riot' EP, Richey had enclosed a photo of Lamacq himself, scrawled with the flattering caption 'Cheekbone Charisma'. Steve, now presenter of Radio One FM's *Evening Session*, then working as News Editor on *NME*, was sufficiently convinced by the contents to recommend the band strongly to Philip Hall (an act which played a major part in persuading Hall to visit Wales and check it out).

When he finally witnessed the band live, however, Lamacq's initial enthusiasm took a rapid nose dive. As he now recalls, the Manics' set at the Bull & Gate, supporting something called The Fury Things, was *not* the iconoclastic holocaust they had promised. 'If they were the future of rock 'n' roll, then I was definitely seeing it in the wrong context. If I'd seen the Albany gig, maybe it would have been different. But the place was less than a third full, and they ran on in their white boiler suits, James pogoing up in the air to reach the same height as Nicky, and they just weren't very convincing. It looked like all the wrong elements of late 70s punk. We'd just been through the whole disappointing Birdland thing, and alarm bells were ringing.'

Lamacq walked out, and strolled the few hundred yards down Kentish Town High Street to north London's other legendary indie dive, the Camden Falcon, to report on a gig by another band whose name posterity fails to record. In his review, he couldn't resist firing a sideways shot at the Manics. 'Further down the road,' he quipped, 'I've just witnessed the Vibrators' revival . . .'

Steve Lamacq was – and to some extent still is – the champion of brash, (s)punky, straightahead indie rock (Kingmaker, Carter USM, Senseless Things), and the avowed eNMEy of anything he saw or sees as hype, contrivance, image and pretension. However, having spent his teens as the only punk in a dead-end Essex village, he actually empathised with the Manics more than his printed dismissal might suggest.

'"Motown Junk" was a *fantastic* record,' he says. 'The irony is that if it came out now I'd be one of the only people playing it. It couldn't be more of a Steve Lamacq record if it was called "I'm Steve Lamacq's Best Friend"! But I couldn't tally that with all the

46

make-up and attention-seeking tactics. I thought the way to get attention was through songs.'

On 15 May 1991, *NME* dispatched Lamacq to Norwich to put his reservations to the band in person. 'No one was taking them to task, so I thought I would. I was being over-negative just because everyone else on *NME* was being over-positive: "Burn the heretic! Non-believer!"'

Steve first hooked up with the band at the hotel before the gig. Nicky, Richey and Sean, engrossed in a Nottingham Forest match on television, nodded politely. James, however, appeared to resent Lamacq's jibes more than the others, refusing to acknowledge him, and later sitting silently at the back of the tour bus.

Norwich Arts Centre was an unlikely venue for a Manic Street Preachers gig. A deconsecrated gothic church down a narrow side street in the cathedral city's antiquated heart, it still had tombstones on the floor, all too visible between the disappointing turn-out (the MSP hype machine had, thus far, failed to conquer Norfolk). Just forty paying punters showed up, including a handful of Preacher clones in leopardskin and glitter, and two old-skool punks who pogoed furiously at the front. On a stage erected where once there had been an altar, James pointedly dedicated 'Starlover' to Lamacq. Thirty-three unspectacular minutes later, he walked off, never to return. 'Plastic punks!' jeered the pogoing pair. 'People ought to pay to get OUT!' complained another. So far, hardly a night to remember.

On the dancefloor, where an audience should have been, roadies began humping gear away. Over in the corner, the four Manics dutifully gathered and sat on flight cases to talk to *NME*. Steve Lamacq kindly gave me a tape of the interview, the majority of which has never been published until now.

STEVE LAMACQ: 'The main thing is, that I think in certain instances the image thing takes over from everything else.'

RICHEY EDWARDS: 'Yeah, but there are so many bands with things to say who got ignored because they were prepared to almost . . . not wallow in the shadows, but not make a big deal of the way they look visually. Y'know, and it really is important, because in rock music and pop music, it's always been vital the way people look. And when bands, like, dress down, or make no attempt at an image, you just get bypassed. You find yourself in a subculture or a clique.'

JAMES DEAN BRADFIELD: 'Just to portray human life onstage, I don't think higher grades or elevates the subject matter of the song. It just allows it to reach one plateau, then it dies out.'

SL: 'Don't you think, following on from the Birdland scenario, the look cheapens what you've got to say?'

RE: 'I don't think Birdland, in their lyrics, had anything to say at all. We've got copies of all our words, if you want a copy. We've got loads of lyrics . . .'

SL: 'But then again, don't you find that, certainly with a live act, you don't get to hear what you're trying to put across?'

JDB: 'Public Enemy are one of my favourite groups, and they've got so much to say and elevate from their works, and when they play live they just try and manifest all that in . . . well, there's this song, "Party for Your Right to Fight", and they say: "This is a live concert, take all the songs at face value and, if you've got the record, therefore you already know what's in the lyrics." I just think in a live set you can only ever hope to give energy. And if you made every message clear-cut, and directed towards the audience every time, it'd be too much like Red Wedge or something. People would think, "Party-line politics."'

SL: 'But surely the whole thing about Manic Street Preachers is impact. I mean, why go and do a cover of *NME* in an almost glam rock/shock type of way, if you're not going to get something across immediately? You see, the real thing I'm keen to know is exactly what some of the things are you're trying to get across?'

RE: 'We, personally, wanted to make music redundant. Because when I was a teenager, all it was was entertainment, just love songs which never changed my life. It's supposed to be the ultimate youth culture, and it says nothing. So if we could become a huge group, I mean a really fucking massive group, sell millions of LPs, then split up, well . . . rock music would continue, but at least it would have been made: a definitive statement, which all bands in the past who were supposed to have meant something never did.'

SL: 'All right, so what do you actually want to say on that album?'

RE: 'I wanna sing about a culture that says nothing, I wanna say the fact that basically all your life you just feel like a nobody, you feel like nothing, you're treated like shit. Just, like, you're completely bored, you're offered nothing, you've got nowhere to go . . .'

JDB: 'Also, we want a chance to attack the obvious targets that people never attack any more. Because they're too frightened to. Because to write about subjects such as the House of Lords, the monarchy, institutionalised corruption, things like that, people just think they've been attacked before, and they think they're just gonna be fucking trodden on. Which they rightly kinda feel. But they're the hardest subjects to write about. And if you can write about those things in an eloquent way, you're tackling the hardest subjects.'

SL: 'So why haven't you done that as a single?'

JDB: ' "Repeat" does. We want that to be a single.

RE: I don't think many young people have any respect for the monarchy, or for the House of Lords any more, but, you know, a complete negative attitude towards these institutions has gone, and all it has been replaced by is reservations. They're prepared to accept that they are there and they will continue. They don't like it, but they accept it.'

JDB: 'We call ourselves a democracy, when in the second chamber there's more than half undemocratic power. And we're questioning those kinds of things. And for it not to slip into boredom is the hardest thing and that's what we're trying to do . . .'

[Cigarette break]

RE: 'All we wanted was a band that spoke about political issues. And we've never had one in our lifetime. Like, the music press pushed The Wedding Present down my throat as the alternative, but all they sang about was love songs.'

NICKY WIRE: 'Cos where we come from, everbody's in love, and we don't want a band that can write about love.'

RE: 'Love is important to most people, but it's not important to us, that's all.'

NW: 'Aah, you're a really lucky bastard! The women are all over you all the time!'

SL: 'So do you believe that your bold image will help you get the things that you say across to more people?'

RE: 'Yeah, I do. Completely.'

NW: 'Sometimes I think it'll take time. Sometimes I think we could end up like The Stooges. But I know that, at the end of the day, we've got much better songs, and the songs always sort of carry through. We wouldn't have got where we were if we had shit songs. Everybody, deep down, likes those songs, and they might think, with the image, "Oh, I'm too scared to like them", or "Oh, with all the hype, I cannot like them", but that's not our problem. That's the only reason we make an effort for an image, and to say a lot of things – we've got total confidence in the songs.'

SL: 'Do you ever feel uncomfortable with the fact that you're almost sleeping with the industry?'

JDB: 'I decided not to get bitter about it. We had an experience when we first came up to London where we met a publisher, and they gave us two young people, and they were dressed casual, and they were going: "This is the record industry now, it's not people in suits any more, we're young and hip", but they were just the same as everybody else. So, y'know, I decided everything was totally fucked up. And we're not working from the same old maxim that you've got to work from within, but you've just got to resolve yourself to sign to a major if you care about . . .'

RE: 'We're prepared to prostitute our art. We're prepared to prostitute ourselves completely just so we get heard.'

JDB: 'Like, our first four months, we were just touring, not doing anything worthwhile.'

RE: 'What were we? We were nothing.'

NW: 'We had the "New Art Riot" EP, we had a "Turn On" in *NME* . . .'

RE: 'We were with Ian on Damaged Goods. We were nothing.'

JDB: 'In small provincial towns, it's enough to be in a band, as a kind of escape . . . but where we come from, it wasn't even enough to be in a band.'

SL: 'Doesn't that fuel the argument that it's all a bit of a chip on the shoulder?'

RE: 'Oh, completely!'

NW: 'We are bitter people.'

RE: 'But I don't see that as a problem that we are, like, spiteful, malevolent, bitter people! But most people's lives are really shit.'

NW: 'Yeah, I wish more bands were like that!'

SL: 'The ideal band for me would be a band that touched on personal relationships, who would go through hard times with you . . .'

NW: 'I watched the telly, there was this concert, and the Bangladesh (flood) victims were on, and I just thought: "I will not allow myself to write a love song." Because what will it mean to those people?'

RE: 'Any government is really happy that the working class reduce themselves to a self-sufficient unit of two, completely obsessed by each other, by the girlfriend and the boyfriend.'

SL: 'The problem then is, I don't see how you can like a band like Guns N'Roses.'

NW: 'Musically!'

JDB: 'We do this thing where we take bands . . . we don't ever put ourselves in the position to be their fanbase. Because we're not fans, in a sense. We realised a long time ago that you can't ask anything from any band because they'll never give you anything. So just take what you want. So we're not fans, we just like those bands: Public Enemy and Guns N'Roses.'

RE: 'Guns N'Roses proved that a rock band can still sell sixty million LPs. And also, a lot of their lyrics, they are completely pissed off. It's called *Appetite for Destruction*, and everybody thinks "Paradise City" is a really shit song 'cos it rhymes "Paradise City" with "girls are pretty", but later on it goes, "Captain America's been torn apart/Now he's a court jester with a broken heart." It's not just shit lyrics.'

NW: 'It bugs us when people don't take the time to look past . . . I mean, I'll never ever see anything in a lyric by any British band that can mean anything to me, so I've got to look further to Guns N'Roses and Public Enemy.'

RE: 'You could easily say the same thing about Public Enemy, couldn't you? Public Enemy: anti-semitic, homophobic. That's two huge problems.'

NW: 'But we divorce ourselves from that and take the good points.'

SL: 'If a band let me down in any way, that'd be it.'

JDB: 'We just never wanted to be in that position, because we knew that we would be in a constant state of being let down all the time.'

NW: 'You can't put your faith in anyone, because they've always let us down from such a young age.'

RE: 'Because, when you're at school, you're led to believe that music is going to change your life, you hope a band's gonna reflect the way you feel, and they don't. All they do is just reduce you to a shit second gear.'

NW: 'You do get this feeling of total depression. And there's nothing you can do to control it, to smash your walls. And that's what we're trying to articulate.'

SL: 'You couldn't find that in any music, any album?'

JDB: 'In each other. It sounds a bit soppy, but . . .'

NW: 'We do really love each other.'

SL: 'So what would you say your chief motivation is?'

RE: 'To write music, obviously, and to make people address issues that are really important.'

NW: 'But James wants to write brilliant songs anyway. He's a talented person.'

JDB: 'I just want to create the greatest record ever . . . boring old tepid muso, aren't I?'

RE: 'It's really hard for us to convince you . . . that we're for real.'

SL: 'Don't you see that, even if you're just a normal guitar group, from the way you look, act, talk, you're setting yourselves apart?'

RE: 'We just really hope that people will address those issues. I mean, like, I don't know how many letters you read in the music papers, but a lot of the ones that seem to be published say: "What a bunch of bastards, they wear eyeliner." And that's full-stop, that's your whole argument! It's 1991, and if people can't get to grips with men wearing make-up, then what kind of society is it? People do come up to us at concerts saying: "Fucking queers, you wear make-up!"'

NW: 'I'm really happy with that.'

SL: 'If I wore make-up around the village where my mum and dad live, I'd be run out of town. I wouldn't get served in the corner shop. It's just the same. You have to accept and deal with the settings . . .'

RE: 'But don't you think it's important that those issues should be dealt with? And, I mean, you can talk about it in a song, but it's different to actually go out there and wear it.'

NW: 'But we don't think it's a big thing. It's natural. We just want to look lethal. Like Pete Townshend did.'

RE: 'Like, in Brighton, we got bottled. For 35 minutes, we got bottled. Non-stop.'

SL: 'After that, I just don't see the joy in it.'

RE: 'Oh, I do!'

NW: 'They loved us at the end of it. Instead of going home and beating up their wife, they got rid of their frustrations on us. And that's much better than going around slapping their fucking wife. And it does happen.'

RE: 'At the end of the concert, James went: "We fucking love you, and if any of you want to fuck us, just come on and do it upstairs." And at least they'll have gone away and thought about it, that they've physically hurt a band for thirty minutes, and they couldn't do a thing.'

NW: 'They carried us off at the end. Look, we make no pretence about hyping ourselves with what we say. Journalists come to us. We didn't make them write about us.'

SL: 'Hang on, I've got your letters at home!'

SEAN MOORE (*en passant*): 'Yeah, but what's wrong with that? We wrote to every band. We were desperate.'

NW: 'We're not ashamed of anything. We want to reach the biggest audience we can because we feel we've got something important to say.'

SL: 'It doesn't worry you, the way you get there?'

NW: 'Well, no! That is the truth. We are total prostitutes. Sluts! If we can get across what we really feel, then that's more important than any credibility.'

RE: 'You can't make a point if the only people who know about you read *NME*.'

NW: '*NME* doesn't mean anything. We can go back home where we come from and no one gives a shit.

Why should they bother about a music paper who put The Happy Mondays or us on the cover, who don't sell any records? It's really depressing for me because we come from a real rock-fan kind of area, and when Steve Clarke died from Def Leppard that was a massive issue to them because he was fucking important. But it got about that much in the *NME*, and Shaun Ryder got a full page for his baby being born. How can anyone justify that? It really makes me sad. Def Leppard are the ones who've sold sixty million albums and had three No. 1s in America, and Happy Mondays are slogging their guts out and they've sold 1,500. There are a lot of people out there who like rock music and are desperate for status, just like all your Mega City Four fans. They're more desperate, because they've got no work, and they've got nothing in their lives.'

RE: 'They've got to learn that suicide is a career, like, thirty years of a career is a slow death, it destroys you.'

NW: 'We've got to be understood in the context of where we come from. We really have.'

SL: 'But you can't treat rock music like that. Surely, if you want to reach as many people as possible, you've got to transcend that.'

NW: 'That's why we chose rock. Because rock is the most obvious art form. We want to be the biggest cliché at the end of rock. That's what we've always said.'

SL: 'The thing which works with all forms of entertainment is, self-deprecation fuels people's belief in you because they think you're for real. And I find that some people don't think you're for real. Therefore they don't take you seriously.'

RE: 'That is one of the points we want to make, is that we do want to make ourselves larger than life, but it's really important to reflect the feelings of fans considerably like yourselves. We're saying: "You don't need big stars to tell you how you feel. We know you're pissed off . . ."' (Breaks off to instruct roadies about where to put Sean's drumkit.)

SL: 'So that's the main thing. That maybe it doesn't seem real to people. So they don't put their trust in you.'

RE: 'You know, where we come from, most people don't even believe in bands anyway . . .'

And so the conversation turned, in futile, unresolved circles.

When Lamacq switched off the tape, Richey took him to one side. 'You got a minute?' he asked. 'Would you mind if we go and sort this out? Come backstage, there's one last thing I'd like to say.'

Lamacq followed Edwards backstage, and clarified his position: 'I just don't think a lot of people will think you're for real.'

'I know you don't like us,' Richey replied, 'but we are for real. When I was a teenager, I never had a band who said anything about my life, that's why we're doing this. Where we came from, we had nothing . . .'

While he was talking, Richey rolled up the sleeve of his 'SPECTATORS OF SUICIDE' shirt, produced a razor blade out of nowhere, and began dragging it across his left arm. 'Believe me,' he implored again, 'we are for real. We're not the next Birdland,' he continued, with a slight stammer. 'We do mean what we do.'

The first cut was the deepest. Fifteen further incisions, of varying depth, followed. On his forearm, Edwards had etched out the now immortal phrase '4 REAL'.

'A lot of people have asked me why I didn't stop him,' Lamacq says now. 'At first, I didn't even notice, because he was maintaining eye contact so I never looked down. And also, I did feel a strange fascination with what he was doing. I couldn't make out what he was writing. We carried on talking for five or ten minutes afterwards. He didn't look in any pain whatsoever. He could almost have been writing it in Biro.'

By now, people were having to step over the pool of blood accumulating on the carpet. Richey went to the Gents to staunch the flow with toilet paper. Lamacq rushed out to find Philip Hall, and told him what had happened. 'It's all right,' Philip smiled, 'he gets like that after gigs.' Lamacq persisted: 'No, no, look.' When Hall saw the scene, he was ashen-faced. Lamacq left the atrocity exhibition behind and stepped outside for some fresh air.

Jody Thompson, coincidentally the *NME* News Editor today (and author of the pocket book *Manic Street Preachers: From Despair to Where*), was a student at the University of East Anglia at the time, and had gone to the gig in the hope of interviewing the band for Livewire, the campus radio station. She had been sitting on the steps, chatting to Nicky, when she witnessed the carnage unfolding. She immediately fetched the Arts Centre's emergency medical kit, and her friend Sandy, who happened to be trained in first aid, bandaged Richey's arm.

'He was bleeding everywhere,' Thompson recalls. 'Steve seemed to be in shock, but for me the full horror didn't sink in. He'd sliced his arm up, and it just seemed surreal.'

Once she had managed to collect her thoughts, Jody questioned Richey as to his motives. 'I was quite angry. I'd lost a friend to suicide as a teenager, and I thought he was trivialising life. I said "What the fuck are you trying to prove?" Nicky said: "It's one of the things he does, just leave it."'

At this point, *NME* photographer Ed Sirrs decided that Edwards's mutilated forearm would make a great news shot, and asked Richey to whip off his makeshift dressing. 'I was livid,' remembers Thompson. 'It could have got infected. It was a really tabloid thing to do.'

According to Sirrs, however, the photo opportunity was Richey's idea. 'He actually said: "'Ere, do you want a photograph of this?" I said "Yeah" and whipped out my camera, and he said: "I'd better take the bandages off." They'd just been put on, so it was mint.'

By now, the crude, angry gashes were beginning to look particularly gruesome. Jody Thompson offers a vivid description: 'You know when you put sausage rolls in the oven and they have those little score marks in the top? That's how his flesh looked where it was pulling itself apart.'

Richey evidently required urgent medical attention, but he made it clear he didn't want an ambulance to be called, and Nicky agreed. Thompson, who happened to live near Norwich General Hospital, offered to pilot the band's minibus in the right direction. 'It was a weird scene. There were a couple of groupie types just waiting in the front, calmly drinking Aqua Libra. Thinking back, they could have been Shampoo. No one seemed to have any sense of urgency. James was watching *Taxi Driver* on video. Sean even made us stop for chips at Kentucky Fried Chicken, then drop him back at the hotel, before we reached the hospital!'

By this time, Steve Lamacq was asleep in the back seat of Philip Hall's car, speeding back to London. 'When I got home, my girlfriend asked me how it went. "Not bad," I said. "Oh, and Richey slashed his arm with a razor blade." It didn't hit me until the next morning.'

Meanwhile, in Accident & Emergency, Richey was refusing to be treated until every patient with a 'proper' – i.e. not self-inflicted – injury had been seen first, despite doctors' concerns that one incision was perilously close to a major artery. (This self-effacing attitude continued when the time came to remove the stitches: Richey rang Cardiff Royal Infirmary to find the least inconvenient time for them, and agreed to turn up at 8 a.m.) At around 2.30 a.m., he was eventually treated by a young nurse who, as luck would have it, had read about the Manics in the press and was quite sympathetic. When he emerged from the surgery, with seventeen stitches in his arm, Richey walked over to a surprised Jody Thompson and asked, 'Do you want to do the interview now?'

When Steve Lamacq arrived at his desk the following day, the phone rang. It was Richey. 'I'm really, really sorry about what happened.' That night's gig in Birmingham was cancelled, and Richey had to leave the stage halfway through the next show because his wounds were weeping. 'Anybody out there play guitar?' joked James.

During the week in question, Mark Thomas, today a well-known stand-up comic, then a freelancer for BBC Radio Five, happened to be recording a behind-the-scenes documentary on a week in the life of *NME*. When the Manics released their version of 'Theme from M*A*S*H (Suicide Is Painless)' from the *NME*-sponsored Ruby Trax charity album, a highly amusing (and revealing) extract from the editorial meeting following the '4 REAL' incident was included on the B-side, under the title 'Sleeping with the NME'.

In the meeting, the to-print-or-not-to-print question is wrestled with by a largely sceptical staff, with the exception of an excitable Andrew Collins, editor Danny Kelly (delighted by the scoop), Ed Sirrs and Steve Lamacq (apparently still in shock); there is also a phenomenal comic performance from James Brown, who in later years went on to edit *Loaded* and *GQ*.

For those who have never heard it, here are the highlights.

ANDREW COLLINS: '. . . And, er, the question is, can we print this picture? 'Cos it is really 'orrible. I find it extremely 'orrible. He's upset, people down there are upset, grown people are upset by this picture. It is an 'orrible picture. Danny's in a meeting, he hasn't seen it yet. He's gonna be jumping around, you know, it's a bit of news, even if you could say it's trivial. Like I say, within our little world it is not trivial. It's quite a thing.'

(Danny Kelly enters.)

MARK THOMAS: 'Do you in any way regard it that you may be responsible for that in any way, because he did it for you?'

STEVE LAMACQ: 'Nah. Not really. He chose . . . he chose to do it. He chose to make his point in that way. I don't think . . . you know, I don't find it kind of . . . feel guilty about the fact that he's done it . . .' (Sighs) '. . . Dunno. It's been one hell of a week now!'

UNIDENTIFIED FEMALE WRITER 1: 'The guy's sick, he really is.'

DANNY KELLY: 'Yeah, I know, but I'm in the publishing caper, aren't I?'

UFW 1: 'There's no way you can print those photos. 'Cos you'll get all their fans doing the same thing.'

AC: 'Rubbish, Karen! It's a really delicate issue.'

SL: 'If more people see the gore, it's probably a good thing.'

AC: 'Well, I'm in charge of gore. I'm Gore Editor.'

SL: 'It says "4 REAL" down there. It doesn't say "T. REX".'

DK: 'Oh my God!'

AC: 'It's a problem, innit?'

DK: 'Oh no, it's not a problem really . . . These things happen, Andrew! We're a newspaper, not . . . not . . .'

ED SIRRS: 'Good man! That's what I wanna hear!'

UNIDENTIFIED MALE WRITER 1: I think they're disgusting . . .'

UFW 1: 'I think they're absolutely . . . sick.'

UMW 1: 'I mean, it's just shock-horror, isn't it?'

UFW 2: 'You wouldn't print a picture of a car crash, would you?'

UMW 2: 'It's self-inflicted.'

UFW 2: 'Yeah, I know, I understand, but it shouldn't be encouraged.'

UMW 1: 'What if we convert them to black and white? The colour's too graphic, isn't it? It's just awful.'

UFW 2: 'If he keeps getting it printed every time he does that, then he's gonna do it all the bloody time. What's he gonna do next? Slit his throat?'

DK: 'Aye, hopefully, well maybe they'll all cut each others' heads off! And that'll be an end to it.'

JAMES BROWN: 'Where are these photographs?'

AC: 'Here it is, if you can handle it. What the butler saw.'

JB: 'Aw, that's nothing!'

ED SIRRS: 'That's my man, that's my man!'

IESTYN GEORGE: 'We were expecting that.'

JB: 'Does it say "T. REX"? He's spelt it wrong!'

UMW 2: 'Dyslexic!'

JB: 'It doesn't say "T. REX", it says "T-R-E-A . . ."'

MARC PECHARDT: 'Well, what do you think, it's coming from Welsh, isn't it?'

ES: 'Yeah, it could be a Welsh statement.'

JB: 'You've gotta print that! It's rock 'n' roll, innit?!'

UFW 2: 'It's self-mutilation, though, James!'

JB: 'I think it's an excellent photograph! Good one, Ed! I bet Mark Ellen (*Select*) will put it in.'

MP (Sarcastically): 'Good man! I don't think we should print it . . .'

JB: 'God, I should! I think more bands should do that sort of thing!'

UFW 2: 'What if some kid carves himself up?'

JB: 'Nah, come on with the "model" stuff, because we have people smoking in the paper every week, we have people like Jack (Barron) who used to work here glorifying drugs for weeks on end, we had the letter E on the cover when E was the national symbol for Ecstasy . . .'

UFW 2: 'Yeah, but all we need is for one child to copy . . . and kill themselves, and you'd be . . .' (makes throat-cutting noise).

JB: 'You couldn't kill yourself cutting yourself on the forearm.'

UFW 2: 'You could if you missed!'

JB: 'If it was bad . . . did he faint, Ed?'

ES: 'Nah.'

MP: 'I just think it's ludicrous and childish and we don't have to . . .'

JB: 'Yeah, but nobody says that about bloody Sid Vicious, do they?'

UMW 1: 'No, but I think all the mileage has gone out of Sid Vicious and . . .'

MP: 'We've been through that before, why should we, y'know, it's like rewriting history, it doesn't have an interest.'

JB: 'Not to you, Marc, because you maybe have seen it before, maybe you're past it!'

MP: 'Yeah, well, maybe, and I'm pleased to be old, I tell you!'

JB: 'I mean, Sid Vicious only took it from Iggy Pop . . . it doesn't seem to be "T. REX", though!'

DK: 'No, it's "4 REAL". It's the letter "4" and the word "REAL".'

JB: 'Aah, right, 'cos it looked like "TREAT" or something.'

DK: 'You're not trying to make a differential . . . I'm not going to spend all day arguing about these pictures, but you're not trying to make a differential between Iggy Pop and him? You don't know how he . . .'

MP: 'No no no, he's talking about Iggy Pop, I'm not making a difference, no.'
JB: 'Me and Ed are saying it's in a fine tradition of self-expression.'
MP: 'You're saying all bands should do that.'
JB: 'I think, if he burnt himself – hopefully, he'll read this – if he burnt himself in Tiananmen Square, we should print it! It's artistic expression, innit?!'

NME did, indeed, run a full-page news story, complete with Ed Sirrs' now-classic photo in full stomach-wrenching technicolour. 'The way James Brown and Danny Kelly saw it,' says Lamacq, 'the Manics were a classic rock 'n' roll band or, at least, they were good for shifting papers.' The piece included a short telephone interview with Richey. Asked to outline his motives, he answered, 'I tried talking to Steve for an hour to explain ourselves. He saw us as these four hero-worshipping kids trying to replicate their favourite bands. There was no way I was going to change his mind. I didn't abuse him or insult him, I just cut myself. To show that we are no gimmick, that we are pissed off, that we're for real.'

Asked if he regretted it, he answered, 'No, because at least now people might believe that we're not in this for personal entertainment. We aren't wallowing in any musical nostalgia like the music papers' Clash/Dylan freaks. We might sound like the last thirty years of rock 'n' roll, but our lyrics address the same issues as Public Enemy.' Lastly, Richey was asked if, in the cold, painful light of day, he felt like a bit of a dickhead. 'No, I feel just like the rest of this country – banging my head against the fucking wall.'

Steve Lamacq's own piece, intended as an on-the-road/interview feature, was almost completely given over to the slashing incident. His last line read simply: 'DON'T BE DAFT BASTARDS.'

The '4 REAL' photo itself stands alongside the most evocative images in rock history: Cobain's pleading panda eyes in close-up, Strummer bent double smashing his guitar, Curtis smoking in the Manchester rain. Like Van Gogh's *Self-Portrait with Bandaged Ear*, to which the photo bears a curious resemblance, Richey's expression seems to carry two opposing meanings: on the one hand, 'My God, what have I done?' and, on the other, a new calm, a precious moment of stillness amid a restless life. As the pupils of his eyes meet the camera, the gaping diagonal of the '4', its sides pulling apart to reveal the muscle below, seems to resemble an extra bloodshot eye, staring out to meet the viewer's gaze.

The incident now tends to be viewed as an early warning of the escalation in Richey's self-destructive behaviour that was to come (admittedly, by devoting a whole chapter to it, I could be accused of perpetuating this perception). Sean Moore now says, 'I regret that it was the start, I feel, of a downward spiral in his life, personally.' But it's worth injecting a little perspective by pointing out that, at the time, it was generally thought of as a bit of a laugh. Nicky, who described Lamacq as 'a parasite', said, 'For me it was the highlight of the tour. It was worth it just to see the look on that journalist's face.' Furthermore, he added, 'Despite what was said, when he did it he was laughing. It hurt him more to get his tattoo done.'

A few weeks later, I ran into Richey and James on Platform Two of Cardiff Central railway station and joined them on the train to Paddington. Richey happily showed me his scars. 'I gouged quite deep on the "4",' he demonstrated, smiling ruefully, 'much deeper than I meant to, but I had to carry on, and so by the time I got to the "L" I was wussing out, only making shallow score marks.' If he were a real man, he added, he would also have spelt it 'F-O-R' rather than '4'.

Within the band, the whole affair was considered no big deal. Shortly afterwards, in an interview, I half-jokingly suggested that, to keep the momentum going, the next time Richey slashed his arm it would have to be live on CNN. Sean, smiling from behind his Game Gear, said, 'We're gonna cut his head off.' Nor was it considered a big deal back in Gwent. 'When I went back home afterwards,' said Richey, 'I would bump into people in the street and they'd say: "Yeah, I did that as well", and they did it because they were so fucking bored.'

Hall Or Nothing (and later, Columbia) had no qualms about using the episode as a selling point: thousands of copies of the Ed Sirrs photo were sent out to stir up interest in the USA, and the inclusion of 'Sleeping with the NME' on a B-side shows that the band members, too, were happy to exploit its iconic power.

For years to come, though, no Manics interview was complete without the question: 'Why did you do it?' 'It's pathetic, isn't it?' Richey confessed to *Q*. 'But this journalist was really upsetting me so I did a shitty and stupid thing. But people like it if you do that sort of shit, don't they? They think it's glamorous. It's sad. I just got very frustrated . . .'

He denied that it was a shameless publicity stunt. 'Not guilty,' he insisted in *RAW*. 'There was an argument with a journalist, which descended so low that it was the only thing I could do. I've never hit anybody in my life. I never would, and the only way I could make a point was by hurting myself. Obviously not to that extent, but it's something I've done since I was a teenager.' And anyway, he argued, 'If I want publicity, I'll cut my hand off. I'll get a front cover then.' (The other Manics would, however, later speculate that he had actually premeditated the whole thing.)

'I sliced up my arm,' Richey told *Melody Maker*, 'because it was the only way I could get through to a 25-year-old who thought like a 45-year-old. I wasn't doing it to be like Iggy or Sid. I couldn't give a fuck for those people. I just pity them. I just did it because you can talk and talk and never make some people understand how much you mean it. Anyway, the fucker was asking for it.'

A few months later, Steve Lamacq ran into Richey again at IPC Magazines, publishers of *NME*. 'He, James and Philip got into the same lift as me. Richey just stared at the floor in total silence all the way to the 25th floor, as if he was somehow embarrassed or ashamed.' With hindsight, Lamacq is surprisingly forgiving about the whole affair. 'It is an amazing rock 'n' roll statement, but part of me thought, "You daft bastard." It did suggest a person who was on a short fuse. I liked Richey, and I did worry about him: would he be motivated to somehow top that later on?'

c) You . . . love . . . us . . .

(FAN-DOM AND FAN-DEMONIUM)

'We won't die of devotion' – 'YOU LOVE US'

*E*VERYTHING LIVE, the video of Manic Street Preachers' May 1997 show at Manchester's Nynex Arena, begins with footage of each member of the band, shot lovingly and lingeringly in Scorsese-style slo-mo to make them look as impeccably cool as possible. At the end of each montage, in the style of a cinema trailer, come the block-capital captions: 'JAMES DEAN BRADFIELD'. Then 'SEAN MOORE'. Then 'NICKY WIRE'.

The camera then pans across a militia of young boys and girls – mostly girls – in pink feather boas, silver plastic tiaras, leopard-print blouses and smudged panda eyeliner. There is one further caption, a fourth Manic Street Preacher. 'THE FANS'.

A 'nice' touch. And somehow it seemed wrong, jarring with the sensibilities: the Manics have never really *done* 'nice'. Yet behind the uncharacteristic sentimentalism lay an immutable truth. The Manics may never have sycophantically courted the devotion of their fans, as lines like 'Don't fall in love 'cos we hate you still' ('Stay Beautiful') and 'We don't want your fucking love' ('Roses in the Hospital') amply demonstrate but, without the 'fucking love' of those fans over the previous decade, the band simply wouldn't exist.

It is a fact that they acknowledge through subtle, low-profile acts. 'We've never been a fan-club band,' says Nicky, 'but we show our appreciation in other ways.' From the early mini-van tours to the arena-filling present, they have always taken time to talk to fans who manage to seek them out. One correspondent on the *Melody Maker* letters page recalled the time he met Richey after a show, who 'delivered an hour-long spiel on why dogs are better than cats, eyes shining, arms waving', just for his benefit. Nicky Wire still grants interviews to fanzines, and tries to fill in every questionnaire they send him. After a gig in Sheffield, the band once gave away guitars and bass worth £2,000 to fans. Wherever possible, they also try to ensure that their fans are treated well and looked after properly. When they heard that someone was harassing female fans camped outside Nynex, they sent security man Steve to scare him off.

Manic Street Preachers is the only British band since The Smiths who – and this is rather old-fashioned – *mean something*. And for the people to whom they mean anything, they mean *everything*. The Manic Civil War between rival Hardcore and Casual fan factions (not 'Old' and 'New' factions, as erroneously reported in the press) is a relatively recent development. For the first five years of the Manics' public life, they had almost no casual listeners at all, but an army of extremely partisan obsessives. In 1992, Nicky told me, 'We get letters from people saying they were never into music until we came along.' The Manics, more than any of their peers, *mattered* to people. At every gig, you could see it in the eyes of the audience, mouthing each line as if it were stolen from their own soul. 'You see them singing every word as if they're praying,' says Caffy St Luce of Hall Or Nothing. 'There's that kind of intensity.'

Intensity. Now there's a word. The media cliché of the MSP nutter, as crystallised by the satirical 'Diary of a Manic Street Preachers Fan' in *Melody Maker*, is easy to mock: sulky teenagers, bedroom-bound social cripples, utterly besotted with their 'intensely intense' heroes. And it isn't all that wide of the mark. In 1994, *Select* carried the following, painfully archetypal personal ad: 'MALE, 23, shy, sensitive, lonely, into Manics, indie, films and intelligence, wants to meet like-minded girl.' I wonder if he ever did . . . Nicky Wire, however, is never one to mock the afflicted. 'Some of those fans get close to "mentalists", as Alan Partridge would call them, but when I look back to 1991 we had no fans, and now we've got people who've been with us for ten years. It's a lovely thought.'

The devotion of the Manics Mentalist is unparalleled. Distance is no object: in 1991, a small posse of sixteen-year-olds hitch-hiked fifty miles from their home town of Waterford to see the Manics in Dublin; they shared one copy of 'Motown Junk' between them. Nor is money: Fiona Bond of *Pout* fanzine estimates that she has spent over £4,000 on Manics memorabilia. Nor is time: the morning before a Manics gig, it is quite common to see fans queuing outside the venue in freezing weather from 6.30 a.m., waiting to stake their places at the crush barrier.

Outside the Reading Rivermead Centre in 1997, a mother, walking past the line of Preacherites in regulation glitter chic, was heard to comfort her frightened child: 'Don't worry, dear, they won't hurt you.' Like their predecessors, the goths, Manics fans are a living paradox: *a flock of individualists*. There is undoubtedly a uniform and, regrettably, feather boas appear to be compulsory – Manic Street Preachers are probably responsible for the deaths of more innocent chickens than Colonel Sanders. On the positive side, it is a highly democratic form of glamour, thoroughly in keeping with the Manics' roots as impudent upstarts who refused to 'know their place'. Can't afford diamonds? Buy plastic jewels from Toys 'R' Us. Can't afford designer T-shirts? Get an army surplus top and a spraycan, and make your own. The Manics have catalysed an aesthetic which can loosely be termed *Glam Anarchism*, incorporating Barbie Dolls and communist badges, Love Hearts and Sartre novels, glitter glue and situationist collage. As a breed, Manics fans tend to be a highly creative, imaginative and intelligent lot (there have, for instance, been several university dissertations written about the band). Caffy St Luce defines the fans as: 'Artistic, daydreamy, thoughtful; some are alienated, but that can be a good thing, but above all really creative. I've never known a band with so many fanzines. They're all really interesting.' In 1992, when Nicky Wire told me, 'We're not interested in people who care about T-shirts. You've seen our merchandise, it's repulsive! They should make their own shirts,' he knew that most of them would do exactly that. As well as a proliferation of MSP-inspired bands with names like The Walking Abortions, The Dead End Dolls and The Little Baby Nothings, and some frankly bloody awful poets, the Manics inspired an explosion in the visual arts. In 1998, conceptual artist Jeremy Deller gathered together many of the best examples in an exhibition titled 'The Uses of Literacy' (Nicky Wire was particularly taken with an impressionistic photo-montage in which he morphs into Christ).

Then there is the revolution in DIY publishing that MSP have unwittingly sparked. It has become rather a cliché that, for every Manics fan there is a Manics fanzine, but the statement contains more than a grain of truth. Manic Street Preachers are almost certainly the most-fanzined band in rock history. The earliest MSP-zine is generally thought to be *Counter-Language*, run by Patrick Jones from America. The first British versions were *Last Exit* (produced by Jacqui and Carrie, a scarily close-knit pair of east London glamour teens with peroxide hair and in white fur, who would soon find considerable fame themselves as Shampoo), and the Exeter-based *Tortured Rebellion*. These were quickly followed by para-Manics 'zines like *The Scream* and Anthony Melder's *Paki Revolution*; these were barely about the band at all, but took the Manics' manifesto as a starting point to disseminate their own theories on political and cultural dissent (in much the same way that Greil Marcus, in *Lipstick Traces*, used the Sex Pistols as an excuse for a meandering history of revolt and heresy through the ages). Of the current crop, *Iconoclastic Glitter* is probably the most comprehensive – and one of the best written – and *TNT* the most gossipy and trivia-packed, although the others are not far behind (I honestly can't remember reading a bad Manics fanzine). It is a phenomenon of which the band members themselves are proud, as Nicky admitted to Darren Broome of BBC Radio Wales: 'The fact that we've got like 25 fanzines and 50 unofficial websites and all the rest of it, it does give you a gratifying smile because those people aren't just dedicated to the band, they're dedicated to the whole lifestyle, the literary aspects, the film aspects, the whole package, really. It's not just liking the music.'

Indeed, in many ways this whole movement is no longer umbilically connected to the music, or to the band, at all. It is beyond their control now. The Manics have started something they can't finish. They could split up tomorrow, and this subculture – these 'Leper cult disciples of a stillborn Christ' ('Starlover') – would continue. Indeed, like a religious cult, it might even grow stronger in the band's absence – after all, the departure of its spiritual leader, the Reverend R. Edwards, only increased the devotion.

There have, to date, been two MSP fan congregations – sorry, conventions – for the faithful. The first was a well-intentioned but poorly attended night on 1 February 1997 (something of a significant anniversary) in difficult-to-reach Blackburn. The second, under the title 'You Love Us' at London's Garage on 8 August 1998, incorporating a general-knowledge quiz, disco, Patrick Jones poetry recital and set from tribute band the Generation Preachers, was wildly successful and may become an annual event.

So the fans don't need the band any more. But the Manics need the fans. In 1998, *NME* asked Nicky Wire to define his feelings towards his audience. 'Actually I feel like a vampire,' replied the spectacularly fanged bassist. 'Because they give me life.'

4. GENERATION TERRORISTS

'In Walkman sounds, hear Sony control' – 'DEMOCRACY COMA'

RICHEY'S ARM WAS STILL IN BANDAGES when he walked through the doors of Sony's Soho Square HQ.

Something of a record-company-signing frenzy had been simmering for months, on the back of the stir caused by 'Motown Junk' and the Manics' disproportionately high press profile. One company, laughably misreading the band's stance, offered to let the Manics smash up their offices and throw anything they liked out of the window if they signed – immediately ruling itself out of the bidding war.

Sony Managing Director Tim Bowen, who had signed The Clash to CBS (as it was then called) in 1977, saw the Manics at a college in Guildford and, although it was a quiet, forgettable night – a closed gig, with the real fans locked outside while apathetic students played pool throughout the set – he left convinced that this was the most exciting band he had seen since The Clash itself. Possibly it was this which persuaded the Manics to sign with him; more likely, it was the fact that Sony/Columbia/Epic was the biggest record company on the planet, home to Michael Jackson, Bruce Springsteen and George Michael (and, of course, Public Enemy), and also because Sony was willing to break the bank to get the Manics' signatures. Another major factor, from Philip and Martin Hall's point of view, was that the Sony employee keenest to sign the Manics was not an A & R man at all but Rob Stringer, a young former Student Union Entertainments Secretary working in Columbia Marketing. With the marketing department behind the band, there would be little danger of its profile slipping into neglect, or of the Manics being afforded low-priority status.

On Tuesday 21 May 1991, Richey, Nicky, Sean and James agreed a ten-album deal (so much for that one-album-then-we'll-split promise) with Columbia Records, worth £250,000.

Heavenly Records bore no hard feelings at losing the band, as Jeff Barrett attests: 'Heavenly actually took quite a hit on the Manics – a £6,000 loss. As soon as they signed to Sony, they paid it back to us immediately, which was really nice, a gesture of thanks. They didn't have to – a lot of bands would have just said, "Bye Bye!"'

Reactions elsewhere were less cordial. Many writers in the weekly music papers (themselves owned by IPC Magazines, Europe's largest publisher) accused the band of 'selling out', and of fulfilling their own lyrical prophecy, 'Revolution soon dies/Sold out for a pay rise' ('New Art Riot'). Andrew Collins of *NME* epitomised the consensus view when he wrote: 'They'll have to cut a lot of corporate 4-arm to convince me that they haven't gone soft now that they're firmly positioned upon corporate dick.'

The band quickly and vehemently defended the move. As James told *RAW*: 'We've never been the trade unionists of rock; we know that we could never reach as many people as we wanted unless it was on a major. We were willing prostitutes.' He later added in *Volume*, 'You don't have a dream so you can cut out little faded pieces from fanzines all your life. You want glossy stuff that's not going to fade.'

Richey agreed: 'The whole indie mentality that grew up from punk onward just seemed so bullshit to us, because the most subversive, really important group in the world were Public Enemy, and they were on Columbia. The level of corruption on an indie label is just on a smaller scale.'

The Manics' view of major label life was thoroughly pragmatic, as Nicky admitted: 'Signing to a major record company is the price of an education; we don't care what they do to us.' Or, as the band would later put it: 'All rebellion is corporate-owned.' It wasn't long before Richey was making barbed remarks such as: 'Sony Records have bought us supposedly because they understand our "art", but not one of their employees in Soho Square on £20,000 a year could tell you what the first track on our album is.'

With their wallets a quarter-million thicker, the Preachers immediately exercised their new-found purchasing power in an orgy of expenditure. James bought a white Les Paul, which he had always coveted, for £800. Sean booked a holiday – his first in eight years – for himself and his girlfriend Rhian. Nicky paid off his gambling debts (estimated at £6,000). Richey's first act of conspicuous consumerism was to visit Hyper Hyper in Kensington and blow £500 on designer punk T-shirts. He also bought a portable CD player. Two months later, a thinner model came on the market, and he bought that as well.

That night, the band was due to play the last night of its tour just around the corner from Sony at the Marquee, Soho's venerable sticky-floored rock mecca.

Officially, they were sharing the bill with Liverpool Marxist hip-hoppers 25th of May and with American rockers The Throbs, but the night belonged to the Manics. All week, enormous 'You Love Us' posters, featuring a Marilyn Monroe collage and the slogan 'OVER DO$E', had been pasted up around central London to advertise the gig, and early copies of *NME* (Londoners can buy it on a Tuesday) had broken the '4 REAL' story. The buzz of anticipation was almost tangible.

The Manics – a monochrome tornado of black eyeliner and white denim (and white bandages) – didn't disappoint. A few songs into the set, James Dean Bradfield made an extraordinary announcement. 'If there are any pretty boys who want to fuck me,' he began, mumbling slightly and trailing off, 'then I'll see you all in the dressing-room after the show.' Years later, he eventually told me, off the record, that he did sort of mean it, but has never acted on it. 'I wouldn't mind going to bed with a boy,' he confirmed to *Melody Maker*. 'The possibilities are endless.'

Vacating the stage to a heroes' ovation, the Manics were quickly back on to play their first-ever encore. They were playing by conventional rockist rules now, leaving the (equally clichéd) punk tradition behind. As 'You Love Us' imploded into the Iggy-sampling ending,

Nicky started giving the band's instruments away to the audience. James, meanwhile, was shattering £800 worth of shiny new Les Paul to splinters. One horrified metaller in the audience was heard to exclaim, 'That's a *Gibson*!'

The jubilant end-of-tour party at the tiny St Moritz bar was attended by an unexpected guest: Linda Duff, pop editor of the *Daily Star*. Never shy of putting two and two together to make 250,000, Duff decided that one slashed arm and one trashed guitar constituted a return to 1976. Three days later, the *Star* ran a double-page shock-horror story entitled 'HIGH PRIESTS OF PUNK – MANIC REVIVAL OF A ROCK RELIGION', including the '4 REAL' photo and a hysterical report which began: 'The Manic Street Preachers are leading the way to resurrect the anarchic craze of punk rock . . .' The Manics, and Hall Or Nothing, were secretly delighted. As Caffy St Luce put it: 'Hats off to Linda Duff, she got there early.' The *Daily Mail* was not far behind, frightening its middlebrow/Middle England readers with a picture of Richey headlined 'IS ROCK MUSIC DESTROYING OUR CHILDREN?'

Back in the real world, it was soon time to return to the hard slog of gigging in hitherto unconquered territory. Much of a depressing Irish mini-tour was spent locked away in the back of a minibus watching rare Sex Pistols videos, acquired from Paul Cook via a mutual friend. James was not taken with the Emerald Isle: 'Ireland is just full of bastards who want to drink Guinness,' he later sniped. In Dublin, Nicky Wire sprained his ankle.

On Saturday 26 May, the Manics played their first-ever festival, 'May Daze', in a big top in Milton Keynes, propping up a distinctly second-division bill (Gary Clail, The Moonflowers, The Dylans). A late addition, they walked on at 4 p.m. – the bar didn't open until 6 p.m. – to a crowd which, from the crash barriers backward, read as follows: Gillian Armstrong (a particularly dedicated fan), one tentpole, Caffy St Luce, another tentpole, Martin Hall. The fabled two men and a dog decided to give it a miss.

Following the '4 REAL' incident, Sony's Japanese headquarters, thrilled by the Manics' headline-making potential, faxed London with the simple request: 'Please tell the band, be more obnoxious.' Within the month, their wishes were granted.

The entertainments committee of Downing College, Cambridge, had decided it would be a jolly hoot to hire this amusing punk-rock cabaret act for their May Ball (actually held in early June, and subtitled, with that inimitable crazy student sense of humour, the 'Jive Bunny Lives Ball'). Whatever reservations the Manics may have had about playing a £150-a-ticket affair for two hundred privileged sons and daughters of aristocrats at a toffs' university – and one which had rejected them as teenagers, too – were outweighed by the thought that the cash being offered would be enough to pay off the remaining debt from their previous tour (they had run up £26,000 in smashed instruments alone).

The first sign that something was wrong came when the Manics spied the ring of hired heavies, recruited from the rugby team, in front of the stage – not to protect the band from the crowd (or vice versa), but to protect the PA system from the band. Four songs into the set, Richey put one foot on a monitor. Instantly, staff pulled the plugs, terrified that he was about to wreck the equipment. Nicky, furious and screaming, threw down his bass and kicked his mike stand across the stage. Sean followed suit, writing off £1,000 worth of drums, while James punched out a rugger bugger intent on proving 'who's the hardest'. A shouting match ensued, with Nicky vociferously denouncing the monarchy (a few junior royals happened to be in attendance). The mêlée was broken up by a swarm of police officers, complete with German shepherd dogs, who escorted the band out through the rarely used ceremonial gates.

Photographs of the fracas provided the Manics with a great limited-edition poster for their next record sleeve. It also provided the *Daily Mirror* with a sensationalist story on the supposed 'punk riot' by 'The Welsh bad boys of rock 'n' roll', including claims that one of the band groped two women (extremely unlikely). 'It was so obscene we walked out in disgust,' said one undergrad. 'It was the best thing all night,' said another.

Tokyo – was that obnoxious enough?

'All our songs offer is NEGATIVITY, CHAOS, DESPAIR. We wanna create so much hate *that we get swept away, we get destroyed'* – RICHEY, PERSONAL LETTER, JANUARY 1991

For the next two months, the Manics were safely under lock and key. The remainder of June was spent in Manor Studios in the Oxfordshire countryside, working on the first Columbia single with producer Steve Brown, a versatile old pro from the 80s who had worked with everyone from Wham! to The Cult. July, give or take a handful of dates in France and Belgium, was spent in pre-production (demoing and rehearsing songs) for that tricky multi-million-selling album. When the band first sat down with Brown to play him the demo of the proposed single, he warned, 'Before you play this to me, as long as there's not like "Fuck Off!" in the chorus, we're gonna be all right.' Which was *exactly* what the chorus contained. 'I think he thought it was some sort of practical joke,' says James.

On 29 July 1991, the Manics' first major label release hit the shelves. At first hearing, 'Stay Beautiful' (originally 'Generation Terrorists') was a straightforward piece of high-octane positive punk, comparable to, say, The Clash's 'Safe European Home' or 'Tommy Gun'. Yet, somehow, it remains one of the most poignantly desolate songs the Preachers have ever written. Despite the irresistible rocket-fuelled melody and a basically optimistic lyric about 'clinging to your sense of total possibility and "sense of waste"' (Richey), somewhere buried deep in the grooves was a beautiful, disconsolate sadness. In *Melody Maker*'s judgement, it was: 'By all canons of musical and aesthetic merit, not a great record . . . but it has a completely different atmosphere from anything else around these days – a bright, eat-the-world recklessness that demands your attention.' But that recklessness – the self-celebratory bravado of couplets like 'We're a mess of eyeliner and spraypaint/DIY destruction on Chanel chic' and the confrontational middle-finger salute 'Why don't you just . . .' (James replacing the words 'fuck off!' with an ironic howl of lead guitar) – was shadowed by a certain bleakness ('All we love is lonely wreckage') as well as by the deeply ambivalent pay-off line (a Kierkegaard quote): 'Anxiety is freedom.' The B-side tracks – the melancholic six-strings-and-tambourine 'R.P. McMurphy' (inspired by *One Flew Over the Cuckoo's Nest*) and 'Soul Contamination' (a splenetic, Prince Charles-like attack on modern architecture) – also reflected this duality. Even the sleeve, featuring misty-eyed *Lolita* starlet Sue Lyons, seemed to mirror the mood. Whereas 'You Love Us' oozed simple up-and-at-'em cockiness, the defining mood of 'Stay Beautiful' was a paradoxical *feelgood dejection*.

With the corporate clout of Sony behind them, and feeling that a chart single was a realistic aim, the Manics invested in their first big-budget video. The shoot obliged James to become a living Jackson Pollock work, repeatedly drenched in multi-coloured paints inside an eerie *Twin Peaks*-style house whose moving rubber and latex walls were constantly closing in (eventually, the house turned into a spider and crawled away). Inexplicably, the video was banned.

Nonetheless, when the band set out for their August tour in the single's week of release, it was in optimistic mood. For the first time many of the dates were sold out, and the early sales figures were sounding positive. Maybe this time, there would be a hit.

For the Manics, though, anxiety *wasn't* freedom.

The four always appeared to be in a permanent state of unrest. James was constantly wound up like a clockwork soldier, always at the edge of two moods, in what William Burroughs referred to as 'a perpetual state of kicking'. Richey, like a speedfreak without the speed, always needed something in his mouth to chew: his fingernails were gnawed almost to the bone. Sean had an even more masochistic habit: he would chew the inside of his mouth to make it bleed, then eat salt-and-vinegar crisps.

It was in this state of anxiety that the band awaited news of 'Stay Beautiful's chart performance. After a Saturday-night gig in Sheffield, their minibus broke down, forcing them to take the Inter-City to London on the Sunday. Caffy St Luce was with them throughout a nerve-wracked journey. 'They had their ears pressed to the radio all the way for the chart rundown. We were playing a general-knowledge quiz to ease the tension but, as the countdown went on, there was still no mention of the Manics. They were still waiting when it got to No. 2, and No. 1. When we got to King's Cross, it was "See ya . . ." through gritted teeth.' It transpired that 'Stay Beautiful' had made its début at No. 44.

Unusually, the single went up the following week to No. 40, making it their first proper hit (albeit for one week only). Perhaps more enduringly, its title has replaced 'Yours sincerely' whenever Manics fans write to one another.

'Regard all art critics as useless and dangerous' – FUTURIST MANIFESTO

Regard all art critics as useful and malleable – this was the Manics' manifesto. From day one, the Manics had written their own reviews, dictated their own agenda, knew exactly which buttons to push. 'We were quite clinical. We were like magpies, collecting information, keeping dossiers on journalists and learning how to manipulate them.' (I have never seen the contents of my own dossier, but it clearly worked.) The result, by the summer of 91, was a press profile absurdly disproportionate to their actual popularity. 'We were at No. 94 in the charts,' said Nicky, 'but everyone had an opinion on us. That was the most brilliant thing we'd done.'

Whatever anyone may have thought of their music, the Manics were a music journalist's dream. They looked fantastic, and they *gave good quote*. Every interview was an abattoir of sacred cows; they scattered vitriol towards other bands with the carefree glee of a USAF chopper over a Vietnamese village. In an early *NME* interview, Richey explained, 'You know how Catholics always hate every other religion, or Baptists hate Methodists more than they hate the Devil? Well, we will always hate Slowdive more than we hate Adolf Hitler.' In amongst all the platitudes of their peers – 'We just make music for ourselves and if anyone else likes it, it's a bonus' – the Manics were a godsend.

They were also incredibly visual, and the papers knew it: 'like exhibits at a Victorian freak show,' the *NME* described them, 'the Elephant Men of Pop'. In May 1991 Richey and Nicky appeared on the *NME* cover writhing semi-naked in gold sheets, Nicky with 'CULTURE SLUT' written on his body in lipstick, Richey with 'HIV' (or, to be accurate, 'VIH', having evidently forgotten that the mirror reverses things) razor-bladed into his chest – not the first time he had practised Gillette calligraphy for that particular publication. The Wedding Present may have sold more records, but you would never get them doing *that*.

However, for every preacher of the Manics gospel – Steven Wells, the Stud Brothers, John Robb, James Brown, myself – there were ten disbelievers. Ian Gittins, reviewing the Paris/Heavenly show in *Melody Maker*, typified the view of many when he wrote: 'A swift blow to the head should see them off.' When John Robb first suggested putting the Manics on the cover, at a *Sounds* editorial meeting, he was sneered down: 'Oh, they're one of *your* stupid bands, aren't they?' I was once threatened with the sack, only semi-jokingly, by the *Melody Maker* Features Editor for giving them a favourable review. The Manics, with their incessant Muhammad Ali-esque frontin', were excellent copy – slap 'em on the cover, sit 'em around a microphone, wind 'em up and watch 'em go – but dare to take them seriously and you would be laughed out of town.

Not that the Manics cared. When *NME* put them on the cover with the headline 'DO YOU REALLY, SINCERELY LOVE THE MANIC STREET PREACHERS? OR DO YOU WANT TO KICK THEIR HEADS IN?' the answer was barely relevant. All that mattered was that they were on the cover of *NME*.

The tactic didn't work everywhere. Gillian Porter, then of press company Maggie Farran PR (and later of Hall Or Nothing), had the unenviable task of selling these scrawny Welsh faggots to the metal mags. 'They couldn't get arrested in the rock press,' she remembers. In desperation, she sent an unmarked promo tape to journalistic friends with no band name, just a sticker reading 'PLAY ME'. It proved a far more effective policy than honesty.

That particular ghetto aside, the Manics had the media in their pockets. They had skilfully manipulated the press into an obsessive relationship, a fatal attraction: the tired cliché 'love them or hate them, you can't ignore them' had rarely been more true.

Wherever the Manics went, violence followed – and there were increasing signs that they were beginning to enjoy it. On 10 August they played Reading's After Dark Club, a tiny, sweaty, low-ceilinged dive, supporting temporarily popular glam-punk racketeers Daisy Chainsaw.

Almost immediately, the sound failed, and a voice in the crowd hollered: 'You wankers!' Wire, never one to shrink from a verbal challenge, responded by trying to provoke a band-versus-audience boxing match. He may not have realised, however, that there were no security staff. All hell broke loose. Fans began punching each other, Rob the soundman and the band, until power was restored. Throughout the truncated fifteen-minute set which followed, missiles rained down. James, wearing Caffy's leather pilot's hat (which he frequently borrowed 'because bottles just bounced off it'), abandoned several songs halfway through to engage in slanging matches and, at one point, fired up on adrenalin, ran screaming towards Nicky, who backed away, visibly shocked and upset by this show of hostility (apparently not intended).

James, in particular, seemed to relish skirmishes such as the Reading Riot. 'Come on, then! We enjoy it!' he yelled to a boisterous crowd in Warwick. 'To us, applause is the worst thing in the world!' Richey, too, seemed to take a perverse, almost masochistic pleasure in bombardment by bottle. Before another Sheffield gig, he confessed to Caffy St Luce that he actually enjoyed being hit on the head. Knowing this, Caffy collected a stack of hard plastic beer glasses and launched them at a maniacally grinning Richey until angry fans, unaware of his little perversion, warned her to 'leave him alone or else'.

The tour concluded on 13 August with the *de rigueur* London date, this time at the Fulham Hibernian, a huge (now disused) hall frequented mainly by Aussie expats. As well as being the Manics' largest headline to date, it was also, rather belatedly, the official Sony signing party.

Among the cigar-chomping industry suits was a small but significant smattering of newly converted Manics kids. One teenage boy, for instance, otherwise sporting the Joe Bloggs-and-Adidas uniform of Madchester, had scrawled the legend 'DEAD FLOWER' across his chest. With each gig, a small but very visible Manics militia, kitted out in glitter, eyeliner and fake fur, seemed to be gaining new recruits. The MSP aesthetic was beginning to catch on. The band's very first British fanzine, *Last Exit*, compiled by Jacqui and Carrie Shampoo, was also on sale that night.

Following support band Dodgy, the Manics took the stage for a set which the *Guardian* would describe as 'brief, violent and exhilarating'. At the end, Nicky Wire was dragged into the audience by adoring fans. 'It felt like the end of an era,' said Bob Stanley, guest DJ for the night, and he was right.

The Manics were no longer anybody's best-kept secret. They were going overground.

It was time to put up or shut up. The rest of August – and September, October, November and December – was devoted to recording the sixteen-million-selling album that they had promised the world.

Reunited with Steve Brown, the band retreated to Black Barn studios. A secluded, ivy-covered cottage in Ripley (near Guildford in Surrey), a Tudor hamlet populated mainly by stockbrokers and ladies with labradors, Black Barn had previously been used by the likes of Black Sabbath, prompting bizarre tabloid rumours that the Manics had been dabbling in black magic to improve their songwriting skills (rumours corroborated by stories that the band had passed the time during the 'Stay Beautiful' video shoot with nocturnal readings from Aleister Crowley, of whom Sean was a fan).

Initially scheduled to take eight weeks with a maximum budget of £400,000, *Culture, Alienation, Boredom and Despair* (the original working title; *Generation Terrorists* came later) eventually took 23 weeks and cost well in excess of £500,000. It was a testament to the perfectionism of James and Sean, and to the band's conviction that it really was now or never – there would be no second chances. While James, Sean and Nicky slaved over a hot mixing desk, Richey – whose musical services were not required – found himself at something of a loose end.

In Guy Peellaert's and Nik Cohn's exquisite picture book *Rock Dreams*, there is a painting of Diana Ross huddled in the back of a limousine, wrapped in white fur and jewels, staring impassively at the underclass from which she had risen in the street outside. I once asked Richey what he wanted to become, and he told me he was saving up for plastic surgery so he could turn into Diana Ross. By the end of the *Generation Terrorists* sessions, I think he had already done it. Nicky described Edwards's behaviour during the sessions to the Stud Brothers in *Melody Maker*: 'All he does is go into London, drives around in the company Mercedes, goes to Soho stripjoints, spends £300 on the band's Amex, comes back covered in lovebites and asks how the track's going. I think that's the thing that's given me the most pride in this band.'

Recounted second-hand, it sounds an incredibly glamorous life. It was only years later, in changed circumstances, that James would reveal the truth about Richey: 'He was royally fucked up in terms of every kind of abuse. He would cry a lot.' On one occasion he started sobbing uncontrollably in the studio, telling Nicky that if the band ever did actually split up, he would be left with nothing.

Richey's epic consumer sprees (sample haul: Vauranet sunglasses, Black Crowes T-shirt, Franz Kafka book, some roses) owed as much to boredom as to avarice. To fill the empty hours while James was laying down guitar solos, Richey occupied himself by decorating several rooms with cut-up fragments of aesthetic debris: Marilyn, Liz, Rotten, Keith, Stalin, Flav, Axl – the usual suspects. When recording was complete, he burnt the lot, along with all the clothes that reminded him of Black Barn, in a ritual pyre.

To keep Richey busy, the others entrusted him with the task of choosing a sleeve design for the album. The record company's suggestion involved the Royal Shakespeare Company's red-velvet curtains parted to reveal a nuclear cruise missile with the words 'GENERATION TERRORISTS' written on the tip in lipstick. Richey politely stated that the band had other ideas.

Initially, he wanted Andres Serrano's controversial *Pisschrist* (a Jesus figure suspended in a vat of blood and urine), but Sony was nervous about using anything overtly blasphemous. His next target was one of Bert Stern's legendary defaced photos of Marilyn Monroe (her last-ever session; Monroe hated the shots so much that she seized the prints, scratched them with her nails and threw paint over them). However, Stern wanted $30,000 – out of the question even for the profligate Preachers.

Another abortive but conceptually brilliant idea was to encase the record in a sandpaper sleeve, so that it would both develop scratches itself every time you played it, and also gradually erode the rest of your collection: a record which would literally destroy rock 'n' roll.

Richey then started visiting London art galleries looking for suitable works. One contender – a cast of a human face made of the artist's own congealed blood – was, ironically, bought by Tory advertising magnate Charles Saatchi that very week. Other possibilities were Grunewald's *Crucifixion*, Dali's *Christ of St John of the Cross*, Rodin's *I Am Beautiful* and Clarence John Laughlin's *The Spectre of Coca-Cola*. Permission was, in each case, refused. The eventual sleeve design was a shot by *Melody Maker* photographer Tom Sheehan of Richey's own torso, with a Prague crucifix around his neck and a rose tattoo on his arm reading 'GENERATION TERRORISTS' (this had to be airbrushed in; his actual tattoo read, 'USELESS GENERATION'). Unfortunately, this design made the band look like some sub-Motley Crüe glam-metal act from Los Angeles; worse still, it came back from the printers an unsightly shade of Spam pink instead of the intended mustard – a mistake which caused the meticulous-minded Richey considerable distress.

The reverse featured a reprise of the 'Collapsed European Stars' motif (see 'New Art Riot'), this time crumpled and in flames – a sceptical statement on the naïve triumphalism which greeted the fall of the Berlin Wall.

'You know the myth of Stagger Lee, that he'd kill for a stetson? The Manic Street Preachers would kill for a Sega Megadrive' – RICHEY, 1991

Video games were a popular time-killer for the band. At one stage Richey was spending eight to ten hours a day playing 'Donald Duck Quackshot', 'Mickey and the Castle of Illusion', 'PGA Tour Golf' and 'Sonic the Hedgehog' on the Megadrive. 'It took me a couple of weeks to do it: to get to the end and kill Doctor Robotnik . . . I should be interested in learning to play my guitar, but Sonic the Hedgehog rules my life. I find that very sad.'

By now, Richey found video games far more exciting than dull old rock 'n' roll. 'In a video game,' he told *Melody Maker*, 'you can murder, maim and impoverish thousands, you can create and destroy whole populations. Put four people playing guitars next to that, and it *has* to be boring!' Some fans complained that this proved that the band was compromising its principles. 'It's sad to see how they're reduced to talking about mindless computer games . . . when they had so many intelligent things to talk about,' wrote one.

In one way, the Manics' much-flaunted obsession with Sega was a calculated cultural statement, designed to offend crusties and their Luddite technophobe sensibilities. In another sense, however, it was merely an honest reflection of a misspent south Wales youth. Nick, Richey and Sean, like almost anyone born between 1967 and 1972, were arcade kids who grew up on 'Space Invaders', 'Donkey Kong' and 'Pac Man', and no amount of fancy books and adolescent academic snobbery could completely breed that out of them (only James, who despises such games, abstained: 'Computers erode the soul. Then again, I'm a simple man. Give me a simple pint') and no amount of fancy books and adolescent academic snobbery could completely breed that out of them. You can take the band out of Wales . . .

The fact that Richey did not play a note on the Manics' forthcoming album was beginning to leak out, and became a national scandal to indignant musicians and critics alike. His guitar (to the horror of muso rock snobs everywhere) was a top-of-the-range Telecaster, but it might as well have been a Slazenger. In many ways, Richey had never left the bedroom-mirror/tennis-racquet stage, forever miming along to the fantasy band he had made a reality.

Melody Maker called him 'the band's guitar holder'; *Select* called him 'a guitarist whose performances were always unplugged' and 'a fifth wheel', comparing him to The Happy Mondays' dancer/tambourinist/hanger-on, Bez. In a sense they had a point about the Bez thing: Richey was a mascot – a totem embodying everything the band stood for, but who didn't actually do anything. This was a man whose very existence placed a huge question mark over the nature of Authenticity in Pop.

On one occasion, a member of The High (a third-division Manchester baggy band) approached Richey and tried to engage him in conversation about instruments. 'When I told him I wasn't interested and that James plays my guitars on the record, he went mad. He was going, "There ought to be a union to stop people like you!"'

Richey's colleagues initially attempted a cover-up. James insisted that 'Richey's not miming; he's playing *very quiet guitar*.' Nicky, talking to John Robb in *Sounds*, lied blatantly: 'People make too much of a thing about music. Like everyone goes on about people like John Squire being guitar heroes, but Richey can play those solos behind his back and jump up and down. It's piss easy.' It has to be remembered here that Nicky – whose bass strap used to read 'REDUNDANT' – was no great virtuoso either.

Richey himself didn't try to hide the truth – in fact, he felt a great degree of glee in the disgust his incompetence caused. 'Why is everyone hung up on an ugly piece of wood and metal and strings?' he protested. For Richey, the guitar wasn't a musical instrument at all, but part fashion accessory, part prosthetic penis. 'I can't play guitar very well, but I wanna make the guitar look lethal.'

The Manics' imprisonment in Black Barn was punctuated by a handful of memorable television appearances.

On 4 September, they were back at the Marquee and back on BBC2. The Yamaha Band Explosion, a week of indie showcases (the Manics shared a bill with Intastella, The Godivas and Five Thirty), was being filmed for BBC2's *Def II*. More importantly, the Manics had access to national airwaves for the first time: the set was to be broadcast live on Radio One.

The Manics had specifically been asked not to swear and, therefore, not to sing anything with lyrics such as, for example, 'Repeat after me/Fuck queen and country.' With delicious inevitability, Nicky Wire took the stage and launched an unprovoked – and patently unbroadcastable – attack on Chapterhouse and Slowdive, while James Dean Bradfield announced, 'This is for our dear queenie,' before barking out the opening line of 'Repeat'. Within seconds, a full can of Coca-Cola struck him on the head, perhaps thrown by an outraged monarchist (one rumour suggested it was a member of Blur), or possibly by an exasperated BBC producer. A trickle of blood ran down James's neck and on to his red plastic Miss Selfridge mac. Carrie from *Last Exit* took a photo capturing the exact moment of impact (she then promptly fainted and had to be carried out by tour manager Rory). James paused, as though considering retribution, then sneered, 'Nah, too fuckin' ugly.' It wasn't the night's only bloodshed: fan Gill Armstrong, standing in front of Richey, cut the words 'Suicide Baby' into her arm.

A brief but electrifying set ended with 'Motown Junk' amid a storm of red glitter (blown from an industrial-sized fan), as the audience, encouraged by James to 'rip it apart', tore a Radio One display to shreds and threw it stagewards, before admirers of both sexes invaded the stage to kiss their favourite Manic.

Some poor band or other had to follow that.

If the offending missile *had* been launched by Blur, or by any other rival band, it couldn't have come as any great shock.

The Manics had erected what the *Guardian* described as a *cordon sanitaire* between themselves and the rest of pop. 'I detest every musician I've ever met,' said Nicky, and the feeling was mutual: 'I can't think of a single band in any interview who've said they like us . . . And I'm really proud of that. I've lost count of the useless fuckers who want to beat us up.' Baggy bandwagon-jumpers Northside were apparently among those keen to trade punches with the Preachers. Richey, typically, was quite into the idea, but it never happened. The Manics didn't mind putting their fists where their – or, to be exact, someone else's – mouth was. On one occasion they got into a scuffle with some 'useless fuckers' called Candyland in Sony's reception area. No bones were broken – just a little office furniture and a Beats International gold disc.

In many ways, the Manics' constant conflict with the predominantly *luv'dup* pop culture of the day bears parallels with that of The Beatles versus The Rolling Stones. Nicky Wire always preferred The Stones, primarily because, while The Beatles were off meeting the Maharishi, Keith Richards had announced: 'We want to kill psychedelia.' Two decades later and in similar spirit, Richey Edwards, in letters to the press, had called for 'a Winter of Hate in the Summer of Love'. The Manics were a timely revolt against the bourgeois complacency of the Thames Valley scene, the slacker sloth of Seattle, the patronising pauper-play of the crusties and the bombed-out backwardness of Madchester's smiley culture. It was, to borrow Public Enemy's marvellous phrase, a *contract on the world love jam*.

While the band toiled away in rural Surrey, another release from the earlier Steve Brown/Power Plant sessions appeared on 28 October to maintain MSP's public profile. Two songs shared a double A-side single. First came the chunky, charged-up 'Repeat', an eight-line anti-monarchist haiku which had been part of the Manics' set for years, and which ran: 'Repeat after me/Fuck Queen and Country/Death sentence heritage/Death camp palace/Royal Khmer Rouge/Imitation demi-gods/Useless generation/Dumb flag scum.' Sharing headline status was 'Love's Sweet Exile', while completing the twelve-inch were the rousing, Ginsberg-sampling 'Democracy Coma' and a live version of 'Stay Beautiful'. Originally titled 'Faceless Sense of Void', 'Love's Sweet Exile' was rather a weird choice for a single, progressing as it does from a drums-only intro to alternating schizophrenically between an unmelodic, almost atonal thrash-metal verse and a highly tuneful, very pop chorus. The hookline 'Rain down alienation/Leave this country' bore more than a shade of Morrissey's 'Come, come, nuclear bomb' (inspired in turn by Betjeman's 'Come, friendly bombs, and fall on Slough/It isn't fit for humans now'). 'Love's Sweet Exile' had begun life as a great pop song, but somewhere in the studio it degenerated into a showcase for James's guitar virtuosity. Nicky Wire recalls a moment from the recording of the single: 'We were all sitting around and playing Sega, and Richey burst out of the control room, really excited, going, "James has just done a solo as fast as Steve Vai!"' It has since become an un-song, written out of history and dropped from the live set, never to return. Nicky now says, 'I think that has to go down as our worst ever record.'

The decision to make the single a double-A was calculated to help its prospects of radio airings ('Repeat' obviously being unplayable), but Caffy St Luce was constantly told it was 'unsuitable for daytime play'. Radio exposure was still difficult for the Manics – few DJs (Craig Cash from Manchester's KFM/Signal being an honourable exception) would touch them. The single nevertheless entered the chart at No. 29, climbing to No. 26 a week later, due largely to an astonishingly homoerotic video, screened on ITV's *Chart Show*, featuring Nicky and Richey naked but for tiny leather thongs ('It was quite hard to pack everything in,' Wire boasts), kissing, embracing and writhing around in an array of S & M paraphernalia including gas masks, blindfolds and ropes. Sean sensibly refused to join in, but was punished by being made to wear a Batman mask.

There was also a riotous appearance on Channel Four's *The Word*. All afternoon the band had rehearsed 'Love's Sweet Exile', but as soon as the On Air light went red, they hurtled into 'Repeat' instead. Chaos erupted as Manics fans in the studio audience began slamdancing, and even Bomb The Bass's chic backing dancers joined in. Floor Manager Jo Whiley (now a Radio One DJ) could only watch powerless, and tearing her hair out. The televised mayhem was enough to earn yet another sensationalised splash in the *Daily Mirror*.

But the Manics knew their markets, and were learning the rules of the game. The following morning they performed 'Love's Sweet Exile' on the children's show *Motormouth*, and behaved impeccably.

With the album all but completed – Steve Brown was adding the final touches at The Hit Factory, the evil bunker of the Stock Aitken Waterman empire (and also, much to Richey's delight, the birthplace of The Clash's début and Iggy's *Raw Power*) – the stir-crazy Manics were unleashed on the nation for a December tour. At least, that was the idea – in fact the first three shows had to be cancelled as Nicky, ever the poorly waif, fell victim to glandular fever.

Once the tour got started, the gigs met with mixed reactions. Portsmouth Poly – the scene of Nicky's first brief foray into higher education – was another case of real fans being locked out while arms-folded students stood and stared. A subdued Nicky claimed that the reason he wasn't jumping around much was 'I've got laryngitis, from kissing too many boys' (yeah, right), but made up for it by yelling, 'How ya doing out there, you fucking sailor slags?!' The next night, at the Cambridge Junction, the response was so delirious that fans actually helped Nicky to smash his bass. After the show, he limped around in a fur coat but with no trousers: his knees had swollen horribly, a legacy of an old football injury, and he couldn't get his skin-tight jeans on.

There was no London date as such, but a secret fans-and-friends-only Christmas show was held on 13 December at the Diorama, a quaint hexagonal miniature theatre near Regent's Park. For the first time, a separate Cult of Richey was visible within the Manics' fanbase. Semi-naked schoolgirls with '4 REAL' written on their arms (in Bic ballpoint rather than Bic razor – a far healthier idea) congregated at Edwards's habitual stage-right position, and thcweamed and thcweamed until they were thick. Meanwhile, members of Fabulous, a third-rate posse of Manics-inspired punk revivalists (managed by *NME*'s James Brown) tried to disrupt the show by heckling throughout, but no one listened.

One member of the Diorama audience had flown all the way from Los Angeles to be there. At the age of 21, former porn starlet Traci Lords was the USA's unofficial Madonna: an under-the-counter Monroe, a word-of-mouth superstar, a goddess in a brown paper bag. Lords (real name Nora Kuzma) had caused a national scandal – FBI busts, questions in Congress, a top story on CNN – when it emerged that 39 of her 100+ adult movies (mostly with punnish names like *Beverly Hills Copulator*) had been made when she *wasn't* an adult: she had shot her first film aged just fourteen. Perhaps unsurprisingly, Traci subsequently spiralled downward into a drink/drugs dependency which nearly proved terminal when she injected a huge amount of cocaine and came within seconds of death (this was assumed by many to be a suicide attempt). Four months later, however, an agent found her 'legitimate' modelling work. With the money she saved, she went into rehab and took acting classes.

In 1991, Lords's self-reinvention as a mainstream actress was just beginning. Ultra-kitsch film director John Waters had used her in *Cry Baby*, but her role in glossy soap *Melrose Place*, her workout video and her singing career were yet to come. Hers was still a fame that was never spoken; it was celebrity without respectability – the kind of fame that didn't get you invited as a special guest on *Sesame Street*. All of this fascinated Richey Edwards, who, prompted by Martin Hall's suggestion, sent Lords a song he had written about female exploitation, 'Little Baby Nothing'.

'I listened to the tape and really identified with the character in the song,' she told *Details*, 'this young girl who's been exploited and abused by men all her life', although it was only later that she realised the song was partly Richey's specific interpretation of Traci herself.

Traci had not heard of Manic Street Preachers and admitted that 'It's not really my kind of music,' but hit it off with Richey and agreed to contribute guest vocals, as much 'for the experience' as anything else. Edwards was deeply impressed by her –'Traci Lords is female power' – as was Nicky, who unforgettably told BBC2's *Rapido*: 'Everybody thinks, "Traci Lords, dirty slut," but she's actually one of the most articulate Americans we've ever met.'

It's the way he said it.

'Historical phenomena always happen twice – the first time as tragedy, the second as farce' – KARL MARX

Re-releasing a single just didn't seem like a very Manic Street Preachers thing to do.

But then again, the Manics had long been applying Malcolm X's 'by any means necessary' as a covert marketing strategy, and so it came to pass that on 16 January 1992 they released a 'new' single: a steroid-pumped, bass-heavy, Guns N'Roses-ified version of 'You Love Us'.

According to Richey, this was because the original run of three thousand had long since sold out and he had been inundated with letters begging for a copy. James offered a musical justification: still disingenuously perpetuating the myth of his own inadequacy, he told me that Steve Brown and Black Barn had enabled him to record 'the big rockist ending that we couldn't do last time. We've learnt to play now'. The reissue could also claim two new B-sides: the exuberant, glam-rocky 'A Vision of Dead Desire' (formerly 'UK Channel Zero') and a live cover of Guns N'Roses' 'It's So Easy'. It also had a new sleeve – a photograph by Tom Sheehan of Richey's Top Shop blouse with Edvard Munch's *The Scream* stuck to it.

'You Love Us' had also, arguably, gained a new meaning. Back in May 91 it was either an absurdly presumptuous claim or, as James put it, 'a sarcastic valentine to the industry'. By now, however, although the band was still more hated than loved, the song was beginning to seem more like a taunt.

The end-of-year readers' polls in the music press showed that the Manics were starting to capture the popular imagination. They were voted Fifth Brightest Hope in both weeklies (*Melody Maker* and *NME*), and *MM* readers also made them No. 1 Hype of the Year (arguably a backhanded compliment), although admittedly there were also strong showings in the Weirdo, Prat, Motormouth and Worst Band categories. Further evidence of the Manics' steady upsurge in popularity had been offered by the fact that, when Damaged Goods reissued 'New Art Riot', this time all 4,500 copies sold out and it shot to Indie No. 1.

With the help of Columbia's marketing clout (HMV chose it as their Single of the Week), the new 'You Love Us' entered the charts at No. 27, earning the Manics their first appearance on *Top of the Pops*. Not for the last time, Nicky Wire reneged on a public promise ('We'll set fire to ourselves on *Top of the Pops*'), but the sight of James topless with 'YOU LOVE US' scrawled across his chest in lipstick was enough to send the Manics leaping to No. 16 the following week. Informed that his single had gone Top Twenty, James apparently shrugged: 'Not good enough.'

The new video for 'You Love Us' was the Manics' best – and, at £38,000, most expensive – yet. Filmed in stylish black and white, it cut rapidly back and forth between James performing 'live' at the end of a fashion catwalk in front of a cinema screen showing MSP icons (Lenin, Malcolm X, Chairman Mao, Traci Lords) and Nicky and Richey getting even more homoerotic than last time around (Wire simulating sex with a pocket TV down his trousers showing a nuclear explosion; Edwards snogging a giant poster of himself, and the pair feeding each other oysters).

I was privileged to be present at the shoot (with careful use of the freeze-frame, I'm just about visible), and witnessed one moment of absolute pop genius. While the rest of the band was miming a 'live' performance, Richey slouched slowly along the catwalk, drugged on his own narcissism, trailing his guitar by the neck, without even the slightest pretence of playing the thing. Looking up at the camera, he hoisted his instrument up for one contemptuous strum before turning away. In those thirty seconds, the entire debate over whether this non-musician deserved to be a pop star was turned to dust.

The scene never even made the final cut. Nor did a shot involving Richey looking unspeakably gorgeous in a white wedding dress, a hand grenade stuffed in his mouth like an apple. I would have married him there and then.

'The most beautiful thing in Tokyo is McDonald's.
The most beautiful thing in Stockholm is McDonald's.
The most beautiful thing in Florence is McDonald's.
Peking and Moscow don't have anything beautiful yet' – ANDY WARHOL

The phoney war was over. It was time to drop the bomb.

Released on 10 February, *Generation Terrorists*, the Manics' long-awaited début album, was an endurance-testing eighteen tracks and 73 minutes long. Although its epic length unquestionably stretched their quality control ('Everybody knows the first album would have been better if we'd left out all the crap,' Richey later admitted), in a way it is fitting that it was a double: in many ways it is two different albums in one.

At least half of *Generation Terrorists* constitutes a testament to wasted youth, a hymn to futility in the tradition of *Low, Searching for the Young Soul Rebels* and *Meat is Murder*, with the Manics cast as desolation angels gazing from bedroom windows over piss-washed, dead-end towns. The rest of the time, they sound ready to dance in the rubble of the palaces of the rich and to feed on their entrails. Throughout its eighteen tracks, they constantly switch between micro- and macro-politics, between paeans to personal despair and critiques of global capitalism (implicitly equating the two), between amphetamine anthems and moments of bruised beauty. This schizophrenia perfectly reflects the adolescent condition, lurching violently from resigned passivity ('we are the useless sluts that you mould') into joyous revolt ('we're gonna burn your death-mask uniforms'), and perpetually at the point where abject ennui ignites into insurrection.

The world was expecting a straightforward sequence of Semtex prayers – 'You Love Us' x 18 – but the band was determined to make an enduring rock classic. 'It has got to be there as a landmark,' said Nicky, 'it's got to be a reference point, it's got to be a full stop.' Indeed, as he later admitted, maybe they tried *too* hard: '*Generation Terrorists* is a fucked-up album because we tried so hard to make some songs Rock FM.'

The sleeve design, featuring Richey's left nipple, was certainly eye-catching, but the most striking thing about the album's packaging came inside the booklet: Richey had chosen an apposite literary quote to accompany each song. (By some distance the most well-read Manic, every time he passed a railway-station bookshop he would buy four or five 'classics' to stuff in his bag, and avidly followed Radio Four's series on controversial novels.) For the first time in ten years, a British band was pointing its fans towards the cultural world beyond rock 'n' roll. In the same way that being a Smiths fan led you to investigate Oscar Wilde, James Dean and Andy Warhol, being a Manics fan made you find out about Orwell, Plath, Larkin and Rimbaud. Manic Street Preachers' record sleeves have arguably done more for youth literacy than has a decade's worth of A-Level syllabuses. As one MSP fan once wrote to me: 'My bookshelves are bulging with stuff they've quoted.'

The sleeve was also the public inauguration of Richey's new name: he had decided, at rather a late stage, to change his name to Richey James. One can ascribe various motives to this identity shift. Perhaps he was rejecting his parental surname in the same way that Cassius Clay had rejected his 'slave name' to become Muhammad Ali. More probably, he just thought 'Richey James' sounded more rock 'n' roll. For the purposes of this book, however, he shall remain Edwards.

The album opens with 'Slash 'N' Burn', a familiar live curtain-raiser built around a headspinningly fiddly rock riff – it might easily have been called 'Slash 'N' Axl' – and some frankly embarrassing lyrics about Third World exploitation ('worms in the garden more real than McDonald's . . .'), although some listeners mischievously took it to be the first rock song about the living hell that is cystitis.

The next two tracks also fall into the category of Horrible Heavy Metal. 'Nat West – Barclays – Midlands – Lloyds', ostensibly attacking the high-street banks' overseas credit policies, probably had more to do with Richey's personal grievances against them (his bank had sent him red letters about a £23 overdraft and repeatedly refused him loans, but soon changed their tune when the royalty cheques started coming in). The marginably more likeable 'Born to End', like the 'Collapsed European Stars' sleeve art, is a comment on the way citizens of former communist countries had been seduced by the cheap glamour of capitalism, and had emancipated themselves from state slavery only to leap willingly into slavery to multi-national corporations. (It is also, in part, another paradoxical *happy suicide* song in the tradition of 'Suicide Alley'.) Richey had noted the rise of anti-semitism and misogyny in the former Eastern Bloc, commenting that: 'All they've got now is better jeans.' And Nicky added: 'Instead of queuing for bread, now they queue for McDonald's.'

Nicky had once stated: 'If we have to write the 'Wild Horses'/'Stairway to Heaven'/'Sweet Child o' Mine' of the 90s, then we'll do it easily, if that's what it takes.' With the fourth track on *Generation Terrorists*, they had finally delivered. 'Motorcycle Emptiness' was a song which had existed in various forms since the band's inception (Richey and Nicky had written it at university, while heavily under the influence of *Rumblefish*, a film described by director Coppola as 'Camus for kids'), but for financial and technical reasons it had yet to be recorded in anything other than rough demo form: 'We had guitars that cost about one quid, a shit amp, it wasn't worth it.' As Richey told *Deadline*: 'Even when people were dismissing us as a tossy two-chord imitation of The Lurkers, we knew we had "Motorcycle Emptiness". No matter how bad things got, we always knew we could write a song like that . . . it was just a question of learning to play it properly.'

With Steve Brown's production, they had finally done it justice: a classy wash of strings and piano underlining a gorgeous guitar motif which Danny Eccleston of *Q* would later describe as 'a high, lonesome figure . . . of the sort that someone in Thin Lizzy might have written on a tremendously good day – roughly six notes that carry the idea of the song far better than the characteristically garbled verse or even the brief, lilting chorus'. Incredibly, however, there had been some talk of leaving the song off the album on the grounds that it was 'too advanced'.

The title, despite James's armchair enthusiasm for Suzukis, has nothing to do with motorcycles; the lyric, incorporating a chorus borrowed from Patrick Jones's 'Neon Loneliness', was a bittersweet critique of the shallow dreams offered by consumerism ('From feudal serf to spender/This wonderful world of purchase power'). Even after six minutes, you never wanted it to end.

Next, after the singles 'You Love Us' and 'Love's Sweet Exile' (the latter prefaced by a brief Patrick Jones poetry recital), came the much-discussed Traci Lords duet. Opening with some Marlon Brando/Kim Hunter dialogue from *A Streetcar Named Desire*, 'Little Baby Nothing' recycles the melody line from 'Suicide Alley' into a windswept American rock epic in the manner of Meatloaf, Bon Jovi or Bruce Springsteen (Richey was an admirer of Springsteen's *Nebraska*), with keyboards by Spike Edney, who did Queen's orchestration (it showed). It was enough for one critic to call them 'a stadium band looking for a stadium. And getting close to finding it'.

The song was originally intended for Kylie Minogue, but she – or, perhaps, her people – turned it down (one rumour had it that PWL demanded percentage points on the whole album, not just on the song). 'We saw Kylie as a manipulative kind of person without really knowing it,' said James, 'but she had a very subtle way of infusing power into her songs – she had people in the palm of her hands.' Nicky could often be seen wearing a Kylie badge, and proclaimed her 'a pop genius'. The song's portrayal of teen-porn-actress-as-exploited-victim was sometimes clumsy, leaving the Manics open to charges of sexism themselves – James as heroic white knight, come to 'rescue' a distressed damsel – but ultimately powerful ('. . . and if I'm starving, you can feed me lollipops'). It was far better suited to Lords' persona than to Minogue's, and, in any case, Traci turned out to have a wonderful Belinda Carlisle bubblegum voice.

Next up was the 'Stars and Stripes' remix of 'Repeat', produced by Nicholas Sansano, Frank Rivaleau and Dan Wood of The Bomb Squad, Public Enemy's engineers (originally, the Manics had considered covering PE's 'Fight the Power'). Although this team actually made four mixes from which the Manics chose the best, the track was hardly up to *It Takes a Nation of Millions* standards. Without wishing to be unkind, one suspects that Sansano, Rivaleau and Wood had tossed it off in their lunch-break and gratefully accepted the fat Sony cheque.

'Tennessee', a glossy version of the band's early B-side, was optimistic but forgettable metal *lite*. 'Another Invented Disease' was pure Guns N'Roses, its title – a pun on AIDS – referring to the conspiracy theory that the HIV virus was manufactured by American germ-warfare scientists, although one wondered where lines like 'I need to feel alone amongst the weeds' (a steal from Sylvia Plath's 'I am solitary as grass') fitted in.

The singles 'Stay Beautiful' and 'Repeat (UK)' were punctuated by a more mellow and reflective version of 'Spectators of Suicide' and 'So Dead'. Another critique of the dissatisfaction bred by western culture, 'So Dead' contained the ear-catching line 'No one fucks as good as Marilyn'. As I wrote at the time, 'the Manics deal in the iconography of the totally fucking obvious (Marx, Madonna, McDonald's, Monroe). No pissing about with minor-league sepia cool, no reverence for Cave or Cohen.' The Manics had little time for the romantic lyrical *auteur*, and respected only the politicised populists: Rotten, Morrissey, Chuck D, Strummer.

The next sound you heard sounded suspiciously like the scraping of a barrel. 'Damn Dog' (written by Billy Mernit/Jacob Brackman) was originally performed by teen actress Robin Johnson as Nicky, singer with The Sleez Sisters in Robert Stigwood's cheesy but endearing 1980 teen movie *Times Square* (two troubled teens meet on psychiatric ward, run away, form band and conquer Manhattan). Likeable enough, but pure filler, B-side fodder.

Things improve after another burst of Patrick Jones verse. 'Crucifix Kiss', a live favourite with a peculiar drums-only chorus, was a furious hymn to atheism, clearly inspired by Richey's traumatic childhood encounters with organised religion, in which Christ is referred to as a 'Führer Nazarene'. 'Methadone Pretty', another live favourite, opened with a Karl Marx quote which encapsulated the spirit of the early Manics in just seven words: 'I am nothing and should be everything.' Similar in mood to 'Stay Beautiful' – an adorable, addictive mixture of victory and defeat – it argued that, in the same way that methadone is a substitute for heroin, people accept a living death ('an MFI wardrobe and two weeks' holiday', as Richey once put it) as a substitute for real life.

'Condemned to Rock 'n' Roll', a somewhat slug-paced six-minute rocker (incidentally, one of Nicky's favourites) ends the album by reiterating its now-familiar theme: the false hopes raised by the spectacle of pop culture, and the emptiness felt when the reality is exposed. The song finishes with the words: 'There's nothing I wanna see, there's nowhere I wanna go.'

'My generation is the soundbite generation. My attention span is incredibly short. My words reflect that' – RICHEY

Generation Terrorists was not written in the English language as we know it, but in a peculiar Preacher patois in which the words 'culture', 'suicide', 'alienation', 'holocaust', 'slut', 'decadence' and 'rock 'n' roll' were more common than the definite and indefinite articles combined.

Some critics described the Manics' crude, compressed headline grammar as 'Sunspeak'. Richey saw this as a compliment: 'We took the abortion language of the *Sun* and turned it to our own means.' This appropriation of tabloid techniques was a classic example of the situationist notion of *détournement*: seizing the products of capitalism and using them as weapons against it.

The band's flexible grasp of syntax, rhyme-free verse and multiple-message songs had more respectable literary precedents in Jack Kerouac's unpunctuated stream-of-consciousness and in William Burroughs's cut-up method. 'Anyone of our generation isn't conditioned to think about just one thing,' said Richey. 'You're always flicking TV channels, always switching radio stations. For us to sit down and write a song about something would be so forced.'

As with The Beatles' Lennon/McCartney, Manics fans love to speculate on which songs are by Richey and which by Nicky. In general, Nicky's songs are more optimistic and easily comprehended ('I think I was like the McCartney to Richey's Lennon . . . I'm a much more hopeful person than Richey') while Richey's are more morbid and impenetrable. As Nicky also put it later: 'Richey was so intelligent that he ended up trying to condense so much that it was unintelligible.'

For the record, 'Roses in the Hospital' and 'Yes' are completely Richey's lyrics; 'This is Yesterday', 'La Tristesse Durera (Scream to a Sigh)', 'Gold Against the Soul' and 'Symphony of Tourette' are entirely Nicky's lyrics. Often, however, as with 'Faster' and 'Little Baby Nothing', Wire came up with the title and Edwards fleshed out the actual lyric. Occasionally, too, as with 'Motorcycle Emptiness', the pair literally sat down at the same desk. 'I used to come up with a chorus and he'd come up with a verse,' Nicky told *Top*, 'and we'd say pretentious things to each other like "We want to put *Rumblefish* to music and make it sound like The Jesus and Mary Chain."'

The words were rarely written with singing in mind. As Stuart Maconie of *Select* put it: 'You got the impression that often they hadn't even been tried out in the mouth.' It was James's task to sift through the lyric sheet and choose what to use and what to lose (Richey's first draft of 'Motorcycle Emptiness' apparently included the line 'under economic clouds of loneliness'). James's often harsh vocals and strange pronunciation ('I sold my medals, it paid a bill' becomes 'I sold my medals, it paid a *BL*') hardly helped, but this was partly deliberate: 'I wanted our message to be so powerful but quite unintelligible, in such a way that people would want to find out more, find out what would drive us to create music that sounded like that.'

Revisionist history has been unkind to *Generation Terrorists*, dismissing it as an ego-puncturing failure. In fact, it soon went Gold and eventually sold three hundred thousand copies – not bad for a début album by any standards other than the band's own – and sold enough to guarantee a Top Five entry in any normal week. Unfortunately, this was the week of the Brit Awards, and the winners shot up the chart, relegating the Manics to No. 13. The album did, however, enter the Rock charts at No. 1, which was some consolation to Nicky: 'It gave us more of a thrill getting to No. 1 in the Rock charts than it ever did getting to No. 1 in the Indie charts.' Indeed, it won them rave reviews in previously sceptical metal mags such as *RAW*, *Kerrang!*, *Riff Raff* and *Rock Power*, a spot on MTV's *Headbangers' Ball*, and a session on Radio One's *Friday Rock Show*.

Perhaps the worst 'review' of *Generation Terrorists* came from two girls in Glasgow, who threatened to kill themselves when it was released. 'I'd rather people killed themselves for us,' said Richey, 'than for a group like Carter or Ned's Atomic Dustbin.'

The album did not sell sixteen million. And the band did not split.

The release of *Generation Terrorists* came amid another tour characterised by hysteria, violence and illness.

At Leicester, a topless female fan prostrated herself at Richey's feet; later, the stage nearly collapsed (the two incidents were apparently unrelated). In Warrington Legends, a power failure left the band performing in darkness (an increasingly common occurrence on the tour: in Colchester, the fuses blew at least five times). Quick-witted as ever, the band changed mid-song from 'You Love Us' to 'You Can't See Us!' After the show, fans fought each other to get into the dressing-room.

Elsewhere, violence involved the band itself. In Sheffield, James told security guards to 'fuck off', which they did. In Cardiff, Nicky told security guards to 'fuck off', which they didn't. What should have been memorable as a triumphant homecoming show (and the live début of 'Little Baby Nothing') nearly went down in history under 'Rock Deaths' when Wire had to be dragged away from a potentially fatal confrontation with an enormous bouncer.

Nicky's warlike mood carried through to the London Astoria. During the second song, 'Nat West . . .', he assaulted a Japanese cameraman with his Fender Precision bass (the show was being filmed for an MTV special) on the grounds that he was obscuring the fans' view. The man was uninjured, but his camera fell shattered to the floor.

At the final date, Nicky's hyperactivity proved to be his downfall. Backstage after the gig, Rachel, his girlfriend, came looking for him, only to be informed by Martin Hall that he wasn't feeling too well. She wearily asked: 'Is it [*pointing to her head*], or is it [*pointing to her stomach*]?' It turned out to be a knee thing. Nicky had damaged his legs jumping over support band The Wildhearts' tour manager, a certain 'Scabby John'. He was eventually found, ice packs on knees, whimpering in the Ladies.

The tour had ended not at Wembley Stadium, but at Northampton Roadmenders. Richey's attitude to this apparent failure was one of phlegmatic realism: 'We read all the classic rock books, which make everything out to be so fast. You're meant to explode overnight, but that never happens.' Nicky was more optimistic. 'Our ego has always been way ahead of our bounds. We have no sense of proportion at all. But we still think it'll happen.'

A mere fortnight later, the irascible, injury-prone Wire and his band were on the road again. After a show in Reading, Nicky's knee condition had deteriorated sufficiently to demand immediate surgery. After a gruesome operation, he spent the rest of the tour on crutches and in excruciating pain. The strain was beginning to show and, at Essex University on 21 March, the rest of the band appeared to be disintegrating in sympathy. A very drunk Richey fell over mid-song, James began coughing up blood (a horrifying viral cocktail of 'flu, tonsillitis and hepatitis).

Nicky in particular was in desperate need of convalescence, and the final two dates of the tour were cancelled. For the other members, however, there was no rest. 'Slash 'N' Burn' had been released as a single on 16 March (backed with 'Motown Junk' and 'Sorrow 16' for those who had missed out first time around, along with a mournful acoustic ballad, 'Ain't Goin' Down'). To some extent, the promotional duties were fulfilled by a video cobbled together from footage of the Astoria gig, and James did his bit with a beautiful solo performance of 'Little Baby Nothing' on Radio One's *Steve Wright in the Afternoon*. *Top of the Pops*, however, required the whole band, and a stand-in was needed. The band's first idea was to use Caffy St Luce, a black woman, as an up-yours to the racist BNP (whose Derek Beackon had won a council election that week). In the end, tour manager Rory Lyons (himself a former bassist with 80s psychobillies King Kurt) stepped into Nicky's Dunlops, covering his face with a pig mask.

By the time April's IRMA Awards – Ireland's prestigious answer to the Brits – came around, the Manics had fully recuperated. They had not originally been invited, and were only whisked to the event by stretch Daimler because Seal had dropped out. Hapless compère Dave Fanning was clearly not an admirer, introducing the band's performance of 'You Love Us' with cheap sarcasm: 'Some music from the Welsh valleys, some nihilistic punk rock from the eyeliner-friendly band, Manic Street Preachers.' It was all the provocation they needed.

Towards the end of the song, a riled James Dean Bradfield spontaneously mutated into the Incredible Hulk, dragging down towers of Marshall amps like Samson in the temple, before diving into a crowd which consisted of the President of Ireland and several hundred fourteen-year-olds waiting for New Kids on the Block. Nicky followed suit, destroying his mike stand, while Richey did the same to his guitar and Sean kicked over his drumkit.

As the four sauntered off, co-presenter Gerry Ryan sneered: 'Well, that was jolly rebellious, wasn't it . . . I believe in years to come journalists will view it as a salient point in the development of rock 'n' roll.' He hadn't seen nothin' yet.

Later, at the celebratory dinner at the Burlington Hotel, suspicious doormen refused to believe that the Manics were guests until Martin Hall and Rory Lyons convinced them. Once inside, the quartet rapidly became horrendously drunk. Nicky – clearly unusually susceptible to alcohol after his long period of abstinence – went around popping all the balloons, and slid under the table on his back before the main course had even arrived.

Richey, meanwhile, emptied three bottles of wine and the contents of the salt and pepper shakers into an ice bucket and spilt them all over the floor. Sean just kept shouting 'booooring!' at the top of his voice. Eleanor, the tweedy Sony Ireland representative, called them 'scum'; the waiters chipped in with 'a disgrace'.

Meanwhile, James had disappeared in search of Dave Fanning, whom he subjected to a verbal (and almost physical) assault. He was dragged away by security guards and ejected from the building. Before long the entire Sony table was physically removed from the premises.

It didn't end there. Back at the band's hotel, Nicky was thrown out of the bar for wearing only his boxer shorts. James collapsed on his bed having drunk so much that he temporarily went blind. Richey got into a fight with an Irish businessman about Catholicism. Sean, ever the sensible one, ended up at a rave with 2 Unlimited.

According to Martin Hall, the whole episode was 'just high spirits from a bunch of lads not used to the Irish way of drinking'; for Richey, however, it provided another example of his dissatisfaction with major-label life. As he told *Smash Hits*: 'What do they [Sony] expect us to be? Phil Collins? They signed us for loads of money for being what we are, and now they expect us to start dressing like them and looking as chronically ugly and boring as them with their crap haircuts and no brains.'

In the same interview, Richey, wearing a T-shirt reading 'I'M TOO DEAD', had advised the readers of *Smash Hits* to commit suicide before they reached adolescence. 'Our manifesto is: "Don't do it, kids." Never get past the age of thirteen.' Perhaps unsurprisingly, the sub-editors drew a red line through that one.

The very fact that Richey was talking to the magazine in the first place was surprising to some. But Richey had no problem with speaking to the kiddie press: 'We've never minded doing teenage magazines like *Smash Hits*, which some bands refuse to do. I just find that incredibly patronising. I know, when I was fourteen, music was the only thing I cared about.' He had also previously stated that '*Smash Hits* is more effective in polluting minds than Goebbels ever was.' This was meant as a compliment: *Smash Hits* was a propaganda tool, and the Manics knew how to use it.

The remainder of that spring was spent touring Europe supporting someone called Peter Hamill, and playing German festivals with crap comedy punks Die Toten Hosen. The Manics were still willing to swallow their pride of necessary (and if it meant playing to twelve thousand people) and, if fan hysteria is any measure of success, it was worthwhile. In Munich, a female admirer rammed their tour bus on the *autobahn*, left her car stranded across two lanes of traffic and rushed over to get Richey's autograph. The band also made its first attempts to crack America – an episode which is described elsewhere, but suffice to say that it was not a good experience. In Nicky's inimitable words, they found it 'a country that floats on a huge sea of shit and piss'. The Manics' most successful foreign invasion took place in possibly the least likely terrain: Japan. A five-date tour – each night a 3,000 seater – had sold out well in advance, 70,000 copies of *Generation Terrorists* had been sold there, and the band had been receiving 200 letters a week from their Japanese fans. However, nothing prepared them for the fan-demonium which greeted their arrival in Tokyo: obsessive fans, many carrying DIY Richey dolls, literally camping outside the Hotel Pacific Meridien, staking the place out to catch a glimpse of the band, and stampeding to follow them if they dared venture out to a club. The T-shirt stall sold out after just two shows; thereafter, fans happily queued just to fill in a *form* for merchandise.

Richey believed that the Japanese saw some of Mishima's hara-kiri spirit in the Preachers' now-or-never, do-or-die manifesto, although it probably had more to do with the Japanese love of cross-dressing and western glamour. The country which had fallen in love with Boy George a decade earlier was enchanted by Nicky's and Richey's kabuki-style *maquillage*: the Manics were rock 'n' roll *onnagata* (men who play women's roles in kabuki theatre).

To a great extent, the admiration was mutual. 'Japan is a culture we can respect,' said Nicky. 'There's no sex crime; four- and five-year-olds can go to school on the train alone. But then women are treated as second-class citizens . . .'

For James, the attraction was mainly visual. As he later told me, Japan was '. . . responsible for my most perfect twentieth-century moment. We were travelling into Tokyo in a taxi, it was pissing down with rain, we were all really tired and silent, we were going over this passover, listening to Joy Division's "The Eternal", and everything all of a sudden went into slow motion. I know it sounds like "my life is a film", but it was. It was the only time music has turned a living moment into moving cinema for me. You always want to write your own script . . . I don't subscribe to that lemming theory about Japan, but the regimentation of the whole situation was perfect. I just remember imagining that everyone could hear this song: the cars in the distance, the people walking to work on the pavement . . .'

On the return from Japan, Nicky Wire (band nickname: Mr Hypochondria) claimed to have contracted malaria. Nobody took any notice.

It was during the Japanese tour that the Manics had filmed the video for their next single. 'Motorcycle Emptiness' was shot in a variety of locations: at Tokyo Station in the rush hour, in Yokohama Temple high in the mountains, and in front of the largest big wheel in world. Having failed to gain the necessary permits to film, the band (Richey looking alarmingly Black Crowe-like with his longer, shaggy hair; James looking like George Michael in pinstripes and designer stubble; Sean looking unusually rugged; and Nicky looking ultra-glam in leopardskin and shades) and first-time director Martin Hall were constantly on the run from police. It was worth the trouble: the video remained in MTV's *Buzz Bin* for two months.

Released on 1 June, 'Motorcycle Emptiness' was something of a breakthrough single. Backed with a fairly pointless cover of Alice Cooper's 'Under My Wheels', a live version of 'Crucifix Kiss' and a haunting acoustic slowie called 'Bored Out of My Mind', this was the song that had many doubters grudgingly admitting, 'I never used to like them, but . . .' Martin Carr, of the Manics' 1997 tour-mates, The Boo Radleys, typifies this phenomenon: 'I thought they were really cool, but in an amused kind of way. I kept buying their records, for some reason, hoping they'd eventually do a good one. It wasn't until they put out "Motorcycle Emptiness" as a single that I decided they were fantastic.'

The single won them another memorable *Top of the Pops* performance: seven hundred red carnations lay on the floor as Sean, Richey and Nicky (the latter in velvet choker and leopardskin gloves) mimed, while James sang beautifully live. Although it only

Manic On The Streets Of London: preparing to storm the 'Death Camp Palace'   MARTIN GOODACRE

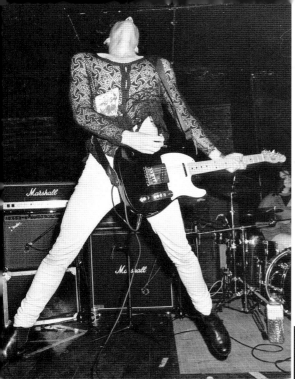

◄ *Author's first Manics gig: Manchester Boardwalk, 1991*

IAN T TILTON

➤ *Note original 'working' songtitles*

IAN T TILTON

➤ *Clockwise from top: Nicky Wire, Sean Moore, Richey Edwards, James Dean Bradfield*

STEVE DOUBLE

∨ *Early Mitch Ikeda shot*

MITCH IKEDA

◄ *Philip Hall,*
1959-1993

PAUL SLATTERY

Roses In The Hospitality:
Richey backstage in
Cardiff, 1991

TIM PATON

➤ *James with Martin Hall*

PIERS ALLARDYCE

➤ *That coveted Bradfield physique*

IAN T TILTON

⋁ *Traci Lords, 'probably the most intelligent American we've ever met.'*

LILI WILDE

*Cracked Actor: Richey rocks
the Brat Pack look*

TOM SHEEHAN

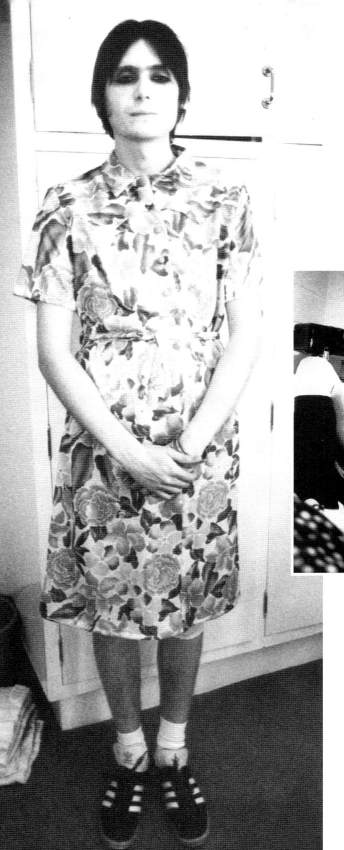

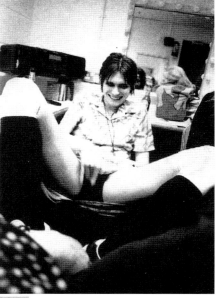

◄ *Condemned To Frock'N'Roll: Nicky Wire*

PAUL SLATTERY

▲ *What does a Welshman wear underneath his dress? Wire reveals all.*

reached No. 18, the song stayed in the Top Forty for a month, becoming the biggest-selling Manics single so far. As Nicky drily remarked: 'I hope one day it may be used in a car advert or something.' Indeed, 'Motorcycle Emptiness' was the track which would eventually turn up on 'Various Artists' CDs bearing titles such as *Drive Time* and available only through petrol stations, alongside Chris Rea and Dire Straits. It even made it on to the Radio Two playlist.

'Don't fall in love 'cos we hate you still' – 'STAY BEAUTIFUL'

On 19 June, the Manics returned from their planetary conquest for a one-off show at London's Town & Country Club (now The Forum) – their largest British headline to date.

For the first time, it felt as though the Manics were a *big deal*. The place was sold out – those new 'Motorcycle Emptiness' fans were there in force – and the band played the song live for first time (many had previously suspected they were incapable of doing so, and that the single had been recorded by session musos).

The four appeared to have been sartorially transformed by their foreign escapades. The white jeans had gone: Nicky was all in black, James was in his Japanese pinstripes and Richey looked the very embodiment of Nik Cohn's description of the young Jim Morrison: 'a marvellous boy in black leathers, made up by two queers on the phone.' If the band had changed, so had the audience. The atmosphere that night was strange: for the first time ever, the crowd reception was one of pure adoration. The undercurrent of mutual antagonism – the Manics' lifeblood – had vanished.

For 'Little Baby Nothing', James, momentarily convinced that he was in Bruce Springsteen's *Dancing in the Dark* video, pulled two girls out of the crowd to sing Traci Lords's part. Nicky was on top motormouth form, opining that 'all males should be castrated', and delivering a special message to Princess Diana, who had apparently been throwing herself down staircases: 'If you're gonna commit suicide, at least do a decent job of it, don't try *five times*!'

Before leaving the stage – there was no encore – Nicky also promised, with a wicked grin, that 'this is the last fucking gig we'll ever do'. I almost believed him. In the bar afterwards, he explained, spitting out the words. 'It was like a *celebration*. I can't handle all these people liking us.'

The following month, the official Manic Street Preachers fan club was formed.

Richey, meanwhile, was becoming something of a *bona fide* sex symbol. The recently launched soft-porn magazine *For Women* asked him to pose for a centre spread. Disappointingly, he declined, explaining: 'Public nudity is repugnant, private nudity isn't much better; the human form is ugly compared to, say, a leopard or a seal' (inviting speculation that he kept back issues of *WWF Monthly* under his bed). Later, he would be more candid about his reasons: 'I have no desire to expose my genitalia. Too small.'

Comics, though, were a different matter. Richey spent many an afternoon in Cardiff's Forbidden Planet and Newport Market seeking out the latest *Shade the Changing Man*, *Bad Company* or *Nemesis the Warlock*, and was thrilled when the Manics began making cameo appearances in *2000AD*. In August, a distinctly Wire-esque character wearing a Manic Street Preachers T-shirt cropped up in *Zenith Part 2: Blind Justice* and, in another issue, a certain 'Clarence' from 'The Crazy Sked Moaners' branded '4 RAEL' [sic] on his forehead with a laser.

The Manics were also offered – and turned down – a few film roles, but their public acting début came soon enough anyway. In August they played a series of Radio One Roadshows at seaside resorts (Porthcawl, Ilfracombe, Great Yarmouth). After one performance, DJ Gary Davies dragged James back out of the trailer to act out a scene from *Neighbours* with two members of the cast.

The band had spent much of the summer on the festival treadmill, sharing bills in France, Belgium and Germany with the likes of Bryan Adams, Lou Reed and truly terrible 70s boogie revivalists The Black Crowes, whose singer, Chris Robinson, once worryingly described by Richey as 'the best-dressed man in the world', had apparently specifically requested the Manics as support (Robinson was horrified when they showed no interest in joining him in backstage rock 'n' roll debauchery, preferring to hang around in tracksuits playing Sega).

Even so, there was still something deliciously wrong about seeing the words 'Manic Street Preachers' among all the grunge mediocrities, press darlings and had-beens on the Reading Festival line-up. The Manics were playing on the Saturday, along with their inspirational heroes Public Enemy, but they were fourth on the bill, below past-their-peak indie plodders Ride and EMF.

The merchandise stall was doing a brisk trade in specially designed Manics T-shirts. The fronts featured a woman carrying a machine gun with the caption 'This is the only answer to rape' (taken from a Class War book I had given them as a present, which in turn had lifted it from the cult movie *If . . .*); the backs displayed a phrase Richey had first used in a fan-club essay about his disgust for crusties: 'Cultural Chernobyl'. Nicky later summarised its meaning as 'Just three years of bastardisation and hatred, and Reading was the symbol.' Either way, 'Cultural Chernobyl' proved a self-fulfilling prophecy.

Just after 6 p.m., when John Peel had completed his traditional announcement of the football results, Marilyn Monroe's 'I Wanna Be Loved By You' wafted over the speakers and the Manics walked out into the sunshine to wild, wild applause. They struck up the intro to 'You Love Us' – and the crowd, clearly, did. The band was taken aback by the adulation, as Nicky told me later: 'The initial reaction of the crowd felt quite exciting for us, it felt like Guns N'Roses or something going out there. There was something good in the air. We were a bit of cleanliness among the dirt.' And James added: 'We were surprised to find out that so many people actually liked us. We felt like a proper band. I don't think we'll ever get over it.'

This breakthrough only encouraged the perverse Preachers to engage in even more audience-baiting than usual: James, bare-chested in white jeans and black Docs, duckwalking his white Strat around the stage, goading and spitting at the front rows, and Nicky – a vision in cerise chiffon, white denim and black feathers – shimmying, sashaying and rubbing his crotch *à la* Michael Jackson. 'You don't half fucking stink, you lot,' he informed the sweaty throng and, acknowledging their protests, added: 'There appears to be some heckling from the cheap seats!' (As he explained afterwards, 'Any mass of people who turn up to see ten different bands must be pretty fucked up. They just go to enjoy the day. They're used to a bit of abuse.')

Then, with eerie predictability, Nicky went just that bit too far. After the last song, he threw his bass offstage, but it rather pathetically failed to make the front row. Instead, it struck a security guard in the photo pit, breaking his arm and gashing his head. 'It was unintentional,' Wire later pleaded. 'I tried to reach the crowd with my guitar, but I'm too puny.' Fearing retribution, Nicky, Richey and Sean fled the site for their lives, leaving a disappointed throng – the largest crowd of the weekend – standing outside the *Melody Maker* Signing Tent. James actually stayed behind and snuck sidestage to watch Public Enemy, but his colleagues were grateful to be safely back in their hotel rooms in time for *Match of the Day*.

In the end, Specialised Security didn't sue (although the organisers withheld some of the Manics' fee). Boss George Cameron quipped, 'Next time I do the Manics, I'll have a couple of guys facing the stage as well!'

Back in June, the Manics had been invited to contribute a song to *NME*'s *Ruby Trax* compilation, which involved the big alternative acts of the day covering No. 1s of the past in the name of charidee (the fortieth anniversary of the Spastics Society).

The band considered a number of songs, including Dexys Midnight Runners' 'Geno' (which they had covered in their Blackwood days), and also 'School's Out', although, having already recorded 'Under My Wheels', James didn't want the Manics to look like an Alice Cooper tribute band. Richey wanted to do 'Bye Bye Baby' by the Bay City Rollers, but he was overruled by Nicky, who chose 'Theme from M*A*S*H (Suicide Is Painless)' instead. In 1980 Johnny Mandel – under the pseudonym The Mash – had added some strangely morbid lyrics ('The sword of time will pierce our skins . . .') to the signature tune from the classic Korean War comedy, creating one of the stranger No. 1 singles in chart history. 'It reminded us of a very gloomy time in our lives,' Wire explained. 'It was No. 1 when there was a Musicians' Union strike and no *Top of the Pops*, which essentially meant there was no music on TV at all.'

On 21 June Manics went into the dirt-cheap Soundspace Studios in Cardiff's docklands, and recorded the song in one day at a total cost of just over £80. No overdubs were used: they just kept playing it over and over until they got it right. Which didn't happen – not exactly. James had misheard the line 'the losing card I'll some day lay', and instead sang, 'the losing card of some delay' (although, to be fair, it is difficult to imagine Johnny Mandel making much sense of James's vocals on 'Another Invented Disease' either).

On 7 September 'Theme from M*A*S*H' was lifted from *Ruby Trax* and released as a single, backed with The Fatima Mansions's bizarre take on 'Everything I Do, I Do It For You', and 'Sleeping with the *NME*', detailed elsewhere. The Manics' treatment of the song, already previewed live at the Reading Festival, was not dissimilar to the Guns N'Roses version (complete with HM rockout ending) of 'Live and Let Die' by Wings – a professional enough job, with only James's sometimes rough vocals betraying the haste with which it had been recorded. Visually, the theme of 'Theme . . .' was flags: another fucked-up flag on the sleeve (American this time), a video filmed in a room full of flags, and a *Top of the Pops* performance in front of a huge Soviet hammer and sickle (which apparently offended a few Korean War veterans).

NME, which had something of a vested interest, declared that: 'James, Richey, Nicky and Sean have taken the theme from *M*A*S*H* and turned it into the least embarrassing rock anthem of all time. It should have been titled "Helicopter Emptiness".' David Cavanagh of *Select*, however, called it '"The Eye of the Tiger" with an even worse widdly-widdly guitar solo. The end of any hope of credibility these men ever had.'

But the most disappointing thing about it all, if truth be told, was that the Manics – a band perceptive enough to write the line 'hospital closure kills more than car bombs ever will' – couldn't see charity rock records for what they are: the crumbs from the table of capitalism, doing the work the government should be doing, propping up the system, and solidifying the benefactor/victim, have/have-not relationship. Indeed, Richey had already told *Indiecator*: 'The thing that really pisses me off about these charity appearances by pop stars is that the minute they come offstage, they're counting their record sales, pissing off to Browns and snorting cocaine out of some six-year-old boy's backside.' Yet it wouldn't be the last time they played the charity game.

Nevertheless, 'Theme from M*A*S*H' was their biggest hit to date, although one suspects that this had more to do with the song than with the artists. After entering the charts at No. 9, amazingly, it went up the following week to No. 7 – much to Richey's delight. It also made No. 1 in the National Jukebox Chart, for what that was worth.

If the Manics didn't like being liked, they were going the wrong way about it.

The Manics reacted to this new level of fame by turning inward, reinforcing their gang mentality. On their October tour, they behaved as what James would later call 'a tight, impenetrable four-person unit; it's like an Enid Blyton nightmare'. ('We've become so close it's almost awkward,' he admitted to *Esquire* years later, 'blokes being that close.') Louis Eliot, then of mod/punk band Kinky Machine, which supported the Manics on the tour (and now of the far superior Rialto), remembers: 'They were like this kind of eight-legged insect that moved around as one.' Unlike the relationships within most bands, which form at college or through an ad in *Melody Maker*, this Cosa Nostra-like closeness came naturally to the four childhood friends. 'We get on too well,' admitted Sean. 'We fit too snugly, like a slipper; we've just got used to each other.'

It was with little enthusiasm that they gathered again to face their public. At the first tour date, in Exeter, Richey turned up camouflaged in a green woolly hat and anorak. Nicky, asked to sign an autograph, reluctantly scribbled: 'I hate life.' The glammed-up Manics faithful, however, couldn't get enough of their heroes. One particularly intense show took place at Warrington's Parr Hall. From the moment the band took the stage to the strains of Ice-T's 'Cop Killer', the hardcore sang along with every word, and screamed like a burning crèche. At one point James leapt into the crowd, and they wouldn't give him back; it was only after he had been chaired shoulder-high around the room that he was allowed to rejoin his band and play on. By the end, fainting fans had to pulled out of the front row for mouth-to-mouth resuscitation.

No Manics tour would be complete without the random act of violence and the Nicky Wire medical problem. At the Cambridge Junction, James was hit by a can of lager. 'Beer?

Is that the best you can do? Why don't you just shoot us down now and have done with it?' was his response. After the final date in Norwich, Nicky once again retired hurt, this time with teeth problems and torn back ligaments.

Another notable aspect of the October tour was the Manics' choice of cover versions. Their rendition of The Clash's 'What's My Name?', as well as being a tribute to a formative inspiration, carried an extra meaning. The phrase dates back to the Ali versus Tyrell fight of the late 70s. Throughout the pre-match hype, Tyrell had offended his opponent by referring to him by his slave name, Cassius Clay. During the later rounds of the fight itself, having gained the upper hand, Muhammad Ali taunted Tyrell, repeating after every punch, 'What's my name? What's my name?' The cynics who had doubted that this band would ever become a *name* were having to eat their words now. Manic Street Preachers: everyone knew their name.

On 15 November the Manics finally released 'Little Baby Nothing' as a single, in what was no less than the *seventh* song to be lifted from *Generation Terrorists*. It came accompanied by 'Never Want Again', a gorgeous, mid-tempo stomper; 'Dead Yankee Drawl', an anti-American rant resurrected from their early days; and the original 'Suicide Alley'. Or, depending on which version you bought, three tracks recorded live in Japan.

There was a medium-sized feminist outcry against the preceding ad campaign, which featured a naked woman with cuts of meat marked on her body. The furore died down somewhat when it emerged that this was a genuine Meat Marketing Board ad from the early 70s, and that Richey was making precisely the same point as his detractors about the objectification of women.

By now, however, it seemed that even Sony could not really be bothered. The vinyl version of the single, and its sleeve, were of such poor quality that it felt like a flexidisc wrapped in Andrex (when I raised this with Richey, he freely admitted that the Manics had had nothing to do with the packaging, or with the two-part CD marketing tricks now being pulled by Sony on their behalf). The song deserved better – as did anyone who paid good money for it. It barely bruised the charts, limping to No. 29, and carried the unmistakable whiff of dead-horse flogging.

The most extraordinary thing about 'Little Baby Nothing' was its video. Directed by Steven Wells of *NME*, it contained almost too much to take in at one viewing. James, guitarless and symbolically castrated, sang in front of The Dead End Dolls, an all-female band made up of Manics fans including Gill Armstrong (the other three Manics apparently 'couldn't be arsed' to appear). They in turn played in front of a wall covered in such slogans as 'White Men Are Sexually Inferior' and 'All Rock 'n' Roll Is Homosexual', and adorned with a pink triangle (as worn by gay inmates of the Nazi death camps), and with a Soviet hammer and sickle made from cut-up Union Jacks. The camera repeatedly cut away to a series of feminist/situationist images: girls in T-shirts reading, 'EJACULATE YOUR DESIRES', 'CARPET BOMB THE RICH' and 'I LAUGHED WHEN LENNON GOT SHOT'; the impossibly glamorous Jacqui and Carrie Shampoo morphing into a pair of lesbian skinheads; a woman pushing a He-Man doll into a liquidiser; and a model who, to be honest, looked more like Cindy Crawford than Traci Lords (Traci was unavailable), singing while the lens crawled along the lipstick graffiti up her leg: 'READ MY LIPS'.

'I can't listen to music too often. It affects your nerves, makes you want to say stupid, naïve things and stroke the heads of people who could create such beauty while living in this vile hell. And now you mustn't stroke anyone's head, you might get your hand bitten off' – V.I. LENIN

On Friday 11 December, bigmouth struck again.

The Manics were midway through playing to a sell-out crowd at London's 2,500-capacity Kilburn National. It had been an electrifying performance, James burning through the now-familiar *Generation Terrorists* set (plus one new song, rumoured to be the forthcoming single, called 'Patrick Bateman'), Richey looking more beautiful than ever in silver PVC jeans, and Nicky – resplendent in a silky shirt covered in Sellotaped Marilyn photos – rapping through 'Slash 'N' Burn' with a weird glint in his eyes. Once again, halfway through 'It's So Easy', a girl had to be carried out for mouth-to-mouth resuscitation.

During a break in proceedings, The Wire stepped up to the mike and announced: 'In this season of goodwill, here's hoping Michael Stipe goes the same way as Freddie Mercury pretty soon!'

The repercussions began before the last chaotic clangs of 'Motown Junk' had faded from the PA system. In the bar and lobby, music-biz luvvies pulled concerned faces. 'Did you *hear* what he said?' 'I know, that was *totally* out of order.' (At the time, the R.E.M. singer was widely, and wrongly, rumoured to be HIV positive.) A war-trial/witch-hunt atmosphere immediately ensued. At the after-show party in a nearby wine bar, Wire was harangued by a journalist from *NME*, who demanded an unequivocal apology. The very same hacks who loved prodding the Manics to 'say something outrageous' in interviews had suddenly come over all moralistic.

Simultaneously, handbags-at-dawn scuffles broke out as members of support band Disco Assassins and New Wave revival combo Trafalgar were ejected after angry protests. 'It only caused a fuss because it was about someone so revered in their own industry,' Wire said later. 'It was like being at a Red Wedge meeting!' By the time I arrived, Nicky's mood was a mixture of stoic resignation and typically black humour. He glanced over at a wheelchair-bound fan, and grinned. 'Ah well, never mind, I've offended the homos, but I'm down with the cripples now.' He meant it in exactly the same sick-but-harmless spirit as the Stipe remark. This time, fortunately, the world wasn't listening.

The furore refused to die. The following night, at Brixton Academy, Huggy Bear vocalist Chris said, 'Fuck Manic Street Preachers, I hope they get cancer.' In the following week's music press, the opinions of such 'celebrities' as Silverfish and Kitchens of Distinction were immediately canvassed, and the majority censured The Wire's 'mindless verbal terrorism' in horrified, pompous tones. In a faxed statement, Boy George bizarrely asked, 'Doesn't he realise that AIDS is not a gay issue?' (at no point had Nicky said that it was), and signed off: 'If suicide is painless, why doesn't he just slit his throat and shut the fuck up?' In *NME*'s letters page, one seething correspondent wrote: 'It is a touch ironic, since half their act is based on ripping off gay culture. Sadly, they expose themselves as just one more bunch of glam-rock lads, dressed up in drag and make-up, but behind it all they're just a bunch of arsehole beerboys like Rod Stewart or Axl Rose.'

Melody Maker's Viewpoint column thundered: 'All that will be remembered is that

Nicky portrays AIDS as a form of punitive justice (just like the fundamentalists and the political right)', and indeed, a handful of Nazis actually wrote to *NME* agreeing with Wire. It took Cass, drummer with The Senseless Things, of all people, to see what was really going on: 'Who cares? We fall for it every time. Nicky said it to 2,000, you said it to 200,000, but it ain't changed anyone's opinion of Michael Stipe. More publicity for the Preachers, more publicity for us, more for R.E.M, you keep your jobs. Everyone's a winner, baby.'

Difficult as it is to believe now, the Stipe affair caused such moral outrage that pressure was put on Nicky to leave the band in disgrace, an option which, for a few weeks, was semi-seriously considered.

Hall Or Nothing acted as his spin doctors. As Caffy St Luce saw it: 'Wire always says things that most people think but keep to themselves. People pretended to be shocked, but they still tried to get into the after-show.' His colleagues, meanwhile, rallied around in an admirable show of collective responsibility – or in what James amusingly terms 'a *Murder on the Orient Express* mentality: we all willingly step forward to stab the corpse.' As he unapologetically explained: 'People should realise that the most important changes come about through talking in really discriminate terms. Language has always been our weapon . . . and if you hurt a couple of "nice" people along the way, or offend them, then that's necessary.' Richey, surprisingly, was more tactful, claiming that the statement was meant to 'highlight the reverence held up to rock stars' and 'the emptiness of liberal arguments about AIDS', and wondered whether there would have been the same outcry if Nicky's remark had been directed at Prince Edward (also rumoured to be gay). 'It's an upside-down view of morality,' he noted. 'Outside London that would've got no reaction at all.'

The truth of the matter was closer to home than anyone imagined. Although he kept it quiet at the time, Wire had just heard the heartbreaking news that the band's manager, mentor, father-figure and friend, Philip Hall, had cancer. Wire was lashing out in all directions. (He now claims, perhaps mendaciously, that Hall encouraged him. 'It's Philip's fault,' he joked in *NME*, 'he told me to do it: "Go on, Wire, say it!" The mad bastard . . .')

Lest we forget, Wire *did* have a point of sorts. It's worth remembering just how hideous the posturing Wembley mournfest that followed Freddie Mercury's demise was: Bowie down on one knee reciting the Lord's Prayer, Extreme's Nuno Bettancourt sobbing, 'This one's for you, Freddie!' Plus, on a more trivial level . . . well, maybe Wire just fucking *hated* R.E.M. Although he regrets it now, he certainly didn't at the time. 'I don't regret it at all,' he told *Tortured Rebellion* fanzine. 'I'm sure Stipe hasn't got AIDS anyway, that's one of the sick things of it all, he's just using it and flaunting his sexuality to make a point again.'

In many ways, the Michael Stipe incident was Nicky's equivalent of '4 REAL'. It was incontestably a turning point, and a public-relations catastrophe. A lot of people who had harboured a sneaking affection for the Manics' mascara-ed motormouth abruptly changed their minds. He'd gone too far *this* time . . .

d) Ifwhiteamerica . . .
(WHY THE USA WON'T LOVE MSP)

*'The USA . . . I completely detest it. It's the most washed-up shithole
I've ever been to in my whole life'* – NICKY, 1992

I T WAS A CLASSIC CASE OF RIGHT PLACE, wrong time.
American rock audiences have always been notoriously sceptical about what they perceive as 'English haircut bands' – anything smacking of contrivance, pretension or hype – and there was no reason why a Welsh version should be given an easier ride. (In any case, to most Americans, it's the same thing: tell them you're from Wales and, if they have heard of it at all, they'll reply, 'Oh, you mean Wales, *England?*')

However, on the face of it, there was no reason why the Manics, with their classic glam-metal image (if you squinted at the panda eyes and ratted hair, if you closed your ears to the revolutionary rhetoric, MSP could almost be Hanoi Rocks) and palatable Guns N'Roses-style sound, shouldn't find an instant niche in the American rock/metal market. After all, 'Little Baby Nothing', for God's sake, could almost be a *Meatloaf* record.

Furthermore, the US wing of Sony was genuinely optimistic about the Manics at first, and very keen to get the band across the Atlantic for gigs. Although an MSP sampler CD was playing well on college radio, Sony's ambitions for the Manics went much further than the alternative ghetto, as a delighted Richey remarked at the time: 'It's not like they want us to go to the East Coast and blitz the college radio scene; they're talking about us going to the Mid-West, the rock heartland. Which is where we've always wanted to have impact, 'cos that's closest to our south Wales smalltown experience.'

On 26 April 1992, Manic Street Preachers arrived in New York for the first night of an American mini-tour. The entire city seemed to take an instant dislike to the band: 'A huge feller with a bike chain chasing our van down the road trying to smash his way in' was hardly a good omen. At the Limelight club (another disused church: see '4 Real' chapter), *Generation Terrorists* posters adorned the walls and the album played softly in the background. A smattering of music-biz types – including a certain Deborah Harry – indulged in a bit of meet-and-greet (or, in cynical US parlance, shake-and-fake) with the band and took advantage of the complimentary bar, while support band Blind Melon bored the locals to tears. A perfectly refined setting. 'This is all very civilised,' scoffed a bemused James, glancing at the scene as the Manics walked on. But Nicky Wire was in no mood for niceties. As brother Patrick Jones (then resident in Illinois, nursing terminally ill cancer patients) remembers, Wire's inaugural address to America was far from friendly. 'Nick screamed: "The only good thing about America is that you killed John Lennon!", and this ageing hippy grabbed Nick's ankle, so Nick swung his bass in retaliation, but where there should have been a head, it just got stuck in a mass of hair. Nick just shouted, "Go back to Woodstock!"' In a further attempt at provocation, he sneered: 'This is what you Americans do best: "Slash 'N' Burn".' The crowd, rather pathetically, responded by throwing paper balls and, eventually, one bottle of expensive imported beer. James offered the whole audience a fight outside. There were no takers.

Chicago on 30 April was a similar story, with Nicky bursting a pillow and showering the crowd with feathers, but this time James got what he wanted: a skinhead invaded the stage, only to be unceremoniously despatched with a Bradfield headbutt. Nicky, in particular, didn't enjoy the US experience and made no effort to investigate American culture, spending most of the tour inside buses and hotel rooms, reading books. Richey felt the same way: 'It's really fucked me up,' he admitted at the end of the trip.

By the time the Manics arrived on the West Coast, Los Angeles was burning. At the height of the LA riots, the band was dismayed to find that its own 'Slash 'N' Burn' was being played by an alternative radio station to celebrate the disturbances (they sensibly refused NME's request to do a photo shoot in the war zone, opting for Disneyland instead). The trip culminated with a showcase gig at the Whiskey A Go-Go, Los Angeles's legendary rock dive. It was fairly well received, and even drew a handful of curious celebrities including Red Hot Chili Peppers and Guns N'Roses (although the latter were probably there to see former member Steve Adler's new band Road Crew, which was also playing). Neat little plastic mats in the shape of Richey's 'Useless Generation' tattoo lay in the urinal troughs.

LA seemed to dig the Manics and, with the indifference of New York and the hostility of Chicago behind them, everything appeared to be in place for a swift and easy conquest. Generation Terrorists was released in an abridged, rearranged form, with some of the more 'difficult' tracks removed ('Born to End', 'Spectators of Suicide' and 'So Dead' were axed purely for their morbid titles, while 'Damn Dog' was considered too profane and 'Motorcycle Emptiness', weirdly, too AOR). 'Democracy Coma' was added to the album. It was also devoid of the arty interludes, intra-song dialogue and literary quotes on the sleeve, just to be extra-sure. How could they fail?

The production of Generation Terrorists was blatantly aimed as a silver bullet to the aorta of redneck Middle America. Some commentators found this cynical pragmatism nauseating. 'At times,' wrote Barbara Ellen in NME, 'the band's struggle to be perceived, aurally at least, as shaggy-haired, blue-jeaned Americans reeks of desperation beyond the Chunderdome.' Desperate or not, the Manics had undeniably perfected a slick, FM-friendly rock sound. Unfortunately, they had chosen the precise moment when America had finally tired of slick, FM-friendly rock sounds. 1992 was, to borrow Sonic Youth's phrase, 'The Year That Punk Broke'. Seattle grunge had replaced LA glam as the predominant rock aesthetic. 'Image', apparently, was dead; The New Authenticity (actually just as stylised and premeditated as anything which came before) reigned. A whole generation was sold on the *Generation X/Slacker* ethos, and a general aura of skulking alternative-ness pervaded everything from teen movies to Pepsi commercials.

Nirvana, Pearl Jam and Soundgarden were the new rock-megastar élite. The *ancien régime* of Extreme, Poison and Motley Crüe – terrified that its dreams of a retirement mansion in Aspen were going up in smoke – dirtied up its sound and made *faux*-punky videos in black and white. Jon Bon Jovi got a haircut. *Generation Terrorists* bombed. It shifted a mere 35,000 units – a drop in the ocean of the US market.

Viewed in this light, if one wishes to be cynical, the grainier, scuzzier sound of *Gold Against the Soul* could be seen as a belated attempt to woo the Grunge Nation (even though the press release threatened to 'piss on the floor of Seattle'). The tactic, if that is what it was, met with only limited success. The Manics' next American tour found them playing depressingly small venues and with supporting bands of which even most Americans hadn't heard (er, Sponge?!). Nor were the US critics convinced. Old-school journalist David Fricke, reviewing a Manic Street Preachers gig at celebrated punk cavern CBGBs, typified the dull, stultifying American view: 'The rhetoric is earnest enough, but mortally wounded by its lack of

Whatever did happen to Noah Stone?

common sense ... A little less racoon-eyes mascara and a little more deep thought, and the Manic Street Preachers could have the makings of a UK glam equivalent of Soul Asylum or vintage Replacements.'

Ironically, on *The Holy Bible*, generally seen as their most forbidding, impenetrable, uncommercial work, they may finally have got it right. A generation in love with the bleak nihilism of Nirvana's *In Utero* and *The Downward Spiral* by Nine Inch Nails might just hear some sort of resonance (the clanging chimes of doom?) in the Manics' morbid, macabre masterpiece – even if its title might not play too well, to say the least, in the Christian Mid-West.

The theory would never be tested. It was on the eve of a promotional trip to launch the *The Holy Bible* in America that Richey disappeared from the Embassy Hotel in London. The visit was immediately called off, and Sony's US wing finally gave up trying. *The Holy Bible* was never released in America, forcing the small army of Manics devotees to track down expensive import copies.

The Manics, it seemed, were doomed to follow in the tradition of T. Rex, The

Jam and The Smiths: Great British Guitar Bands that never really meant anything Over There. At best, they might become a Morrissey-esque cult act, adored by the trendy Anglophiles in Hollywood and Manhattan, but they would remain ignored by the vast expanse in between. And one has to ask the question: are they even that bothered?

To a great extent, they only have themselves to blame. According to Sarah LeClaire, a Virginia-based music journalist on *Slash* magazine (and one of that extremely rare species, an American Manics fan): 'Their ambiguous sexuality had a lot to do with it. American rock audiences are nauseatingly notorious for their love of testosterone and all its associated evils. OK, Guns N'Roses wore eyeliner and *they* were huge, but they also let it be known that they'd fuck your daughter the moment the opportunity presented itself. Meanwhile, in one of the Manics' first interviews with the American press, Nicky said: "I've had glandular fever from kissing too many boys . . . your *son* might prove to be far more intriguing to us Welsh waifs than your daughter!", which wouldn't have gone down too well with the Seattle-ite grunge fans.'

Tanya Pacheco, an American fanzine writer, agrees. 'It's doubtful that the Manics would ever be able to woo the States because the American music scene is one that cherishes and praises positive stupidity, simple chords, moronic lyrics and shameless patronising by mediocre pop stars.'

There are a handful of American Preacher-zines (*Manicfesto*, *Scream to a Sigh*) but, in the States, Manics fandom is a difficult and time-consuming labour of love. With the exception of the devotees named here, no American of my acquaintance has even heard of them. Sarah LeClaire had to work incredibly hard to find a copy of the début album. '*Generation Terrorists* received no discernible push from Columbia in the States. It was released with the minimum of fuss. I had to search every record store in a thirty-mile radius before I found a copy. When I told one proprietor the name of the band, he said, "Have you tried the gospel section?"'

The Manics' attitude to America is, like so many other things about them, self-contradictory to the core. It was an attempt to fuse two polar extremes of American pop culture – the seedy wastrel ardour of LA's Guns N'Roses with the righteous revolutionary ardour of New York's Public Enemy (force White Trash and Black Panther together, and watch the sparks fly) – which provided their initial concept, their whole *raison d'être*. They had grown up in love with sleazy West Coast glam – a yankee drawl is often detectable in James's singing voice – and the majority of their literary and cinematic idols (Tennessee Williams, Sylvia Plath, Marilyn Monroe, Marlon Brando) were Americans.

And yet, one could be forgiven for thinking that the band in general – and Nicky in particular – despised America and everything it stood for, with enough dogmatic zeal to shame the most doctrinaire Cold War KGB agent. One of their earliest songs, 'Dead Yankee Drawl', is a clumsy but vehement assault on the racist reality beneath the shiny surface of the American dream: 'Smothering justice seen through Red Indian eyes/Silent race war of sweet Hollywood lies.' 'Ifwhiteamericatoldthet-ruthforonedayitsworldwouldfallapart' reiterates the theme – a vicious critique of 'the stars and stripes and an apple for mommy', this time from the imagined perspective of a black militant.

And if there's one thing Americans never take kindly to, as Damon Albarn for one can testify, it is snotty Brits coming over, sneering at their culture and telling them how they've got it all wrong. Something to do with the Boston Tea Party, apparently . . .

Yankophobia sometimes seems to run through The Wire like letters through a stick of Porthcawl rock. Asked by BBC 2's *Rapido* to outline the reasons for working with Traci Lords, his answer was a giveaway. 'Everybody thinks, "Traci Lords, dirty slut,"' he memorably explained, before adding, tellingly, '. . . but she was probably the most intelligent American we've ever met.' As if Americans were some sort of intellectually inferior sub-genus, like the Epsilons in Huxley's *Brave New World*. More recently, he described the USA as 'the Devil's joke, the Devil's flycatcher'. Although his Anti-Americanism is, one presumes, founded in cultural disgust rather than in actual racism, Nicky is now increasingly frank about his contempt for the New World, openly admitting, 'Aah, I fuckin' 'ate Americans,' and remaining ultra-vigilant for signs of the creeping Americanisation of British culture (he once puritanically berated me for wearing an LA Kings hockey shirt instead of one from his beloved Cardiff Devils).

Nevertheless, when the time came, in 1996, for the Big Comeback, the Manics decided to give the world's biggest music market one last try, especially since 'A Design for Life' had been receiving encouraging airplay and fairly regular rotation on MTV. There is, however, or so rock folklore has it, only one failsafe method of cracking America: tear a whole year out of your diary, and tour until you drop. Then do it again. In September, Sony booked the band as main support on Oasis's first major American tour, just as the Gallagher phenomenon was gathering momentum in the States. They would be playing to fifteen thousand people every night, so this time, surely, they would have to fall over to miss.

Instead of promising to outsell Guns N'Roses and subsequently failing to outsell Bikini Kill, the Manics' new humility had taught them to do things the hard way, in a time-honoured slog. While Oasis and Screaming Trees took days off, the Manics played their own club dates at tiny venues like LA's Troubador club, and in-store performances at the Sunset Boulevard and New York Virgin Megastores. To some extent, the policy worked: 'A Design for Life' was playlisted by the major radio station KROQ. However, it never translated into sales. 'We played to loads of people,' sighed James, 'and sold shit, nothing.' Not that it was all hard work. Placed third on the tour bill (Screaming Trees were second), the Manics' half-hour set was over by 8 p.m., providing them with a fatal amount of free time. Sean, harmlessly enough, stayed in his hotel room watching films and playing Nintendo, but James, who had not drunk for five weeks, fell spectacularly off the wagon.

Once again, disaster struck – but, for once, the Manics weren't involved. After only a handful of dates, Liam Gallagher freaked out, quit Oasis and flew home to London (supposedly 'house hunting'), leaving brother Noel to play one date as lead singer before the tour limped to a premature and ignominious end. Nicky handled the situation with characteristic black humour: 'People not turning up, people disappearing: it's good that it wasn't us this time.' He later told *Select*: 'The day before the tour ended, Liam was showing me his knuckles, and they were all bruised and scraped. He said, "We had a great fight last night on the bus." And I was like, "Ooh yeah, sounds familiar!" '

Oasis, and the Manics, returned to the UK. Two weeks later Liam Gallagher had calmed down, and the whole tour returned to the USA, much to Nicky's secret chagrin (he got through it by permanently wearing a French Foreign Legion *képi* with a damp flannel underneath, to 'cool his brain'). But it was too late. The Manics' US campaign – and the *Everything Must Go* album – was dead and, by now, Nicky was beginning to accept defeat. 'When we started, we did want to conquer the world,' he told *NME*, 'but that was just a young boy's dream.' Some things just seem fated never to happen.

With their next album, the Manics got off to an even worse start. It was reported that *This Is My Truth Tell Me Yours* had been rejected by Atlantic, by Virgin America and even by the US division of Epic after one cursory hearing. Atlantic said: 'We can't take this to radio. It's too down.' As *Rolling Stone*'s David Fricke explains: 'Just look at the title "If You Tolerate This Your Children Will Be Next". How many US radio DJs can even take the time to say that? Unless they know it's a hit they won't even bother. It's too many syllables for those guys.' The band reacted angrily to the story, indicating that the album was likely to be picked up by Virgin America for a spring 1999 release.

In the meantime, *NME* asked the Manics realistically to assess their chances of breaking the USA. Although James didn't seem so sanguine about the Manics' poor performance, Wire cheerfully announced: 'Zero! We are the smallest-selling band in the history of the world in America!'

There is no shame in this. There are some things one would say to a roomful of friends that one wouldn't say to a stadium full of strangers, and the same applies at national level. Some of our greatest pop groups – not least that Smiths/Jam/T. Rex trilogy – have spoken crucial truths to the specific, self-contained audience of the British Isles alone. For now, the Manics belong firmly in this honourable tradition.

IfwhiteAmericaheard*ThisIsMyTruthTellMeYours*foronesecond . . . itwouldprobab-lyshrugandswitchchannels.

5. GOLD AGAINST THE SOUL

'At last men came to set me free;
I ask'd not why, and reck'd not where;
It was at length the same to me,
Fetter'd or fetterless to be,
I learn'd to love despair' – BYRON

THE 1992 BREAKTHROUGH OF THE MANIC STREET PREACHERS – Revlon Revolutionaries wrapped in animal print and Miss Selfridge, reeking of fake Cacharel and spilt Babycham – had scrawled 'DRESSING UP' in lipstick capitals across pop's agenda for the first time in a generation. Proletarian scum dressed as dandies, these paupers/pierrots made a dazzling contrast to the posh kids slumming it in DMs and dreadlocks, and to the recidivists in trainers and hoods who dominated the landscape.

To James Brown, 'they looked like your sister's turned her Barbie into the New York Dolls'; to Steven Wells of *NME*, they were 'a kamikaze dive-bomber flown by Andy Pandy and his transsexual friend'. In part, this was a rebellion against their reality. 'If we looked like we felt,' Nicky told *NME*, 'then we would have come onstage like Joy Division. We made a massive effort to be a glamorous band, because inside we know we're not particularly glamorous really.' Grey realism was never the Manics' masterplan. 'We never wanted to look like The Fall or all those other 1978 bands like Magazine,' Richey told *Melody Maker*. 'Disgusting! We wanted to look like Duran Duran and sound like The Sex Pistols.' It was this instinctive understanding of the importance of visual impact that made the Manics a fundamentally POP thing, regardless of the rock noise they made (the true pop experience goes far beyond mere aural sensation: every great pop group creates its own parallel universe, where image and imagery, statements and manifestos are as crucial as sonic thrills).

Indeed, as Richey saw it: 'Glamour is not necessarily a superficial thing.' More than mere window-dressing, it was crucial to the Manics' gender-political *kulturkampf*; they were on a mission to eradicate masculinity. 'The worst thing about the Thatcher years,' Richey once told me, 'was that gender barriers were re-established. You had to be either laddish or . . . *Sharonish*.' And the Manics were unquestionably Sharonish (some of those blouses certainly looked like Letitia Dean's cast-offs). According to Richard Smith in his excellent collection *Seduced and Abandoned*: 'The Preachers fly in the face of fashion by playing "manly" rock music while coming on like absolute jessies.'

Even their choice of drink was effeminate. There is a telling early photo of the Manics in a dressing-room, a crate of Tennents Pilsner lying untouched on a shelf, and Nicky brandishing a glass of Babycham at the camera. While the cream of Madchester was supping Boddingtons, the Manics were swigging the 'Cham – that sweet fizzy plonk so beloved of 70s secretaries on the razz (they always requested a stash on the rider, but most venues ignored it, presuming it was a joke). 'It's better than a pint of Websters,' said Sean, 'and it doesn't make you fat.'

'The female is a female by virtue of a certain lack of qualities' – ARISTOTLE

Perhaps non-coincidentally, it had become increasingly clear that the Manics had an abnormally high percentage of girl fans, much to the scorn of the macho indie world. (To this day, almost every Manics fanzine editor is female.)

'We get loads of girls at our gigs,' said Richey, 'and we get criticised for that because people think that's too poppy: "Ooh, you've got girl fans", so we can't possibly be serious. That is soooooo patronising because these people are saying that girls aren't real fans, like they can't possibly like or understand the music and they're not going to have fifteen pints of lager, have a big mosh down the front and have a curry on the way home. And they should be at home reading *Jackie* and thinking about blokes. It's crap! In terms of sensitivity and intelligence, girls understand so much more than men. How they can condemn 50 per cent of the population of the entire world is completely beyond me.'

Indeed, as Nicky told me, their quantity of female followers was actually a matter of considerable pride to the band. 'One of our biggest achievements is the percentage of female fans we appeal to. Women can be bored and fucked off like men. They write the most interesting letters. Most girls are more rebellious than boys: smoking and shagging in the toilets at school, but it's seen as the divine right of the male to be a tortured artist.'

One reason for the Manics' girl following was quite simple: their undeniable pin-up potential. As Caffy St Luce puts it: 'It'd be a lie to say there isn't a lot of sex involved. I mean, none of them are donkeys.' As much as any boy band, MSP were willing and able to objectify themselves, to pout and pose for the cameras: Richey, for all his intellect, didn't mind being consumed purely as a piece of totty, a *himbo*. He once told me, with reference to Brad Pitt in *True Romance*: 'He does make a good poster, and you can't do much better in life than that.' Sony may have owned the whorehouse, but the Manics were their own pimps.

However, the explanation for the female fanbase goes deeper than their looks and their she-male appearance alone. If the Manics had a gender, it was female. Miranda Sawyer, writing in *Select*, called them 'one of the few male bands who have any valid ideas about women'. If their lyrical affinity with prostitutes, porn stars and anorexics was sometimes clumsy ('Little Baby Nothing') and was open to accusations of patronising attitudes, more often ('4st 7lbs', 'Yes') it was uncommonly empathetic. As Nicky put it, 'I think they see us raging on their side.'

The Manics loathed masculinity, both in themselves and in others. 'The horror of ourselves is 95 per cent confined to men,' Nicky once told me, 'and it's men who've got to change. They are the perpetrators of 95 per cent of the world's violent crimes. We've got to face up to ourselves; we've got a brain capable of controlling it, our biology, our bestiality, and we should. Men are the beasts of the race, the fucks of the world.' Even the physical fact of their maleness repelled them. As teenagers they were distraught when they had to start shaving, while their schoolmates were desperate to start growing moustaches.

Put simply, Nicky and Richey were *feminised males*. Richey, in particular, always struck me as emotionally and psychologically female. His identification with Sylvia Plath and with the SCUM (Society for Cutting Up Men) leader and would-be Warhol assassin Valerie Solanos didn't appear to be once-removed or theoretical, but direct. Equally, his fixation with skinny supermodels seemed somehow utterly non-sexual. When he covered his walls in collages of Ione Skye, Twiggy and Kate Moss, I always got the impression it was not out of lust, but out of empathy and aspiration: less a workplace Page Three calendar, more a shrine to his heroines. He didn't want to screw them, he wanted to be them.

Richey's perennial 'problems', too, were all glaringly *unmale* traits. When he got drunk, he didn't smash things up or look for a fight as a man might do, but quietly drowned his sorrows in his room, like a housewife with a bottle of gin. It was a similar story with his anorexia (rare in males, although not as rare as one might expect) and cutting. Statistics show that 99 per cent of self-mutilators are female, a fact explained by Caitlin Moran in *The Times*: 'To externalise rage, men turn on someone else. Women internalise it, turn it on their self [sic].'

For the first half of 1993, the Manics maintained an ominous public silence. In private, they had been working on the one thing they said would never happen – a second album.

Work had actually begun in secret back in the summer of 92, when they had holed themselves up in Outside Studios in deepest Wales to write new songs. By December they were ready to lay down demo versions, first at Impact Studios in Kent, then continuing into January 1993 at House in the Woods, a gothic manor turned residential studio near Cobham in Surrey (the Manics made a rule of using residential studios whenever possible so that they wouldn't have to meet other bands). Between sessions, they stayed in a rented flat in Shepherd's Bush.

They had entrusted their now-regular engineer Dave Eringa with the job of producing the demos, and were pleased enough with the results to invite him to produce the album itself. This caused a problem, in that Sony was not happy about allowing a relatively unknown 21-year-old to take on such a high-profile task. A band-versus-label stand-off ensued, but the Manics won, and Eringa got the job.

On 25 January 1993, the Manics and Eringa booked into Hook End Manor, an absurdly luxurious, palatial studio complex in the Berkshire countryside. As well as having recording facilities, the Manor boasted a swimming pool, a gym, a snooker-room and live-in caterers. The surroundings had an inevitable effect on the Manics' state of mind. 'We got sucked into MTV-land for a while,' Nicky later reminisced. 'All we did was sit on our arses all day.' In comparison with Cwmfelinfach's SBS or Cardiff's Soundspace, it was like making an album in Hugh Hefner's mansion and, at £2,000 a day, it didn't come cheap.

The mixing-desk capacity was a massive 48 tracks, and there was a special stone room for drums, which Sean exploited to the max. On one song, 'Life Becoming a Landslide', 25 mikes were employed for the drums alone. On another, 'Roses in the

Hospital', he created a huge drum sound by asking the engineers to leave the barn doors open, and to place the mikes in the courtyard outside. Unfortunately, his improvisation backfired: he kept hearing ducks quacking in his headphones, and had to keep leaping from his stool every five minutes to shout: 'Shut the fuck up!' (to the ducks, the engineers, or both). On another track, 'Nostalgic Pushead', he again made use of the Manor's facilities by going to the snooker-room, fetching a cue ball, dropping it on to a frying pan and recording it as percussion.

Although a small number of auxiliary musicians were drafted in – keyboardist Ian Kewley (ex of Paul Young's band Q-Tips), Shovel (percussionist with M-People) and strings arranger Nick Ingham – the majority of the album, unlike its predecessor, was recorded as a band. In other words, drums, bass and guitar recorded simultaneously rather than in sequence (James, however, for reasons of shyness and atmospherics, preferred to record his vocals alone in a blacked-out studio lit with candles).

He, in particular, could hardly be accused of 'sitting on his arse all day'. He switched into workaholic mode, often working a nineteen-hour day (staying up until 6 a.m., sleeping for five hours, then getting up again at 11 a.m.), perpetually imploring a bleary-eyed Eringa: 'Let's just go the extra mile.'

Even Richey was allowed to play a few basic guitar parts on one track, 'La Tristesse Durera (Scream to a Sigh)', while his colleagues hid in the control room and laughed their socks off, before retreating to his room with a pile of books and a bottle of red.

Richey really needn't have bothered.

The partition of responsibilities within the Manics was Marxist division of labour in action ('from each, according to his ability, to each, according to his needs'). 'A band should be a positive division of labour,' postulated James, 'people should do what they're best at. I'm not going to let Richey try a solo just because I think it'll do his self-esteem a load of good, because he can't do it.'

'We're very unique in the way that we have two musical geniuses and two complete incompetents,' said Nicky, who rates himself 'as a bass player 0, as a lyricist 5'. It is, certainly, extremely unusual for the lead singer to be only the third most recognisable member of a band, and this was never part of the original plan, as James later confessed to NME: 'I never wanted to be the singer. I always wanted to be a really good guitarist and always wished that Richey had a voice . . . it's always best to have the coolest fucker in your band as the singer. It is, it's the rule!'

He was realistic about the necessity for his 'wingers', Wire and Edwards, to act as the band's public face. 'Richey and Nicky never rely on me to look aesthetically pleasing, and that's a pressure in itself. When your frontman goes out there not looking remotely pretty, that's a big gap for them to fill.' I once wrote: 'The Manics are sexy in the same way Professor Stephen Hawking is sexy: the way the voice box is disembodied from the intellect, which smiles on with mute benevolence.' In retrospect this was unfair to James, but it does illustrate the peculiar Edwards/Bradfield, lyricist/singer dynamic.

There was something touching, something 'He Ain't Heavy, He's My Brother' about the Richey/James (and, latterly, Nicky/James) relationship, the way the 'poet' (to put it crassly) entrusted his most precious works to the broad shoulders of the 'artisan'. The trust had to travel both ways: James needed at least to comprehend – if not necessarily to endorse – the work's meaning. 'I have to totally understand everything I'm singing. It's not just a throwaway thing. I think of myself as a redeemable Roger Daltrey.'

'The nobility of man lies in making himself the conqueror of matter' – PRIMO LEVI

Then again, perhaps this strict delineation of roles was the essence of Richey's problem: 'The thing about Richey,' said James, 'is he's never seen his own worth in the band – you can tell him his worth a million times but he thinks it's down to his guitar playing or something.'

In addition, unlike the other three, Richey had never exorcised the boredom of his childhood by joining a band. For long stretches of time, there was absolutely nothing for him to do.

'The rewards for what we do are, like, nothing,' he told *Atomic* magazine. 'We get to do things like shopping and buy stupid little things, but tomorrow morning we will be bored again. When we first got signed, it was fucking heaven on earth. We thought we were never gonna have another boring two seconds again and it's just not true.'

So he would go to his room, lie on his four-poster bed, read his books, listen to his Suede album and drink himself to sleep with a litre of Smirnoff. The next morning, he would avert a hangover by the most masochistic method imaginable: working out in the gym and swimming in the pool. 'I don't get hangovers. I never stop drinking, I suppose. When I stop I get really ill for days. In the morning I get up and do exercises: sit-ups and push-ups.' It was a policy of purifying the body by day, poisoning it by night.

It may not have matched the delicate waif-poet image he liked to cultivate ('A lot of people can't watch *Aliens*, or Roman Polanski's *Repulsion* . . . I can't watch sport'), but Richey was by nature a well-built, sporty Welshman who grew up playing football and rugby, and idolised Muhammad Ali and Chris Eubank. By 1993 he was doing fifteen hundred sit-ups a day and pumping iron regularly; he even took weights on tour.

As well as being another form of body control (to join cutting, starvation etc.), he admitted that his exercise obsession came down to vanity. 'I want a flat stomach,' he told *NME*. 'I wanna six-pack. I wanna stomach like Brad Pitt.' Richey was every bit as much a victim of social body-fascism as the supermodel-fixated anorexics he described in his songs. (There was a grim irony in the fact that someone whose laser intellect could see straight through every other media construct should so easily fall prey to the Beauty Myth.)

His fitness regime completed, Richey would allow himself one jacket potato with grapes (his only meal of the day), before startig to drink all over again.

This precarious balancing act was clearly not working. Richey was in a particularly bad way when Andrew Collins visited the studio for a *Select* feature. After mumbling a few sentences of stream-of-unconsciousness gibberish, Richey passed out mid-interview.

It was now, for the first time, that Nicky publicly described Richey as an alcoholic. Speaking to *Melody Maker*'s Everett True, he confided, 'I can honestly say that I've seen Richey (and James) become confirmed alcoholics over the last eighteen months.'

Yet somehow it seemed wrong, at the time, to portray Richey as an archetypal tragic alkie. For a start, he wouldn't drink just anything. He was allergic to tequila: on one American tour, a journalist from *NME* was treated to the bizarre spectacle of Richey's arm swelling up, the '4 REAL' scars rising like pastry in an oven, after he had drunk several Jose Cuervos. He tended to stick to vodka, on the grounds that 'It's just the best-looking drink, clear and pure – just like me.' Unlike Nicky, he appeared to have a resilient constitution; appeared able to handle it. He simply loved drinking, took comfort in it, and spoke about it poetically, as Nicky remembers: 'There was something comforting about hearing him wax lyrical about an ice cube dissolving in whisky . . .'

One evening in 1993 I met up with Richey in the deserted Hall Or Nothing offices for an interview. He offered me a whisky, and I accepted. He picked up two glasses, both of which had recently been used as ashtrays, and filled them to the brim. Apparently oblivious to the grey cigarette ash floating in our drinks, or maybe past caring, he knocked his back. Not wishing to appear rude, I did the same.

Sometimes, his drinking had comic results. On tour, he calculated his alcohol intake to reach a peak of alcohol-rush come stage-time, but on one occasion was faced with a conundrum: he had to play two shows in one day. In between sets, he stuffed himself with piles of kiwi fruit in a doomed attempt to sober up. Another similar 'miscalculation', at a festival, ended with Richey falling asleep on James's shoe. 'I've got memories of Richey that people wouldn't even want to know,' Nicky would later tell *Melody Maker*, 'like this time in a bar in Portugal when he started doing the moonwalk in front of all these people, and I remember thinking: "He's not tortured tonight, he's pissed!"'

Nonetheless, despite his ominous statement (to me) that 'Things which could potentially fuck us up just seem deserving of the Shane MacGowan school of drinking', there was nothing Mac-Gowan-esque about Richey. He was never an embarrassing drinker. I often saw him drunk, but never 'pissed'; trembling, but always articulate.

'Look at Edwards. He's gone!'

Richey's drinking, like his cutting, was not always seen as an ominous precursor to his downfall: it was treated as a bit of a laugh. In 1991, I covered the 'You Love Us' video shoot for **Melody Maker**, *and witnessed this telling incident.*

As the evening wears on, Richey's performance becomes progressively more . . . loose. His walk has acquired a distinct wobble, and he can't hold a pose without giggling. Somebody mentions a bottle of sherry concealed behind his white Marshall stack. Suddenly, he vanishes.

Nicky bounds up to me, flashing that grin that can't decide whether it's a Cheshire cat or an alligator.

'This is brilliant! I can't believe it! If I was ever worried that this band wouldn't split up, I'm sure of it now. This video will be the last time you see the four of us together on a TV screen. Look at Edwards. He's gone! He's up there with Ronnie Wood!'

He is. He's the man on the moon. The Keith Moon. When I finally find him, he is trying on a gorgeous black-velvet tuxedo, with a Dalmatian-spot fur collar and a purple lining. It's straight out of a 1972 **Top of the Pops**. *Nice jacket, Richey. 'Yeah,' he smiles. 'In Rod We Trust.'*

There was, however, one classic danger sign: his habit was generally indulged in private. 'I drink alone,' he said, 'which isn't maudlin. I feel maudlin enough when I wake up in the morning anyway. I get in bed, drink vodka and flick channels. It sounds sad but it's the most pleasurable thing I can think of doing. And Tuesdays and Thursdays you've got *The Prisoner*, *If You See God, Tell Him* and *Top of the Pops*. And *The Late Show* . . . I guess I drink three-quarters of a bottle of vodka a day. I don't hate myself enough to be bombed out of my brain all day long. I just start at seven in the evening. I like four hours to pass slowly, till I feel my legs are dead and I can hardly move my head. It's a blur.'

By the end of the Hook End Manor sessions, Richey was looking sufficiently unwell for his band-mates to take action. In top secret, they booked him in for a weekend at a private health farm.

> *'Poignancy (and this is why its domain is the minor key) is the exquisite meshing of two contradictory feelings. It's a piercing beauty, or a sweet sorrow. Anyone who's ever treasured their pain, tried to prolong it, toyed with exacerbating it or been driven to dwell on inside it long after recovery was an option, preferring the company of ghosts to the dreamlessness of everyday sociability – that person understands poignancy'* – SIMON REYNOLDS, WRITING ON MORRISSEY

The word 'poignancy' derives from the French for 'fist'. The Manics' next single, 'From Despair to Where', was the most poignant thing they had written so far. It *fisted* you.

Released on 7 June, 'Despair' began with an unusually intimate, confessional, almost gospel-like intro – James, *a capella*, uncomfortably up close and personal, singing, 'I write this alone in my bed/I've poisoned every room in my house . . .' – before thundering into a rock classic which someone, possibly myself, described as 'existentialist Thin Lizzy'.

At the heart of all great existentialist literature (from *L'Etranger* and *The Goalkeeper's Fear of the Penalty Kick* to *Generation X* and *Less Than Zero*) is the feeling that the world is becoming *too much* – 'life becoming a landslide' – bringing with it a desire to withdraw, to secede, to go to sleep. Richey, asked what he would like to be, once replied, 'Any animal that hibernates.' The only other new song on the single, a ravishing acoustic lament for a loveless marriage, was entitled 'Hibernation'; the remaining two tracks were the original Heavenly recordings of 'Spectators of Suicide' and 'Starlover'.

It had long been clear that the Manics' plan to catalyse a youth insurrection, *as they always knew*, was doomed, a vainglorious King Canute stance against a tide of Manchester/Seattle-led apathy. 'I don't think any bands are dangerous,' Richey acknowledged. 'I mean, there's no one point when music could ever ignite something truly daring or revolutionary. Music doesn't send kids into the streets with guns.'

This delicious defeatism was not completely new: it had always been present at the heart of the Manics, from their very earliest demos ('Killing Myself From Inside'), B-sides ('R.P. McMurphy', 'Spectators of Suicide') and even A-sides ('Motorcycle Emptiness'). But now they were wearing their sadness on their sleeves. Above all, 'From Despair to Where' was an anthem to alienation (Richey had spoken of 'a sense of being displaced'), and lines like 'There's nothing nice in my head, the adult world took it all away' and 'I try to walk in a straight line/An imitation of dignity' were Richey's/Nicky's most concise expression yet of their sorrowful souls, melancholic without being maudlin. As *Melody Maker*'s David Bennun brilliantly put it, 'They relish their melancholy as a connoisseur would a fine wine.' They were *melancho-holics*.

Many fence-sitters found this new spirit of inward-looking despondency more palatable than political demagoguery: 'Despair' made 'Single of the Week' in a hitherto-unbelieving *Select*. For a comeback single, though, it made a disappointingly small chart splash, entering at a lowly No. 25.

The video to the song heralded the unveiling of a subtly different, more 'sensible' image for the Manics. Blouses, lipstick and slogans were out, Brat Pack film star was in: Matt Dillon sideburns, tight black Ts, pinstriped suits, designer stubble (spoilt only by Nicky Wire's white-plastic women's sunglasses, which looked as if they had been the prize in a seaside lucky dip). Inexplicably, the video was also full of albino German shepherd dogs. The original idea had been to use sheep, in a nod to a film the band had seen about Brunel called *Exterminating Angel*, until the words 'goal' and 'open' sprang to mind.

They could run, but they couldn't hide. Performing the song on the ITV children's show *Gimme 5*, the Manics were unaware that viewers at home were being treated to an animated puppet called Nobby the Sheep, dancing for the cameras.

The very existence of a new Manic Street Preachers single hinted, to the amusement of many but to the surprise of few, that – despite their famous kamikaze vow to split – there was indeed going to be a second Manics album. Caffy St Luce, rewriting history somewhat, now claims: 'They said they would split up *if* they sold sixteen million. Bear in mind that, at that time, Carter USM were as big as it got.' James was more frank: 'Our fault,' he admitted to *NME*. 'If you make a record as good as *Appetite for Destruction* [by Guns 'N' Roses], it sells. If you don't, it doesn't.' Nicky may have wanted 'to be nailed to history as soon as we can', but the process was becoming more of a long, slow screw.

Nicky had always circumnavigated tricky issues such as this by invoking a Contradiction Clause which proved useful over the years: 'We're the only band who reserve the right to contradict ourselves', or, 'From the start, we always said we'd be sluts' (shades of David Bowie's famous quote: 'If you're going to work in a whorehouse, you'd better be the best whore in it'). Talking to *Melody Maker*'s Taylor Parkes in 1994, Nicky clarified the issue further: 'We were really saying, "Let's forget notions of contradictions when it comes to bands." Everyone fucks up, everyone lets you down. Contradictions are meaningless. There's nothing to betray.'

'When we are victorious on a world scale I think we shall use gold for the purpose of building public lavatories' – V. I. LENIN

And lo, on 20 June 1993, *Gold Against the Soul*, the treacherous second Manic Street Preachers album, was released. Its duty, according to a Richey-penned press release, was 'to piss on the floor of Seattle'. It was a disingenuous claim. Although the Manics were hailed by many as the antidote to grunge, Richey was an avid devotee of Nirvana and Pearl Jam ('I think Pearl Jam are the closest America will get to The Smiths'), as well as of earlier proto-grunge bands such as Pixies and Faith No More and, musically, it was beginning to show. *Gold* was basically the Manics' way of saying, 'All right, world, have it your way.' The Route One approach to world domination, via classic Stones/Guns N'Roses *obviousness*, had failed. If they were ever going to win over the Def Leppard fans in the Blackwood Pot Noodle factory, and their equivalents across the globe, first they would have to swallow their pride and court the approval of the middle-class indie kids and disaffected grungers who, realistically, formed their constituency. And so, in contrast to the trashy flash of the garish *Generation Terrorists*, *Gold Against the Soul* was a concerted attempt to be a little bit tasteful, classy even (if *GT* wanted to be Guns N'Roses' *Appetite for Destruction*, then *Gold* was trying to be their *Use Your Illusion*).

The sleeve, designed by Japanese photographer Mitch Ikeda, reflected the band's new understated style. Ikeda, a well-known name in his native Japan, had decided to spend insane amounts of time and money following the Manics, and soon became semi-official group photographer – to date, he has taken over 10,000 pictures of the band. (Sample Mitch quote: 'Difference with Manic Street Preachers is other bands talk about peace like bad hippies. Manics speak only of truth, and truth is more powerful than peace.') His cover shot, a multi-limbed torso with its head replaced by three roses, was based on Yukio Mishima's *Bareki* (*Killed by Roses*). The inner sleeve featured 'Song for Those Who Died in Vain', a poem by Holocaust survivor Primo Levi; its use had actually delayed the album's release for a month while clearance was sought.

The *Gold* cover's burnished bronzes and subtle shades of sepia were in direct contrast to the bright pinks and blues of the band's début. For the first time, Sony, as if suddenly realising that Manic Street Preachers was a product which could be marketed to proper, grown-up people, plastered posters of the sleeve all over the London Underground.

In Steve Lamacq's opinion: '*Gold Against the Soul* is their worst record . . . but all my favourite [punk] bands made terrible records to impress America.' It is now the one album the band cannot bear to listen to (it is apparently the fans' least favourite, too), and appears doomed to go down in history as the sound of surrender: 'We were sucked into the stupid fucking new eclectic age we're supposed to be living in,' James told *Sky*. 'I just feel really thick for allowing ourselves to be subconsciously compromised.'

Nonetheless, the album is far from devoid of musical merit: shiny killer hooks are worked into a gorgeous matt finish, like evening sunshine seen through smog. It opens with the arid, parched guitars of 'Sleepflower', a magnificent piece of minor-chord metallica about Richey's terror of insomnia: 'At least a beaten dog knows how to lie/I feel like I'm missing pieces of sleep??' Sleeplessness was a genuine problem for Richey; on tour, for instance, he would often sleepwalk over to Nicky's bed in the middle of the night and start mumbling. Indeed, if *Gold* had a spiritual home, it was Richey's Blackwood bed (the next track, 'From Despair to Where', even opens with a reference to it).

Track three provided evidence that the Manics, behind all the callous, cackling bitchiness of their public outbursts, had always been a deeply *humane* band. 'La Tristesse Durera' (Scream to a Sigh)' – the title, meaning 'The sadness will last forever', was taken from a suicide letter sent by Vincent Van Gogh to his brother Theo – was written from the perspective of an elderly war veteran (and partially inspired by Patrick Jones's poem

'The Sympathy of Petals'). Rock songs about senior citizens are few and far between – Dexys' 'Old', Pulp's 'Help the Aged' – but Nicky and Richey handled the subject matter beautifully: 'Wheeled out once a year, a cenotaph souvenir/The applause nails down my silence . . .' Weirdly, given the band's anti-dance stance, 'Tristesse' was propelled by a monster of a Madchester beat (Paul Moody of *NME* would later call it 'the last great baggy single').

The album's pivotal track was 'Life Becoming a Landslide', a handsome rock requiem for lost youth. Although, to some degree, 'Landslide' was another expression of the Manics' feminine empathy (its opening line was 'Childbirth tears upon her muscle'), the phrase 'I don't wanna be a man' should not be misunderstood: what it really meant was 'I don't want to be an *adult*.'

'The only perfect circle on a human body is the eye. When a baby is born it's so perfect, but when it opens its eyes, it's just blinded by the corruption and everything else is a downward spiral.' That was Richey in 1992. In the same year, he told *Smash Hits* readers to 'stay five years old forever!' He had developed an unshakable conviction that the onset of puberty spoils everything; that, to quote a later song, *nothing turns out like you want it to*, that nothing is within your control. (Richey's favourite Clash song, 'Lost in the Supermarket', went, 'I wasn't born so much as I fell out . . .') 'Children smile at nothing at all,' he told *The Times*. 'It takes a lot to make an adult smile.' On 'Landslide', Richey – for it is very much a Richey song – is at war with his own chromosomes, lamenting/resenting the grim inevitability of sexualisation (even his anorexia can be seen in this light: anorexia shrivels the genitals to a pre-pubescent state). He also, for the first time, explicitly expressed his uniquely dystopian, pessimistic view of love: 'My idea of love comes from a childhood glimpse of pornography [a true story: see Chapter 1]/There is no true love, just a finely tuned jealousy.'

Elsewhere, *Gold* could be too eager to please. 'Roses in the Hospital' was a shameless stadium rock rewrite of Bowie's 'Sound and Vision', replete with a cheesy drums 'n' vox, handclaps-over-heads breakdown reminiscent of Queen's 'Radio Ga Ga' – a false sense of community from this most alienated of bands – and a fade-out which pointlessly quoted The Clash's 'Rudi Can't Fail' *ad nauseam*. 'Any other group in the world would get the audience to clap during the quiet bit,' explained Sean apologetically, 'but we physically can't do it! We can't bond with the audience.' The title 'Roses in the Hospital' was a quote from *Times Square*, clearly something of a Manics obsession (they had already covered 'Damn Dog' from its soundtrack on the previous album). By now, Nicky was even painting a bankrobber-style mask across his eyes, in the style of the 'Nicky' character from the film.

'Nostalgic Pushead' (which surely must rank as the least graceful MSP songtitle ever), and the hilariously anthemic 'Drug Drug Druggy' (when James later admitted that there had been record company pressure to write 'radio-conscious songs', this must have been what he meant) were sister songs. Both featured thematic reprises of the Morrissey-esque discophobia that Wire (and we can be fairly certain it was Wire) had first displayed on 'Destroy the Dancefloor': the former with its chorus line 'slavery to the beat', the latter with 'dance like a robot when you're chained at the knee'. They were also deeply *anti-London* songs. Richey and Nicky – especially Nicky – frequently vented their disgust at the superficial vanity and moral degeneracy of metropolitan life.

Sometimes the results were clumsy ('My tie is Paul Smith or Gaultier/My cheeks blood red as my favourite port/But hey, cocaine keeps cholesterol at bay . . .'), but occasionally the imagery was stunning: 'I am the raping sunglass gaze of sweating man and escort agencies . . .' In the same vein was 'Yourself', a sustained attack on a vain, ageing male ('Free scent burns your skin/But no smell can really cover sin/Too many teenage holes to fill'). Presumably they had a specific person in mind, and it's odds-on that he was a Londoner.

There was one high point before the end. The nihilistic funk-rock *noir* of 'Symphony of Tourette', inspired by a television documentary Nicky had watched about Gilles de la Tourette syndrome, which causes violent verbal and physical tics, and involuntary swearing, was brilliantly unnerving. ('"Children can be cruel", she said/So I smashed her in the fucking head.') Up to this point, however, the album is utterly apolitical, ditching the invective for introspective, solipsistic, private issues. Robert Burton, in *The Anatomy of Melancholy* (1621), argued that both the general and the microcosmic human condition was one of melancholy. The Manics had simply slipped from the general to the microcosmic.

According to Wire, this was because other acts, such as the Riot Grrrl and New Wave of New Wave movements – ironically, both directly inspired by the early Manics – and bands like Rage Against the Machine, had taken up the torch of rock rebellion. As if to overcompensate, however, the closing (title) track was a clumsy, rambling resumé of the entire contemporary political scene, filled with couplets which would be obscure in two months' – let alone in two years' – time: 'Close the pits, sanctify Roy Lynk, an OBE . . .'

If *Gold Against the Soul* was an experiment in the art of compromise, by charting at No. 8 (five places above its predecessor) it was a qualified success. Humbled by failure in the USA (and, by their own standards, in the UK as well), the Manics had concentrated their efforts on becoming a *better* rock band rather than just a bigger one.

Before the *Gold Against the Soul* tour had even begun, Nicky Wire's big mouth had once again got the band into trouble. After telling *NME* that New Age Travellers were spoilt rich kids who should be rounded up by the police, he was condemned by representatives from Shelter and the New Gypsy Council. And far worse controversy was to come.

The Manics had chosen a daring value-for-money support bill for the tour, comprising two bands which were fairly big in their own right: Credit to the Nation, a politicised teenage rap crew from Walsall who had scored a hit with the Nirvana-sampling 'Call It What You Want'; and Blaggers ITA, ska-punk anarchists, some of whom were alleged to have had shady pasts in the racist British Movement, but who were now advocating Anti-Fascist Action. To illustrate the tour's triple-pronged assault, Richey appeared on the *NME* cover with Credit's MC Fusion and Matty Blagger.

There was no little irony in the fact that, just as the Manics had ditched angry polemic in favour of Jovi-style anthemic rock, they had hired such a militant underbill. 'We were just trying to make it an exciting tour,' said Nicky, 'not to have three American noise bands or three indie bands; to try to do something different.'

After a 'secret' warm-up at The Marquee on 23 June, under the hardly mysterious name Generation Terrorists (James showing off his custard-coloured bleach job), the tour began in earnest on 1 July at the Town & Country Club in Leeds. The gig itself was relatively uneventful, save for the bizarre presence of fellow Columbia artist Nick 'Heartbeat' Berry, and for the CS gas canister that was detonated afterwards.

At a post-gig club, *Melody Maker* reporter Dave Simpson was confronted by members of Blaggers ITA. Simpson had made reference to the fact that Matty had once been a member of the British Movement. An angry discussion ensued for several hours, before things turned very nasty. Philip Hall, explaining the incident to the press, summarised it thus: 'Matty and the journalist had a heated argument which lasted over a few hours. Matty insisted he just pushed him a bit. The Blaggers are very apologetic that it has embarrassed the Manics.' This author, having witnessed the horrific facial injuries which endangered Simpson's eyesight, can only presume that if Matty 'just pushed him a bit' he doesn't know his own strength.

Nicky, Richey, Sean and James condemned the attack on Simpson as 'brain-dead machismo' but, unbelievably, the Blaggers were not thrown off the tour. Six days later, at Southend Cliffs Pavilion, I questioned them about the incident. 'There's nothing good or brave about violence,' said Wire. 'It's just sad. But I think it's in the nature of life. I don't think it's good conduct at all, but I don't think by having a band on your tour you're associating with them as such. I don't think it's fair to pin us with the consequences of other people's actions. We're the last people in the world ever to use violence [*give or take the odd Japanese cameraman?*]. We use it with our words, and that's the best way to use it. But I'm sure it'll all come out the wrong way again: "Nicky Wire Says Smash All Journalists' Heads In!"'

'I don't believe in bullying, full stop,' said James. 'The most honest answer I can give you is there's no way I can throw them off the tour. There are so many accusations flying at that band at the moment that you have to give them the platform to go up there and perform, rather than make them look like sacrificial lambs. That would be the ultimate middle-class patronage, or cop-out. We always said we don't agree with their means. I told them the day after: "I don't like bullies and I totally disagree with what you did." I didn't realise the extent of what had gone on. No matter what they think, that is a different kind of fascism. I think they do regret it, and that does make a difference. I've been on the receiving end of violence, I've been a connoisseur of violence in my younger days, now and then, and I knew that, if I indulged myself much more than I did, I'd begin to enjoy it. I think an intelligent person steps back from something they can potentially enjoy. I think it's OK to admit that.'

James's logic was perverse: the Manics did ban the Blaggers' entourage of friends/minders/heavies from subsequent shows, but felt unable to deal with the Blaggers themselves. (However, Fun-Da-Mental, scheduled to share a bill with Blaggers shortly after the Manics tour, found it perfectly easy to cancel.)

That unpleasant chapter apart, it was a fantastic tour. Looking back, these were the best times to be following Manic Street Preachers: rolling into a railway station in a strange town, gradually spotting more and more like-minded devotees in leopardskin and eyeliner arriving at the venue, and making new friends and meeting familiar faces: Gillian, Caffy and the Halls, Rory and the road crew, Jacqui, Carrie and the other fanziners, even Patrick Jones moonlighting on the T-shirt stall.

The band was at the very apex of its live form, its sound expanded by the presence of Dave Eringa on keyboards. They were now playing a set which could boast eleven singles, and which *NME*'s David Quantick described as 'a greatest-hits back catalogue the size and power of the Soviet navy'. The Manics – deeply imbued with a working-class understanding of their role, first and foremost, as *entertainers* – have always, always played Greatest Hits sets. 'When we were younger we hated going to concerts and hearing songs we didn't know, they just drift over people unless you're a really hardened fan . . . It's also the fact that we don't like practising anyway! When we decide to do a new song or resurrect an old song it takes us fucking years!'

The Manics' first outdoor appearance of the summer took place on 18 July at the inaugural Phoenix Festival, held on a disused airstrip near Stratford upon Avon.

Originally, the Manics had been offered a prime slot at the Glastonbury Festival, *but* . . . Nicky Wire takes up the story. 'First of all it was a headline or co-headline with Suede. Within two weeks it was: "You can't go on before Suede, so you're below Teenage Fanclub." Then it was: "You're below Belly as well." After five weeks we were on at two o'clock in the afternoon! And it certainly doesn't reflect our record sales or following: it's just other bands' paranoia. It is a massive problem. They think we're going to spoil their party or blow them away. Because we are a bit of an exciting live band. Musically we may not always be totally efficient, but we're certainly entertaining.' The fact that so many scaredycats were reluctant to follow the Manics was a genuine problem. 'We're probably at our most potent when we're pitted against other bands,' James told me. 'That's when we're most like our own selves. Perhaps other bands realise this. The minute we get added to a bill, every other band says, "Can we play Friday?"' Eventually, the Manics gave up on Glastonbury altogether, settling instead for Phoenix in England and Feile in Ireland.

At Phoenix, things were only slightly better. Although they would have been the ideal warm-up band for headliners The Black Crowes, they were instead shunted to a derisory 4 p.m. slot, in between Living Colour and an Aboriginal dance act called Yothu Yindi. 'I can't imagine a bigger nightmare than seeing a band like us in the daytime,' said James. 'The Disney veneer of rock music is ruined by festivals.' The Manics gave it their best shot, a dragged-up Nicky simply divine in a floral A-line dress, leopardskin headscarf and *those* white plastic shades, camping it up for all he was worth (one cruel writer compared him to Dot Cotton from *EastEnders*). Hecklers, shouting 'Get yer tits out' to Nicky, and 'You sex god!' to Richey, received short shrift from James: 'Shut up, you fat little cunts!'

If festival organisers had a problem with the Preachers, the feeling was mutual. 'I've never liked festivals,' Nicky told *Select* later, 'I don't understand the idea behind them, or why people want to come. It's not something I would do . . . but we don't want a world full of me, I'm a miserable sod.' In any case, he told *The Face*, he would rather play a sports stadium than a hippy festival. 'Some fucking twat of a dancer covered in beads playing a fucking didgeridoo – I just can't handle it. It's not me.'

James agreed: 'People who go to festivals and roll around in mud, actually doing things to return to the earth, I think is really strange. Having a mud fight isn't a million miles away from having a food fight, and I don't like food fights. I don't come from public school. We never wander around and look at any of the pottery stalls or onyx rings or artefacts you can buy. We just stay backstage at the Portakabin gettin' bloated. At Phoenix we just turned up and got the fuck out.'

So why, I asked, were they doing it in the first place? After all, they had vowed never to play a festival, and here they were, playing yet another. 'Just another Manic Street Preachers broken promise!' laughed Nicky. 'Once you've played with Ringo's All Starrs in Belgium and the stage collapses, it's quite easy to master British festivals.' More to the point, it was just another facet of their new realism. The world-conquering plans had failed, so they needed to win over The Kids the hard way. 'We thought that we would benefit from an explosion,' James admitted, 'but that explosion never happened. It's a sad fact of our existence. We do it for purely mercenary reasons.'

The 'last great baggy single' was released on 19 July. 'La Tristesse Durera (Scream to a Sigh)' was indeed a great song, even if it only made No. 22, but it had usurped the place of another. Six months previously, Nicky Wire had promised me that the much talked-about 'Patrick Bateman' would be 'the meanest, most motherfucking horrible single there's ever been'. Instead, it was relegated to being the meanest, most motherfucking horrible B-side there's ever been. Columbia was apparently not happy with the content, and James, as he later admitted, wasn't happy with the sound: 'It's far too metal. The lyrics are great, but the music? Naaah.'

An ambiguous, equivocal analysis of the cult of the serial killer (with specific reference to Bret Easton Ellis's *American Psycho*, a Wire/Edwards favourite), 'Patrick Bateman' starts with a snatch of 'The Star-Spangled Banner' before turning into an ugly, lumbering Americanised metallic monster, juxtaposing the innocent sound of a children's choir with self-consciously shocking lines such as 'I fucked God up the ass' (repeated twice) as well as more typical Manics fare like 'I am melancholy flower turned into stone'. Hardly surprising they (or Columbia) bottled out.

Welsh gigs, for the Manics, were normally celebratory, triumphant ticker-tape homecomings for the local heroes – in Cardiff and Newport, at least. In August, they toured Wales with the Radio One Roadshow, playing resorts like Porthcawl alongside indie bands like Pop Will Eat Itself, and were well-received just about everywhere.

In Swansea, though, things were different. On Saturday 7 August, they headlined the Heineken Festival, a free open-air event in the city's picturesque Singleton Park. This time, the Manics' welcome in the hillsides consisted of a stage full of broken glass before they even came on. All day, as the Heineken trailer doled out free lager and cheap wine to a crowd estimated at between eight and twenty thousand, fights had been breaking out spontaneously, and a poor supporting line-up (Pele, The Tansads and a few local bands) constantly needed to dodge flying bottles and cans.

By the time the Manics walked out to face a few hundred eyeliner kids chanting '*Maaar-necks, Maaar-necks!*' and several thousand sceptical armfolders in Kappa, the stage was so deeply covered in shards of broken glass and other debris that it had to be swept clean. They were a spectacularly un-Swansea sight: Nicky, his now-legendary floral dress clashing with his Adidas Sambas, resembling Grace Kelly stretched by a fairground freakshow mirror; his band-mates respectively *Taxi Driver*'s Travis Bickle, *Rumblefish*'s Motorcycle Boy and the cute one from The Monkees. From the very first chords of 'Slash 'N' Burn', a persistent shower of tin and glass rained down. Eventually, one missile reached the part the others couldn't reach. As 'Drug Drug Druggy' faded out, a bottle of Liebfraumilch made a graceful arc through the spotlight beams and caught Nicky Wire full on the head. As he stumbled offstage to be attended to by a guitar technician, James barked, 'One concussed, three to go! Well done, you brainless wankers!' While the band left the stage in disgust, organiser Mike Eddowes appealed for calm, melodramatically – but, it transpired, accurately – announcing that, if one more bottle hit the stage, the Manics would never play Swansea again.

This, naturally, only encouraged the hoolies. Within seconds of the band's return, another bottle whizzed two centimetres past a guitar technician's head and shattered on the stage. James, in disbelief, demanded an apology to the technician. 'We don't fucking need this. Just one more, and that's fucking it.'

For a moment, there was an uneasy silence as a blue strobe flickered over his pecs. Then the Manics raged into the remainder of their set (shortened by two songs – one of them, ironically, 'Roses in the Hospital' – with a raw, incendiary power unseen since their riotous early gigs. Never before had the line 'Why don't you just FUCK OFF!' been delivered with such venom, never before had 'You Love Us' borne such ferocious irony, and the punk-rock version of 'Motorcycle Emptiness' had to be heard to be believed. At the end, Richey, his fluorescent necklaces illuminating a homicidal glint in his eye, climbed a speaker stack, held a precarious Jesus Christ pose, then performed a perfect Olympic tuck dive into the tenth row.

A pale, shaken Nicky, who had bravely played on till the death, was rushed to Singleton Hospital with a mild case of existential nausea. Wire was possibly an unwitting victim of the fierce and perennial rivalry between Swansea 'Jacks' and East Walians from the Cardiff/Newport area (police identified the troublemakers as a group of football supporters in town for the Swansea City v. Watford fixture), and of the fact that several thousand punters – and not specifically a MSP crowd – had been drinking steadily since 5 p.m. In Wales, that's a lot of Heineken.

The following morning, in his Holiday Inn room, I asked Richey what he made of it all. 'Most bands look forward to their homecoming gig' he told me. 'Croeso y Cymru! [Welcome to Wales]. I don't expect roses and petals at my feet, but the amount of grief we get here is non-stop. Anything from Welsh bands complaining about us betraying Wales by not singing in Welsh, to gangs of four blokes in Cardiff pouring lager over me and saying: "What are you gonna do about that?" Tom Jones doesn't get it!'

Richey, of course, took aerial bombardment in his stride. 'Cans are easy. I've learnt to hit them with my guitar. And plastic glasses I can catch in my mouth! But bottles are something else. In a way, I wish they'd hit me, instead of one of the musicians!'

One Saturday in September, Nicky Wire broke the hearts of lanky transvestite fanciers everywhere by marrying Rachel ('my first love, and my last') in a small, private ceremony (band, family, friends and the Hall brothers) in Blackwood. 'I've always believed in marriage,' he told *Sky*. 'It's about the only thing I do believe in, and it's very un-Manics, I agree.' Mr and Mrs Wire moved into a terraced house in the shadow of a mountain.

At around the same time, James Dean Bradfield's life was moving in the opposite direction. He was in the process of a painful break-up with his long-term girl-

GOLD AGAINST THE SOUL

friend; they had been together for two and a half years, and had been engaged. Sean's life, in this respect, was stable as ever: he was still seeing Rhian, who had by now moved to Bristol to study and work.

Richey, meanwhile, did have a girlfriend of sorts (although he never referred to her as such): a glamorous, stunning model-type from London called Jo, who could usually be seen on his arm at after-show parties, braving the jealous glares of female fans. She was, he claimed, the only person he had slept with in 1993 and 'the one person I've found attractive for two years. But I barely see her, and we just talk.'

For their next open-air show, the Manics would leap from tragedy to farce. On 18 and 19 September, they were booked to open for Bon Jovi, Billy Idol and Little Angels at the Milton Keynes Bowl. An incongruous line-up to say the least, which James justified thus: 'The reason we're doing it is because I've got two friends outside the band – one's a drama student, the other works in the Pot Noodle factory – and, for them, it would be a dream to be within ten yards of Jon Bon Jovi. If I turned it down, they'd think I was a wanker. He's one of the only *bona fide* stars you'll see in *Casey Casem's Top Ten* in ten years' time.' The Manics, like anyone within a twenty-mile radius of Newport, had grown up listening to *Slippery When Wet*, and when James told Bubble, his Pot Noodle-manufacturing friend, about the gig, he did indeed go 'absolutely bullshit'.

It didn't stop the experience seeming weird. 'It is the most absurd, Camus-esque thing we've done,' admitted Nicky. Yet in some ways it made sense. Musically the Manics had made huge strides towards stadium territory, but culturally, they were still an indie concern. This show would be a smart move in their bid to court the *Kerrang!*-reading heavy-rock audience. James, however, predicted: 'We're not going to win any of those fans. We're gonna sound worse that day than we ever have in our lives!'

His misgivings proved eerily accurate. The Manics took the stage at 3 p.m. in an already mud-soaked Bowl and, playing it safe to win over the mainstream soft-rock crowd, toned down their confrontational, in-your-face attitude. The tactic backfired horribly: they met with a muted response somewhere between bewilderment and total indifference. James later described it as 'terrible', and vowed never to play in daylight again. 'We always had this perverse attitude that the best situations are the most bizarre ones. We enjoyed putting ourselves in situations where we couldn't win. It was obvious as soon as I walked onstage that I shouldn't be doing it.'

One Manic, at least, was determined to enjoy himself. 'They were offstage by 4 p.m.,' remembers Hall Or Nothing's Gillian Porter, 'and Richey and I started drinking pints of vodka and tonic. Everyone else wanted to leave, but we said: "We are going to see Billy Idol." Richey was mobbed for autographs as soon as he got out there, which he loved. You should have seen him drunkenly punching the air during "Rebel Yell". He suffered for it the next day, though: very quiet, very moody.'

Nicky, second time around, decided to give the metallers a mouthful to chew on: 'For victims of American aggression everywhere,' he mischievously began (opening for this most All-American and Reaganite of bands), 'from Somalia to Vietnam . . . "Slash 'N' Burn!"' By the end, however, even he had admitted defeat, making the parting shot: 'Roll on Bon Jovi. It'll be better than this shit!'

'Every form of addiction is bad, no matter whether the narcotic be alcohol or morphine or idealism' – CARL JUNG

Released on 20 September, a re-recorded version of 'Roses in the Hospital' was the next single, with the band having wisely decided that the chorus line 'We don't want your fucking love' might reduce its chances of airplay. Of all the *Gold Against the Soul* singles, this one fared best, reaching No. 15.

It also signalled an unexpected *rapprochement* with dance culture. For the first time, a twelve-inch remix single was issued, featuring six mixes from the painfully hip likes of Ashley Beadle. The CD version, alongside the down 'n' dirty 'Us Against You' and the more mellow 'Donkeys', included a version of the Happy Mondays' 'Wrote for Luck', which the Manics had performed on the spring tour. It was, on the face of it, an incredible, pigs-flying, ravens-leaving-the-Tower choice of cover. Despite their loathing of baggy and its drug-drug-druggy culture, however, the Manics had always had an ambiguous attitude to the Mondays, who clearly loomed large in the Wire imagination. Although the Manics had set their uptight selves against the loose clothing and loose morals of what they called the 'scum fuck retard zerodom of Madchester', Nicky approvingly likened the Mondays semi-criminal, don't-give-a-fuck attitude to the Sex Pistols' 'get pissed, destroy' nihilism. Originally, Shaun Ryder had actually been lined up to duet with James on the track, but kept missing appointments and blowing them out.

This touched on a contradiction at the heart of the Manics. Paradoxical creatures, *decadent puritans*, they had never quite walked it like they talked it when it came to the middle part of the sex/drugs/rock 'n' roll equation. In their early days, they had written a letter to *Melody Maker*'s Stud Brothers heralding their 'heroin-tainted rock 'n' roll' and ending with the promise 'heroin supplied', and claimed in a Simon Reynolds interview for *MM* that they used speed to fuel their frenzies of reading and letter-writing ('it's sexless and it helps you concentrate'). And yet both their albums contained vituperative attacks – in 'Another Invented Disease' and 'Drug Drug Druggy' – on drug use.

Richey, pressed for his views on drugs, said, 'Ecstasy is too designed to make you happy. People I know who've taken E just want to be friends with everybody. I've got so much more respect for people who stick a needle in their veins . . . Someone who's drunk a bottle of whisky is more fucked up than someone who's smoked a spliff. But if you're gonna do it, do it properly. Take smack.' Whether he actually acted on his own advice is doubtful. Although, referring to this era, he later claimed, 'I drank and did drugs,' it is unclear whether he meant anything stronger than Prozac. Give or take an occasional spliff with the road crew, Richey's *anaesthetic aesthetic* was far more old-fashioned: if it didn't come in a bottle, he wasn't interested. When Nicky saw Richey smoking weed for the first time, he was horrified. 'No one spoke to each other for the next five hours,' he told *Select*. 'I suppose our reaction was a punk leftover. I almost considered the band to be over. The mad irony is that if he'd been smacking up, we'd have been: "Oh, that's all right!"'

To this day, misconceptions about the Manics' attitude to narcotics plague the band. Nicky has received numerous 'Legalise Cannabis' petitions from the *Independent* and from Creation Records, asking for his signature. He refuses every time. 'That's not gonna cure all the ills of the world is it?!' he told *NME*. 'That's not gonna sort out the NHS, sort out unemployment!' Speaking to *Select*, he went even further. 'I'd rather have a law to stop people talking to me when they're on cannabis,' he raged, 'because they bore me shitless. Put those cunts in prison.'

In October, the Manics got their passports out again for tours of Japan (another sell-out) and Germany.

On their travels, they took time to visit the Peace Museum in Hiroshima, and the still-preserved Nazi concentration camps at Belsen and Dachau. Both were moving experiences which left an indelible impression on their minds. 'The human capability to inflict pain on its own race,' Nicky told *Melody Maker*. 'That's what we would like to write about.'

While in Germany, Richey went through what, in his own words, he called 'a bad period'. In addition to his heightened drinking, he had added a new form of self-abuse to his repertoire: he had started stubbing cigarettes out on his arm.

As soon as they arrived in Britain, the other three sent Richey back to the health farm.

All things considered, 1993 had been something of a nowhere year. Good album, good concerts, sure – but now, when they were on *Top of the Pops*, on magazine covers, when even mums knew their name, NOW was exactly when they should have been spewing their manifestos like never before. This was their big chance to stamp the MSP message on to the public consciousness. As I wrote at the time, 'Circumstantial evidence suggests that Manic Street Preachers (1993 Model) want to (sub)merge, blend in, become Just Another Rock Band. In which case I'm disappointed: they should never have lost the momentum (MORE hatred, MORE eyeliner, MORE outrage, MORE everything).'

Instead, they lost their early momentum, and seemed to cruise through 1993 as if on autopilot, settling for a year of consolidation rather than of confrontation. As well as being more humble about themselves, they were even being nicer to other bands, and were publicly regretting their bitchy past. 'I think we did it badly,' said Richey, 'in that we alienated a massive record-buying public before we even had a record in the fucking shops. There's a certain type of indie fan who was going: "I'm not buying their records, they're cunts." We can really understand that.'

Nowadays, James refers to the *Gold Against the Soul* era as 'the most unfocused period of our history'. In 1993, the Manics had softened up, compromised – as James accepted at the year's end. 'We thought we could resist record-company pressures. All we wanted to do was to go under the corporate wing, but you do get affected, and we lost the plot a bit before . . .

'Now,' he promised, 'we're back to speaking in tongues.'

e) He's a boy . . .

(LOVE, SEX, GENDER AND RICHEY EDWARDS)

'Don't wanna wake next to your stretched skin . . .' – 'LAST EXIT'

N 1992, DURING AN INTERVIEW with the University of York's radio station, Richey Edwards made the extraordinarily dishonest claim that Manic Street Preachers were a walking orgy of bisexual depravity. 'We realised that sex and love is a completely useless commodity, so if anybody wants to fuck us they can,' he began. 'We're just total prostitutes . . . and we're willing to be used. Any boy. Any girl. Any time. We fuck each other!'

In the same year, Richey french-kissed Therapy?'s very manly, bearded singer Andy Cairns at a party (but then proceeded to shag a girl back at the hotel later), chose a T-shirt slogan that read, 'ALL ROCK 'N' ROLL IS HOMOSEXUAL,' and told Andrew Collins of *Select*: 'I've been homo for a long time . . . fuck knows, I mean . . . 12 per cent?' Nicky Wire confirmed that 'Richey's virtually bisexual'. Edwards was also, undeniably, a magnificent homoerotic icon. 'You may be embarrassed to admit it,' said *Young, Pretty and Fucked* fanzine, 'especially if you're a bloke, but I bet you'd love to fuck Richey . . .'

The weight of proof is hardly formidable, but there is enough *prima facie* evidence for the question at least to be asked. Was Richey Edwards, to any extent, gay? The answer is . . . almost certainly not. As far as the T-shirt is concerned, Edwards explained his point as being that most great *art* is homosexual, citing Allen Ginsberg's *Howl*, Jackson Pollock's *Map of the United States*, Tennessee Williams's *Suddenly Last Summer*, Michel Foucault's *Archives of Pain*, and Quentin Crisp's *The Naked Civil Servant*. (Of course, an academic appreciation of gay art and culture does not require one actually to *be* gay.)

If Gore Vidal is correct, and there are no homosexual and heterosexual people, only homosexual and heterosexual *acts*, then arguably Richey never lied (the stubbly snog with Cairns gets him off the hook). Whichever prefix one chooses to apply, however, Richey was simply not a very *sexual* person, more Celibate Rifle than Sex Pistol. After his first childhood glimpse of pornography (see Chapter 1), Richey had to rush outside to be sick (James, also present, found the experience quite arousing).

'I didn't spend my teens wanting to fuck,' Richey later claimed. Not that he didn't do plenty of fucking. In later life, Edwards was no Morrissey. His spiritual sexlessness didn't manifest itself in some pseudo-puritan vow of chastity. On the contrary: he was regularly to be seen after gigs sneaking off into a toilet cubicle with whoever happened to be at hand, whether they were five years younger or twenty years older than himself. But the expression in those coal-black eyes was not one of decadent joy, but something closer to *duty*. In many ways, for Richey, debauchery merely provided escape from boredom (he loathed life on the road). I once saw him being chatted up by a pair of hard-bitten serial rock groupies in the bar of Cardiff's Holiday Inn. He was deeply in awe of the fact that they had previously slept with the likes of Hanoi Rocks, Motley Crüe and Dogs D'Amour. Minutes later, he escorted them both up to his room, grinning his head off – not out of lust (barely conceivable in the circumstances, to be brutally honest) – but in obeisance to his rock 'n' roll destiny. His heroes had been there, so now Richey, *a sexual tourist*, must go there too.

Richey, who once described sex as 'nature's lukewarm pleasure' was once asked whether he used condoms. 'I gain no pleasure from sex anyway,' he replied, 'so wearing condoms doesn't bother me.' He simply couldn't see what all the fuss was about. 'I don't think there's a sacred essence to sex. To say that the body's greatest reward is to come, and sperm . . .' And if he only wanted to 'sperm', he didn't need anyone else's help. Clearly a believer in the Woody Allen line on masturbation ('Don't knock it, it's sex with someone I love'), Richey said, 'Sleeping with someone is just a change from wanking. Personally, I get as much pleasure out of wanking. I could just as happily go back to the hotel, sit on the bog and have a good wank. It doesn't make any difference to me.'

Most musicians spend their entire careers in the pursuit of easy sex. Even dear old Nicky Wire once said, 'Sex is absolutely crucial to this group.' The Manics never really walked it like they talked it, though. 'We're not a band that has group sex filmed on a camcorder to watch on the bus the next day,' he admitted later. 'It's always personal, one-to-one in a bedroom.' Richey claimed to have fucked every night on the European and British tours of spring 1992, but didn't have sex once on the subsequent American tour, and then got stuck in again on the Japanese leg. For six months between December 92 and June 93, he gave up sex altogether. One female fan I know was privileged to sleep with Richey during this period, after a gig in Southend. But it was only that: she literally *slept* with him. Like an old man who hires a prostitute not for sex but for company, Richey just wanted someone to talk to. He lay on the bed all night fully clothed.

Richey's Sex Tourism – literally, *wanderlust* – led him in some unorthodox and potentially perilous directions. His fascination with the waif look, for instance, together with statements like 'Every man wants to shag a thirteen-year-old' bore dodgy paedophile overtones. He once made the inside of the tour bus feel a little more like home by covering the walls and ceiling with pictures of Kate Moss and other, similarly slender, childlike stick insects. 'I just think she's pretty,' he told journalist Simon Witter. 'She looks delicate, that's what I like about her. I'm not the sort of person who could like Cindy Crawford. That's not my type of look.' This might explain the attraction that the delicate, slender, childlike young prostitutes of Bangkok held for Richey. He had no moral problem with prostitution itself (or, if he did, he managed to live with the double-think). 'I don't regard paying for sex as being different to sleeping with a groupie,' he argued. 'It's all done on the same functional level.'

Richey's fellow Manics got their functional kicks in more harmless ways. Since that childhood glimpse of pornography, James remains an occasional porn user, and has been known to visit sex shops in Hamburg and Amsterdam when on tour. 'It's helped me through my fallow periods,' he admitted. 'Everyone goes through a dodgy period when they can't pull anything. Porn just gives you a quick relief. It just sends you to sleep.' Richey, too, used to buy porn at service stations, but it did little for him, as he confided to *Select*: 'Men with non-erect dicks, man on top of woman, woman on top of man . . . it bores the fuck out of me.' He even watched a hardcore bestiality video called *Animal Farm* (with a cast list featuring chickens and ducks) on the tour bus, but claimed to be bored after five minutes.

So what did it take to turn him on? He admitted to being aroused by J.G. Ballard's *Crash*, Yukio Mishima's *Confessions of a Mask*, Dennis Cooper's *Frisk*, Octave Mirbeau's *The Torture Garden*, the film *Tetsuo: The Iron Man* (in which a man turns into a machine, and fantasises about an ideal male and female lover). Fetishism and masochism: the erotica of pain and imprisonment. These are the extremes to which Richey's cold-blooded, passionless tourism led him. Intensive promiscuity, monastic celibacy, groupies, prostitutes, machine sex, car-crash sex, masochism, fetishism, paedophilia, bestiality, gay sex, straight sex, DIY sex, porn: Richey Edwards tried, watched or fantasised about them all . . .

. . . and walked away bored every time.

'I wish somebody did love me . . .' – RICHEY
'I love you, Rich!' – NICKY, *GIMME 5* INTERVIEW

If casual sex were merely a diversion for Richey, could love have 'saved' him?

From the beginning, Manic Street Preachers was determinedly, didactically *anti*-love. 'We'll never write a love song, or a trip-out, or a ballad,' they told *Snub*. 'We want to sing about all the issues other bands ignore. Institutionalised racism, sexism, homophobia . . . We've got no respect for bands who sing about love.' For the Manics, like their heroes Public Enemy before them, life was too short and time too tight to waste on banal boy/girl lyrics. 'We got into music when the Miners' Strike was happening, and that had a massive bearing on us: you couldn't write about going out with a girl because you'd only gone out with a girl for about a week. You had to write about what affected you, directly or otherwise.'

For many years – in fact, until Richey was gone – they remained true to their word. But for James Dean Bradfield (engaged), Nicky Wire (married) and Sean Moore (long-term relationship), this anti-love stance was mere rhetoric. For Richey Edwards, it was a matter of sacred political principle. He believed that love was intrinsically counter-revolutionary: the division of the working class into manageable units of two. 'Once you fall in love,' he told *Melody Maker*'s Simon Reynolds, 'or get a girlfriend pregnant, you've got no chance, you've got responsibilities. There's no way you can ever do anything. Once you're reduced to a couple, alone together between your four walls with your TV set, you're cut off.' One also suspected, as with Chuck D, that Richey had never progressed beyond the blushing, boyish 'Ugh, girls smell!' stage of pre-pubescence. There was to him something embarrassingly soft, and disagreeably girly, about being in love. In 'Comfort Comes', he compared love to 'a crutch'. According to him, it is weak to love, and strong to live without it.

Richey despised what he saw as the inevitable dishonesty and hypocrisy that love entailed. 'People go through the same rituals time and time again. You can see the lies dripping from mouth to mouth,' he said in disgust. 'I find love a very alien concept. People I know who are in long-term relationships have always been unfaithful, and I find the whole lie just really tiresome. That's why I've never been involved in any relationship. I find other people attractive, so it's kind of unfair to walk around with one partner. It's just being honest, really.'

This, in all probability, was the heart of the matter. Richey knew himself well enough to know that he simply didn't have what it takes. ' "A well-preserved virginity shows a limited capacity for love," ' he once quoted. 'Who said that? Kenneth Williams?' Although Richey's virginity was far from well-preserved, his capacity for love, he knew, was limited. When he said that 'Infidelity is a sign that you can't deal with self-hatred', he did so in the knowledge that he already had more than enough self-hatred to go around, and didn't need another reason. When he told *Smash Hits* that 'Men and women just aren't compatible – men are too selfish', he was all too aware of his own instinctive selfish streak, which showed itself in the tiniest ways (offer him a cigarette and he would automatically take two from the packet without asking).

Richey's Spock-like refusal to acknowledge emotions (one of his nicknames within the band was 'Android') often brought out some of his finest and most entertaining epigrams. 'Our lips kiss empty, we fuck futility,' he wrote in an early letter to *Select*. 'Today I would rather fall in love with a washing machine than a woman,' he later wrote in a diary for the same publication.

'There is no greater stupidity than for people . . . to marry and so surrender themselves to the small miseries of domestic and private life' – KARL MARX

But did Richey condemn himself to a loveless life at the expense of his own mental health and happiness? He had always sneered that 'being in love is just someone to share your boredom with' but, after Nicky's wedding in 1993, Richey, inspired by the marital bliss he saw in his friend's life, began to think that maybe he *needed* someone to share his boredom with. One night, he announced that he was going to get married by the end of the year: doing so, he touchingly believed, would solve all his problems. Terri Hall pointed out a fundamental flaw in his plans. 'Richey,' she asked, 'have you got a girlfriend?' And if he had, might things have turned out differently? When he was hospitalised in 1994, James suspected that they might have done. 'Richey's never been in a relationship, and I should say that's something to do with it.'

The package left behind in Room 516 of London's Embassy Hotel on 1 February 1995 contained a note for his sometime companion Jo, the woman he had never publicly described as his girlfriend. With heartbreaking irony, Richey Edwards's last written statement contained the three words he had never felt able to speak.

It read: 'I love you.'

6. LIFE BECOMING A LANDSLIDE

'We sit in straight lines, do what we are told, like seats on Lockerbie, deck chairs on the Titanic' *–* RICHEY, PRESS RELEASE, 1992

I T WAS IN PORTUGAL, playing a few pre-Christmas dates, that the Manics heard the news. Throughout his two-year battle with lung cancer, their manager, Philip Hall, had carried on working for the Manics and for his other bands. As recently as August, in between undergoing chemotherapy at the Cromwell Hospital, he had taken on the monstrous task of organising the Reading Festival.

On 7 December 1993, at the age of 34, Philip finally succumbed to cancer. A show at Brixton Academy on 10 December, which would have been the Manics' biggest yet, was cancelled out of respect.

Hall's funeral, on 14 December, was the first Nicky Wire had ever been to.

There was precious little time for mourning. On 22 January 1994 the band was back in the back of a van for a two-week UK tour, this time with a somewhat less controversial support line-up: The Wildhearts, Compulsion and Eve's Plum. The rescheduled Brixton date, a sell-out, was played on 28 January. The backdrop to the stage – several hundred square metres of military netting – didn't seem significant at the time.

On 7 February, two days after the final date, Columbia squeezed the last drops of gold from the album. 'Life Becoming a Landslide' crawled to No. 36 and dropped straight out again, the Manics' mushrooming live following failing to translate into record sales. It remains the lowest-placed MSP single since the band's major-label début. There was little call for promotional work and no invitation to *Top of the Pops*, and the video was edited together from black-and-white 'live' footage. 'Landslide' was a deserving A-side, but the most interesting thing about its release was tucked away on the CD. 'Are Mothers Saints', a beautiful, mid-tempo, free-and-breezy melody, was good but nothing new (in fact, it was not dissimilar to 'Motorcycle Emptiness'). There was also a crude, punky 1-2-3-4 cover of 'Charles Windsor', McCarthy's call for the execution of the heir to the throne, and yet another tribute to a formative influence. However, the remaining track, 'Comfort Comes', with its taut, discordant guitars, mechanical, martial drumming and arid, freeze-dried vocals, sounded like nothing the Manics had ever done before.

Finally, they had found what they had been looking for throughout 1994: a direction.

* * *

By the early part of 1994, the other three Manics had followed Nicky's example and bought homes of their own.

Sean had moved to a house on the outskirts of Bristol to be with Rhian, who had been studying then working there for some time. Richey had bought a flat on impulse, driving through the 'regenerated' (i.e. gentrified) sector of Cardiff's docklands with Nicky one day. A third-floor yuppie apartment overlooking the water, it provided Richey with the one thing he craved: absolute solitude. Apart from the swans, which would sometimes fly in at dawn (Richey would feed them bread), he was completely alone. For the first few months, he didn't even have a phone. His only regular contact with the outside world was the weekly trip to his mum's in Blackwood to get his laundry done (he did own a washing machine, but he couldn't work out how to use it).

James was last to fly the nest, but he moved the furthest – all the way to London's Maida Vale (which he nicknamed 'Media Vale', on account of the unusual preponderance of celebrity neighbours). He said that he did it '. . . because Richey bought a flat in Cardiff, Nick lives with his wife, Sean lives with his girlfriend and I started feeling like Ronnie Corbett in *Sorry!* I was comfortable living at home with my parents. I was 25 and I couldn't put a plug on, I couldn't change lightbulbs or sew. Now I'm educated domestically. Although I still can't get rid of the bachelor smell in the flat.' The other reason for escaping to the big city, he later admitted, was that he was finding it difficult to live surrounded by the ghosts of his broken engagement.

Soundspace Studios were located in the part of Cardiff's docklands which hadn't been 'regenerated' yet. Although only half a mile from Richey's flat, the only *nouveaux riches* to be found around Soundspace were sleazy businessmen, kerbcrawling for hookers in their Rovers.

It was in these shabby surroundings, in stark contrast to the Byzantine luxury that spawned *Gold Against the Soul*, that the Manics decided to lock themselves away to record their third album. Columbia had offered to send them to Barbados; the band told the company to 'fuck off'.

The decision was highly significant: the Manics were seizing back control both of their career and of their fate. 'It was a release,' James told *NME*, 'in that we knew what we were doing and we had the courage to actually go to a crappy studio and do it. So we were really happy that we'd taken control again.' They even had the confidence to refuse a big-name producer, opting to produce the album themselves with the help of the relatively unknown Mark Freegard.

As James later told *Volume*: 'It was recorded in this really shit studio in the red-light district of Cardiff. It was really bleak, seedy, perfectly suited to us really. We didn't want to get into that decadent rock-star rubbish. We wanted to communicate ourselves honestly.'

Soundspace, which the Manics had sporadically used for rehearsals (and for 'Theme from M*A*S*H'), had a number of advantages. For Richey and Nicky the studios were close to home, and for Sean and James they were a short walk from Cardiff Central station. They were remarkably cheap: at £50 a day, *one-fortieth* of the cost of Hook End Manor. More importantly, the surroundings perfectly matched the mood of the new songs. A few rough-and-ready first-floor rooms of irregular shapes (the Manics' studio was a narrow triangle), Soundspace was ideal for the tight, claustrophobic sound the band was looking for, as previewed on 'Comfort Comes' (Sean was particularly keen on the compressed drum sounds he could make in the confined space). James called it 'Method Recording'. Even the proximity of prostitution echoed one of the songs Richey had written.

Richey Edwards had been going through a spell of songwriting hyperactivity, and Nicky was happy to allow these lyrics to dominate the new record, in something like a 70/30 split. As far as the actual recording went, however, Richey was as much of a spare wheel as ever, reverting to his late-80s role as band chauffeur: driving the foursome to and from the studio, getting off his face, and sleeping on the settee. 'Richey would come in at about twelve o'clock,' said Nicky, 'collapse and have a snooze and say: "Leave me alone, I've had a big drink" in a nice Welsh voice. Then he'd get up and do a bit of typing and we'd record for a bit, then go around Cardiff and have a shop.'

In comparison with the sprawling, through-the-night *Gold Against The Soul* sessions, there was an order and routine to the making of that album's successor. 'I used to commute in on the train,' said Sean. 'Regular work: drum till six and then go home. It was like a little office job.' In the evenings, the honest day's toil done, they would join the city's other workers in the pubs and clubs of St Mary's Street. 'Me and Richey would go out after in Cardiff,' James told *NME*, 'and have a really good drink and stuff, go to the dodgy disco, and we'd have a good laugh. A bit of pullage, all that kind of stuff. Try and get girls. Really ordinary things.'

The Manics paid tribute to Philip Hall on 2 March with a one-off show at the Clapham Grand, a fine old Victorian theatre in south London. The concert, with support provided by The Pogues (another band on the books of Hall Or Nothing, which was now being run by Philip's widow Terri and brother Martin), was a charity benefit for Imperial Cancer Research.

It was a straightforward Manics set, with no new material and the mandatory Nicky Wire mouth-off ('I know this is supposed to be a benefit, but I fucking hate Blur') – until the encores. For the first time, the Manics were joined onstage by a guest musician. Suede's Bernard Butler, who had lost his father to cancer, added his trademark guitar histrionics to 'Motorcycle Emptiness', Suede's 'The Drowners' and a version of The Faces' 'Stay with Me'. It was a fitting union: Suede, who had emerged at the same time as the Manics and whose fanbase overlapped with theirs, were the only other British band sharing their mission to bring glamour and intellect back to pop.

There was something contradictory about the Manics' apparent sympathy with animal-rights causes (demonstrated in Richey's love for dolphins, in their opposition to fox-hunting, by their donation of tracks to Greenpeace and Save the Dolphin compilations, and by Nicky helping his mum's pony-welfare charity) and their playing a benefit gig for one of Britain's top three supporters of vivisection but, in the circumstances, one could understand emotion overcoming principle.

Imperial Cancer Research benefited to the tune of £20,000.

'And in these plagued streets of pity, you can buy anything' – 'YES'

In late April the Manics flew to Thailand, where, due to some pop-geographical anomaly, they were huge: it was a case of platinum discs, stalker fans – the full *Hard Day's Night*.

On arrival, they were mobbed and bedecked in flower garlands at a Sony-organised signing session, which took place under a banner reading, 'FROM DESPAIR TO BANGKOK'. (In the circumstances, 'FROM BANGKOK TO DESPAIR' might have been more apt.) It was a bizarre situation: the fiercely royalist Thai people falling for the fiercely republican Manics. The band had been warned that, if they dared to play 'Repeat', or any other anti-monarchist song, they risked execution.

On 22 April, they played the first of two nights at Bangkok's Mah Boonkrong Hall (2,000 capacity, but 3,000 crammed in). Before the show even began, there were worrying signs that the organisers didn't quite understand the Manics ethos: the stage was flooded with *Spinal Tap*-esque dry ice. Throughout the ninety sweat-soaked minutes between 'From Despair to Where' and 'You Love Us', a battle raged between rabid fans in DIY retro 'punk' gear and security guards, who mistook their pogoing and moshing for an attempted riot and tried to suppress them with electric cattle prods. Nicky, in the heat of the moment, screamed, 'Long live the King! May he reign in Hell!', and James, against all advice, launched into 'Repeat'. Wire apparently spent a sleepless night convinced he would be clamped in leg-irons in the morning.

On the second night the band was asked to play more quietly, on the grounds that the roof of the hall downstairs was in danger of collapse. For the first hour, it was indeed a quieter, less eventful show. While James played a few acoustic numbers, Richey and Nicky both left the stage for a costume change.

In the dressing-room, Richey found two presents left by fans. The first was harmless enough: a big fluffy Snoopy. (Richey, having taken to wearing goggles and a grey communist flying hat with huge ear-flaps, already looked like something from *Snoopy Vs The Red Baron*). The other was an expensive set of carving knives, with an accompanying note: 'Look at me while you do it.'

Nicky walked back out in a floral dress, which was rapidly torn off by the front row, leaving him standing in nothing but his jockey shorts. Richey also reappeared with a different look: his chest was cross-hatched with fresh, running knife wounds. According to Wire, Edwards was actually annoyed by the fan's gruesome request, and he speculates that Richey actually did it for the benefit of the photographers (*NME* and *The Face* were present). Shortly after Thailand, at a *Select* photo shoot, Richey had to be restrained from cutting himself for the camera.

Before coming home, the Manics had a free night to kill in Bangkok, which is known with no little irony as the City of Angels. Nicky hid in the chilled air of his hotel room, praying for the trip to end – he couldn't handle the unfamiliar food and returned weighing less than nine stone (his ideal weight being thirteen-and-a-half stone). The remainder of the band, entourage and journalists visited the notorious Pat Pong district and ended up in a strip joint, watching underage girls pole-dancing in high heels. A couple of vodkas and a beer later, Richey, bored with the floor show, left the club and walked the streets alone.

After wandering aimlessly for a while, he approached a young prostitute and paid for a handjob. 'I'd never been with a prostitute before,' he later told *Club* magazine. 'I've never had a girlfriend, so I wasn't being unfaithful to a memory. It was something I wanted to experience to see whether it would make me happy, and it didn't really. I couldn't really expend any emotion on it. It just helped to pass a few hours.'

When Barbara Ellen of *NME* heard the story, she challenged Richey to reconcile his actions that night with his lyrical attacks on Third World exploitation. 'All developing economies abuse their young,' he offered in justification. 'When Britain was a developing economy we sent our children up chimneys and down coal mines and out into the street to steal. This is just abuse on a wider scale.'

In restrospect, the Thai tour was, by general agreement, the beginning of The Troubles. Nicky, who feared the band was becoming a 'freak show', said that it was 'the first time that I felt something was going wrong'.

The Manics were starting to unravel.

The causes of Richey's descent into severe alcoholism are open to speculation. The death of Philip Hall was an obvious catalyst although, as James later said to *Select*: '. . . now, Richey says he would have probably ended up the same way regardless'. Richey was also deeply affected by Kurt Cobain's shotgun suicide on 8 April. Shortly afterwards, Guy Debord – another Richey hero – shot himself in the heart (within three days, two of Debord's close friends were also found dead, prompting rumours of a suicide pact). Richey had been surprised, the previous year, by how much the death of actor River Phoenix had upset him. He was beginning to comprehend the notion that fame can be fatal. Amazingly, he had even grown bored with his Sega. He needed something else to occupy his hands and to fill/kill the empty hours.

Whatever the reasons, by the time the band returned from Thailand, Richey and his 'birding and boozing buddy' James were both drinking heavily. James was aware of the irony of these committed puritans seeking respite in the bottle. 'I know that's at odds with our old image, the conspiracy theory that getting out-of-it is just a way to keep you down, but . . . I discovered the art of switching off. Which I do by enjoying myself.' James's drinking habit followed a more traditional, socially acceptable pattern than Richey's: Jameson's and Coke after Jameson's and Coke – in company. James has an almost *Cheers*-like sentimentality regarding pub life and the male bonding that goes with it, and is reluctant to leave a bar until the shutters are pulled down on his fingers. 'He's always late,' complains Wire, 'always the last one out the door.'

In contrast, and as had been the case for some time, most of Richey's drinking was conducted in private: just him and a litre of vodka. He drank, he said, for two reasons: to make the day shorter, and to assuage his fear of insomnia (his favourite poem, Philip Larkin's 'Aubade', dealt with precisely this fear). A terror of lying awake at night led him to use vodka to smother the thoughts splitting through his mind. 'I get paranoid about not being able to sleep,' he told David Bennun of *Melody Maker*. 'And, if by about eight o'clock at night I haven't had a drink, I get massive panic attacks and I'll be awake all night, and that's my biggest nightmare. I know that until one in the afternoon I'm going to be shaky and have cold sweats. By six o'clock I feel good, but by eight it starts coming around again. I can't stomach the thought of not sleeping. That's why I drink. It's a very simple choice.'

This was fine in theory, but doomed in practice. Despite Richey's claim, alcohol is known to increase depression and morning anxiety, leading to a classic vicious circle. Asked what distinguished him from an alcoholic, Richey replied, 'That's someone who wakes up and needs a drink straight away. My need is more functional. By about midday

I need a drink to stabilise me, but I've got to drive the band to rehearsal, so I can't have that drink. But on tour I drink all day, just so I don't have to think about going onstage. That's why, as a live band, we fuck up so many times.' One function that Richey's drinking did not fulfil, however, was to aid creativity: 'Some people maintain that the best writing is done by alcoholics or junkies. That's crap: the more addicted you are, the less time you have to write.'

Was Richey addicted? By his own definition, perhaps not. *Dependent*? Certainly. As anyone connected with the band unanimously agrees, it was at this period that Richey started going off the rails. 'He was never *on* the rails,' says Caffy St Luce in retrospect, 'but at first you always refuse to believe it when your mates start to deteriorate.' Not that they would necessarily have been able to do anything about it anyway. 'You do all you can,' James later told *Sky*, 'but you can't put someone in a straitjacket. It's a cliché, but you can only be there for the fall.'

Even though, after Thailand, the band had sent Richey to the health farm again, he had stopped taking care of his body: no more workouts. However, paranoid about developing a beer belly, he needed another method to keep his figure. 'He was still obsessed with getting a flat stomach,' said Wire, '. . . so he stopped eating.'

'The slave begins by demanding justice and ends by wanting to wear a crown. He must dominate in his turn' – ALBERT CAMUS

The first time you heard 'Faster', you knew something had changed. There was a startling new militancy – a new extremity, a new *urgency* – to Manic Street Preachers. The stakes had been raised. It was like hearing members of a band with guns to their heads and microphones in their faces, forced to condense everything they believed into one final four-minute edict. The Manics were playing for dear life, rather than worrying about unit sales in America.

Released on 6 June by Epic (the Manics had moved across to Columbia's sister imprint when their friend Rob Stringer became label head), it began with the voice of John Hurt from *1984*, skewered by an ear-piercing squeal of feedback: 'I hate purity. I hate goodness. I don't want virtue to exist anywhere. I want everyone corrupt.' A half-second hiatus, then the whole thing exploded. Driven by an uptight, atonal two-note riff (essentially the earlier B-side 'Comfort Comes' turned upside-down; that song was actually included, perhaps for comparison, on the Japanese CD), 'Faster' had James Dean Bradfield singing alternate lines unnervingly close-up and then distant; in your ear then in the room next door. Hurtling yet controlled, wild yet disciplined, this was music to do sit-ups to.

The words, like the sonics, were lean, pared-down and to the point. Although Wire has since said that it was 'a joint effort', it is near-impossible to view 'Faster' as anything other than a Richey song (a perception heightened by the Mitch Ikeda sleeve photo of him admiring his own emaciated torso in the mirror). From the very first words, 'I am an architect [i.e. a creator] they call me a butcher [a mutilator/destroyer]', this is Richey's great song of self-justification.

That said, there are various possible readings of 'Faster'. As Wire admitted: 'It's the first time we've written a song and not completely understood what we've written.' Even the title is ambiguous. Nicky said it referred to 'society speeding up' but, given its personal background, one could be forgiven for reading it as 'he who fasts' (i.e. starves).

According to Richey, the point of the song was that morality is merely obedience to the ruling caste. He said that the song was inspired by Yukio Mishima, the Japanese artist/poet/philosopher whose élitist, quasi-Nietzschean notions of nobility are usually – if simplistically – interpreted as being right-wing. Certainly, the most obvious interpretation is that 'Faster' is a declaration of absolute, intransigent, tunnel-vision certainty. In the chorus, Richey proclaims his superiority to Norman Mailer, Henry Miller, Sylvia Plath, Harold Pinter and the entire membership of Mensa. This was the mother of all boasts: Plath, in her last eighteen months of life, hit a terrifyingly prolific streak in which she would write three poems a day (and not doggerel either – it was considered her finest work). This kind of adamant proclamation of one's own strength, according to many psychologists, is a classic symptom of imminent collapse.

Another intriguing possibility is that it was the Manics' considered response, eighteen years on, to the Sex Pistols' 'Anarchy in the UK'. Was 'I am an architect' a conscious reply to 'I am an antichrist'? Did the nihilist mantra 'I know I believe in nothing, but it is my nothing' deliberately echo 'Don't know what I want, but I know how to get it'?

Other lyrics in the song had more clear-cut origins. One line, 'If you stand up like a nail then you will be knocked down', is an ancient Chinese proverb; another, 'Self-disgust equals self-obsession, honey' came from a drunken discussion with Richey's close friend Gillian Porter. He had been holding forth at tedious length about his feelings of self-disgust, when Gillian sardonically burst his bubble. 'Self-disgust? More like self-obsession, honey . . .'

Just as 'Motown Junk' was anti-baggy, in mood and content, 'Faster' was an anti-slacker anthem. As James explained to *Melody Maker*: 'The media are so into this idea of "Generation X" at the moment, this fucked concept of teenage discontent. But they're just celebrating, these kids, saying, "Ooh, we've always had money, but the second they took the spoon out of our mouths we decided maybe we never really liked our life after all, and – hey – maybe we won't get a job." And they'd never fucking publish anything by some scummy junked-up bastard from Manchester, they're only concerned with willing underachievers from the upper-middle classes.'

Whatever its true meaning, 'Faster' remains arguably the Manics' finest moment (challenged only by their next 'comeback' single, two years later). The second track, with which 'Faster' shared double A-side billing (a live version of 'New Art Riot' and the shabby, punky 'Sculpture of Man' made up the numbers), was almost as good. 'P.C.P.' – its title was a four-way pun on Political correctness, the Portuguese Communist Party, Police Constables and the drug PCP/'angel dust' – kicked off in a storm of gothic, Banshee-esque guitars and rumbling, tumbling drums, before suddenly switching up three gears into streamlined, minimal power-rock to which the word 'punk' cannot do justice. The track was mistaken by some for a contribution to the New Right's tiresome anti-PC backlash, but it was actually a protest against PC's Orwellian/*Fahrenheit 451*-style eradication of language, inspired by a Mick Hume anti-censorship article Richey had read in *Living Marxism*. It also attacked the New Puritanism – Richey still could not decide whether he was or was not a puritan himself – as a subtle form of fascism which condemns the very people it aims to save.

'Political correctness is more sinister than anything anyone can ever accuse us of,' he told Peter Paphides of *Time Out*. 'It's all about language. It's all aimed at the working class. I read the *Guardian* and *The Times*. I also read the *Sun* – it uses language that is accessible. Lenny Bruce said that being scared of words is also what gives them their power. The word "nigger" is not frightening. You know, his famous quote where he just says "Nigger nigger nigger nigger nigger"? PC just builds more walls. "P.C.P." is an important song in understanding what we do. It could be construed as quite a right-wing point of view but then, at the same time, every left-wing party seems to be advocating censorship of some kind. Which I can't really agree with. Like that Ken Loach film, *Hidden Agenda*. That got pulled off Channel Four, after the Warrington [IRA] bombing, but then it gets shown a month later! Now, I don't think that's even being sensitive.'

'Faster' ended, with no apparent relevance, with the voice of Albert Finney's ageing thespian in *The Dresser*: '227 Lears . . . and I can't remember the first line.' *King Lear*'s first proper line, incidentally (give or take some irrelevant scene-setting), is 'Meantime, we shall express our darker purpose . . .'

Given its uncompromising style, the single sold gratifyingly well, reaching No. 16 in the charts, but any celebrations were overshadowed by another piece of terrible news. Midway through the promotional schedule, Richey heard that one of his best friends from university had hanged himself.

One of a handful of people outside the band in whom Richey would confide was Gillian Porter (long-time Manics publicist, first for Maggie Farran PR then for Hall Or Nothing). Richey doted on Gillian – he was sometimes to be seen literally carrying her bag – and held her in far higher esteem than he did the majority of music-biz types, not least because she could drink him under the table. It was Gillian whom he rang in the small hours when he heard the news, and to whom spent four hours crying down the phone.

In public, Richey put on a brave face. The very next day, I met him at the filming of a mini-gig for Channel Four's *Naked City*. As we debated the rights and wrongs of political correctness at great length, he seemed fine. You wouldn't have guessed he had a trouble in the world.

> '*A good soldier has his heart and soul in it. When he receives an order, he gets a hard on, and when he drives his lance into the enemy's guts, he comes*' – BERTOLT BRECHT

The BBC switchboard lit up like a Christmas tree before the Manics had reached the first chorus. For the *Top of the Pops* performance of 'Faster', flanked by two ominous Olympic-style oil-burners, James Dean Bradfield had decided to top off a quasi-paramilitary outfit with a black, IRA-style balaclava. Although he looked seriously scary, the effect was spoilt somewhat by the name 'James' embroidered above the eyeholes, rather as if his mum had made it. The outfit caused national outrage: over 25,000 people rang or wrote to complain, a *TOTP* record. 'I don't think they'll be inviting us back in a hurry,' said Nicky.

As well as having a new sound, 'Faster'/'P.C.P.' heralded a new look for the Manics:

military chic. In the video, all four band members were kitted out in army-surplus fatigues, resembling some non-aligned 1970s terrorist cell like the Baader-Meinhof Gang or the Angry Brigade (which tied in perfectly, of course, with the song's nihilistic lyrics).

Military uniforms in rock were already something of a cliché (The Clash *circa* 'Sandinista' being just one example), but the Manics were not simply making a meaningless fashion statement. It was not simply an image change, but almost a sex change: from feminine to masculine. It was also intended to signify the new mood in the band, as Nicky, speaking to a German magazine, explained: 'We used to wear the same clothes when we started too: white jeans and spraypainted blouses. It gave us the feeling of unity. After *Gold Against The Soul* we felt we were losing our grip on the band. We didn't know which direction we were heading. The uniforms represent the control and discipline that we are trying to get back.'

James, of course, who had longed to join the army during the Falklands War, needed little encouragement to get togged up like an Action Man. Another factor was Richey's growing fixation with *Apocalypse Now* and the Marlon Brando character, Colonel Kurtz. In Coppola's Vietnam masterpiece, the further upriver and the further from sanity Kurtz travels, the more devoted acolytes he gathers. Make your own Richey analogies . . .

Although Nicky and Richey could claim military backgrounds of a sort, their fathers having both been in the army, there was arguably something hypocritical about the Manics wearing second-hand, unearned war medals they presumably hadn't earned (unless the MOD were suddenly bestowing *For Valor* VCs for services to rock), the very ones that the war veteran in 'La Tristesse Durera' sells to market stalls in order to pay the bills.

The Manics didn't just choose the prettiest medals in the shop, however: everything had a meaning. Richey's was a Soviet War Veteran medal, which he chose because he saw the beautiful but failed dream of communism as analogous to the band's early dreams. Similarly, although James's naval gear may have made him look like Sinatra in *On the Town* (or perhaps a bottle of Matey), it wasn't just any sailor suit, but the uniform of the battleship *Potemkin*, which played a crucial role in the Russian Revolution. The band's new logo reinforced the point, incorporating a hammer and sickle with the letters 'CCCP', although the significance of Sean's sky-blue UN Peacekeeper beret was less clear.

Just as the Manics were beginning to resemble some clandestine fascist corps themselves, they reinforced their opposition to fascism.

On Saturday 28 May they played at an anti-Nazi carnival in Brixton's Brockwell Park, to one hundred thousand people who The Wire would previously have derided as 'Jeremies' (The Levellers were headlining). The band did have their reservations about the anti-Nazi cause: 'If you give any government the power to silence a political party, however dodgy, they will end up abusing that power,' said Richey. It was surprising, somehow, to see the Manics aligning themselves unambiguously with a good cause in the world outside at a time when they seemed to be turning inward towards solipsism and when their every statement was equivocal (as *Melody Maker*'s Taylor Parkes wrote at around this time: 'The Manics' triumph is that, where they could have been the full stop at the end of rock 'n' roll, they chose to be its question mark'). However, they weren't planning to make a habit of it, as Nicky told *Melody Maker*: 'We're not The Levellers, and we're not going to do a benefit concert twice a week for the rest of our lives. This is the first time we've agreed to do something like this, and that's enough of a statement in itself.'

A month later, on 24 June, the Manics played the most un-Manic venue imaginable: the Glastonbury Festival. (The Levellers, ironically, were playing simultaneously in the adjacent field.) The irony was not lost on Wire: 'They should build some more bypasses over this shithole,' he crowed to a field of shocked hippykids. The Manics looked spectacular, with James in his navy suit and balaclava, and Nicky in camouflage fatigues and facepaint, and the headlong aggression with which they assaulted their set gave the show a dramatic, life-or-death feel (intensified by the fact that, during 'From Despair to Where', rain poured through the stage roof on to the amps, posing a serious danger of death). By the reckoning of every witness, it was the Manics at their finest. The band members themselves, however, were hyper-critical. 'It just seemed like the worst gig we'd ever done,' said James later, 'it was like a cabaret for post-degree students.' Richey agreed when he saw the Channel Four footage. A sound technician, under the impression that Richey was the lead guitarist, turned him right up in the mix. Edwards was mortified.

Although rumours regarding Richey's health were now beginning to seep out, the Manics didn't hide away: Richey and James were both to be seen cheerfully socialising in the VIP bar, and James spent several hours watching USA 94 in the football tent (making bizarre pretend-African chants every time Nigeria got the ball).

Indeed, to the casual observer, Richey seemed to be on top form. That month, the Daily Mail's professional controversialist Julie Burchill held a dinner at Soho media drinking den the Groucho Club in honour of Douglas Coupland, author of the era-defining slacker text Generation X. The guests were supposed to comprise Britain's brightest young minds (TV's Caitlin Moran, the Sunday Times teenage columnist Emma Forrest, Alan Coren's journalist daughter Victoria), handpicked to worship at the hem of Coupland's napkin. Richey Edwards walked in, pale and emaciated, wearing a pink 'Fairy' T-shirt and carrying a handbag, and sat down right next to Coupland. The author turned to Richey and indulgently enquired: 'So, what do you do then? Are you part of Generation X?' For a moment, Edwards stared at him with an expression combining cold pity and disgust, then, slowly and deliberately, turned his chair away from Coupland and didn't say a word to him all night. A magnificent performance.

To the band, however, it was increasingly clear that all was not well. After Glastonbury, the Manics returned to Portugal. As Sean later pointed out, it was already far from their favourite country: 'The first time we went there, Philip died.' This time, Richey's mental state was visibly disintegrating. He would talk psychobabble all day, and involuntarily burst into tears at regular intervals.

Nicky later described Richey's unhinged behaviour to NME: 'We had to put him to bed one night 'cos he just burst out crying in the car. And then he phoned me up at about half-three in the morning and – you know those terrible commercial presentations you get? Some American twat showing you how to flatten your stomach or summat? – and we were watching that together, and it seemed so bleak and nondescript. We didn't have a row or anything, but he kept yapping and I was really tired. The next morning, he comes up to me and says, "Here you are, Wire," and he gave me a fucking Mars bar . . .'

'Well, my own work, I am risking my life for it and my reason has half foundered because of it'
– VINCENT VAN GOGH, THE DAY BEFORE SHOOTING HIMSELF IN THE GROIN

Suicide and pop music have always been inseparable.

Pop, it might be said, is about the creation of impossible desires for unattainable things. The flipside, with unerring logic, is massive disappointment, inconsolable sadness. *Top of the Pops* or top yourself: terminal adolescence. It's a medium constantly concerned with sex, which in turn is fundamentally linked with violence: both are things that we do to each other when words are no longer enough. Unfortunately, they are also both things that people sometimes do to *themselves*.

Manic Street Preachers' fascination with suicide barely needs stating: 'Suicide Alley', 'Spectators of Suicide', the 'SUICIDE BABY' shirts, Richey advising *Smash Hits* readers to kill themselves, and so on. Like Morrissey before him, Richey believed that to take one's own life is the strongest statement anyone can make, and the single way in which we can truly take control of our own existence. 'It's a strong thing to do. It's only the thought of hurting the people who are left that stops you from doing it. Even if it's people in the band. We all rely on each other.'

Nor was he unaware of the attraction of dying young and leaving a good-looking corpse. One afternoon in 1993, Richey was driving to the coast to take his dog Snoopy for a swim when he heard the news of River Phoenix's death on Radio One. He nearly crashed the car. 'River Phoenix dying upset me more than the BNP getting in power. I know it's morally wrong, but it did. When I phoned James, we both said: "The fucking bastard!" He's . . . I wouldn't say he's *immortal*, but he's there forever. He's picture perfect, he's never gonna get old or grey or wrinkly.'

A high percentage of Richey's heroes and icons had committed suicide. Yukio Mishima, who carefully staged his own ceremonial hara-kiri in 1970 to urge the Japanese to revive pre-war notions of honour and nobility; Sylvia Plath, who, although young, successful and talented, suffered from the blackest depression and committed suicide aged 31; Tony Hancock, whose suicide note, 'Things just went wrong too many times', Richey described as one of the most beautiful things he had ever read. Vincent Van Gogh, Primo Levi, Kurt Cobain, Bobby Sands, Ian Curtis – the list goes on.

Not that a theoretical fascination with the subject is any evidence of genuine suicidal tendencies. Nicky Wire had studied suicide as part of a sociology course for two months, and has 'never felt the urge: there's always too many people I want to piss off'. Richey, too, wasn't sure that he could ever make the fatal step from theory to practice. 'It's something that everyone thinks about. Everyone has their bad days. I wouldn't say it's a question of guts, but . . . It's hard to imagine how low you could be to actually do it. It's quite a threatening thought.'

One hot July night, shortly after returning from Portugal, Richey phoned Nicky from his Cardiff flat. He was talking psychobabble again, and said a few things which Wire found strange and disturbing, even by Edwards's standards.

The next day, Richey's parents and Wire phoned to check that he was OK. There was no answer. At first, his parents assumed Richey had gone away, but Nicky suspected something was amiss. Eventually, Graham and Sherry Edwards went to the flat and let themselves in. As soon as they opened the door, it was clear that something was wrong. The flat, uncharacteristically, was in a terrible mess (Richey had been going through a fanatically tidy phase). When they found him, he was in an appalling state: he had subjected his body to a violent two-day binge of drinking and cutting.

It did not come as a complete surprise, as James later revealed: 'He said a couple of things to Nicky one evening that Nick thought were a bit funny, and the next day we couldn't get in touch with him and we knew.' Richey later played it down, saying that he had been a 'drama queen' and denying that the episode had been a suicide attempt. 'In terms of the S-word, that does not enter my mind. And it never has done, in terms of an attempt. Because I am stronger than that.' This time, though, his wrists were butchered rather than merely slit.

'I was raped by orderlies, gnawed on by rats, and poisoned by tainted food.
And I survived.
I was chained in padded cells, strapped into straitjackets, and half-drowned in ice baths.
And I survived.
The asylum itself was a steel trap, and I was not released from its jaws alive and victorious. I
    crawled out mutilated, whimpering and terribly alone.
But I did survive' – FRANCES FARMER, 'WILL THERE REALLY BE A MORNING?'

This time, it was too serious for another trip to the health farm. Richey, by his own admission, needed psychiatric treatment, and asked Hall Or Nothing for help.

The first step was to have him admitted to the local NHS psychiatric hospital, in Whitchurch, Cardiff. Whitchurch, by all accounts, was more like an old-fashioned asylum than a modern psychiatric hospital. Richey later described it in *One Flew Over the Cuckoo's Nest* terms: neglected patients staggering down the corridors banging off the walls, the lobotomies replaced by sedatives. Nicky visited him every day, and Sean and James, who lived more distantly, visited once or twice during his stay. They found him, drugged up to his eyeballs with Valium and Librium, stuttering and barely able to talk, but still writing his notebooks. 'It was horrible,' said James. 'People have got this strangely romantic *Cuckoo's Nest* image. It's not even that disciplined, it's just a flotation tank for people who can't cope. They're in stasis, in limbo, kept stable with dosages.' Sean, speaking to *Select*, confirmed this: 'They had no money, and they just knock 'em out with drugs. It's not treatment. I don't think he ever saw a psychiatrist.'

When his band-mates visited, any mention of the band itself was off-limits. 'To be honest,' said James, 'we were all quite numb to any sort of discussion about the group's future because we were too concerned about Richey. He's a friend first and foremost, so we never entertained any discussion about the group until he brought it up himself. We couldn't walk out of the hospital and say, "OK, what about this concert on Tuesday night, then?"'

Richey did bring it up himself, offering partially to quit the band. Nicky, James and Sean told him that whatever he wanted to do was fine with them – become a lecturer, writer, anything – if it helped him to recover. After much discussion, they hit on a compromise: Richey would contribute artwork and lyrics, but would cease to be a visible, performing part of the Manics set-up. However, as soon as he had seen them to the door, Richey changed his mind. Later that evening, he rang them in tears, saying that he *had* to be in the band. He expressed his feelings of guilt that he would be missing several important festivals, and even promised to start practising guitar. He made the decision, he later told *NME*'s Stuart Bailie, 'Because it's not enough for me just to do the words. I kind of think I'd be cheating on them, 'cos the touring part is the worst bit – the bit that no band really enjoys. It's the thing that makes it feel like a job, because you know what you'll be doing in three months' time at two o'clock in the afternoon.'

After just eight days in the hospital's cheerless surroundings, the band's concern for their beloved friend overcame their principled stance against private medicine. They decided to check Richey out of Whitchurch, and into the best clinic they could afford.

In public, a façade of normality was maintained – with one of the most abnormal records the Manics have ever made. Released on 1 August, 'Revol' began with a (small-g) 'gothic' intro similar to that of 'P.C.P'. The remainder, however, was truly bizarre, scary bubblegum-metal on helium, with Richey's degree in Political History coming to the fore as he listed totalitarian leaders next to unusual sexual images: 'Mr Lenin, awaken the boy/Mr Stalin, bisexual epoch/Khruschev, self-love in his mirrors/Brezhnev married into group sex . . .' and so on. The chorus invoked slogans belonging to Hitler (*lebensraum*) and Bismarck (*kulturkampf*), and barked disciplinarian instructions in German and Italian: 'Raus! Raus!' ('Get outside!') and 'Fila! Fila!' ('Form a line!'). Released with the obligatory rare oldie (the original 'You Love Us'), the now-unsurprising slow, moody number ('Too Cold Here') and a handful of live tracks, a baffled public sent 'Revol' to No. 22 and then straight back down again.

Nicky Wire, inexplicably, now loathes 'Revol' (although it remains hugely popular among hardcore fans as an example of just how mad the Manics once were, to believe that something as extreme as this could ever be a commercial single). Originally titled 'Revol/Lover', it was a 100 per cent Richey song, and mystifying even to Nicky, who could only speculate that it was an analogy between failed personal and political relationships: as every revolution fails, so all love fails. The titular use of puns, anagrams, palindromes and acronyms is something of a Preachers' trademark ('Another Invented Disease'/A.I.D.s, 'Spectators of Suicide'/S.O.S., 'P.C.P.', 'Enola/Alone'). One might, at a push, add to the list 'Love's Sweet Exile', included live from Bangkok on the 'Revol' CD (could it really have been a terrible pun on popular sugar substitute Sweetex? Did Richey and Nicky spend hours wrestling with the words 'Hermesetas' and 'Nutrasweet' before the eureka moment hit them?).

On Wednesday 3 August, the music papers hit the streets bearing the official announcement that Richey was being treated in a private London clinic for 'nervous exhaustion' – a standard rock 'n' roll euphemism covering a multitude of sins (medical-dictionary definition: 'a number of physical and mental symptoms including loss of energy, insomnia, aches and pains, depression, etc.'). James explained that: '[Richey] has always had too many vices to cope with – too much drugs, too much alcohol, the self-mutilation thing – which he uses as a release. He believes in a strong mind, strong body, and his mind overestimated the reaction to his body.' Nicky told *Melody Maker* that: 'Richey just reached a point where something clicked. His self-abuse has just escalated so fucking badly – he's drinking, he's mutilating himself, he's on the verge of anorexia . . .' James added, 'We all saw Richey's problems getting to a stage where things were going to get very nasty, and now he's going to see a psychiatrist to try to nip that in the bud. That's the true story. Those are the facts.' Rumours of Richey's suicide attempt were neither confirmed nor denied. (By now, there were also rumours – which turned out to be false – that he had attempted suicide again in hospital.) The other Manics jokingly called Richey 'a nutter' in interviews to defuse difficult lines of questioning, and made light of the situation: 'Some things will have to change,' said James, 'but that's OK. I'll have to find a new drinking buddy.'

None of which excuses the cynical nature of much of the subsequent press coverage. The *Guardian*, incredibly and unforgivably, postulated the theory that the whole thing was just another Manics publicity stunt. 'Even we wouldn't stoop that low,' said James. It was even suggested, mischievously, that Richey James's hospitalisation had had the same effect as Kurt Cobain's suicide (instant canonisation, waves of empathetic adoration, a sudden, respectful recognition that he *did* mean it, that he was '4 REAL' after all) with the difference that Richey was still around to enjoy it.

These reactions infuriated Nicky Wire, who later told Jon Savage in *Dazed & Confused*: 'That's the old Kurt Cobain thing, with the coma, everybody was kind of laughing and thinking he couldn't do it, and then a few weeks later he's dead. I think that jolted people a bit . . . There is that thing, that failed suicide can fuck you up more than anything. Every failed suicide tries to do it again, virtually . . .'

'The only freedom left is the freedom to starve' – RICHEY, MSP NEWSLETTER, DECEMBER 1992

Martin Hall had found a clinic for Richey: The Priory, a whitewashed neo-classical mansion in Roehampton, south-west London (a stone's throw from the tree where Marc Bolan's Mini came to its fatal halt). One of the Priory Hospitals group, and the self-styled 'leading provider of acute psychiatric care in the UK', The Priory has treated quite a roll-call of celebrity patients, including Spike Milligan, Shaun Ryder, Sinead O'Connor, Paul Gascoigne and Fleetwood Mac's Peter Green (the north London branch, in Southgate, has treated mass-murdering Chilean dictator General Augusto Pinochet, U2's Adam Clayton, TV's Paula Yates, and comedienne Caroline Aherne). At over £300 a day for a private room with en-suite bathroom, it is a sanctuary beyond the budget of most mere mortals.

The most urgent problem to deal with was Richey's dramatic weight loss. 'He was down to about six stone, which, for a 5ft 8 ins 25-year-old, is pretty grim,' said Nicky, kindly remembering to lie about Richey's age. The clinic's Eating Disorders Unit treats anorexia by focusing on body image. According to its Dr Desmond Kelly: 'In the process of being very thin, people's image of themselves becomes very distorted, so that, for instance, as they gain weight, their ability to judge distances becomes better. For most of us, with poles which restrict entry to a road, we can judge whether our car can fit through: we have an accurate perception. As you get thinner, your perception of width changes, so many people perceive themselves to be fat when they are not.' The origins of the condition, however, may not be purely psychological. Two years too late for Richey, it was announced that scientists had found a brain-trigger for anorexia.

Whatever the causes, Nicky, who witnessed Richey's anorexia first-hand, called it 'a kind of suicide where you don't have to die. Any association with self-abuse and self-control is pretty romantic in a naïve sort of way, but obviously the reality of anorexia is much worse than the idea. It's like a slow death.'

When they visited Richey, the other Manics decided that gentle mockery was the best approach. 'I'd say to him, "You're just a fucking nutter anyway" in an offhand way,' said Nicky. James's cajoling was even more blunt: 'I can say to him, "Oh, you're not exactly *compos* tonight, are you?" and he'll go, "I know, what can I do?" and I'll go, "You can just fucking stop it, you cunt!" You've got to get a sense of perspective at the end of the day. So I just go down there every night and give him a good kicking. He said to me, "You know, if you took just one of these tablets you could really open up your creative senses," and I said, "No, Richey, I don't really think so."'

Gillian Porter, too, refused to allow Richey to dwell on his illness(es): 'I smuggled in coffee and got him talking about other things, like which gigs I'd been to. He was trying to play guitar as well, which was fucking hysterical!' Richey had, indeed, made good his promise to learn guitar. James took a guitar in every night and gave him intensive lessons; Richey even bought a Nirvana songbook and got Sean to teach him 'Come As You Are'. Other Priory pastimes included group drama therapy, much to Nicky's amusement: 'I can't see Richey putting up with that "I am a cushion" stuff, somehow . . .'

Although The Priory was undeniably more comfortable than Whitchurch – patients were allowed to wear their own clothes, buy cigarettes and so on – in the long term it was arguably more damaging, and not just because Richey left with a 65-a-day smoking habit. As well as tobacco dependency, the doctors had put Richey on Prozac, the controversial anti-depressant. A patented product of the Eli Lilly pharmaceutical corporation of America, Prozac is extremely well marketed, and the fourth-biggest-selling drug in the world with a turnover of $2.6 billion per annum. One of many schools of thought on depression is that it derives from a simple chemical imbalance, a deficiency of seratonin in the brain, and it is this which drugs like Prozac attempt to remedy. It didn't help Richey, though. To paraphrase someone else's song, *the drugs didn't work*.

By far the most controversial part of Richey's treatment, however, was the Twelve-Step Programme. Part of the Twelve Steps and Twelve Traditions developed by Alcoholics Anonymous in 1952 (Richey was obliged to join Alcoholics Anonymous at The Priory), the Programme, which still uses leaflets published in the 1970s, is heavy on religious notions of repentance and salvation. Summarised in shorthand, the Twelve Steps involve the following:

1. Admission of one's own powerlessness.
2. Encouragement of a belief in a higher power (God, AA or other), while attacking 'intellectuality and self-sufficiency'.
3. Warnings against the misuse of willpower, so that the patient agrees to turn his or her will over to the higher power.
4. Requiring patients to make 'a searching and thorough moral inventory' of themselves.
5. Stressing the need for confession to someone/God.

6. The patient being ready for the higher power to remove these defects, and to move towards God's will. Rebellion may be fatal.
7. The patient humbly asking the higher power to remove his or her shortcomings. Humility is encouraged ('Value of ego-puncturing . . . Pain is the admission price to new life').
8. The patient preparing to make amends to others by making a list; avoiding extreme judgements.
9. Making direct amends to produce peace of mind.
10. The patient continuing to assess him- or herself, and to correct defects.
11. Meditation: 'Actual results of prayer are beyond question.' One must pray for knowledge of the higher power's will, and for the strength to carry it out.
12. Having achieved spiritual awakening, the patient must carry this message to others, and practise these principles in all of his or her affairs.

You don't have to know Richey Edwards all that well to spot a few glaring problems here. 'Intellectuality and self-sufficiency' were at the core of his being – remove these and you leave a cadaver. Making too severe a 'searching and thorough moral inventory' of himself was part of Richey's problem, not a potential cure. He already had humility in spades – if anything, he needed an injection of self-esteem, not a course of 'ego-puncturing'. And meditation? *Richey*?!

The portion which caused Richey the most difficulty was Step Two, which asks the patient to fixate on a higher power than himself, on 'a god of your own understanding'. Richey, an atheist since his negative childhood experiences of organised religion, had a problem with imagining any Christian deity. Shaun Ryder had used his grandmother instead. Richey tried that, and then his pets, but discarded both: they die on you. Eventually he reluctantly settled on nature. 'Mine's not going to be my dead grandmother or my pet cat,' he said, 'and it's not gonna be the Big Man upstairs. The closest I can get to it is nature, probably – but then nature is very cruel.' The problem, of course, is that the relationship with a fictional 'God' is a one-way thing. As Frances Farmer, another survivor of the Programme, wrote, 'I have God here, but He was never there.'

Many have attacked the Twelve Steps for being Victorian or (in the Christian sense) Revivalist. Certainly, it is terrifying that modern hospitals are still using this kind of thing. Furthermore, the therapy-speak seems far too Americanised for Richey's British sensibilities. James later derided it as 'Pseudo-religion. If he'd become a born-again Christian, I think it would have been better. We all think that The Priory filled him up with a lot of shit. All the things The Priory stood for, in one way or another, Richey had ridiculed viciously in the past . . . Deep down, he knew it was crap.'

Nicky Wire went even further. 'The Priory ripped out the man and left a shell. They say they've got a cure in places like that, but all they do is completely change the person you are. I don't think that's a cure. And you could see him struggling with this, wondering if this was the only way. They loved him in there, because he's so intelligent and sharp-witted, and he got into it, played along with them. But they ripped the soul out of him. The person I knew was slowly ebbing away . . .'

'The more sensitive you are, the more certain you are to be brutalised, develop scabs, never evolve. Never allow yourself to feel anything, because you always feel too much' – MARLON BRANDO

Young, successful, popular, talented, fairly rich and very good-looking – most of us would kill for such a life. So what was eating Richey Edwards? None of it, somehow, brought him satisfaction. 'Whenever I talk about Richey,' said James, 'I think of that quote from *Rumblefish*, y'know: "He's merely miscast to play, he was born on the wrong side of the river, he has the ability to do anything but he can't find anything he wants to do."'

One recurring theme in Richey's life was the contrast between his idyllic childhood and his disappointment with the adult world. 'It's strange,' said James. 'Richey never had as many setbacks as a kid as me, he's more acutely intelligent than me, he's more beautiful than me – and yet he has more problems. Problems that I'd just snip off with fucking scissors in two seconds flat really get to Richey.'

This was the heart of the matter. Andrew Mueller, writing in *Melody Maker*, described depression as 'a vicious sclerosis of the spirit'. One might expect that Richey had it made but, wrote Andrew, 'depression – which isn't the same as being depressed, which happens to everybody – suspends your perspectives, acquires its own impetus, one totally divorced from reality. It's beyond such commonly suggested remedies as pulling your socks up or snapping out of it, which would be like trying to leap free of quicksand.'

Arguably, though, Richey's illness was not classic manic depression – the quasi-physical illness which descends like a stormcloud quite regardless of external circumstances – at all, but the same sort of cause-and-effect depression which we all suffer. Richey was disproportionately affected by . . . *everything*.

In *The Secret Life*, H. Granville Barker wrote: '. . . the whole world's turmoil is but a reflection of the anarchy in your own heart'. In Richey's case, the reverse was true. He, much more than most of us, turned his insides out, and allowed the outside world in. To Nicky, the nihilistic superbitch, the world was a sick joke, to which the correct response was to laugh your head off like The Joker in *Batman*; whereas Richey couldn't help taking it all to heart. Global tragedies and personal ones affected him equally.

'I think he just feels things so fucking intensely,' said Nicky. 'He always had this vision of purity, or perfection, a kind of childlike vision, that became completely obliterated. A misprint on a lyric sheet, or whatever, would just upset him so much . . .'

Richey's extreme sensitivity recalls Dr Anthony Clare's description of Spike Milligan: 'a man with a skin layer missing'. Richey was not insane, mad, or any of those old-fashioned words. He was, in the literal sense, a *clairvoyant*: one who sees, and feels, (too) clearly.

Too sensitive for this world Richey may have been – but the mortuaries are littered with people who had that problem. What set him apart was his ability – and his driven, messianic desire – actually to articulate the horror. Although the romantic Marcel Proust line on the madness/creativity interface ('Everything great in the world is done by neurotics: they alone founded our religions and created our masterpieces') has its dangers, the basic premise is valid. To put it crassly, if Richey hadn't been the way he was . . . would he have been able to write those songs?

Before Richey's hospitalisation had been officially announced, the fans knew something was wrong. On Saturday 30 July the Manics (billed under Blur in the second tent) were due to play the inaugural T In The Park festival, which was to be held in a country park near Glasgow. For the first time since 1989, only three Manic Street Preachers walked out onstage.

'We could have cancelled the tour,' said James, 'but he wanted us to carry on playing while he was away. But it's not the same.' Once was bad enough, but the publicly stated hope was that Richey would be ready for Reading. Eventually, it became clear that he was nowhere near full health – but the Manics were going to play the Reading Festival without him. For many fans, this just didn't feel right – a criticism acknowledged by Nicky. 'When we played Glasgow without him it was horrendous. It just felt like a massive spiritual betrayal, and it looks pretty certain now that we're going to have to play Reading without him as well.' What most fans didn't realise was that the band had to play these shows to raise money for Richey's not-inconsiderable medical fees (his ten-week course of rehab ran up a total bill of nearly £20,000).

Nicky had warned: 'We'll be so fucking resentful that he isn't there [at Reading] that a lot of fucking anger is gonna come out, I tell you.' As well as the Richey situation, in the back of the Manics' minds was the fact that Saturday 27 August 1994 would have been Philip Hall's 35th birthday. The three-piece Manics appeared midway up the evening bill (before Ice T and Primal Scream; after Radiohead and Pulp), and James's resentment and anger were beginning to show before he had even played a note: 'I wish I could tell you some jokes like Jarvis Cocker,' he sneered, adding, 'We haven't turned into one of those "power trios" like The fucking Jam or anyone like that.'

Some sections of the crowd, some of them even Manics fans, but perhaps unaware of the seriousness of the situation, began a sickly chant: 'Richey's in the hospital . . .' The Manics responded with a set of breathtaking belligerence, including a meaning-loaded cover of Nirvana's 'Pennyroyal Tea', a never-more-beautiful Nicky – a pierrot in snow fatigues – annihilating his bass while James led a chorus of 'You Love Wire!' At the end, Wire scaled the speaker stacks and *fell*, rather than dived, into the crowd.

The Manic Street Power Trio played three more festivals, in Cologne, Amsterdam and Dublin, but the UK tour, due to begin on 5 October, appeared to be in jeopardy. 'If he doesn't do that,' said James, 'I don't know if we'll do it, really. There's only so far you can go with the "soldiering on" mentality.' Asked whether the band could ever continue without Richey, he answered, 'No, in any shape or form.'

Nicky Wire, meanwhile, was clearly feeling the pressure himself. 'The last six months have been absolutely fucking nightmarish,' he told Taylor Parkes of *Melody Maker*. 'Right now, I don't wanna go out, I don't wanna make any friends; at the moment all I want to do is make enemies. I've never felt this much fucking contempt for everyone and everything in my entire fucking life.'

f) True force

(JAMES DEAN BRADFIELD – BRUTE WITH CHEEKBONES)

'I loved it when Julian Clary said: "All I've ever wanted is a brute with cheekbones." Because I think that's all anybody ever wants, really, a brute with cheekbones' – RICHEY EDWARDS, 1993

I T'S THE JIMMY NAIL FACTOR. It's the brickie buying Bryan Adams's 'Everything I Do, I Do It For You' for the missus on St Valentine's Day. It's Popeye the Sailor Man bashfully thrusting a fistful of roses at Olive Oyl. It's the bit of rough with a sensitive side, it's the regular guy with a heart of gold. James Dean Bradfield has got it, and women, of course, just eat that stuff up (the Bradders-centric fanzine, *Caught in the Crossfire*, is dedicated almost entirely to fans' sexual fantasies about the singer).

And for those of us who *don't* want to smother James' pecs in clear honey and lick it off – well, he still has a certain *something*. It's the inexplicably moving spectacle of a man who resembles a particularly tough scrum-half opening his mouth and singing with the beauty of a violated angel. Out of the strong comes forth sweetness – and, after taking singing lessons from Tona De Brett, he has learnt to harness that sweetness more and more. De Brett later said, 'James, God bless him, is a sensible, down-to-earth, meat-and-potatoes sort of bloke.' And none of his training could tame James's warm-up routine. The more lily-livered kind of singer might prepare for performing with a few scales and some hot honey and lemon. But James? 'He normally screams his head off,' say his band-mates, 'and then he has a whisky and a fag.'

The meat-and-potatoes part, though, is deceptive. James is no Popeye. With his first pay packet he had a tattoo done – but it was a picture of a dolphin. He may sometimes come across like the noble savage in Huxley's *Brave New World*, but he is far too intelligent and self-conscious for that. This is a man who once slung his guitar behind his back, whipped out a comb and slicked back his hair in the middle of a solo – so don't tell me he doesn't have poise.

Despite his twinkling eyes and mischievous grin, James, with his 5ft 5 height, baby teeth and what he describes as his 'permanent Ray Reardon' (he has one of those fascinating hairlines that always looks as if it's about to recede out of view, but never quite does), is hardly archetypal sex-symbol material. He has always seemed heroic, like a noble worker on a Soviet propaganda poster – but *sexy*?

Nicky Wire, asked whether he found James pretty to look at, answered, 'He's very 50s classical . . . He thinks he's Robert De Niro sometimes.' (On his kitchen wall, James has a photograph of Robert De Niro standing next to Joe Strummer: his spiritual parents.)

He is touchingly self-deprecating about his looks. When he was a child, he says, he looked like Joe 90, and now compares himself to another animated character: 'When everyone looks at me I'm just a little short Welsh Smurf onstage trying to play guitar.' Onstage, he did in fact change the words of 'A Design for Life' to 'I wish I had a bottle/Right here in my average, not-so-pretty face'. Asked who would play him in a film of his life, he didn't answer De Niro or Brando (whose tight white V-neck he has appropriated), nor even Robert 'Begbie' Carlyle (to whom he occasionally bears an uncanny resemblance), but Bill Murray or a young Jack Lemmon. The film would, he said, be called *Atrophied in the Winter* – presumably a reference to a private shrivelling problem. Not that he is above vanity. His intermittent running fetish arises from a desire 'to stay beautiful' and, when his stomach is flat enough, he needs little encouragement in stripping off to the waist and engaging in what *Select* called 'chronic rock posturing'.

On more than one occasion, reviewers have compared James to a garage hand (the mechanic street preacher?), and I can't imagine that he protests too strongly. For all the Manics' situationist 'Destroy Work' slogans, James actually has (and has always had) a deeply ingrained work ethic. Even the badge on his school blazer read 'Endeavour'. For most bands, the adjective 'workmanlike' would be an insult; to James, it is a virtue – something to aspire to. When *Select*'s Andrew Collins flattered James by telling him how driven he always seemed, James replied: 'My dad's a carpenter. *He's* a driven man!' If Nicky is a mammy's boy, James is a dad's man. 'We're funny like that,' he said. 'Really traditional. We look up to our fathers because they could do more physical things.' James is a devout believer in the dignity of labour, and there is something navvy-ish, something sleeves-rolled-up about the way he takes on an unfair share of the Manics' musical workload without complaint. 'He is Axl, Slash and Strummer,' wrote *Sounds Info*, 'all rolled into one short-arsed Valleys boy.' To this day, James helps roadies hump the band's heaviest gear into the venue.

The new, blokey Bradders would not nowadays repeat his legendary early onstage Marquee invitation for any pretty boys to come backstage and 'fuck him up the arse'. Although he resents the implication that being a *Loaded* reader automatically makes him some kind of sexist blockhead ('I mean, I read it, but I don't frame every copy or anything – I read *Hello!* as well, but I'm not a fucking wannabe aristocrat'), seen in the right (i.e. wrong) company, James is every bit the New Lad. As he confessed to *Select*: 'It actually worries me that I still like being in a really blokey environment. I always get bored of the company of women really quickly.' But the fact that it worries him at all speaks volumes.

'I don't believe one should devote his time to morbid self-examination. I believe one should become a person like other people' – TRAVIS BICKLE, *TAXI DRIVER*

James, who once said that he thought androgyny was 'really important' but that his cheekbones wouldn't allow it, thinks nothing of singing lines like: 'I wish I had been born a girl' and, as recently as 1995, cried at *The New Adventures of Lassie* ('It had Smashing Pumpkins on the soundtrack. I always cry at dog films'). He is a double agent, a secret ambassador for girliness and arty poeticism in the world of Real Men.

Outwardly, however, he was the opposite: a Rambo between two Rimbauds, right down to the 'KILL 'EM ALL – LET GOD SORT 'EM OUT' T-shirt with its racist connotations (the slogan dates back to grunts in Vietnam who thought all slanty-eyed gooks deserved to die). James's fascination with militarism began with the Falklands War, which made him want to join the army, and he once expressed a bizarre admiration for Napoleon, 'for the way he retook France'. His image, accordingly, often teetered on the interface between moddy and squaddie, and you could tell that he, of all the Manics, was the most delighted when the band opted for the *Combat Rock* look.

If James *were* a soldier, he'd have to be a lone mercenary. Despite the legendary tightness of the Manics gang, and despite his famous sociability, James Dean Bradfield, like his celluloid namesake, is a loner at heart. Nowadays, the garrulous façade which he has cultivated disguises the stammering shyness for which he was once known. In 1991, however, Hall Or Nothing sent a delegation of music-biz types in the Manics' coach (driven by Richey!) to see the band play a gig in Sheffield. When James saw all the strangers, he didn't want to get on board and took the train instead. As a child, he had developed a brief obsession with the SAS: not so much for macho, militaristic reasons, but for 'the independence of it . . . you could go out and pretend to be a tree! I grew out of that.' Maybe, but as an adult he admitted that, if he gave up the music business, 'I'd work for the Forestry Commission back in Wales. I'd do something really isolated that didn't involve any handshakes.'

James never went in much for team sports either, preferring the loneliness of the long-distance runner to the camaraderie of combined effort. Once, when asked who he would most like to be, he named Wakkuri, a Kenyan athlete. James used to run six miles every morning, and at one point claimed to be averaging one hundred miles a week. He made a valiant attempt at the four-minute mile (he got his time down to 4.36), and completed a marathon in three hours ten minutes.

'. . . right now, though, there's a maniac on the mike like a rottweiler with treetrunks for veins, and eyes that don't appear to want to stay in their sockets, just waiting to be let off the leash . . .' – PAUL LESTER, *MELODY MAKER*

Physicality is central to James, and aggression is part of his make-up. 'I've never been a subtle person,' he said. 'I believe in high intelligence and high aggression, and I believe the two mix very well.' When Nicky and Richey were heckled by homophobes at a photo shoot in a rural pub, James surprised everyone by asking the ringleader outside. Nowadays, he tries to contain his aggression (although not so long ago he decked someone who stole a cab from him on Charing Cross Road, and the old fire is still there in interviews. In 1998, he told MTV that, had Cardiff

Arms Park been renamed Princess Diana Stadium as was briefly suggested, 'I'd have fucking blown up the fucking place myself' – and you believed him). Instead, he channels his violence into his performance: witness the way he launches into songs as if he's punching an assailant in the head.

Sometimes, however, James barely seems in control of his body at all, like an overwound clockwork toy. It is no coincidence that the tattoo on his arm reads 'ANXIETY IS FREEDOM'. One Manics myth has it that as a teenager, James underwent a failed operation to calm an overactive thyroid gland which continually pumps his body full of natural amphetamines. This is completely untrue, but it is understandable how such rumours take root. Like Paul Gascoigne, James often seems to exhibit symptoms of a mild form of Tourette's Syndrome (the nervous condition which causes physical and verbal tics, including involuntary swearing). One former flat-mate recalls the way in which James is given to pacing the house, hyped up, shouting 'Fuck! Fuck! Fuck! Fuck!' at televised sport. On Monday 19 May 1997, he inadvertently became the only person ever to swear on the Radio One *Breakfast Show* – and to do it twice. His first accidental expletive flew out during an acoustic set; then, playing Mark Radcliffe's quiz game 'We Love Us' (named in a tribute to 'You Love Us'), he became frustrated when he couldn't name the keyboardist on 'Motorcycle Emptiness' (Richard Cottle): 'Richard, oh, oh . . . FUCKING HELL!'

James doesn't seem to know his own strength. Sometimes he'll say something inaudible, with a mischievous smirk and then, before you can say, 'Er, what?', he's jovially punching you in the ribs, saying, 'Ah, doesn't matter.' And the punch will *hurt*. Caffy St Luce remembers a similar incident at Philip Hall's funeral wake. James started to squeeze her hand, on which she was wearing a huge gold ring. Caffy started to cry – not out of sorrow, but in *pain*. When he saw her tears, he just squeezed even harder.

'I like sex and rock 'n' roll,' he once said, 'but I've never taken drugs.' Just as well. If he took stimulants, James Dean Bradfield might explode in a splatter of Welsh smurf-flesh.

'James, he's an old soul flying about the universe' – MITCH IKEDA

Ultimately, James remains an enigma to me; I have never really figured him out. I once asked him what he would like to do with the rest of his life if the Manics didn't exist. He said he intended to buy a BSA motorcycle and travel the Silk Route across Asia, he wanted to become the editor of a weekly music paper, and he wanted to open a sports bar in Cardiff called 'JDB's'. It was unclear in which order he would do these things, and unclear which claims – if any – were true. Probably none. He was taking the piss.

Louis Eliot of Kinky Machine/Rialto, who enjoyed many a good-natured verbal skirmish with James on tour, says: 'He seemed an odd cross between this seething articulate punk rebel, and the slightly conservative, home-loving guy who went on about how much he respected his mum and loved his dog.' When a fanzine asked him to name the worst thing about 1997, he replied: 'Spent too much time away from my mother and father and dog.'

Despite his boy-about-town bachelor lifestyle and love of the London nightlife, he goes home at least once every three weeks because his mum does roast potatoes like no one else. He's half Michael Caine in *Alfie*, half Ronnie Corbett in *Sorry*.

And all of the above? Absolute rubbish. Or, at least, it is if you believe James. As he recently told *The Face*, he regrets – even resents – his public persona. 'The image I always gave off was a bit of a staid blue-collar Springsteen vibe,' he admitted. 'My neck was bulging "passionate" veins. I think that's what came across . . . I don't like the word "passionate". I don't like the word "brave". I don't like any of those words. It's heroism . . . I think I gave off a *stoic pugnaciousness*. And I never felt like that,' insisted the brute with cheekbones . . . stoically, pugnaciously, *heroically*.

7. THE HOLY BIBLE

'This is not a book, it is a prolonged insult, a gob of spit in the face of art, a kick in the pants to truth, beauty, God' – HENRY MILLER, *TROPIC OF CANCER*

IN JAMES DEAN BRADFIELD'S FAVOURITE FILM, *The Medusa Touch* (1978), Richard Burton says: 'I'm bringing the whole unholy edifice down on their unholy heads.' In Richard Edwards's album, *The Holy Bible* (1994), James sings, 'Do not be ashamed to slaughter . . . you will be buried in the same box as a killer.'

Released on 30 August, *The Holy Bible* was the sound of *intolerance*. It was described in *NME* as 'a vile record', and not without reason: listening to it felt like waking up in a charnel house. Other writers used the word 'millencholia', a fashionable term signifying millennial paranoia, also with some justification. It did feel like the end of the world as we know it – *apocalpyse now*. Yet *The Holy Bible* was not born from vileness nor paranoia alone. Rather than being an easy attempt to stir up cheap 'politically incorrect' (yawn) controversy, this was an intelligent, sustained attack on the liberal consensus. During the writing of the album, Richey confessed to an appreciation of the aesthetics, if not the ethics, of fascism, and told me of his admiration for Dr Hassan El Turabi, who had implemented a hardline Islamic code of Shariya law in Sudan (amputation for theft, etc.). Richey made a favourable comparison with the working-class puritans in nineteenth-century Britain, whose religious morality drove them to attack what they saw as an excessively liberal government. When I pointed out that it was easy to applaud such attitudes from a distance, he replied: 'But I *am* from a distance.'

It had always been a little simplistic to define the Manics as a socialist band, since their sentiments were often very right-wing. It was not even strictly accurate to portray them as humanitarians. As *Melody Maker*'s Neil Kulkarni wrote: 'The Manics are ferocious humanitarians who hate humanity. They don't. Then do. Then do/n't.' They had, however, always been a deeply *moral* band. *The Holy Bible* was a masterpiece of misanthropy, but one with righteousness on its side. Richey had found himself identifying strongly with Johnny, David Thewlis's deeply ambiguous, flawed avenging angel in Mike Leigh's *Naked*; as well as with that other great cinematic angel of death, Travis Bickle in *Taxi Driver*. If Bickle prayed for 'a real rain to come and wash all the scum off the streets', here it was. The album was a merciless Doomsday judgement on what e.e. cummings called 'manunkind'.

* * *

In mood as much as in message, *The Holy Bible* was an intensely sombre record, overcast by the same stormy skies which darkened Van Gogh's last works. It was gothic and, quite often, literally *Goth*: more than one song could easily have been early Cure, Sisters of Mercy or Bauhaus. Nicky Wire called it 'gothic with a small "g". It's quite a morbid album', going on to compare it to PiL, early Joy Division and Cranes. This was no coincidence: Richey, in particular, had been regularly listening to Cranes, while the other three had been overdosing on Alice in Chains, Bowie's *Low* and *Heroes*, and Joy Division.

Unlike much goth-rock, however, there was nothing florid, epic or expansive about *The Holy Bible*. This was compressed metal, the sound of tungsten under unendurable torque. Taylor Parkes of *Melody Maker* captured its quality perfectly: '*The Holy Bible* sounds as though it was created under so much pressure that songs that would once have been fat, rampant anthems have buckled, been crushed and flattened, broken down, emerging as thin, white hot-strips of purest vitriol.' *Select*'s Roy Wilkinson employed a strikingly similar image, describing the album as: 'a ruthlessly efficient scrapyard car-crusher, compacting their careering arena rock into murderously concise packages'.

Unlike the sugared-pill/Trojan horse approach of its two predecessors (which carried uncomfortable messages via melodic, commercial rock), in *The Holy Bible* message and medium are inseparable: the music, discordant and irregular, is onomatopoeic for the content. The lyrics are also brutally succinct: each song is a dwarf star of ultra-compressed imagery, a horrific, harrowing tour of the most shameful corners of the dying twentieth century (dictatorship, prostitution, anorexia, suicide, genocide). *Select*'s Andrew Male called it 'post-punk body horror', while Roy Wilkinson noted that 'The album is full of bodies, distorted, twisted, and sometimes literally, wrenched out of normality.' Almost every review mentioned Nirvana's *In Utero*, with its internal language of rapes, cancers, and abortions, as a reference point.

The album was written with 'an almost academic discipline', said James. 'We sat down and gave ourselves headings and structures, so each song is like an essay.' The four were intensely proud of the results: the entire lyric sheet was reproduced in full as a music-press centre-spread advertisement. For the first time, no attempt whatsoever had been made to make the lyrics scan or to fit the tune; indeed, many sentences started in one line and end in another. There was a certain arrogance implicit in Richey's and Nicky's impenetrable mental shorthand (obscure allusions, omissions of crucial verbs, asyntactic gibberish), although you *did* always get the general idea.

The sleeve image was a striking painting by 24-year-old artist Jenny Saville. *Strategy (South Face/Front Face/North Face)* is a triptych of views of a grotesquely obese odalisque, 'staring, absorbed yet detached, at her own reflection' (*Q*). Richey, who had seen the work in a magazine, tried to buy it from the Saatchi gallery, but was originally quoted a £30,000 price tag. After a thirty-minute telephone discussion with Saville, in which Edwards explained every track in detail, she let him use it for free. The design and logo (featuring reversed, Cyrillic-style letters) were openly plagiarised from Simple Minds' *Empires and Dance*. James had been giving copies of that album ('one of the coldest records in the world') as presents, and perceptively drew a connection between the Minds' methodicism and the situationists' cold anti-lyricism.

Approximately 35 minutes into *The Holy Bible*, the voice of J.G. Ballard archly announces: 'I wanted to rub the human face in its own vomit . . . to force it to look in the mirror.'

In just these nineteen words, Ballard unwittingly defines the whole album. This was the ultimate *uneasy-listening* experience. 'We knew, from the moment we started working on it,' said Sean Moore, 'that it wasn't going to be played at parties.' A classic Mooro understatement. *The Holy Bible* was the sound of a group *in extremis*, at crisis point, hurtling towards a private armageddon. 'I don't see it as a record,' Nicky would later tell *Select*, 'I see it as a state of mind. One we were all in.' Nonetheless, it was very much Richey's album (the lyrical duties were split roughly 70:30) – this time it was Nicky's turn just to stand there looking fantastic. As Caitlin Moran, with tangential reference to Richey, wrote in *The Times*: 'Just as a woman's body irrevocably changes shape after she's been pregnant and had a child, so I now believe that musicians' heads warp and bend and change shape after certain songs have been in there.' If this is true, in what tortured, unnatural shape did the gestation of *The Holy Bible* leave Richey's head?

The title of the opening track, 'Yes', was a hollow joke on the fact that 'We were like the TSB: The Band That Likes to Say "Yes"', but the subject was a profession even older than banking. The band's 1994 tour programme contained shorthand pass notes, written by Richey, on all the songs on the album. Next to 'Yes', the notes read, 'Prostitution of the Self'. And as Nicky told Taylor Parkes of *Melody Maker*, the Manics' 'Culture Sluts' stance had caught up with them. 'We feel that we've prostituted ourselves over the last three or four years. Marlene Dietrich said that she had been photographed to death. Red Indians believe that, every time they are photographed, a bit of their soul goes. We came to a point where we felt a bit like that.' The exploitation, of course, runs both ways. With reference to the song's shockingly graphic chorus, 'He's a boy, you want a girl, so tear off his cock/Tie his hair in bunches, fuck him, call him Rita if you want . . .', Wire explained, 'You can get to a position in a band where you can virtually do anything, in any kind of sick, low form. It's not something we've particularly indulged in . . .' (had he forgotten Bangkok already?). Richey had certainly researched his subject – the 'T' in 'I "T" them, 24-7 all year long' was, he later told me, hooker slang for 'tossing off' – but, in place of first-hand experience, he had derived his info from a Channel Four documentary entitled 'Pimps, Pros, Hookers and their Johns', a piece of dialogue from which introduced the song.

In the context of *The Holy Bible*, 'Yes' had an uncharacteristically poppy, upbeat melody, but any radio-friendly qualities were sabotaged almost immediately by the uncompromising songsheet: the fourth word is 'cunts'. It remains one of Richey's most perfectly realised lyrics. Amid all the prozzie metaphors were moments of poignant self-analysis: 'I eat and I dress and I wash and I still can say thank you/Puking, shaking, sinking, I still stand for old ladies/Can't shout, can't scream, I hurt myself to get pain out . . . the only certain thing that is left about me/There's no part of my body that has not been used.'

After such a stunning overture, it was inevitable that whatever followed would seem disappointing. 'Ifwhiteamericatoldthetruthforonedayit'sworldwouldfallapart' (the unwieldy – and incorrectly punctuated – title is a quote from Lenny Bruce) was a disjointed, mock-heroic rocker with a weak, ill-conceived lyric attacking the inherent racism of US gun laws. (The programme notes read: 'Glorify gun culture until The Massacre gradually moves from the inner cities to the suburbs.') The hookline, 'fuck the Brady Bill', referred to firearm restrictions which, according to Nicky, 'would disenfranchise black communities who generally don't have licences. The white rednecks in America do have licences.'

Track three, 'Of Walking Abortion', is perhaps *the* definitive *Holy Bible* track. The walking abortions of the title are taken from a description of the human male by Valerie Solanos, the founder of the Society for Cutting Up Men (SCUM), who famously shot Andy Warhol. It was a perfect starting point for Richey's most unflinchingly misanthropic lyric yet: a pessimistic, anti-Rousseauvian view of human nature linking man's inherent weakness with the rise of fascism. 'There's a worm in human nature,' said Nicky, 'that makes us want to be dominated.' Worms, like moths, are a recurring MSP image (compare 'Slash 'N' Burn') – hence the line 'Hitler reprised in the worm of your soul'. Richey's well-thumbed Political History folders had clearly proved useful once again as he listed obscure Hungarian politicians to illustrate his argument (the programme notes helpfully explain: 'Horthy and Tisu: eastern Euro antisemite/fascist. Walking sideways unable to make a decision of any consequence. Modern life makes thought an embarrassment'). 'We are all of walking abortion,' runs the chorus, before adding, with grim humour: 'Shalom! Shalom!' There is something brilliantly queasy about the non-sequiturial lurch from portents of Nazi revivals into the Hebrew peace greeting. The listener is not permitted to feel excused: the song ends with the accusatory chant: 'Who's responsible? You fucking are!'

The harsh, scathing Dark Metal of 'Walking Abortion' is followed by a rare interlude of calm. At first, I mistakenly took the moody power-ballad 'She Is Suffering' to be the first rock record about menstruation – a patronising echo of Soren Kierkegaard's 'What a misfortune to be a woman'. In fact, the 'she' has been variously defined as signifying beauty (a homage to Mishima's doomed pursuit of an absolute ideal of beauty, or to the Rilkean idea of beauty's terrible power) or desire. '"She" is desire,' the programme notes clarified. 'In other Bibles and Holy Books, no truth is possible until you empty yourself of desire.' Or as Nicky explained: 'It's kind of like the Buddhist thing, where you can only reach eternal peace by shedding every desire in your body.' Richey, though, was not at peace, but cursing the hormonally driven desires in his own body.

'Archives of Pain', another bicep-bursting, anabolic-steroid-pumped doom-rocker, takes the judgemental tone of 'Walking Abortion' one step further into vengeance fantasies: 'If hospitals cure, then prisons must bring their pain . . . tear the torso with horses and chains . . . sterilise rapists, all I preach is extinction.' Beginning with the voice of the mother of one of the Yorkshire Ripper's victims, the song is a reaction against the glorification of serial killers, both fictional (Hannibal Lecter) and real (Jeffrey Dahmer) – a radical *volte-face* from a band who had themselves glorified Patrick Bateman (or, at least, copped some easy shock value by naming a song after him). The title came from a chapter in David Macey's *The Lives of Michel Foucault*, which Nicky had been reading (Wire and Edwards both studied Foucault at university), about the idea of punishments matching the crime. 'It isn't a right-wing song,' said Richey, 'but a lot of people don't like seeing a rapist getting off with a £25 fine.' A joint effort, Richey and Nicky took longer over this song than over any other.

After the now-familiar (but still bloody weird) 'Revol' comes a Richey lyric even more uncomfortably personal than the opening track. '4st 7lbs' was Richey's autobiographical narrative on anorexia, barely concealed behind the third-person format of a young girl's diary. Brainwashed by media images of 'Kate', 'Kristin' and 'Emma' (models Moss, McMenamy and Balfour), and by the advice of 'Karen' (Krizanovitch, *Sky* agony aunt), the girl follows the deadly internal logic of anorexia until she reaches 4st 7lbs (the weight generally said to be the threshold of death). Like the narrator him/herself, James's musical accompaniment progressed in phases from turbulent beginnings (an intro which recalled The Jam's 'Eton Rifles') to placid serenity. Unusually, given the album's condemnatory context, Richey refuses to criticise the victim. According to the programme notes, the song was all about 'finding your own self-worth and admiring yourself for it, whatever that involves'. Nor was he romanticising her plight – or, not exactly, although couplets as exquisite as 'I wanna be so skinny that I rot from view/I want to walk in the snow and not leave a footprint' made it seem almost attractive. As with his interviews, the astonishing thing about '4st 7lbs' was Richey's ability to analyse with clarity an illness from which he himself was suffering. By the end, the listener felt like a voyeur in the worst kind of pornography, and slightly unclean.

The Manics' experiences in Belsen, Dachau and Hiroshima back in 93 bore not one but two tracks on *The Holy Bible*. The first was 'Mausoleum', a song which had been knocking around in various forms for some time but had yet to be recorded. An attack on revisionist historians ('Holocaust is one of the few examples where even truth is being questioned,' the programme notes explained), it opened with the chilling line 'Wherever you go, I will be carcass', before peaking with the refrain 'No birds, no birds/The sky is all swollen black/Holy mass of dead insect . . .'

In much art – Van Gogh's *Crows in the Cornfield*, Hitchcock's *The Birds*, Poe's *The Raven* – birds are often symbols of impending doom. In 'Mausoleum', it was precisely their absence which created this mood. Indeed, the song was originally to be called 'No Birds', until someone pointed out to James that PiL had released a track with that title on *Metal Box* and he came up with the new title at the last moment (just to make extra-sure, Nicky wrote to me in my capacity as an ex-goth to ask whether I had ever come across any song by a goth band titled 'Mausoleum'). 'Dachau is such an evil, quiet place,' said Nicky. 'There's no grass, and you don't even see a worm, let alone any birds' (Wire on worms yet again!). Musically, 'Mausoleum' is schizophrenic: parts of it almost have a boogie dynamic (the intro bears a worrying resemblace to The Wonder Stuff's 'Give Give Give Me More More More'), while other parts are as classically gothic and terrifying as Carl Orff's *Carmina Burana* as used in *The Omen*.

After 'Faster' came another rare shaft of light. 'This Is Yesterday', a soft-rocker reminiscent of The Jam's mellower moments ('Ghosts' in particular), was the only song which could also have sat happily on *Gold Against the Soul*. A nostalgic lament for halcyon youth, it was as simple and straightforward as the similarly titled slowie by The Beatles.

The next track lurched to the opposite end of the human age spectrum. 'Die in the Summertime' was written from the viewpoint of an OAP who wants to die remembering childhood bliss, rather than adult sadness. As was the case with Kurt Cobain's 'I Hate Myself and I Want to Die', most commentators in the post-modern, ironic 90s assumed that, well, of course he didn't *literally* mean he wanted to die in the summertime. Even Nicky Wire was fooled. 'I think this [song] and "4st 7lbs" are pretty obviously about Richey's state of mind, which I didn't quite realise at the time. Even if you're quite close to someone, you always try to deny thoughts like that.' The song also had a more trivial meaning: the Manics genuinely loathe summertime. 'I hate summer,' Nicky told *NME*. 'I'm sure I get the reverse of Seasonal Affective Disorder. I can't fucking stand it and just wish it was dark at six o'clock.' Sean agreed: 'I remember one summer me and James just closed

➤ *Portrait Of The Artist As A Young Boy: Richey Edwards, some time in the 70's*

WALES NEWS & PICTURES

⋎ *Richey in his teenage Bunnyman phase, with Snoopy*

WALES NEWS & PICTURES

➤ *From top, Sean Moore, James Dean Bradfield, Nick Jones*

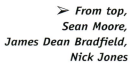

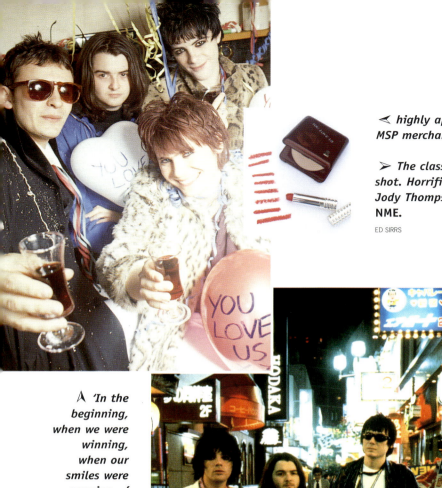

◄ *highly appropriate MSP merchandise*

➤ *The classic 4 REAL shot. Horrified onlooker: Jody Thompson, now of NME.*

ED SIRRS

⋀ *'In the beginning, when we were winning, when our smiles were genuine ...'*

➤ *'Under neon loneliness ...' Tokyo 1992*

PAUL SLATTERY

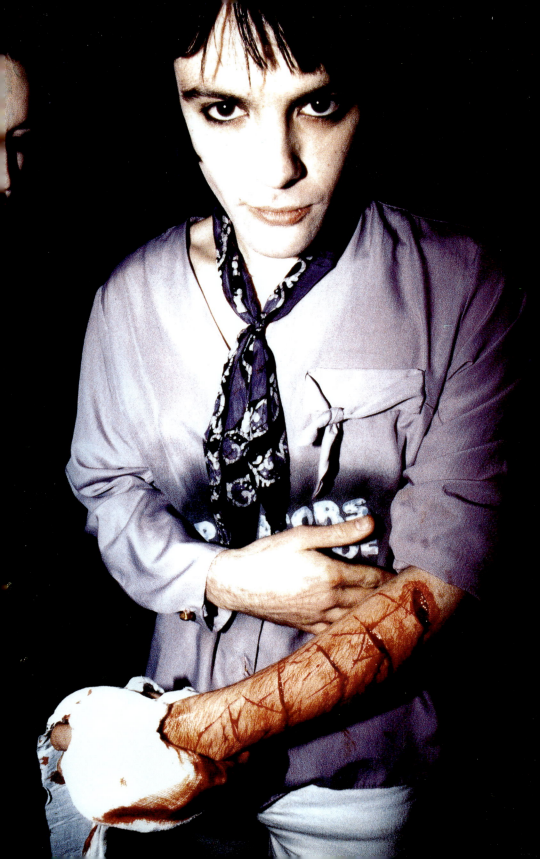

'YOU LOVE US' VIDEO SHOOT 1

∨ *Richey: Suicide Bride*

∧ *Man(ic) In The Mirror*

∨ *Making love to his ego...*

**'YOU LOVE US'
VIDEO SHOOT 2**

◀ *Old Nick: Horny Devil*

ⱽ *James under the spotlight*

➤ *One size fits all: Nicky and Richey*

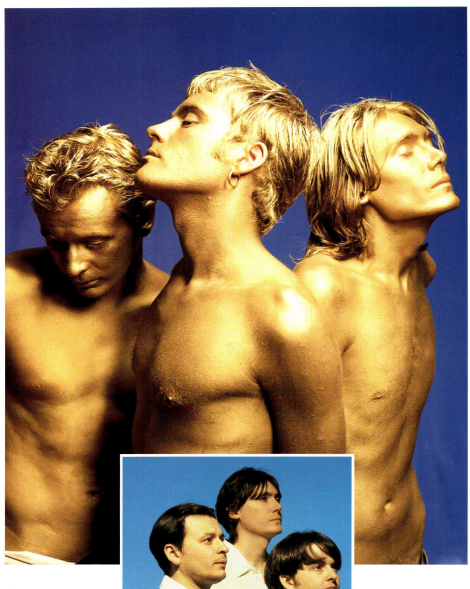

▲ *The Three Disgraces: Melody Maker session, Jan 1994 (note JDB panty line)*

STEVE GULLICK

◄ *1996: Rumours of a new 'Kraftwerk' direction proved unfounded*

STEVE DOUBLE

◄ *Is it Grace Kelly, or is it Hilda Ogden?*
MICK HUTSON

▽ *James' 'controversial' balaclava* MICK HUTSON

⋏
'Faster'/'PCP'
ephemera

^ **Rocking the Kop: Hillsborough Justice Concert, 1997**

MARK McNULTY

v **Sucking up to the establishment: Brits 1997**

PATRICK FORD

➢ **a Brit Award, yesterday**

the curtains every day and didn't go out at all. We stayed in, we watched Wimbledon and played records until the sun went down.'

The twelfth track, a six-minute monster called 'The Intense Humming of Evil', began with a brass band playing a death march, before turning into what sounds like the roar of a big machine cranking into life. A sister song to 'Mausoleum', James apparently considered its original draft to be 'not judgemental enough', and requested a rewrite. 'You can't be ambivalent about a subject like that,' he told *Q*. 'Not even we are stupid enough to be contentious about that [the Holocaust].'

Then 'P.C.P.', then that Albert Finney sample . . . then nothing but the whirr of the CD player coming to a halt as you attempt to take in all that you have just heard. Apparently there was once a book with the same title. But you needn't worry about that.

1994, the year when rock's new-found hedonism finally caught up with itself, the year of Kurt Cobain's suicide and any number of ODs, breakdowns and near misses, was christened 'The Year Rock Cracked Up', or 'Year of Death of Destruction', by phenomenon-spotters in the media.

The Manics were speeding down the same freeway, whether they knew it or not. As Keith Cameron of *NME* noted: 'James, Nicky, Richey and Sean have always seemed like innocents abroad, like little children who knew about snow but were still blissfully unaware that it could fall in blizzards and do you harm.'

Yet the Preachers, of all people – apostles of Monroe, Plath, Cobain – should have known that self-destruction was part of the deal. It was an essential requisite of the fans' voyeuristic, vicarious love. *You have to fuck up*. In their kamikaze bid to become the ultimate crash 'n' burn rock spectacle, they had made a Mephistophelian pact – had sold their souls for rock 'n' roll – and the clock was ticking.

While the other Manics had only ever toyed with the rock 'n' roll myth, Richey actually believed it. 'We were all attracted to the glamour of suicides and alcohol and beauty,' Nicky told *Select*, 'that *Rumblefish* thing of self-destruction. It's just that Richey took it a lot further. Richey took a lot of things further than us.' In his heart of hearts, though, Richey knew that he wasn't actually a very rock 'n' roll person. As he had confessed to *Select* some years earlier, aged just 23: 'I'm an old man now . . . I read the *Independent*. I watch *Question Time*.' Which meant he had to try even harder.

To some extent, Richey's behaviour throughout 1994 was '4 REAL' writ large. He felt obliged to walk it like he talked it. 'Some of the lyrics were so self-fulfilling for Richey,' Nicky told *NME*, 'like "Die in the Summertime". I'm sure he felt that "People are gonna say I'm a fake if I don't do something about it."'

'If you become sick, don't try to carry on as if you are not . . . The return to work should be gradual' – 'OVERCOMING DEPRESSION', A LEAFLET BY DR DESMOND KELLY OF THE PRIORY HOSPITAL

In early September, Richey, despite medical advice, obeyed his work ethic and his guilt at letting down his friends, checked out of Roehampton and rejoined the band. The Manics were at Blue Stone Studios, a converted Dyfed farmhouse retreat recently vacated by Take That, to rehearse for an eleven-date tour of France supporting Therapy?, Richey's old snogging partners.

Although he had been slashing again (Stuart Bailie of *NME* witnessed fresh scars all over Richey's arms), he generally seemed to be getting better, give or take a few eccentricities: he had begun insisting on being called Richard. He was, at least, eating properly, and was actually making an effort to learn the songs.

Not that he wasn't still prone to 'days of wobbliness', as James put it. At a photo shoot for a *Select* porn issue, he expressed deep reservations at being asked to paint on the old eyeliner one more time and sprawl provocatively on a studio floor covered with hand-picked erotica. By the end, he was almost in tears. The line from 'Yes' that ran 'the only way to gain approval is by exploiting the very thing that cheapens me' was beginning to make sense.

Still, it was mutually agreed that Richey should come on the French tour – the reasoning being that, even if he wasn't getting noticeably better or worse, at least his mates could keep an eye on him. The tour itself was not a particularly successful one, the French audiences seeming distinctly underwhelmed by the Manics. 'You develop an instinct for when a whole country doesn't get it,' James told *Melody Maker*. 'If there was any way we could have done this tour and bypassed France, we would have done.' However, Richey's colleagues believed the experience did him good: he seemed to be happier.

Throughout the jaunt, Richey was a ghost member of the Manics. In the dead hours before and after gigs, while the crew played pool or table football, Richey would pass through unnoticed. Nobody caught his eye; nobody spoke to him. When he wasn't around, his absence wasn't commented upon. Most of the time, he stayed locked away on the tour bus, like the mad aunt in the attic in a Hammer horror movie. He would pass his time listening to the *Hole* album, choosing the Manics' set, and adorning their set lists with ornate doodlings and literary quotes (Shelley: 'When will return the glory of your prime?/No more/Oh, never more!'). He was able to ensure that the full gravitas of *The Holy Bible* carried through into the live show: the set may have blazed out of the blocks with 'P.C.P.', 'Faster' and 'Revol', but before long it would grind into 'The Intense Humming of Evil'.

Onstage, Richey barely moved, apparently concentrating on his guitar parts, which were now turned up moderately high in the mix. He was even seen soundchecking. He was now providing what James would affectionately describe to the sound engineer as 'a bit of clatter behind me'. Richey himself told *Time Out*'s Peter Paphides: 'I can play a bit but, compared to James, I can't play much at all. Most people

1. PCP
2. FASTER
3. REVOL
4. THE INTENSE HUMMING OF EVIL
5. YES
6. MOTOWN JUNK
7. SHE IS SUFFERING
8. PENNYROYALTY
9. REPEAT
10. YOU LOVE US
– BORDEAUX –

"I ALSO HAD NIGHTMARES. SOMEHOW ALL THE FEELINGS I DIDN'T FEEL WHEN EACH THING HAD ACTUALLY HAPPENED TO ME I DID FEEL WHEN I SLEPT." —ANDREA DWORKIN.

Richey-penned set list, France 1994.

think I go onstage and I'm not even plugged in at the back, but I do actually make a noise. Either that or there's someone behind the curtain, crouched down playing my bits.'

At one show, he smashed his guitar so enthusiastically that he bloodied his nose in the process. He wasn't slashing, though. Believing that he had let the band down badly in the past, he tried to maintain some self-discipline. 'The first day,' said James, 'I was really, really nervous. I was so on edge, I kept thinking: "If you cut yourself up now, son, everything will be wasted." He has wanted to cut himself on this tour already, but hasn't. And that's a first.'

'It was Christianity which first painted the devil on the world's wall; it was Christianity which first brought sin into the world. Belief in the cure which it offered has now been shaken to its deepest roots; but belief in the sickness which it taught and propagated continues to exist' – FRIEDRICH NIETZSCHE

There was increasing evidence that Richey had indeed found God in The Priory. He carried a book of biblical quotes everywhere and chose a different motto to live by each day, recited prayers before each gig, painted the words 'LOVE' and 'HATE' on his knuckles (another Priory ritual) where once, in happier times, he had painted 'Icon', and said that he wished he'd written 'The Cross', Prince & The Revolution's Christian rock plodder. His colleagues, however, are far from convinced that he truly believed it all.

Religious imagery had always been central to the Manics' iconography (right down to the 'Preachers' in their name). Both religion and pop, as the Manics understood, rely on irrationalist idolatry. 'Whatever percentage aren't going to church nowadays,' Richey told me, 'it's still the ultimate icon.' Nicky pointed out that: 'In every hotel room in the world, the only constant is the Holy Bible.'

But whereas religion had never been a major part of Nicky's life, it was deeply ingrained in Richey's psyche. He had always respected parts of the Bible, particularly the passages in Isaiah concerned with misjudging people. Other parts, he said, like the turn-the-other-cheek message of Luke, chapter VI, he had never been able to take on board. Thus, a man who could write a song as vehemently secular as 'Crucifix Kiss' and quote Sylvia Plath's 'I talk to God but the sky is empty' on a record sleeve could just as easily find himself, if not exactly born again, then certainly a latent convert.

Ultimately, this was a conflict Richey would never fully resolve. The Priory's crypto-religious methods had left him confused rather than cured.

The Holy Bible – the rock record, that is – had not been selling very well at all, despite widespread critical acclaim. On 3 October, to boost its profile, Epic released one of the less-harrowing tracks, 'She Is Suffering', as a single. An incredible three separate CD versions were made available, including mixes of 'Faster' and 'La Tristesse Durera' by The Dust Brothers (later to become the Chemical Brothers), a pair of former history students turned dance *cognoscenti* whom James knew through the Heavenly Social clubland clique. The other tracks were a ponderous strum-fest called 'Love Torn Us Under' and two live covers, 'The Drowners' and 'Stay with Me', with Bernard Butler from the Imperial Cancer benefit. Cursed with a video which Nicky described as 'absolute shite beyond belief' (lots of black-and-white shots of women looking miserable), even a beautiful acoustic rendition by Nicky and James on MTV could not push the single any higher than No. 25 in the charts.

By this time the Manics were back in the UK, and began a national tour on 5 October at Glasgow Barrowlands, supported by Sleeper and Dub War. There were some eternally memorable shows, including one which produced audience delirium at Wolverhampton Civic Hall, and a perspiration-drenched final date on 20 October at Cardiff Astoria, a way-too-small pressure cooker of a nightclub (even the chrome pillars seemed to be sweating). The set list, kicking off with 'Revol' (like 'P.C.P.', an excellent choice of curtain-raiser), leant heavily on *The Holy Bible*, but also featured an unaccompanied James Dean Bradfield rendition of Burt Bacharach's 'Raindrops Keep Falling on My Head' from *Butch Cassidy and the Sundance Kid*. Picture Paul Newman and Robert Redford, knowing that the game is up and that the Bolivian army is about to turn them into bullet pizza, leaping into that final poignant freeze-frame . . . and let the analogies flow.

The behaviour of the more obsessive kind of Richey fan, presented with their hero for the first time since his sojourn in The Priory, became more extreme than ever: breaking into his hotel room, dressing in his clothes, drinking from his stale coffee cup, stealing his used bars of soap – even rolling around in the bed he slept in. But even the sane spectator's gaze couldn't help being drawn towards Richey in morbid fascination. 'How unwell is he? Will he fuck up tonight, before our very eyes?' The truth was that Edwards's appearance had acquired a horrific glamour. It seems almost perverted to say so, but Richey looked simultaneously bloody awful and bloody fantastic. His finest features – that methadone-glossy hair, the hungry jawline, that sparkle of destiny in the eyes – were still intact. But draped in a ten-sizes-too-big workman's boiler suit or in a 'THEY FUCK YOU UP, YOUR MUM AND DAD' T-shirt (the first line of Larkin's 'This Be the Verse'), with an outrageous bottle-ginger rent-boy fringe, a thick brushstroke of eyeshadow over each eye, a streak of pink lipstick on his cheek, stubble like coal-miner's dust all over his face, and a solitary silver hoop in one ear, he looked uncannily like John Hurt as Quentin Crisp in *The Naked Civil Servant*. Plus, it must be said, Andy Pandy.

At around this time, Caitlin Moran of *The Times* described Richey as '. . . the most untouchably beautiful person I have ever seen in my life. His hair has that "rock-star" glow. His skin is translucent, and punctured only by two huge, soft-brown Bambi eyes. He has the kind of bone structure that would make Kate Moss's agent weep. This is beauty beyond lust.' And yet, his teeth, already yellowed by nicotine, showed the telltale decay caused by a bulimic's regurgitated stomach acids; his arms were dappled with calluses whose vintage varied from seven years to the previous day; and those eyes were less Bambi-cute, more rabbit-in-the-headlights terrified.

It was a precarious tightrope act, but compelling to watch. Richey was frighteningly thin (straight-up/straight-down, no arse, prod him and he'd snap), but – and this was wonderful – he was *posing* again. No one threw guitar hero shapes quite like Richey Edwards. Sometimes, he would suddenly look uncertain (in *NME*'s Stuart Bailie's marvellous phrase, the Insecurity of the First World), glancing around to Nicky, James and Sean for reassurance, mouthing the words silently to himself as if they were his personal epitaphs. Then, just as suddenly, he would turn into Old Richey and hurl his guitar into an amp stack.

His curious exhibitionism perplexed his band-mates, as Nicky later revealed. 'It's a well-known fact that anorexics try to cover up their condition with baggy clothes all the time but, on the first day of the British tour, Richey walks in and he's wearing the tightest pair of girl's leggings that I've ever seen in my life. He still wanted the rest of the world to know that he was completely fucked up. Everyone knew already. I said, "Why are you doing that? You haven't got to prove to the world how fucked up you are!"'

The Twelve-Step Programme, clearly, hadn't completely diminished Richey's vanity. In Sheffield, he embroidered his arms with three new tattoos to join his existing 'Useless Generation'. There were two intricate circular diagrams, one with the words Hemisphere, Jerusalem, Land, Water, Hemisphere, Hell, Mount and Purgatory (apparently derived from the seven concentric circles of Hell as depicted in Dante's *Inferno*), the other bearing the names Caina, Antendra, Ptolomae and Judecca, with the condemning additions 'Traitors to their Lovers, Traitors to their Guests, Traitors to their Country, Traitors to their Kindred'. Obscure biblical/classical references, and more fuel to the rumour that Richey had found God in The Priory. The third tattoo read 'I'll surf this beach', a quote from *Apocalypse Now*.

Coppola's Vietnam epic had by now annexed Edwards's imagination. In Cardiff, the Manics' dressing-room was a dimly lit cavern of green-and-red camouflage netting, in which Richey could be found, lurking in the furthest recesses, holding court like Colonel Kurtz. He had also taken to carrying around exactly the same model of camera as does the crazed photojournalist, played by Dennis Hopper, in *Apocalypse Now*. There was no evidence that Richey's fascination with the art form of photography, or his ownership of the necessary equipment, would lead to a mastery of the technique – but then the same could be said of his love of rock 'n' roll.

Meanwhile, the media fascination with him was reaching fever pitch. Over the next six months, a mini-industry thrived around what was crassly termed the 'Culture of Despair'. Music papers and Manics fanzines alike were filled with people claiming they 'knew how he felt' and, for some idiot style-chasers, it was fashionable to be fucked up: rehab was the new rock 'n' roll, detox the new drugs, and the Betty Ford Clinic the hippest club in the world. In a cover story entitled 'Manic Depression', *Melody Maker* made the timely point that, while it may be an attractive cultural myth that genius is pain, suffering should not be aspired to: 'There's nothing wrong with wanting to be like Kurt or Richey – eloquent, charismatic and glamorous figures both. But it is wrong to want to feel like them, and there's a big difference. If you already do feel like either of them, you'll know that.'

'It's been a drama-queen year, and I thought this would be a mustard-cardy year, kind of relaxed. but it was more a beer-gut year, and I ended up regressing' – JAMES, *SELECT*

The soulless chrome-and-mirror financial ghost town of Frankfurt-am-Main provided the launchpad for another Manics support tour on 7 November, this time with Suede. Richey had been an admirer of Suede from the time of its début single, 'The Drowners', and the two bands had many similarities. Both had emerged in the early 90s as a glamorous, intelligent British alternative to grimy US grunge, and both had barely survived career-threatening difficulties (Suede's guitarist and co-songwriter Bernard Butler had recently quit amid much acrimony, and had been replaced by Richard Oakes, an unknown seventeen-year-old).

From almost every perspective, whether professional or personal, the tour was a disaster. Once again, the Europeans didn't appear to 'get' the Manics. On one occasion, they were not even given the chance to do so: at the Lyon Transbordeur, a promoter's mix-up meant that the Manics took the stage half an hour before the venue's advertised opening time. The audience comprised myself, *Melody Maker* photographer Tom Sheehan, members of Suede, and the Manics' loyal road crew. On a personal level, Nicky had lost his suitcase, missed his wife Rachel desperately, developed a thyroid cyst on his neck (possibly a side-effect of pills he was taking for other ailments) and had to fly home mid-tour for treatment. It was, he said, 'four weeks of Hell', and 'probably the worst time of my life'. James felt 'like a caged animal' (more than once, I saw him punching the walls in rage), and the tour was no picnic for Sean, either. Worst of all, it was extremely damaging to Richey's state of mind. 'In retrospect,' Sean told Paul Moody of *Dazed & Confused*, 'I think it was the wrong decision, because touring, especially on that European tour with Suede, proved to be very detrimental to his health and personality.'

When he was not onstage, Richey spent almost all his time in the back of the tour bus, wrapped in a blanket like a convalescing war veteran, playing soccer on the Sega, and ostentatiously crumbling chocolate in a bowl (to show that this was all the sustenance he needed). The Manics masked the seriousness of the situation with typical gallows humour, heckling Richey with cries of 'Mr Blobby!' at a photo shoot, and mocking his 'fat arse'. Even Richey could see the funny side, reading a joke about anorexia and Slimfast aloud from a magazine.

Richey had successfully beaten the bottle, but was getting through thirty cups of coffee and 65 cigarettes a day instead and was, according to Nicky, 'on the verge of madness . . . fucked out of his mind'. The rest of the band needed alcohol to alleviate the stress. 'James was pissed all the time,' said Sean, 'and stayed in bed till five. I had my moments.' Yet it was always a case of *pas devant l'enfant* – Nicky, James and Sean never drank in front of Richey. 'We have to watch how we govern ourselves now,' said James. 'Without being corny, Richey and I were, if not quite birding and boozing buddies, something like that. We'd go out and stay up after gigs. We can't do that now. It's just not on the agenda. We don't want to be unfeeling dickheads.'

In fact, James went drinking on his own, often staying up all night and not resurfacing until 7 p.m, just before showtime. That was OK, he reckoned – the others, he was convinced, disliked his company anyway. After the show at the Bataclan in Paris, I joined him as he headed out for a cathartic drinking session, running in front of cars on the Boulevard de Rochechouart and growling at the traffic. The evening ended with a vignette which provided a beautiful précis of the situation. While James, myself and various record-company types drank into the early hours at the legendary Pigalle bar, Lili La Tigresse, the Manics' tour bus quietly pulled up outside, Nicky and Richey sleeping soundly within.

Richey, never a believer in the old one about travel broadening the mind, rarely bothered to explore the culture of foreign cities. 'It's really patronising to spend one day somewhere,' he told me, 'and say "I really understand this city." Like Norway: "Well, they've got Ibsen, but on the other hand they've got whaling."' The band did its best to make the Kafka-esque absurdity of the touring ritual as painless as possible. 'Me and Richey stayed in a Hotel Ibis every night,' Nicky later told *Select*. 'The only nice thing was waking up together and having breakfast together, with a bit of French bread and apricot jam. That was the only smidgeon of normality during the whole tour.'

Despite this, there were increasing signs that Richey was unready for it all, and his behaviour began to deteriorate in familiar patterns (one member of the Manics' entourage quit at the end of the tour, citing the grounds that having to kick down a toilet door and find Richey's body was not part of his job description). Richey had long been intrigued by Steve Clark, the troubled Def Leppard guitarist who once smashed his fingers on a washbasin so that he wouldn't have to go onstage. In apparent emulation, Richey bought a butcher's meat cleaver on the Suede tour, with the horrific intention of hacking off his own fingers (how he would have managed to mutilate his other hand remains unclear). Thankfully he was dissuaded, and the cleaver confiscated.

Nicky expressed his unhappiness in a more peaceful manner, but was equally distressed. One night, he told James that he'd had enough and wanted to quit the band. James was surprisingly agreeable to the idea, but proceeded to get blind drunk that night and by morning had forgotten the conversation ever taking place. 'He went out, got wazzed out of his brain and couldn't even fucking remember what I'd said to him,' Wire later told *Select*. 'Everybody was totally oblivious to everybody else's needs.'

In the afternoon before the Paris show, I borrowed the Manics for a *Melody Maker* photo shoot in a location I considered somehow appropriate: the catacombs. Known as L'Empire des Morts, the catacombs comprise two miles of subterranean tunnels whose walls are made up of the femurs and skulls of the proletariat of Napoleonic Paris, reinterred in nameless piles to make room for the artists and aristocrats in Montparnasse cemetery up above.

If you see one human skull, stained brown by the now-rotted flesh, the natural response is shock. If you see 10,000 skulls, you quickly become desensitised. I had already visited the catacombs, so I knew what to expect, but watching the Manics' differing reactions as I led them through the labyrinthine corridors of human remains was fascinating. The two members of the band's musical wing were shocked by the death all around them, James worrying about bringing on some sort of Egyptian-style curse, Sean having Auschwitz flashbacks. Nicky, typically, resorted to humour: 'It looks like a Nutty Bar . . . No, actually it's more like Kellogg's Honey Nut Loops.' Richey, at first, was deeply phobic and lagged several yards behind the rest of us, but, gradually, he forced himself to confront his fears. The first step was casually to rap his knuckles on a skull. A few minutes later, I turned around just in time to catch him pushing his face near another skull's lifeless jaw, smiling to himself, and kissing it.

The Manics' set in Amsterdam was, by common consent within the band, 'a crap show'. In the dressing-room, everyone sat in depressed silence except Richey, who seemed oddly happy. Nicky lifted up Edwards's shirt and was distraught to discover that he had carved a vertical slash down his chest. The local press was due to arrive at any minute, but Sean, the consummate professional, took the journalists to a club instead, pretending that nothing had happened. Nicky, meanwhile, sat Richey down in his hotel room and talked the situation through: why was he doing this?

The situation came to a head – literally – back in Germany. The show in Hamburg on 13 December was, as far as the Manics were concerned, the last date. The band's live agent had offered them further dates in Prague and Vienna, and Richey, strangely, was all for continuing, but he was overruled. Nicky and Sean couldn't face any more. It proved to be the right decision. The morning after the Hamburg show, Nicky awoke to find Richey outside the hotel, banging his face against the wall, blood running down his cheeks, repeating the words 'I want to go home' over and over again, like Dorothy in *The Wizard of Oz*. In that instant, the tour was finished.

'The passion for destruction is a creative joy' – PARISIAN GRAFFITO, MAY 1968

And yet it was in a perversely confident frame of mind that Manic Street Preachers arrived back home from their European nightmare. After all, if they could survive that . . .

Their final public engagements of the year were a trio of pre-Christmas dates in London at the Astoria Theatre on 19, 20 and 21 December. As anyone privileged to attend even one of these shows can attest, they were three of the most extraordinary rock 'n' roll shows the capital has ever seen. The atmosphere inside the Astoria was remarkable. The warmth of fan-love which greeted the band was heightened by a note of nervous tension so powerful you could almost taste it. Nobody knew what to expect. What we witnessed, in restrospect, was the absolute climax of Manic Street

SJM CONCERTS present

MANIC STREET PREACHERS

+ *Special Guests*

MONDAY 19th DECEMBER 1994
DOORS 7:00pm
Tickets £9.00 (In Advance)
THE ASTORIA
157 CHARING CROSS ROAD
LONDON   TEL:- 071 434 0404

01172

Preachers Mk. 1. Here was a band firing on all cylinders, with every element – music, manifesto, image, excitement – peaking in one synchronised tumult. They were, said *NME*, 'the only band on earth to radiate intelligence like Stephen Hawking squared AND provide dumb rock thrills like a hundred Axl Roses'.

There was an indefinable mood of finality about the whole thing (as well as the hits and *The Holy Bible*, the Manics were playing long-lost Heavenly B-sides, which seemed somehow ominous). Their three breathtaking sets were, by turns, comic and dramatic, emotionally draining and hilariously funny. Comedy was an attribute which I had hitherto never attached to the Manics (who had always had a sense of their own ridiculousness but, crucially, no sense of irony whatsoever). When, at the suggestion of a female friend, James played an unaccompanied version of Art Garfunkel's 'Bright Eyes', your first reaction may have been a chuckle at the thought of cartoon rabbits; yet it was in such an intensified atmosphere that, as soon as he got to the line about 'following the river of death downstream', you were choking back the tears (incidentally, the song was originally written by *Wombles* songwriter Mike Batt, about the death of his father). Even the spectacle of James in a Santa hat singing Wham!'s 'Last Christmas' (and, as is his tendency when performing covers, having neglected to learn the words first) was oddly touching in the circumstances.

Acoustic interludes aside, the Manics – lean and battle-fit in blacks and combats – tore through their set with do-or-die velocity. There was a physical explanation for this: for three nights running, the sound through the Astoria's onstage monitors reached dangerous frequencies, and engineers seemed unable to fix it (simply turning the volume down didn't work). As a result, the band's noses kept bleeding uncontrollably. James, in particular, was thoroughly pissed off. Each night they left stage in a fraught, hyped-up state of mind, with the exception of Richey who, perhaps predictably, loved it.

The final night was the most thrilling and memorable of all, and mostly for the encore. 'You Love Us' disintegrated into the traditional orgy of destruction but, this time, the sound of breaking wood was accompanied by the tinkle of glass and LED monitors. The foursome were sacrificing their real equipment, not the cheap versions they usually trashed. The total bill came to over £8,000. 'If we could have,' Sean told *Select*, 'we'd have trashed everything into tiny pieces and said: "That is *it*. We can't do any more. We haven't got any instruments to play, we haven't got a stage to play on. That is it."' It was a cathartic, symbolic, but above all *joyous* act. 'That last five minutes of the last gig when we smashed eight grand's worth of gear and lights were five of the best minutes I've ever had in my life,' Nicky enthused to *NME*. 'It was just brilliant. We were transported back to the days of "Motown Junk". Beautiful. It meant more than any of the songs. Until we saw the bill.'

First to bite the dust was Nicky's Fender Jazz bass. Next, James, who had been performing the song directly towards his band-mates with his back to the audience, snapped his guitar in two and stormed off, declaring: 'I fucking hate that song anyway.' Richey, meanwhile, had been pummelling his forehead repeatedly against the metal microphone grille until its criss-cross pattern was imprinted on his bleeding brow, mouthing the words silently as he did so. By the time Wire and Bradfield had left the stage, Edwards was beating himself about the head with the splintered neck of a guitar. For an instant, with a sickly grin – the same grin which had demonised his face that night in Bangkok when he slashed his torso with knives given by a fan – Richey paused in front of Sean's drum riser. He hesitated for a few seconds, gaining resolve, before finally – and much to Sean's apparent annoyance – divebombing balletically into the precious Yamaha 9000 drumkit.

Then he was gone. I haven't seen him since.

g)I hurt myself to get pain out

(RICHEY EDWARDS AND SELF-HARM)

'Once, I remember well, my life was a feast where all hearts opened and all wines flowed. Alas the gospel has gone by! Suppose damnation were eternal! Then a man who would mutilate himself is well damned, isn't he?' – ARTHUR RIMBAUD; SCRAWLED ON RICHEY EDWARDS'S BOILER SUIT, PARIS, NOVEMBER 1994

ROSE OF LIMA (1586–1617)
'Born at Lima (Peru) of a Spanish family of moderate wealth, subsequently impoverished through unsuccessful speculation in the mines, she chose not to marry in spite of parental persuasion, but took a vow of virginity. Extreme forms of penance, sometimes self-inflicted, matched the love of God which radiated from her presence to those who came into contact with her. She lived as a recluse in a hut in the garden and experienced both trials and consolations of an extraordinary kind. After a long illness which seems to have had psychological as well as physical elements, she died at the age of thirty-one. Perhaps her life is best understood as an attempt to make reparation for the widespread sin and corruption in contemporary society.' – OXFORD DICTIONARY OF SAINTS

WHETHER RICHEY EDWARDS WAS FAMILIAR with Rose of Lima is doubtful – he grew up a Methodist, not a Catholic – but the similarities between their lives are uncanny.

If, in his absence, Richey has arguably become something of a Christ figure (see Chapter 9), towards the end of his known existence he was already well on the way to canonisation. The details of Richey's life and, more importantly, the *reactions of others to it*, betray many of the hallmarks of saintliness – for sainthood (or, to be more specific, martyrdom) entails a great deal of pain. Saints, typically, need to have *suffered*. By this logic, every time Richey took a blade to his flesh, he was polishing his halo.

There are broadly two classifications of saint: those who lived lives of pious solitude, and those who ventured into the world to amass acolytes and disciples.

To a degree, Richey Edwards straddles both categories, but it is the latter – his Pied Piper/*Life of Brian* ability to inspire imitative behaviour – which has, literally, left the deepest scars.

Young, Pretty & Fucked fanzine editor Beeza Seed raged against the auto-abusive Cult of Richey: 'I'm sick of seeing fans with "4 REAL" carved into their arms, or hearing of shaven-headed fans eating virtually nothing, wallowing in despair AND ENJOYING IT!'

In the same issue, Dave, aged nineteen, wrote: 'Richey Edwards is to blame for a whole generation of kids thinking it's cool to be a loser. All this cutting your arms is bollocks. If it's that bad, cut your throat, mate, don't bore us with it all! At the very least, switch role models from Richey to James, and have a pie.'

Tessa Norton of *Firecracker* fanzine agrees: 'The Cult of Richey is very insular, focusing on your own problems. It's almost a rivalry syndrome: "Oh, my sore throat's worse than yours." It's insulting to people who genuinely do have problems. It's like going up to a disabled person and cutting your leg off.'

'Scratch my leg with a rusty nail/Sadly, it heals' – 'DIE IN THE SUMMERTIME'

The Manics themselves felt partly responsible. As Sean told *NME*: 'A lot of the stuff on *The Holy Bible*, I feel that it's done a lot of harm rather than good in some cases, just in terms of self-abuse.' It was understandable that the band should have negative feelings towards this phenomenon. After Richey's disappearance, many slashers continued to send disturbing letters to the remaining Manics, often written in their own blood ('You just feel powerless to help these people,' said Nicky), until it reached the point where Caffy St Luce had to stop passing them on.

And Sean did have a point. Some indubitably did it for fashion reasons. Others, perhaps, were merely diverted into slashing from other forms of self-abuse: if it hadn't been for Richey's example, they might have headed for drugs, anorexia or alcohol instead (admittedly, at least two of these are also possible outcomes of Richey-worship). The tabloids, too, had at least a germ of a point with their lurid 'Slasher Cult of Rock Star Richey' exposés.

Invariably, though, it was cart-before-horse, egg-before-chicken stuff: cause and effect were the wrong way around. Although much of the slasher blood spilt in 1994/95 doubtless came from the veins of self-dramatising wannabes (at the height of The Troubles, one individual was advertising a 'self-abuse autobiography' alongside the usual MSP-zines in the *Select* classifieds), a great many cases, it must be acknowledged, were '4 REAL'.

Two separate television documentaries on self-harm focused on Manics fans. *Inside Out* (Channel Four, 1995) dealt with MSP superfan Gill Armstrong, while *Damage* (Channel Five, 1997) featured Shara, a Berkhamsted teenager with an enormous tattoo of Richey's face across her stomach. Like hundreds, maybe thousands, of others, they didn't cut their arms because Richey did it – they empathised with Richey because they were already cutting their arms (and gained the courage to 'out' themselves as a result).

'At a time when I felt alone and depressed,' wrote Helen of Ashford on the *Melody Maker* letters page, 'it was comforting to know that someone out there felt the same . . . he hasn't encouraged me to harm myself, he's just made me feel less alone.' The music papers were inundated with 'I thought I was weird for doing it' letters from people Richey had helped to come out of the cutting closet (the knife drawer?). Sometimes the empathy was cultural as well as personal. As one Thai fan wrote in *NME*: 'We understand why Richey cut his arm. Part of our culture is to cut ourselves, out of frustration.'

Although Richey was not the first celebrity cutter (in 1995, following years of speculation, Princess Diana revealed that she had used self-harm as a means of alleviating stress during her marriage to Prince Charles), he was the first with whom young sufferers could identify. He even helped some to stop altogether. I remember opening the mail at *Melody Maker* to find razor blades from former self-mutilators, asking us to dispose of them on their behalf.

Self-mutilation has been described as 'the hidden epidemic of the 90s'. It was once estimated that seven out of every one thousand Americans, almost all of them female, regularly slash themselves. In a survey in the UK, it was discovered that an estimated fifteen thousand people cut, burn and bruise themselves, although, since most keep their behaviour private, the true figure could be higher. Again, the perpetrators are mainly women (almost twice as many as men). The reason is that women are more likely to internalise problems and to exact punishment upon themselves, whereas men release their anger on others.

In this respect, as in so many others, Richey Edwards was a big girl. 'I've never hit anybody in my life,' he once claimed. 'I never would, and the only way I could make a point was by hurting myself.' Richey was a believer in the underrated British virtue of repression, reserve and keeping it all bottled up. 'I'm too polite,' he said, 'and I find that I can't express what I feel when I'm pissed off. I have these frustrations and it's the only thing I can do that will make me feel better.' He also, perhaps strangely, perceived social class as a factor: 'Working-class resentment is always turned on itself. Nobody seems to realise that.'

Although most mutilators are women, it is men who are more prone to absolute self-destruction, i.e. to suicide. One of the most common misconceptions about self-harm is that it constitutes direct evidence of suicidal tendencies. Dr Michael Crowe of Bethlam Hospital, Kent, whose controversial methods include actually allowing patients to cut, insists: 'Cutting is usually not suicidal in nature.' Moreover, Richey's self-destructiveness had clearly defined limits. To be blunt about it . . . he never touched his face, did he?

'All I want is for this pain to seem purposeful' – ELIZABETH WURTZEL, *PROZAC NATION*

One theory has it that self-mutilation has roots in childhood. Children are taught from an early age to associate wrongdoing with punishment in the form of pain, and are also aware that injury elicits attention from adults.

And attention – for the look-at-me fakers and the real sufferers alike – is crucial. Just as the scars of stigmatists like Padre Pio are a physical manifestation of their piety, so the scars of self-mutilators are evidence of their internal pain. 'If I've got these scars on my arm,' wrote one, 'there must be something properly wrong.' As Dr Alan Cockett of Orchard Lodge, Somerset, explained on the Channel Five *Damage* documentary: 'It's a signal to the outside world that "I am in pain and nothing you have given me so far has helped."' This doesn't always have the desired effect. According to Emma Borton of the Samaritans: 'Self-inflicted pain focuses inexpressible emotional pain. But it is a non-expressive verbal scream that can make others shut their eyes in horror and incomprehension.'

In this respect, Richey was unusual. Although the '4 REAL' incident had had plenty to do with attention (Sony even used photos of the wounds to attract attention in America), in general the scars on his arms – which one writer described as 'a lurid-pink testimony to a sustained programme of self-mutilation' – were not a cry for help. 'They're just my war wounds,' he joked, making light of the carnage. On the contrary. As James Dean Bradfield said at the time: 'It's almost like a badge to show that he's emotionally strong enough to deal with problems in his own way' – a subtle but vital distinction between Richey and the 'look at me, I'm suffering' school.

Vincent Van Gogh, asked why he had shot himself in the groin, replied: 'I am free to do what I want with my own body.' Richey Edwards, asked why he lacerated his arms, replied: 'Where is the rule that the body is sacred – thou cannot mark thine own skin?'

Like tattooing, piercing, branding and any other kind of corporeal modification, self-harm is partially a form of *physical graffiti*, a way of vandalising nature, defiling and disfiguring the perfection your mother brought into the world, a fuck-you to God. Richey described pierced/tattooed Modern Primitive types – wrongly, in my view – as 'just walking mathematicians of their own misery'. Count the holes, count the pain? That is rarely the spirit in which it is intended. Rather, it is the bodily equivalent of Marcel Duchamp scrawling a moustache on the *Mona Lisa*'s face.

In all probability, there are as many reasons for self-mutilation as there are self-mutilators. For some, it is all about *pain management*. 'Physical pain can be dealt with,' wrote one slasher. 'I know the cause, I know it's going to stop eventually, and, while I'm in physical pain, the emotional pain lessens.' Others say they find the sight of blood reassuring – it reminds them that they are 'real', alive (controlled blood-letting is known to have a calming effect, causing a reduction in heart rate).

So what was Richey's bag exactly? He once claimed – and this, apparently, is quite common – that he didn't actually feel *pain* while cutting, in the traditional sense of intense displeasure. Could it have spilt over into actual pleasure?

> '*An angel's gold spear pierced my heart. The utmost pain, the sweetest pleasure. I desired the pain to last into infinity. It was the sweetest caressing of the soul by God*' – BERNINI, *LIFE OF ST THERESA*

The term 'masochism' is derived from Leopold Von Sacher Masoch, the nineteenth-century Austrian novelist who wrote on the subject of what he described as 'the euphoric agony'.

It was another famous masochist, French journalist/art critic/novelist Octave Mirbeau, who captured Richey Edwards's imagination. In his classic 1899 text, *Le Jardin des Supplices* (*The Torture Garden*), Mirbeau, who (like Richey) oscillated between extreme right and anarchist left politics, used decadent sadism as an ironic metaphor for power relations in society.

If Richey – who banged his forehead against walls, enjoyed being hit on the head, and empathised with the defendants in the Justice Templeman case (they were imprisoned for taking part in consenting acts of sado-masochism) – was a masochist, it was not in any clichéd 'bring out the gimp' sense. He was a passive masochist: he quite liked the idea of being beaten up, he once told me, and wouldn't raise a hand to defend himself.

For Mirbeau, masochism wasn't primarily about sex. But for Edwards . . . speaking to *Select* about his mania for maiming in 1994, he famously said: 'I find it attractive. I find it . . . sexual.' He once compared cutting to '. . . when the air is really muggy and a good thunderstorm clears the air'. The meteorological nature of the metaphor clouds its underlying sexual subtext, but it is definitely there. For men, ejaculation is literally about *release*, and it is well known that a quasi-sexual pleasure can be gained by holding in urine until it is actually painful, then pissing it out. In a similar way, slashers often 'save up' their feelings of frustration for a cutting binge.

Hence Saint Richey's most damaging legacy: he made cutting oneself *sexy*.*

Helplines
The Bristol Crisis Centre Helpline (available Friday and Saturday 9 p.m.–12.30 a.m.), tel: 0117-9251119.
The Self Harm Association, 526 Harrow Road, London W9 3AT, tel: 0171-625 5683.

Recommended reading: *Women and Self-Injury* by Lois Arnold

*To which one must add a coda which ought perhaps to be attached, like a Parental Advisory sticker, to every interview, photograph and record Richey Edwards ever made:
DON'T TRY THIS AT HOME.

8. ARCHIVES OF PAIN

'There's no part of my body that has not been used' – 'YES'

I N NOVEMBER 1994, I joined the Manics on their European tour in order to cover two French dates, Lyon Transbordeur and Paris Bataclan, for *Melody Maker*. There was no promise of an interview; a basic live review/on-the-road piece was all that I was expected to deliver. In Lyon, I tentatively asked Nicky whether he thought Richey might consent to being interviewed alone. By the time I reached Paris, I was told that the answer was yes.

Looking back, the aspects which still astonish me are the absolute clarity with which Richey was able to analyse his problems, and his capacity for keeping a detached perspective on his illness – to act as doctor and patient at the same time. His intellect, as ever, made me feel pathetically inferior; his own low self-esteem and humility made me feel humbled in turn. I came home with enough material for two cover stories, and, in my opinion, the best interview of my journalistic career. A full transcript follows.

'I'm weak, all my life I've felt weak compared to other people, if they want to crush me they can – but I know I can do things that other people can't.'

THE HORROR, THE HORROR
I have been summoned.

It's pitch dark in here. There has been a power failure on the silver Phoenix tour bus, and I am led stumbling to the back. What little light remains in the Rue de Voltaire outside is screened by heavy velvet curtains. Through a tiny gap, Richey Edwards's face is intermittently illuminated by a flickering neon sign. I feel like I've walked into the scene in *Apocalypse Now* when Martin Sheen finally meets Brando's Colonel Kurtz.

'Hello, Simon. I heard you wanted a chat.'

PEOPLE SEND POSTCARDS, AND THEY ALL HOPE I'M FEELING WELL
I hear you think you have been misrepresented.

'Um . . . I wouldn't say any more than usual. I can't think of anything specifically. It's difficult for me to talk about something like that without seeming really petty.'

The way it all blew up in the media, it would be easy to imagine that you just suddenly flipped out and lost it one day, spent two months as a complete nutter, then, equally suddenly, you were cured. Presumably it's a little more gradual than that.

'I think that is an assumption that an awful lot of people do make, and it's completely wrong. That never happens. You don't wake up one morning and say: "Oh, bad day!", and, like, here we go. It is something very gradual, and I don't think you even realise what's really happening. You've got a different perspective on yourself and what's actually going on. It's fairly difficult to explain.

It just comes to a point where . . . your mind thinks that it can cope but maybe your body can't carry on. You can't physically do anything, which is what happens: you actually can't move. And again, people think, at the minute you check out, everything's OK. Which it's not. At all. I've got a good smile . . .'

He smiles a good smile.

'. . . Not as good as Nick's, admittedly. With him, everything's always OK, everything's all right, everything's fine. That's just the way it is. With most people, it's not worth saying how you really think, feel. People say: "How are you?" and if you go: "Actually, I'm fucking feeling shit", they don't wanna know. So instead it"s: "Feeling all right. Feeling fine." That's just the way everyone does it, me included.'

It saves a lot of embarrassed silences.

'Yeah, of course.'

INSANITY #1: I'VE BEEN TOO HONEST WITH MYSELF, I SHOULD HAVE LIED LIKE EVERYONE ELSE

I suppose I veer towards the liberal, romantic view of madness: that people who are unusually sensitive and creative are especially prone, and are misdiagnosed as 'insane'.

'Um, I don't think . . . I mean . . . a lot of letters I've got have said: "Oh, it's natural, it always happens to poets." Which is fucking bullshit. When you're in the places I've been in, the first place especially [Whitchurch Hospital in Cardiff], it's just any job, any occupation. Housewife, bricklayer, plumber, somebody who works for South Wales Electricity Board, whatever. It doesn't pick or choose people who pick up a pen. When you write something down, it's not like, here we go. It's something nobody really knows anything about, apart from that some things work and some things don't, to stabilise you again. It's very romantic to think: "I'm a tortured writer", but mental institutions are not full of people in bands. They're full of people with so-called normal jobs. Or *were* full. 68,000 beds have been closed down in the last couple of years, which I wouldn't have been aware of unless I was actually in one.'

I often think that the 'insane' are those who have ceased to block out thoughts, which most of us do, to be able to get on with life. We're all borderline cases, just about holding it together.

'I think people who get through the day, every day, are far stronger than me. Getting completely paranoidly – if there's such a word as "paranoidly" – upset about tiny little things is nonsense. Maybe I'm in the luxurious position of not allowing that to worry me, because I haven't got children to feed, I haven't got payments to make to an ex-wife, I haven't got to worry about my rent or my mortgage. So my mind is not cluttered with the day-to-day necessities of staying alive. I'm not worried about: "If I don't pay this bill today, the gas is gonna get cut off." Because I just chuck some money to somebody, and it gets paid.'

You sound as though you feel guilt.

'I haven't got guilt about that at all. I lived with my parents till I was 25. I was never bothered about being a home-owner or anything like that. I saw my flat one day, and I bought it the next, just like that. I hadn't thought about it before. I was just passing by, and Nick said: "Oh, let's go and have a look at these", and I thought: "This is all right." I asked her how much it was, she told me, so I said "I'll buy it." And I just moved in. I didn't really know what to do, I just paid the bills. I don't feel guilt about that.'

INSANITY #2: ENDLESS HOURS IN BED, NO PEACE IN THIS MIND

Then there's the Victorian view of 'asylums', full of irredeemable cases walking up and down *Cuckoo's Nest*-esque corridors, banging off the walls.

'I think NHS hospitals are full of people banging off the walls in long corridors. Long, endless corridors. In communal wards, nobody sleeps. They can give you as many drugs as they want, but the noises in there are pretty horrendous. Then the next day, you wake up, have your drugs and sit in a big communal room, and you don't hardly see any fucker. And then you just, if you're like me, try to keep out of everybody's way. Know your place. Don't get in anybody's shadow.'

Did you ever think, 'I don't belong here'?

'I think I had just as much right to be there as anybody else. When I got taken to hospital, they didn't know who the fuck I was, y'know? I'm not in Take That, I'm not even in The Stone Roses, I'm in a moderately successful British band. I wasn't there in my Manic Street Preachers T-shirt. They didn't have a clue.'

In the eyes of those who do have a clue, however, your breakdown has put *The Holy Bible*, indeed everything you do, into a different, revisionist perspective. Like, 'Oh, he was 4 REAL after all.' [At this moment, I do not mention Kurt Cobain. I don't need to.]

'Mmm. I can understand that. It's fair enough. You get judged by what you write – although I always thought we were more than just what we wrote. Everything else about us always came before our words, and our music to a certain extent. But, you know, that's our own fault, and that's the way the media's gonna judge us.'

Even your apparently objective, second- or third-person lyrics seem to refract back on to yourself. 'All art is autobiography', and all that.

'Yeah, I can understand that. If I use "we" or "you" or "they", it doesn't necessarily mean what it says. But I think most lyric writers would say that. It sounds really corny to say: "Yeah, I can identify with a prostitute", which is not *exactly* what "Yes" is about, but there's certain things I do feel affinity with. Not prostitution, but the nature of the things that happen to her body physically. People have still got the stupid idea, you know, that I'm a loud, aggressive person . . .'

I don't think anyone thinks that, Richey.

'. . . that, by the things I've done, I'd be hyperactive, talking all the time, running round going "*rrarrarrarr*", smashing people in the face, kicking down doors, which is not the case. I've never destroyed anything in my life. Apart from a few guitars.'

I AM STRONGER THAN MENSA . . .

Today, Richey has been walking the streets of Paris with some Rimbaud lines about mutilation scrawled across his arse.

'Rim-bored. Rim-bough. How do you say it?'

'Rimbaud' I say, in French.

'I insist he's called "Rim-bough". Sounds better than "Rambo". Like Americans always say Van Gogh "Van Go".'

That other self-mutilating, asylum-dwelling artist . . .

'And make the "Go" go on for ever: "G-o-o-o-o-o". It's "Van Goff" to me. I know it's wrong but I don't care. One thing I am fucked off about, being misrepresented, is I don't think people believe I read books. I think they don't even – it's all "they" all the time, isn't it? I don't know who "they" are – but they think the quotes just come with the sleeve, and I don't even choose them. I am not stupid. I might come across as stupid. That's nothing to do with academic qualifications. I think there's a difference between intelligence and knowledge.'

Shades of the David Thewlis character from *Naked*, here . . .

'There are plenty of people with letters after their names who only know figures and dates. It's possible to know a lot of facts but not know anything at all. I think you can have no qualifications to your name and be one of the most intelligent people in the world.'

SCRATCH MY LEG WITH A RUSTY NAIL . . . SADLY, IT HEALS

I have a theory that all self-mutilation, right down to tattoos and even ear-piercing, springs from a desire to symbolically, and permanently, vandalise the perfection your mother brought into the world.

'There's something in that. Also – this is a bit of a superficial argument – as the belief in God has faded, there has been a reversal to tribalism, you know, piercing, branding. I know it's vain, but I don't think it's to do with loving the body. It's to do with detesting the body. That's why you choose to mark it. It's also a question of knowing you can do it to yourself. A tattoo does not hurt. It's just like a pinprick. A piercing does not hurt. But knowing you can actually do something which the body does not like . . . I'm weak, all my life I've felt weak compared to other people, if they want to crush me they can – but I know I can do things that other people can't. Then they turn round and say to me: "I don't wanna do it anyway." Which is not really my point.'

Does it take a certain skill to hurt yourself just enough without severing a major artery?

[He laughs, confused.]

'A certain skill?'

It sounds flippant, but I mean it. A discipline.

'Mmm. Probably does. Go on, say it. What were you going to say? You may as well say it.'

It is often said that anorexia and self-mutilation are attempts to exert control in a life that has lost all control. It's a bit of a cliché . . .

'No, but it's completely true! The best thing is knowing that no one can do fucking anything about it. When I was in Whitchurch . . . People can't actually hold you down and force food into your mouth. They just can't do it. And someone can't be near you 24 hours a day to stop you doing something to your body. And ultimately they've got no right to anyway, because it is your body. Justice Templeman saying cruelty is uncivilised – he should take a look around.'

SCHIZOPHRENIA #1: I WANNA BE SO SKINNY THAT I ROT FROM VIEW

On '4st 7lbs', you want to 'walk in the snow and not leave a footprint'. But surely, the very fact of doing what you do exhibits a desire to leave a mark on the world?

'Well . . .'

Am I taking it too literally?

'NoNoNo, there's definitely something in that. In terms of never wanting to be noticed, I've never wanted that. When I was young, especially, I used to keep myself to myself. I don't feel I have the right to intrude on anyone else, and I don't think anyone should necessarily want to listen to me. I think my lyrics are valid. I can't speak for the music, all I can talk about is my words. I think I'm a good lyricist. I don't think I'm up there with the greats, but I'm doing all right. So I guess it's egotistical to publish your lyrics, but we always publish them because I want people to read them. So I guess I wanna be noticed in that sense. In another sense, I wanna pay the fuckers back. There are so many people I would love to . . . just shove something down their fucking throats.'

Around the time of 'Faster', you seemed to find a new urgency. As if you suddenly realised: 'This is not a rehearsal.'

'I think we did realise that. With the second album it was: "Yeah you're on a major label, yeah you're good, you can go to a beautiful studio, spend a hundred grand doing the artwork, yeah you get a swimming pool, yeah you get a four-poster bed, yeah you get food cooked for you." It's all bollocks. When we started writing new songs for The Holy Bible, none of them sounded like they belonged in a place like that. So we just decided to do it in the demo studio in Cardiff. Which was not great, but I'd just gear my day so I could pick the others up in the day while I was still sober, get them down there, try to finish my words for James, get them so he could actually fit them in the lines [never a MSP strong point], get everybody else back home, then just get off my 'ead.'

SCHIZOPHRENIA #2: SELF-DISGUST EQUALS SELF-OBSESSION, HONEY

You deride self-obsession. Yet on the notes which accompany '4st 7lbs' you say 'Anorexia = Vanity' – just another form of self-obsession.

'I don't necessarily understand the contradictions myself, but in Ecclesiastes there's a line: "All is vanity", and I do really believe that. I think everybody's first love is themselves. Some more than others. Some can divide themselves, and give something of themselves to another person. Which I've never been able to do, because I've never trusted another person enough to do that. I don't feel strong enough that I could cope with the rejection if they left me. A lot of people don't cope with it, if something like that happens. I would not allow myself to be used like that. And also I'd feel humiliated.

'And like it was all done deliberately, if you know what I mean. Maybe I think about things too much, but everything that happens to me I do feel is deliberate. And that's been the same since I was a child. If something happened in Infants' School I'd be convinced everybody was against me. Which is self-obsession, because the world does not revolve around you. People don't give a fuck. People don't do things because it's you. When I'm driving in my car and traffic lights turn red, I think it's because I'm in the car. I feel persecuted. I feel that if anybody else had been in the car, they'd have gone through.'

Isn't it always the way? You wait an hour for a bus and then three come along at once.

'I've always felt that. When I got my A Levels, I got straight As, but I thought they weren't as good as other people's straight As, that they would look at me as if their As were better. We didn't get percentage marks, so three As weren't enough: I wanted to know I'd got, like, 95 per cent. Three As is meaningless unless you're arrogant enough to think you're as good as them. Which I'm not. I need to see it written down to know.'

The Government's educational 'league tables' might have an unexpected friend here.

'If they had 98 per cent and I got 95 per cent, I could handle that. It's knowing that they've got an A and I've got an A – what the fuck does that mean? If they're a confident person, they're gonna walk all over you. If I had 1 per cent more . . . they could still walk over me, but I'd feel better.'

It sounds as though the flipside of vanity is an inferiority complex.

'That's what it is. I think so. Linked with a "victim mentality", maybe.'

For twenty minutes, I have been stuttering, trembling and obsessively checking that my tape recorder is on, that the pause button hasn't slipped, and that the microphone is correctly plugged in and is making a reassuring whirring noise. And *he* feels inferior.

'But say if I was in a pub and someone attacked me, and I knew I'd done nothing wrong, I would quite happily take a beating without doing anything, and feel really superior. I would never hit somebody back if they hit me. If I'd done something wrong it's different. But if I was minding my own business, I could easily take a kicking. I'd think: "I don't give a fuck 'cos you are scum, you're way down there and I'm above you 'cos I can take it." It's a bit biblical, "turn the other cheek" and all that, but I like people like Gandhi. And when I see people get picked on, when I see them vainly throw a punch back, half-heartedly, I think they've lost. Any chance they had has gone because they've lowered themselves.'

SCHIZOPHRENIA #3: I HATE PURITY. I WANT EVERYONE CORRUPT.
I can't figure out your feelings on puritanism. Sometimes it seems to disgust you, but surely anorexia is an extreme form of puritanism?

'Oh yeah. Again, I think my views are completely flawed. My idea of purity is completely split down the middle. It's in denial with its own logic. The idea of not eating food, the idea of a political prisoner, say the Maze Block [which housed Irish Republican prisoners] going on hunger strike, when I was young, I thought it was so beautiful, the best thing anyone could do. It's all about injuring yourself to a certain extent. But for a reason, for an absolute reason. That's why I liked Bobby Sands [IRA martyr and Republican icon who died during the Maze hunger strike]. That's why I thought he was a better statement than anything else that was going on at the time, because it was against himself.'

An arm, belonging to a passing James Dean Bradfield, reaches out of the darkness and hands me a Coke. A Diet Coke.

'I like the idea in "Archives of Pain" I took from Michel Foucault, when he advocates a return to nineteenth-century values of execution and capital punishment. You know, it appeals to me, but you shouldn't only bring back capital punishment. It should be compulsory that your body be kept, have oil poured over it and be torn apart with horses and chains. It should be on TV, and four- or five-year-olds should be made to watch it. It's the only way. If you tell a child: "That's wrong", he doesn't really learn. But if you show a body being ripped to shreds, after *Blue Peter*, he's gonna know. But then, that's really right wing. Which I'm not. On things like censorship I think everything should be allowed on television. You know, I mean anything. I don't know who believes that any more. Every left-wing party says there should be some degree of censorship, that some things are bad taste. But it's unjustifiable for anyone to decide what is bad taste.'

AND SUICIDE IS PAINLESS . . .

Richey's spell in hospital began, one lurid rumour goes, after a suicide attempt.* The myth goes like this: he tries the old slit-wrists and hot-bath method and, surprised to wake up the next morning and find himself alive, phones his mother to say: 'I've done something a bit stupid . . . I think you'd better call an ambulance.' Is this true? And what of the statistical evidence that a high percentage of attempted suicides eventually succeed?

This is the question I *don't* ask Richey. As soon as I get home, I feel a complete coward. He seems like he wants to talk, like he wants to set the record straight. I know he would have answered. I do, however, question him on another rumour: that, while in hospital, he 'found God'.

'Found God? The Big Chap?! No. It's something that interests me, but you've only got to look at our name, we've got "Preachers" in our name. I was made to go to chapel till I was thirteen. On our first album you've got "Crucifix Kiss", a cross on the cover, a quote from Nietzsche about Christianity, so it goes deeper . . .'

Than the typical rock 'n' roll religious imagery?'

'Madonna uses religious imagery, and I think that's totally justified. I think she was fucked up by the Catholic church. Pearl Jam use religious imagery, and I can see through it a mile off. It's just really sad. And also, I've spent my whole life studying history, and most events are shaped by some antagonism or fundamentalist belief in God. I dunno if I'm agnostic, atheist or a believer, but I think there's something in people that's really flawed in that sense. Why spend all your time denying something which you believe doesn't even exist? "It's all bollocks, it's all bollocks, he's not there." If you don't believe it, don't even bother talking about it. But it's obviously something that's there in the middle of man, just there to think about. It's a question of, everyone knows they're gonna die, so everybody wants to know where they're gonna go. That's why everyone wants to die "a happy death", to quote Uncle Camus.

"'The cut worm dies in peace,"' he adds. 'William Blake.'

*My recounting of the suicide rumour displeased the other three Manics somewhat, despite (or because of) the fact that it turned out to be broadly accurate. The next time I saw them, they gave me a slightly frosty reception. At the time, I felt guilty. My only remaining regret, however, is that I didn't pursue the issue further, and ask Richey directly.

The above article has since gone down in history as Richey's last British interview. This, in fact, is not strictly true: it was the last *solo* interview published in the British press. *Time Out*'s Peter Paphides came on the same French trip, and interviewed Richey the following morning for a feature on the band as a whole.

Peter has kindly made Richey's quotes available to me, the majority of which have never before been published.

'Here, chewing your tail is joy' – 'SMALL BLACK FLOWERS THAT GROW IN THE SKY'

PETER PAPHIDES: 'Do you feel that you've been misrepresented?'
RICHEY EDWARDS: 'Apart from the band and a few people close to me, no one knows what happened. That's because I chose not to talk about it. There has to be some kind of privacy. Inevitably, I'm bound to be misrepresented, but that's something that everybody has to deal with, whatever job they do. I often meet people and their preconception of you is so different because they think you're violent when you've done things that look aggressive. I've never raised my voice to anybody, but most of my interviews read like a Scorsese script. It's like there's tables flying, bottles broken and you're going: "Fuck you! Fuck you!"'
PP: 'One reason behind your popularity, I think, is not so much the self-loathing, because that's not so uncommon, but your ability to articulate a certain kind of dignity in that state of mind.

'It's strange that people who despise their body, the way they learn to deal with it, is to punish it. It's really quite traditional in terms of flagellance [sic], and, like, just go back through history. Caged zoo animals do it quite well. Baboons chew their own tails, but then that's an artificial environment. They also fix an imaginary point on the wall and constantly walk up to it, stop and then wander back. But they never cross that line. I do see an enormous amount of dignity in self-determination and self-discipline. It goes back to what I was saying earlier about purity and, at some point, some of my beliefs could be construed as quite fundamentalist, Islamic almost. But it's not. It's quite alien to that. It's much more individual.'
PP: 'It could be argued that although you consistently extol the virtues of self-discipline, you might be gleaning some perverse joy from all this.

'It's hard to say. The people that seem to test their body the most are people that are so aware of it, every ounce of flesh. I do believe that if I'd been born with blue eyes, my life would have been completely different. I wouldn't have ended up going to university, I'd be married and I'd be a bank manager. It's the arbitrary factors that determine your life. There's a certain kind of beauty in taking complete control of every aspect of your life. Purifying or hurting your body to achieve a balance in your mind is tremendously disciplined. I've never raised my voice to anybody. When I read about myself, sometimes it's like there's tables flying, bottles broken and me going, "Fuck you! Fuck you!" But my life isn't a Martin Scorsese film. I've been hit lots of times for no reason, but I've never thrown a punch back. If I refuse to do that, then I might get beaten up badly, but I would still feel better than the person who's doing it to me. There's a Latin quote that I can't remember – it's actually in *Green River Rising* – that strength is restored through wounding.'
PP: 'But how do you control the actual physical pain of cutting?

'It's not something that you train yourself to do, like walking on hot coals or something. You just get to a point where, if you don't do it to yourself, you get a feeling that something really terrible is going to happen, and when that moment comes, it's the logical thing to do. It doesn't hurt. You're not screaming and shouting. A couple of days later you feel like a sad fuck, but that's part of the healing process; after that you feel really good. People that harm themselves, be it through anorexia or razors, know what they're doing. Which is why I get annoyed when Lord Justice Templeman, presiding over the Spanner trial, says that "cruelty is uncivilised". How can any member of the ruling classes say that when you consider the backgrounds they come from? Or how little children get blown up in Northern Ireland and you can't even scratch yourself?'
PP: 'Do you think of yourself as a strong-willed person?

'Completely. But not about certain things that should matter more. Like, I'm not disciplined about playing guitar, in terms of sitting down and making myself practise. That's something I should definitely do.'

PP: 'How have the members of the band changed over the years?

That's hard to answer. I think we're naïve, but perhaps not so much now. I think maybe from when we started, everybody is pretty much the same as they were before, just a little more extreme. Nick always used to be happy to lie in bed all day and watch the world go by, and that's exaggerated even more, he's got more time to do that. In terms of what I believe in, that's become stronger as years go on, because the more you read the more you can justify things to yourself. Like, self-harm was something I always thought about. Like, when you're young you're always scratching yourself with compasses, then the more you read, you can cite logical or intellectual defences of your behaviour.'

PP: 'How do you address the problem of not sleeping?

'Well, when I went to the doctors last time, they told me that no one's ever died from lack of sleep. I have my doubts, though. It's not a world tragedy. Again, it's very self-obsessed: "They can sleep, I can't, I am persecuted, etc. . . .". In the past, if we were getting a flight at 6 a.m., I would just start drinking earlier in the morning on the previous day, in order to pass out earlier, thereby allowing myself to wake up early. I didn't like fucking up. I've never missed anything through abuse, because I would always know what we're doing the next day. That's what happens in the band: nothing is spontaneous. So now I just think, I wake up when I wake up. And now I don't drink at all. The last thing I wanted to do was end up a fucking alcoholic mess like Shane MacGowan. I don't want to be like that. I want to be at least semi-aware, semi-conscious. The whole thing about things like self-harm is that you are aware of what you're doing: that's how you justify it. So it kind of gets pathetic if you're a drunken mess. I find it really odd, that mentality that says you have to fall over in a bar to be a drinker, you know? If I fall over and piss myself, I wanna do it in my own flat. Not where people can see me. I used to look forward to my holidays from the band. Just two weeks in my flat with a bottle. That's when we write. But if I'm left with a paragraph after a whole world tour, I'm grateful. Most of it is bollocks . . .'

The journalists returned home; the Manics moved on to Germany. Richey Edwards would never speak to the British press again.

h) Little drummer boy

(SEAN MOORE – AN APPRECIATION)

'Those who speak do not know, and those who know do not speak' –
CARLOS CASTENADA, QUOTED BY RICHEY EDWARDS WITH
REFERENCE TO SEAN MOORE

WHAT DO YOU CALL SOMEONE who hangs around with musicians? A drummer! What do you call a drummer with ambition? A roadie! How can you tell when there's a drummer at the door? Because he speeds up and comes in before you're ready! How can you tell when the drum riser's level? Because the drummer's drooling out of both sides of his mouth! What's the difference between a drummer and a drum machine? You only need to punch the information into a drum machine once! A drummer walks into a shop and orders three plectrums, six guitar strings and two tambourines. The proprietor asks: 'You're a drummer, aren't you?' The drummer says: 'Yeah, how did you know?' The proprietor answers: 'This is a fish and chip shop!'

. . . And so on. And *ha bloody ha*. Drummers are the mothers-in-law of rock, a laughing stock, the butt of a billion lame jokes, (literally) sitting ducks, and generally portrayed as knuckle-dragging neanderthals who comprehend just three concepts: 'fire', 'food' and '1-2-3-4'. The alternatives are barely more appealing: 'the mad bastard' (Keith Moon) or 'the loveable character' (Ringo Starr).

Sean Moore fits none of these categories, although perhaps he does have one role model. It was once written that: '. . . of all the Manics, it is Sean who is the band's Charlie Watts, having been going steady for eight years'. A good comparison, but for reasons far removed from the longevity of his relationship. Nor is it simply because, like Watts, 'Mooro' is also, at first sight, the least rock 'n' roll member of his band, right down to his mastery of the trumpet (a less rock 'n' roll instrument it would be difficult to name; one pictures him, cherubic cheeks puffed out and ruddy, like *Neighbours*' tuba-tooting Harold Bishop) – and he don't care. Like the sardonic sticksman of The Rolling Stones, Sean views the entire rock 'n' roll circus with a mixture of detached amusement, world-weary boredom and out-and-out cynicism. 'Everything's so crap. I feel a lack for anything. If I could isolate myself away from everything, then I would. I'm disillusioned by everything.' Moore's disdain for the rituals of rock 'n' roll is absolute: he finds the tour/promotion treadmill a trial, greeting strangers for whom he has no liking with a fixed smile on his face but with laser-sharp loathing in his eyes; and he once spent an entire *Sounds* interview silently collecting twenty-pence pieces for the parking meter. His cynical attitude has nothing to do with adolescent petulance, but almost certainly stems from an early resignation to the fact that, no matter how significant his talent and how great his contribution to the Manics, he was never going to be taken entirely seriously.

Sean Moore is basically the cat in *Hong Kong Phooey*, quietly making things happen but taking none of the credit. James is a phenomenal guitarist, yes, but Sean is a great drummer, 'the group's musical heart and beat' (Simon Reynolds in *Melody Maker*), a muscular metronome with a brain. It is also worth noting here that Sean co-writes all the Manics' music (how many archetypal comedy drummers can claim that?). Listen to the awesome martial rigour with which he drives 'Faster', or to the subtlety and grace with which he guides 'Motorcycle Emptiness' – to pick two random examples – and it is clear that the silent partner in the Bradfield/Moore partnership (a bond strong enough to allow the band to carry two self-confessed musical incompetents) is every bit as crucial as his all-singing, all-riffing cousin.

'The best shag in the whole of Wales' – JAMES ON SEAN

When Manics fans voted for their 'Sexiest Man of the Year' in the music press, James Dean Bradfield and Nicky Wire made the first and second place; Sean was nowhere to be seen. There is, however, a small but growing Cult of Sean among the hardcore fanbase, and he does have one fan club on the internet (at: http://www.geocities.com/sunsetstrip/lounge/9134/geobook.html). He once made the cover of *Terrible Beauty* fanzine, but only on issue four (it was his turn). *Pout* once devoted a whole chapter to the Manics' reluctant sex cymbal. The tone, however, is usually a mix of irony and patronising support for the underdog (the words most commonly used are 'Awww!', and 'Bless!'). This is not what Sean Moore deserves. When I first met the Manics, it was he with whom I sat in the hotel bar, discussing politics, pop and twentieth-century culture into the early hours, while Richey the Intellectual was busy chatting up the girls. Hall Or Nothing's Caffy St Luce, asked for a few words on Sean, offers simply: 'Still waters run deep.' And yet, to the outside world, he will always be 'just' a drummer, and – worse than that – a comedy drummer.

A lot of it comes down to physiognomy and to the heartless hand of Mother Nature. Cruelly, as a child, Sean was actually taller than James, yet as an adult he has always been childlike. 'I'd hesitate to call them angry young men,' wrote Bob Stanley in *Melody Maker* in 1989, 'because I don't believe the drummer was even born in 1977.' In 1998, *NME* asked Sean if anyone had ever tried to ruffle his hair. 'Uh, maybe on occasion,' he reluctantly admitted. Now 28 and still ageless, a growing lad who takes his vitamins first thing every morning, this 'baby-faced PJ Proby lookalike' (Bruce Dessau, *Vox*) found it difficult to get served in bars long into his twenties. His drink of choice, incidentally, is Blackcurrant Hooch . . . like a thirteen-year-old on the park swings.

I say 'childlike' rather than 'boyish' because there is something *girly* about Sean. He actually has a far more natural androgyny than his lipstick-wearing side-kicks (*Smash Hits* once printed a picture of him next to one of Helena Bonham Carter, and 'amusingly' switched the captions). Even as a child he was often mistaken for girl and, in 1995, his appearence was still enough to confuse Eunice, a 37-year-old mum interviewed in *Young, Pretty & Fucked* fanzine. 'Are they all boys? That one looks like a girl!'

This may explain why, when Richey and James experimented with facial hair, Sean *really* went for it, piercing his eyebrow into the bargain – it was a rebellion against his own boyish/girlishness. Behind his shades (aviator, Lennon, ski), hats (Soviet, UN, bobble) and beards (stubble, goatee, grizzly), and with his radio mike, Sean has often seemed to be in hiding, craving obscurity. He looks like the member of Metallica that even Metallica fans can't name.

Sean is also a little self-conscious about his figure. He once stormed out of a *Melody Maker* photo session for which he was required to strip naked and be covered in gold spraypaint, and, during the Manics' glam era, he often declined the others' requests to participate in provocative dress. As Nicky Wire remembers: 'It was always "Come on, Mooro, get this fucking blouse on!" and "NO! FUCK OFF!" '

Sean's quest for anonymity has been highly successful. The handful of facts known about him are pitiful splinters, mere jetsam. He has a sewing fetish and enjoys DIY. He is into Aleister Crowley. He believes that the world is controlled by computers (the irony being that he is addicted to them). He would rather play his Sega than talk in interviews (to this day, Moore carries a notebook with his highest Game Boy scores in it). He is the only member of the band who can read a map, and consequently the only one who ventures out on sightseeing visits when on tour. At home, he is never seen on the Bristol club scene. His idea of going out is riding his Vespa to Weston-Super-Mare, having tea on the beach, and riding home again. He is fanatical about ironing. One persistent rumour insists he has webbed feet.

And . . . well, that's about it. His private life is exactly that. Nicky and Richey have never even been to his home (or homes – Sean actually owns two houses: one for him, and one next door for his girlfriend). At home, he is almost as domesticated as his bassist. 'I'm obsessed with everything being parallel,' he told *NME*. 'Parallel and in its place.' Nicky, famously, has three Dyson vacuum cleaners, but Sean owns two. When he can't sleep on the tour bus, he does the washing up.

Sean's most famous personality trait, diffidence aside, is shopaholism. Where the rest of the Manics' casual spending – Nicky's slot-machine habit, Richey's clothes mania, James's generous drinks rounds – have arisen from boredom (they spend the money *because it's there*), Sean's spending is never casual. He wields his Gold Amex like a weapon, and is often seen strolling into venues laden with Our Price and Body Shop bags, and with gadgets, electronic toys and the latest Nicam home cinema. 'I can honestly say I've shopped in nearly every city in the UK,' he boasts. Nicky Wire explained the Moore Method to *NME*: 'Sean does this thing where at the start of the tour he says: "Oh, I couldn't pack last night, so I've only got one bag with me!" Then by the end of the tour he's got two brand-new suitcases packed with stuff. Every tour!' On a trip to New York, Sean bought the complete works of Martin Scorsese on Laserdisc; shortly afterwards, he went into another shop and bought the entire contents of the Laserdisc department. 'If the band split up,' Nicky once jokingly told him, 'you'd always have the chance of opening up a second-hand Dixons with all the goods you have.' Sometimes Sean doesn't really seem to want the goods themselves. He once bought an expensive Mac Powerbook laptop, but has only ever used it for card games. 'He'll buy "Comme des Garons",' verifies Wire, 'and con himself that it's better quality. It's secret retail therapy.'

Speaking to *The Face*, Sean explained how the therapy works. 'I want everything to look like it's just come out of the wrapper. I love the smell of, say, a Walkman when you first unwrap it. If it gets a scratch on it, that's it. That's the way I am. And I've always got to get hold of the next best thing. I don't care about money.' However, he does like to splash it around. On the quiet, Sean is a bit of a *flash bastard*. As Guto from Super Furry Animals told *Iconoclastic Glitter*: 'You're in a bar with Sean and he'll buy the entire top shelf, like, because he can.'

Introducing the band onstage, James's description of 'Seanus Moorus' (when it doesn't involve his glossy bob and a plea for bottles of Pantene) is invariably something like: 'A genius consumer, a man whose spending power is so gargantuan you all want to be his girlfriend.' Sean Moore owns things you didn't even know existed (a digital video disc Walkman?!). He was one of the first people in Britain to own a Tamagotchi. In 1997, playing the 'We Love Us' quiz on Radio One's Mark Radcliffe show, he won an electric foot spa. Almost inevitably, he already had one.

'Sean is brutality personified: he pisses everybody off because he doesn't like anybody or anything' – JAMES

Of course, put any of the above analysis to Moore himself and, with a look suggesting that he has just smelt gas, he will make you feel even smaller than he is. Moore holds his thoughts and feelings close to his chest. If Nicky believes in lashing outward, Richey believes in lashing inward and James believes in catharsis, Sean believes in the old-fashioned British virtue of emotional continence. *He keeps it all in.* Last time I met him, I asked Sean – a devoted Liverpool supporter – what it was like playing to 30,000 people at Anfield, the home of his heroes. With heavy sarcasm – although one can never be sure – he shrugged: 'It was just another gig.' (Before the show, a clearly ghostwritten statement from Sean had read: 'As a lifelong Liverpool supporter, I've always wanted to appear at Anfield and I hope my performance on the day matches some of those I've seen from the team.') There is just one recorded instance of a Sean Moore emotional outburst. In 1992, shortly after the Manics first hit the Top Twenty, he received a letter from his estranged father, wanting to be friends. Sean disappeared to his room and smashed it up with a pool cue. 'He said it was because of drink,' said the others, 'but we think it was because of that letter.'

Sean's reticence can easily be mistaken for hostility. As Manics superfan Gill Armstrong once wrote: 'Sean . . . seems to have an invisible wall up around him, an aura of "Go away".' This is partly down to his protectiveness and fierce loyalty towards his band-mates, as if adhering to *omerta*, the Mafia's code of silence. Not that the speak-no-evil chimp doesn't let the occasional jewel slip between his fingers. He is a rock 'n' roll Calvin Coolidge, a man of few words, but whose rare gnomic utterances reveal a deliciously mordant wit.

Shortly after the '4 REAL' incident, I had pointed out that, to keep the hype momentum going, the next time Richey slashed his arm it would need to be live on CNN. Sean, master of the pomposity-puncturing soundbite, looked up from his Game Gear and said: 'We're going to cut Richey's head off.' On another occasion, I asked: 'Where's Richey? Gone to bed?' Sean replied: 'Richey doesn't go to bed. He goes to the abyss.' At the time of writing, Sean Moore is possibly the only person in rock who doesn't take Manic Street Preachers entirely seriously.

9. FROM DESPAIR . . .

'I think, the older you get, life becomes more miserable. Y'know, all the people you grew up with die, your parents die, your dog dies, and your energy diminishes' – RICHEY, IN AN INTERVIEW ON MTV

AT SEVEN O'CLOCK IN THE MORNING, on Wednesday 1 February 1995, a silver Vauxhall Cavalier left the car-park of the Embassy Hotel, took a right turn off Bayswater Road towards the Westway, followed the Westway on to the M4, then sped along the lonely westbound lane out of London, away from the sunrise, and passing the tailback of commuters coming the other way. Within three hours, the driver, Richey James Edwards, would be over the Severn Bridge and back at his flat in Cardiff bay.

This much we know. This much, at least, is certain.

The four Manic Street Preachers had spent a 'quiet, calm, nice Christmas' back home in Blackwood. They saw a lot of each other, exchanged presents, and sat around watching videos together (including one of their own gig at the Clapham Grand), just like old times. After the horrors of 1994 – James, asked by *Select* to describe the year gone by in three words, had answered 'bag of shit' – it was a blissful interlude of calm.

Then, one day, Richey slipped back into his auto-abusive ways. He asked for a bowl, and began ostentatiously crumbling two bars of chocolate into it. 'Among us, we'd take the piss out of it,' James would later tell *NME*, 'and he would take the piss out of himself as well. It had an edge to it, but it wasn't all po-faced. I mean, if ever there was a little crappy film based on the life of Richey, that scene would be [*melodramatic American accent*] "What the fuck's wrong with you, man!"'

At least he wasn't drinking, and, partly as a result of that, he had been writing prolifically, if incoherently. Over the festive break, Richey handed a folder of around sixty lyrics to Nicky, who pointed out that it wasn't really worth giving them to him, photocopied them, and passed them on to the band's musical wing in the form of Sean Moore. 'They were pretty heavy going,' says Sean. 'There wasn't a lot to pick out, to be honest. Most of it was very fragmented and rambling.' And, according to Nicky, unsuitable for use as rock 'n' roll lyrics: 'The lyrics in the last file he gave us were more poetry of a sort. There was a lot of ranting.' None of them would ever see the light of day.

In early January 1995, the Manics checked into the House in the Woods studio (where they had worked in January 1993) in Surrey. As well as working on a contribution to the upcoming *Judge Dredd* soundtrack, they demoed a handful of rough tracks – early acoustic versions of 'Elvis Impersonator: Blackpool Pier' and 'Kevin Carter' – for their fourth album, which was already sounding more melodic and uplifting in mood than *The Holy Bible*.

Richey appeared to be on top form again. 'He was back to being Iggy/Keith Richards,' said Nicky, 'as opposed to Ian Curtis.' Richey's writing, like his state of mind, had improved. James was concerned that 'because of Richey's undergoing treatment he'd turn into Peter Gabriel lyrically, and I didn't want our songs to turn into psychobabble. But he's kept his own voice, which is admirable.' Richey was even, incredibly, coming up with musical suggestions, sending James a note which read: 'Idea for next album: Pantera meets Nine Inch Nails meets *Screamadelica*.'

When the four left the House in the Woods, Richey presented the others with little gifts: a copy of the *Daily Telegraph* and a Mars bar for Nicky, a CD for James, something undisclosed for Sean. And more lyrics.

After Surrey, Nicky took his wife Rachel for one of their semi-regular breaks in Barcelona. When he returned, James told him some alarming news: Richey had gone missing. His mother had assumed that he was in London with the band, while the band had assumed he was in Blackwood with his mother, but he wasn't with either. This time, the disappearance proved to be a false alarm: Richey turned up a day later.

Richey was once asked to name his most prized possession, to which he answered, 'My dog.'

On 14 January 1995, that most prized possession was dead. Snoopy, his childhood pet, had finally passed on at the advanced age of seventeen. Later that day, Richey drove his sister Rachel to the local garden centre to choose a tree to commemorate Snoopy. Rachel was surprised and amused to see a radical alteration to Richey's appearance. 'I remember it being so cold at the time,' she later told the *Mirror*. 'Richard had shaved off his hair, and had been wearing a bobble hat to keep warm. He took it off and gave it to me to wear and the pair of us looked totally ridiculous, me in the hat and Richard with no hair . . .'

When the siblings returned to the family home to plant the tree, Rachel noticed some unusual behaviour in her brother. 'Looking back, there were a few odd things that happened around that time. That day Richard had a little camera, and he took pictures of Mam and Dad, which was odd because he had never done anything like that before. As I went to leave Mam and Dad's house that day, Richard did a very strange thing. He looked at me up and down. I said, "What's the matter? Is something wrong with my belt?" He just said nothing, but now I realise he knew it would be the last time he ever saw me, which makes me think he had everything planned out.'

It would be the last the Edwards family ever saw of him.

'All is vanity' – ECCLESIASTES

The Manics had cancelled a tour of Japan in early 95, for what were vaguely described as 'business reasons'. However, one particularly dedicated Japanese journalist, Midori Tsukagoshi of *Music Life* magazine, determined to get a Manics feature no matter what, travelled from Tokyo to Cardiff on 23 January for what would turn out to be Richey's final interview.

The photographs used to accompany the *Music Life* feature were shocking. With his shorn locks, emaciated physique and striped pyjamas – he was now spending all day hanging around the house in his bedwear – Richey looked eerily like an Auschwitz inmate. Coincidentally – *perhaps* – he was wearing the same black suede Converse sneakers found on the corpse of Kurt Cobain (when he fetched Tsukagoshi from Cardiff Central station, Nirvana's *In Utero* was also playing on the car stereo). There was even something disconcerting about the décor of his flat. With its pot plants and Laura Ashley settee, it looked as though it had been furnished by someone else, not by Richey: an estate agent's show flat rather than a home.

In his conversation with Tsukagoshi, Richey actually appeared motivated and focused: 'When I wake up every morning, I know what I want to do. That's to write better and better things. I want to articulate my inner feelings better.' The aspects of the interview which have been most discussed since, however, are the two dramatic acts of self-purging revealed by Edwards.

Firstly, he claimed that he had thrown a huge pile of his notebooks into the nearby river – a final *Bonfire of the Vanities*, a farewell to all that, *everything must go*. 'I got rid of a lot of my notes. Sunk it in the water. I had all these ideas for songs in the notes. Since after Christmas I'd been writing a huge amount, but when I read them over, for about 80 per cent of the things, I didn't think: "This is great!" Nicky Wire, incidentally, suspects that the claim was fictionalisation on Richey's part. 'He never chucked anything into the river. That's just not true. And there was never a ritual burning of lyrics or anything. Those were just rumours that built up.' Even if he did do it, the act was possibly less dramatic than it may have sounded. 'I'm the type to write everything down on notes,' Richey explained to Tsukagoshi, 'so if I kept everything it would stack up to the ceiling.' Furthermore, he later contradicted himself by saying that he had thrown the notebooks into the garbage bag, not into the River Taff.

Secondly, there was the matter of his shaven head. At first, he said his fringe was irritating him in his sleep, so he took a razor to it one night for something to do ('I'd do anything to be able to sleep'). He also said it was connected to the death of Snoopy (according to psychologists, shaving one's head is often a sign of grief). 'I think you can say that shaving my head did have great meaning to me,' Richey admitted. 'I mean, you know I have a really vain streak. I really loved my hairstyle. For the last six months I'd grown it long, parted it on one side, dyed it a reddish orange, and really liked it. I was almost in love with my hairstyle. But one day, in the end, I just felt like abandoning things like that.'

What was the truth? The Snoopy theory is not inconceivable. The death of a pet may seem a relatively trivial matter, but it may have been the straw that broke the camel's back. 'He did love his dog,' confirms Wire. 'That was a Manics thing. We all had dogs (Lucy, Dixie, Suki and Snoopy). We used to stroke each others' dogs. And they all died.' Of course, if this theory is correct, Richey would have had to shave his head between learning of Snoopy's death and driving his sister Rachel to the garden centre.

Then there's the theory that obsessive haircutting is a common precursor to suicide, two Richey icons being prime examples: Yukio Mishima had shaved his head shortly before ritually disembowelling himself, as had Ian Curtis before he was found hanged. Rachel Edwards, though, remains sceptical: 'There has been a lot of talk about Richard shaving his hair off to be like Ian Curtis . . . but Richard was always changing his hair. That was very normal for him.'

Maybe the prosaic truth is that the skinhead look was merely Richey's latest hairdo (a theory supported by the fact that one neat tramline was etched into its left-hand side). According to one insider, Richey had initially tried to cut his own hair into a new style, but made such a pitiful hash of it that he had had to go to a barber shop to have the lot shaved off.

'*Wanna get out* . . .' – 'SMALL BLACK FLOWERS THAT GROW IN THE SKY'

From this point onward, all one can do is consider the facts – sickeningly stark, horribly naked – and draw one's own conclusions.

On 29 January, the Manics booked into the House in the Woods once again for a couple of days' rehearsal. They were preparing for an American tour, their first in three years. Looking back now, Nicky Wire sees tiny signs that something was wrong. During this period, Richey repeatedly phoned him, often on the sole pretext of checking the time. 'He'd call me late at night,' says Nicky, 'and talk about *Apocalypse Now* or *Naked* for two hours, trying to get some sort of idea across, and he just couldn't.' This inability to express himself, says Wire, made Richey feel unbearably frustrated.

Others didn't notice anything wrong at all. Epic MD Rob Stringer – of all their Sony cronies, probably the closest to the Manics – saw Richey at the House in the Woods. 'He was in really good spirits. They'd just been rehearsing and everything was going great. They'd done six new songs and he'd written two of them.' Richey told Stringer he was really looking forward to going to America.

On 31 January, the rehearsals over, Nicky and Sean went back to Blackwood and Bristol respectively. James and Richey, meanwhile, drove to the Embassy Hotel on Bayswater Road, west London (a regular Manics stopover since the *Generation Terrorists* era), en route for America. These two were to form an advance guard, arriving in the USA for a brief week-long round of interviews to promote *The Holy Bible* and the forthcoming tour.

Before checking into the hotel, they sat in the car outside while James played Richey a demo of a song they had co-written, 'Small Black Flowers That Grow in the Sky' (a delicate acoustic lament about caged zoo animals with the haunting refrain 'Wanna get out . . .'). Richey loved it.

Messrs Bradfield and Edwards were given adjoining rooms. They took half an hour to freshen up, after which James walked into Richey's room to find him in the bath. James suggested they give it another half-hour, then go browsing on Queensway, the nearby shopping centre. Richey suggested a trip to Whiteley's cinema, and James agreed. When James returned, at about 8.30 p.m., Richey had changed his mind, saying that he felt like staying in, and that he would call James in the morning. James went to meet a friend for a drink, and got to bed at 11.30 p.m. Richey, meanwhile, phoned his mum. He told her that, actually, he wasn't really looking forward to going to America.

At the appointed hour, Richey failed to meet James in the lobby, as they had agreed, to travel to the airport. This was unlike Richey, who prided himself on his professional discipline. He had never missed a flight or been late for an appointment. When he failed to respond to telephone calls or to knocks on the door, Bradfield asked the hotel porter to unlock Room 516.

Richey was nowhere to be found. The room was empty save for a curious-looking box left on the table, wrapped in the manner of a birthday present, covered in literary quotes, collages and enigmatic pictures, including Bugs Bunny and a photo of a strange Germanic-looking house. Inside the box was an assortment of books, together with videos of *Equus* and *Naked*. The package was addressed to Richey's sort-of-girlfriend, Jo, with a note reading simply: 'I love you.'

Nicky and James have since analysed the box and its contents in maddening detail. 'Me and James saw the picture of the house,' said Nicky, 'and it was like: "Is that where he is? It looks like a mad house in Bavaria. Perhaps he's there." And the front cover is Bugs Bunny, so I thought perhaps he's in Disneyland [unlikely – Bugs Bunny is a Warner Bros character].' Also abandoned in Room 516 were one packet of Prozac, assorted toiletries, and a packed suitcase containing all of Richey's clothes.

'Oblivion is privilege. It has a fee' – MANICS PRESS BIOGRAPHY, *CIRCA* 1993

At ten o'clock the next morning, Martin Hall reported Richey missing to the Metropolitan Police at Harrow Road, who circulated his details to police stations nationwide. Simultaneously, the Manics hired the services of a private detective to try to track Richey down.

Accompanied by Richey's father and by Nicky Wire, the police visited Richey's flat in Cardiff, where they found his passport (which he was known to have had with him in London, thus proving that he had been home), and a ticket from the Severn Bridge tollgate (the time on it proving, heartbreakingly, that they had missed him by just a few hours). They also found his remaining Prozac, and his credit card. Subsequent investigations showed that, although he had left his card behind, Richey had been drawing out £200 from his building-society account every day for the two weeks prior to 31 January (making a total of £2,800), but that he hadn't touched his account since. This wasn't that unusual, perhaps: as Hall Or Nothing's Gillian Porter pointed out: 'If *you* were going to go away to America in the morning, you'd probably have a bit of money on you.' Sadly, the much-talked-about cash withdrawal may not be quite the ray of hope it has widely been taken for. In fact, the explanation is probably rather more mundane: Richey had just ordered a huge desk, worth around £1,400, for his flat from Cardiff department store D.H. Evans. Mistrusting credit cards and cheques, and preferring to operate on a purely cash basis, perhaps he was simply stockpiling the money to pay for his new piece of furniture. Admittedly, however, the purchase of a desk does suggest that Richey was at least planning a future life, if not a disappearance.

Initially, his absence, although an inconvenience, was not viewed as a cause for undue concern: after all, he had done it before and shown up again. James went to America to promote *The Holy Bible* on his own. Yet this time, somehow, everyone knew it might not be a false alarm. The US tour, a punishing thirty-date schedule due to start in Tucson on 20 March and then to criss-cross the States, was cancelled. 'It would have been pretty bad if Richey's body had been found while we were on tour,' James explained in *Select*.

Dates in Vienna and Prague were also cancelled, as were the Manics' plans to record a song for the *Judge Dredd* soundtrack. A Japanese promoter tried to sue them on the grounds that 'I'll lose honour', to which an understandably short-tempered Nicky replied, 'I don't care about your fucking honour!' Meanwhile, 'Yes', the Great Lost Manics Single, was put on hold. A sleeve was even prepared, parodying an old TSB ad: 'MSP: the band that likes to say . . . "Yes".'

Nicky Wire conducted his own private investigations, 'phoning every big hotel in Britain looking for a Richard Edwards. He found one in Swansea, and was ready to travel there, when the person turned out to be a middle-aged businessman. The Edwards family did their share too, phoning Richey's closest friend outside the band, Byron James, for information, and placing a small ad for three consecutive days in the local paper: 'Richard, please make contact, love Mum, Dad and Rachel.' But every lead drew a blank. After two weeks, a meeting between Wire, Bradfield, Graham Edwards and police detectives reached a decision: it was time to go public.

On Wednesday 15 February, Cardiff Police issued the following announcement: 'Police are anxious to trace Richard James Edwards, aged 28 years, a member of the pop group Manic Street Preachers, who has been missing from the London area since Wednesday 1 February 1995 when he was seen leaving the London Embassy Hotel at 7 a.m. It is known that on the same day he visited his home in the Cardiff area, and is still believed to be in possession of his Vauxhall Cavalier motor car, registration No. L519 HKX. Richard's family, band members and friends are concerned for his safety and welfare and stress that no pressure would be put on him to return if he does not

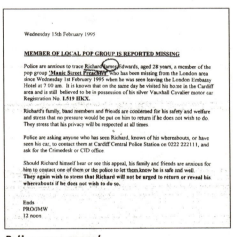

Wednesday 15th February 1995

MEMBER OF LOCAL POP GROUP IS REPORTED MISSING

Police are anxious to trace Richard James Edwards, aged 28 years, a member of the pop group 'Manic Street Preachers' who has been missing from the London area since Wednesday 1st February 1995 when he was seen leaving the London Embassy Hotel at 7.00 am. It is known that on the same day he visited his home in the Cardiff area and is still believed to be in possession of his silver Vauxhall Cavalier motor car Registration No. L519 HKX.

Richard's family, band members and friends are concerned for his safety and welfare and stress that no pressure would be put on him to return if he does not wish to do. They stress that his privacy will be respected at all times.

Police are asking anyone who has seen Richard, knows of his whereabouts, or have seen his car, to contact them at Cardiff Central Police Station on 0222 222111, and ask for the Crimedesk or CID office.

Should Richard himself hear or see this appeal, his family and friends are anxious for him to contact one of them or the police to let them know he is safe and well. They again wish to stress that Richard will not be urged to return or reveal his whereabouts if he does not wish to do so.

Ends
PRO/JMW
12 noon

Police press appeal.

wish to do. They stress that his privacy will be respected at all times. Police are asking anyone who has seen Richard, knows of his whereabouts, or has seen his car, to contact them at Cardiff Central Police Station on 0222-222111, and ask for the Crimedesk or CID office. Should Richard himself hear or see this appeal, his family and friends are anxious for him to contact one of them or the police to let them know he is safe and well. They again wish to stress that Richard will not be urged to return or reveal his whereabouts if he does not wish to do so.' The Metropolitan Police at Harrow Road also issued an appeal, with the description: '5 ft 8, slim with a skinhead haircut and pale complexion.' Although the description mentioned Richey's 'USELESS GENERATION' tattoo, it failed to make any reference to his '4 REAL' scars under the section on 'Distinguishing Features'.

That day, Graham Edwards appeared on Red Dragon Radio's Adrian Masters show, appealing for Richey to get in touch. 'All we know is that he left the Embassy Hotel in London on the first of the month, and he left without giving any reason, and just sort of disappeared into thin air. Obviously everyone in the family is concerned, and we just want to get in touch with him to know that he is OK. We've phoned all his friends and all the acquaintances we can think of, and nobody seems to have been in touch with him at all. All I'd like to say is, Richey, if he's listening, please get in touch, just a phone call or a postcard just to let us know you're all right. If he needs time to be on his own, then that's OK with everybody, but if he does have a problem that we can help with, he'll have strong support from his family and also from his band, Nick, James and Sean.'

Nick, James and Sean themselves released an official band statement: 'Richard's family, the band and management are unavailable for comment, and we would like to ask you to respect their privacy, and for your help and sensitivity regarding this matter.' Wire did, however, tell Ceefax: 'If Richey doesn't want to come back that's fine. We just want him to give us a call or send us a postcard.' Sherry Edwards, speaking to the *Daily Mail*, echoed this sentiment: 'Wherever Richey has been in the world he has always got in touch. Whether it was a quick telephone call or a postcard, we always knew how he was doing.' Not this time.

'Solitude, solitude, the eleventh commandment' – 'YES'

Sightings quickly began to emerge. David Cross, a nineteen-year-old college student at Gwent College of Higher Education, claimed to have met Richey on 5 February outside a newsagents at Newport bus station, and to have had a brief conversation with him about a mutual acquaintance, Lori Fidler (a particularly rabid MSP fan from New York, and Cross's penfriend).

The police, meanwhile, were maintaining an optimistic outlook. 'Although there is still no news on Richey,' Welsh police announced on 16 February, 'there is no evidence that he has come to harm.' The next day, however, Avon & Somerset Police found what, for many, was evidence that Richey had come to harm. In the car-park at Aust Motorway Services, on the English side of the Severn Bridge, an empty silver Vauxhall Cavalier was spotted. The registration was checked: L519 HKX. It was Richey's car.

No one knew exactly how long the Vauxhall had been in the car-park, although closed-circuit footage appeared to show that it had been there for several days, and had been unattended since St Valentine's Day, when a parking attendant had given it a ticket. The car appeared to have been 'lived in': cassette tapes were scattered on the seats, and the battery had been completely run down. There was also a carrier bag, containing photographs Richey had taken of his parents.

To be pedantic, the car did not belong to Richey as such, but to Manic Street Preachers (Richey himself owned a more modest white Ford Fiesta). The band had bought the Vauxhall second-hand from a car salesman, and it was left in Richey's custody because he was the only band member who could drive. Once the police had finished examining it, it was parked in the street outside Graham and Sherry Edwards's home, but then ghoulish souvenir hunters began stealing hubcaps and other removables. The remaining members of the band decided to sell it back to the original dealer, an elderly man who had no idea of the car's history or significance. L519 HKX gained a new registration plate, new hubcaps and a different badge.

* * *

It was difficult to know exactly what to make of this discovery. Police said that they were 'keeping an open mind'. James Dean Bradfield later told *NME* that: 'The conclusion you come to from that is that he couldn't have used the car much more. So if he left it until the 14th and the battery was flat . . . perhaps he just walked off and hitch-hiked. There's a myriad of options.' Nicky Wire had previously still believed there was a good chance Richey would turn up. When the car was found, he thought Richey was either dead, or would be gone a long time. 'If it had been there from the day he went missing,' he told *NME*, 'then I think it's pretty likely that he'd be dead, to be honest with you. But I don't think he was there that day. Otherwise, it would have had a ticket earlier. The battery was flat because he'd been playing tapes and everything. He'd been sleeping in there, obviously.'

The proximity of the Severn Bridge, and the river itself, lent weight to the possibility that Richey had killed himself. Official prognoses were mixed. Welsh police said that bodies in the Severn eventually tended to be washed up in the tide. However, Coroner's Officer Mike Cross, whose jurisdiction covered the bridge area, said it was perfectly possible for a body never to be recovered, due to the strength of the current and to the fact that the Severn flows directly into the Bristol Channel and the Atlantic Ocean. DI Frank Stockholm of Cardiff Police ordered a search of the Severn Estuary, but full dredging was impossible: the Severn, which has the biggest tidal range of any river in the world, was at its height. Rachel Edwards visited every coastguard along the Severn Estuary, but drew a blank.

Nonetheless, it was the bridge-jump theory, almost inevitably, which proved most popular with the tabloid press when the media was informed on the Wednesday morning. The Severn Bridge was hyped up, in many reports, as a 'notorious suicide spot'. This is true only to the extent that bridges in general are notorious suicide spots (as a matter of fact, Clifton Bridge in nearby Bristol has, historically, been far more popular); but the subtext was unmistakable: forget it, he's dead. A very sleazy piece in the *Sunday Mirror*, headlined 'IS RICHEY THE WILD REBEL OF ROCK ALIVE OR DEAD?', ended with the melodramatic, italicised cliffhanger '*Friends fear his demons told him to leap off that bridge, and the dark waters closed over him.*' Not that part of you didn't fear the worst, but the tabloid reportage of this 'cult rock guitarist' was full of ill-informed cliché. Most of it placed him in the lineage of such famous excess-all-areas fuck-ups as Hendrix, Morrison and Vicious (but, as James once pointed out: 'I think if he'd become a lecturer, the same thing could very easily have happened, in a more private way. I don't think it's a natural extension of being in a rock group. It might have accelerated it, but that's all'). Even supposedly decent, moral papers like the *Guardian* were not above squeezing some juicy sensationalism from this human tragedy, running a Richey-related story on the cover of the *Guide* supplement asking, 'CAN ROCK LYRICS KILL?' and even sending reporters to Blackwood to doorstep the Edwards family. Gillian Porter was amazed by their approach. 'A guy from the *Guardian*, of all places, rang me at home, really cheerful, going, "Has the body been found yet? What do we reckon, then, is he dead? Jumped off the bridge, then, has he?"'

The family, meanwhile, continued to make public appeals on television, radio and in the press for Richey to get in touch. Rachel Edwards, who looks unnervingly like her brother (the same eyes, the same mouth), was particularly close to him. 'I've got so

many fond memories of him,' she told LWT's *Missing at Christmas* in December, 'being my brother and being so close in age . . .' Rachel has devoted her life to the search for Richey. 'Richard is the first thing I think of when I open my eyes in the morning,' she told the *Mirror* in 1998. 'I cannot get on with my life or make major changes because I keep hoping he is going to walk through the door as if nothing has happened.' Once again, Rachel made a poignant public plea to Richey. 'I realise that as time has gone on it must seem more difficult for you to return . . . We all love you so much and just hope that whatever has happened, you are no longer in pain.'

The more the Richey story gained momentum through 1995, the more the alleged sightings flooded in. Richey Edwards I-Spy became a macabre popular pastime. Members of the public claimed to have spotted Edwards in, among other places, Cambridge, Whitby, Brighton, Liverpool and outside the Passport Office in Newport. Lucy Winter, a sixteen-year-old from Skipton, north Yorkshire, saw a Richey lookalike appearing haggard and ill, and told the police, but to no avail.

One of the most intriguing testimonies came from Newport taxi driver Anthony Hatherall. At 7 a.m. on 7 February, Hatherall picked up a young man broadly matching Richey's description outside the King's Hotel, a fine old Victorian building in the centre of Newport. Claiming that he worked for a haulage company and was looking for his boss, whose car had broken down, the young man asked Hatherall to drive around Gwent following his directions. Hatherall asked for cash upfront, and the man gave him £40.

The man, described as 'tall, slim and gaunt', carried no luggage and spoke in a possibly fake Cockney accent which repeatedly slipped into a Welsh one. As soon as he climbed into the car, he asked if he could lie down in the back seat, and kept his head below window level, which immediately made Hatherall suspect that he was in some sort of trouble – perhaps on the run from the police. The man instructed Hatherall to drive to Uplands, then to Risca, staying off the major roads. He then asked for the nearest railway station, but there wasn't one nearby, so they headed to Blackwood bus station. The passenger immediately declared, 'This is not the place,' and directed Hatherall instead to Pontypool and New Inn railway station, where he got out to make a phone call. Finally, he asked to be driven back over the Severn Bridge to Aust Services via the scenic route, which he pointed out on an A–Z map. The final fare was £68.

James Dean Bradfield has cast aspersions on Hatherall's account, dismissing it as 'mythical'. There are certainly some inconsistencies (for instance, slim and gaunt Richey may have been, but *tall*?). Somehow, though, the story is strangely believable, if only because one wonders what a sensible fortysomething cabbie with no rock 'n' roll connections had to gain by making it up.

As the months went by, the geographical spread of the sightings grew wider. Richey was 'seen' as far afield as Germany and America. In May, a German friend claimed to have received a postcard from Richey marked 'London Feb 3'. Frustratingly, the German refused to present the postcard to substantiate the story (and one has to ask: if Richey really wanted to disappear, would he have been so careless?). LWT's *Missing at Christmas* also threw up eight new sightings. These included drinking at a gay pub in Brighton, begging in Liverpool, and busking (er, busking?!) in Cambridgeshire. Richey was also apparently spotted by a pair of Manics fans, reading in Books Etc on London's Charing Cross Road.

Whilst the majority of these 'sightings' were doubtless reported in good faith, there was inevitably a handful of sick, malicious hoaxes. 'At first, it was mostly telephone stuff,' remembers DC Tom Gorringe, one of the first officers to work on the case. 'There were a lot of crank calls.' Some of the pranksters even got hold of the Edwards family's home phone number, as Rachel told the *Daily Mirror*: 'We have suffered some of the cruellest hoaxes possible. Someone called up and said: "Hello, Mam, it's me", and then they put the phone down. But there is only one reason we won't change our number, and that is in case Richey decided to pick up the phone one day.'

'Every great band has to lose a member' – THE STUD BROTHERS, *MELODY MAKER*

Perhaps the least welcome repercussion of the many awards received by the Manics after their comeback was that every newspaper editor ordered their hacks to come up with a Richey story, no matter how flimsy. Undoubtedly the most famous was the yarn touted around by one Vyvyan Morris, a 48-year-old part-time lecturer in Media Studies at Neath College and a veteran of the Swansea music scene, known locally as 'Spiv'. Talking about 70s Welsh rockers Badfinger on a radio programme, Morris digressed to claim that he had seen Richey Edwards in the Indian resort of Goa on 6 November 1996. The story was repeated by *Wales on Sunday* on 2 March 1997, before being picked up by several other newspapers.

Goa is a former Portuguese colony (it is actually a separate state on India's western coastline), and a popular hangout for backpackers, hippies, druggies and ravers. It has been described as 'the best place in the world to lose yourself'. Vyvyan Morris was wandering around a market in the Goan town of Anjuna when he made his alleged sighting. According to his account, he had momentarily lost his girlfriend, who was carrying their camera (conveniently, a cynic might say), when he saw 'Richey' wearing a kaftan top and jeans, and carrying a tote bag. He had 'quite matted, longish hair', was fuller-figured than the 'amphetamine gazelle' he remembered, was visibly sunburnt, and looked 'a bit out of it'. 'Richey' then stood up and got on a minibus. Morris approached a man with whom 'Richey' had been talking, Jeff Reid, originally from Bath but a Goa resident for twenty years. Reid told Morris the man was called 'Rick', and was a newcomer who had been in Goa for eighteen months.

The morning after the Manics' triumph at the Brit Awards, the *Daily Mail* ran a follow-up story with a banner flash across its front page: 'MYSTERY OF THE POP STAR WHO VANISHED ON THE BRINK OF FAME'. The *Mail* had actually sent a journalist out to Goa, who met a bar proprietor called Manuel in the fishing village of Arambol; Manuel claimed that Richey had joined him to play guitar. In Anjuna, a Dr Jawahorlal Hendricks claimed to have treated a patient called Richey Edwards for a serious lung infection. An unnamed hippie, shown a photograph of Richey, claimed to know him as 'Steve'.

There were several glaring problems with the Goa theory. For a start, by his own admission, Vyvyan Morris had only actually met Richey once, in a brief encounter backstage at Swansea's Singleton Park, three years earlier. Secondly, were we really supposed to believe that Richey could remain incognito in a resort frequented by thousands of young, pop-literate Brits (and that he could keep his scars and tattoos hidden by long sleeves in such a hot climate)? Thirdly, the notion of Richey playing guitar was hard to swallow. With all respect, unless he had packed Bert Weedon's *Play in a Day* in that tote bag . . . 'Put it this way,' Nicky Wire told *NME*. 'When you get the supposed "sighting" of Richey in Goa I'm not fucking jumping up and down thinking: "That's him!" because I know it's not him . . . Some Swansea journalist dickhead who just happened to be on holiday in Goa saw someone looking like Richey playing a guitar – well, that obviously means it's not Richey straightaway! Unless he's doing Fall covers: "Nng! Nnng! Nng! Nnnnng!"'

At the time, however, the *Daily Mail* story was greeted with guarded optimism. 'We're not planning to fly out there,' said Sherry Edwards, 'but we're keeping an open mind.' PC Chris Coleman also admitted that: 'This looks like the best lead yet.' Privately, Hall Or Nothing called Interpol on to the case, just to be sure. As Terri Hall pointed out, however: 'In the past few months, Richey has supposedly been seen in seven different countries, like Germany, Poland and the USA. If anyone genuinely feels they have definitely seen Richey, they should call the police immediately. What use is four months later?'

On the other hand, perhaps there is more to the Goa theory than meets the eye. Rachel Edwards had already heard of other Goan sightings before Morris produced his account, and PC Michael Cole, the man currently in charge of the Richey case at Paddington's missing-persons desk, has received several since. 'There has been more than one sighting from Goa,' reveals PC Cole. 'For what it's worth, and my opinion isn't worth any more than yours, I'd say that's where he is. Only because so many people, unconnected with each other, have come up with the same sighting. If anybody was actually pursuing him, I'd say that would be the best place to look. But we wouldn't have any powers to pursue him here, let alone in India.'

It is far easier simply to vanish than you might think. The National Missing Persons Helpline estimate that a quarter of a million people in the UK go missing per year. The vast majority come home again within a matter of days or weeks, yet there remains a sizeable core of people who disappear without trace. At any given time, the NMPH is working on about fourteen thousand such cases, long after the initial police trail has cooled (the organisation has publicised Richey's case through advertisements in the *Big Issue* magazine and on their Teletext site). According to spokesperson Sophie Woodforde: 'It's surprisingly easy to disappear within the UK, if you so wish. Just move to a new town, assume a new identity and find a job.' Nicky Wire draws comfort from this fact; as he pointed out to BBC2's *Close-Up* arts series: 'People move from Newcastle to Middlesbrough and aren't seen for 25 years.' This, he thought, was more likely in Richey's case than going abroad: 'It all seemed more like Reginald Perrin than Lord Lucan.'

Not everyone agrees. DS Stephen Morey, who worked on the Richey case and has twelve years' experience in the Met, shockingly went public with his belief that Richey is dead. 'I would say it would be relatively difficult to have remained this anonymous for this period of time in this country,' he told the *Guardian*. 'For me, personally, he is no longer with us.' But PC Michael Cole, Morey's successor on the Richey case, believes that it is: '. . . very, very easy to disappear. Obviously it requires that you have certain support systems. It's very hard to do it otherwise.'

And to leave the UK? 'It would be almost as easy to disappear to Europe,' says Sophie Woodford, 'by buying a One-Year Passport [in 1995, it was still possible to get this simply by walking into a Post Office with your Birth Certificate], which is very difficult for police to trace.' Indeed, shortly after Richey's disappearance, writer/actor Stephen Fry disappeared following a breakdown, and later turned up in Belgium. To go further afield – Goa, for example – Richey would have needed a full EC passport to replace the one he left in the flat. 'It's very easy to get a passport through the back door,' says PC Cole, 'by buying it illegally. I'm not saying that's what he's done. That's just conjecture.'

Whether or not it would have been easy for Richey to disappear, did the police try hard enough to find him?

According to a police statement at the time: 'Obviously if it was a vulnerable juvenile who had gone missing, we would continue to search actively for him or her until they had been found. But you have to accept that every adult has the right just to go missing.' And so, although Richey's disappearance was publicised and investigated, he was not being actively pursued. I asked PC Michael Cole to explain this policy. 'The criterion for that is that there is nothing to suggest that he was physically or mentally ill when he disappeared, and there was nothing to suggest that there was anything suspicious about his disappearance. He's a grown man who's decided to walk away from a situation he didn't want to be in. Quite often, for any number of reasons, a person decides to walk away from their life and start again. And it would be an infringement of civil liberties to pursue them. Normally we'd confirm where he was for our own interests, and confirm to the interested parties that he's safe and well, but not disclose where he is. That's our general line in these cases. Obviously there are no absolutes, but without absolutes we can only go on what we've got, and that's all there is.'

I asked PC Cole whether more would have been done if Richey had been either mentally subnormal, or a psychiatric patient who was considered a risk to himself (or the public). 'Definitely. The way the system works is that there are a number of categories, and one of them is "Limited", which means that the details are circulated, but that's as far as it goes.' Which, it must be said, seems far from satisfactory. There was, after all, plenty of evidence to suggest that Richey was mentally ill when he disappeared, and that he may have posed a threat to himself.

A BBC Radio Wales *Eye on Wales* documentary about Richey's disappearance (17 March 1997) criticised a lack of coordination between the Avon & Somerset, South Wales and Metropolitan Police forces. PC Cole is the first to agree. 'There isn't even a Met-wide policy, let alone a nationwide policy.' Cases of this kind are further complicated by the fact that there is a high turnover of staff in police stations, and also because files are regularly handed from one officer to the next to the next, thus damaging continuity. At the London end, the case was first investigated by DS Tom Gorringe and DS Regan, then by DS Stephen Moray, and is now in the hands of PC Michael Cole under the supervision of DCI Silley (the report is kept in a safe because of its high profile). In Wales, it is a similar story: when I rang the Cardiff Central Police Station, I was unable to find even one existing member of staff with first-hand knowledge of the Richey Edwards case.

Then there was the matter of video footage. Rachel Edwards hit out at police handling after *Eye on Wales* revealed that 24-hour Severn Bridge surveillance camera footage existed, but that detectives had not studied the tapes until that very week, over two years too late. 'I have been told by a police officer from the Met that the tapes had been destroyed, and now, two years down the line, I find out that they were there.' Rachel was subsequently allowed to see the tapes, according to Scotland Yard spokeswoman Jackie Jones, 'to put the minds of the family at rest'. Although the image of a figure was apparently visible on the murky film, there was nothing conclusive either way.

PC Cole, however, claims that the delay in examining the bridge footage was no major oversight. 'The footage came from a camera that is 150 feet in the air. It is designed for traffic flow, nothing else. You would be hard-pushed, even with video enhancement, to tell if you're looking at a lorry, a bus or a car. I can say categorically that the idea that you could identify somebody from that is arrant nonsense. It was laughable. The local police said you must be on another planet to think that. If there were any figures on the bridge, they would be so far away as to be unidentifiable. I doubt if we would be able to tell if the figure were a man or a woman.'

Richey James Edwards, sexually ambiguous to the last.

With every anniversary, awards ceremony or hit record comes another upsurge of interest in the Richey Edwards story. The coverage tends to be at best clichéd and sentimental, and at worst ghoulish. As something of a known authority on the Manics, I am often called upon to contribute. On one occasion, a radio news programme tried to make me the mouthpiece for its trite take on the situation. 'Will you say: "He lives on through his music?"' they asked. "No, I will not,' I replied.

One programme I did say 'Yes' to, to my eternal regret, was 'The Vanishing of Richey Manic'. A half-hour documentary made by Teliesyn, a Welsh production company which no longer exists, the programme was broadcast on 5 October 1996, the day on which the Manics' autumn tour began, as part of Channel Four's *Fame Factor* season. Disappointing and, in places, downright tacky, it was littered with fist-chewingly naff 'reconstructions' (a shaven-headed man in pyjamas staring meaningfully into the river, the camera swooping over the barriers of the Severn Bridge and down towards the water, as if re-creating a suicide jump), and spooky, portentous voice-overs ('. . . and he was never seen again'). The only Manics music was 'Theme from M*A*S*H' (the only MSP single not written by the band, and therefore not requiring its publishing permission), and the only Richey footage Teliesyn had unearthed was an MTV interview from 1994: 'All we've ever been interested in doing is making a record which encapsulates a mood and a time, and then it can be a full stop, you know, bye bye.' The 'bye bye' bit, hilariously, was made to fade into an ominous echo: 'BYE BYE, Bye Bye, bye bye . . .'

The choice of guests was also perplexing. Steve Lamacq (and, I like to think, this author) provided a degree of sense, but what the fuck Shaun Ryder and Boy George were doing in there was as much of a mystery as anything surrounding the missing rhythm guitarist. 'I think if he is alive it would make the whole story much more interesting and much more intriguing and exciting and we could all drag it out for a lot longer,' George chortled fatly, as if discussing an enjoyable episode of Miss Marple. Most commentators seemed handicapped by the belief that Richey was just another typical rock 'n' roll burn-out, overdosed on drugs/food/sex/alcohol/religion/whatever. They raised the names of Curtis and Cobain (correctly), but also of Hendrix and Morrison (incorrectly). As Nicky Wire reminded *Select*: 'Ian Curtis and Kurt Cobain were the two Richey icons. The Hendrixes and the rest were just decadent. But Kurt and Ian meant to do it – took control. That was more fascinating to Richey.' Nor did MSP fans Becky Craig and Jessica McGinney give a particularly good impression of the band's followers in general: 'Everything I said, I said because he said it, everything I did, I did because he did it. I'm not sure whether that's a good thing . . .'

At the Cardiff date of the Manics' 1996 tour, Rachel Edwards, apparently under the mistaken impression that I had been responsible for the programme itself, accosted me, understandably furious, and said: 'That wasn't my brother they were talking about there.' I could only agree. James and Sean, too, were upset that I had been involved. Not as upset as I was. I could understand their anger but, I insisted, I am a pop critic, and commenting on rock 'n' roll is what I do for a living (and, for the record, I still stand by everything I actually *said* in the programme). I received £200 for my troubles and, if I weren't perpetually broke, I would have sent it back by now. However, I had entered into the project in good faith, swayed largely by the fact that Steve Lamacq, whom I trusted, was also involved. Indeed, I had already turned down the approaches of two other television companies when I smelled a rat and suspected them of planning a dodgy and tasteless show. In contrast, Teliesyn at least *talked a good programme*. Sadly, they did not make one.

'The Vanishing . . .' was a wasted opportunity and an unfitting tribute. Richey deserved better. The fans did. We all did.

There is one question I get asked more than any other by Manic Street Preachers fans: 'What do you think happened to Richey?'

Depending on my mood, I normally reply: 'I dunno, what do *you* think happened to him?' The truth, to be honest, is that I still believe that Richey Edwards walks among us. I respect the views of anyone who, having examined the facts in this chapter, comes to completely the opposite conclusion. What I cannot abide, though, are those who have no knowledge of the man or of his life, but who blithely enquire: 'So, what about that bloke who jumped off the bridge, then?'

There is certainly enough evidence, if you want it, to support the theory that Richey at least initially *intended* to stay alive. Some might call this denial but, despite the pessimistic conclusions of the likes of DS Stephen Morey, it is at least as likely that Richey is alive as that he is dead. As PC Michael Cole affirms: 'There's nothing to suggest that he isn't alive.' And, facts aside, instinct is as valid a response as any. Nicky Wire has said that 'Deep down, it's my feeling that he's alive. But that's not based on any logical evidence. I just try to tell myself that he's done what he wanted to. Whatever that is.'

Sophie Woodforde of the National Missing Persons Helpline, who is very familiar with Richey's case, says: 'After a while, you develop a sort of instinct for these things, that maybe the person wasn't getting on with their parents or whatever, but that doesn't seem to have been the case with Richard. On the other hand, you have to ask whether he would want to put his family through that distress.' A fair point, and some sceptics wondered why, if Richey was alive, he hadn't thought to make contact. (The answer might be quite simple: like many depression sufferers, Richey had a paradoxical mix of self-hatred and absolute self-centredness.)

Journalist and Gold Blade musician John Robb says of Richey: 'He's the one person I've met in a rock 'n' roll band who would want to read his own obituary.' Martin Carr, mainman of The Boo Radleys and long-time Manics fan, puts his view even more simply: 'Richey doesn't feel dead.'

'It isn't dying that's sad. It's living when you're not happy' – OCTAVE MIRBEAU, *THE TORTURE GARDEN*

Nicky Wire accepts the *possibility* that Richey may be dead – he isn't stupid – citing the fact that 27 is the optimum age for young men to commit suicide, and is a cursed year for rock stars (Jimi Hendrix, Janis Joplin, Brian Jones and Kurt Cobain all died aged 27). That said, rock history is also littered with disappearing acts. When Joe Strummer walked out on The Clash in the early 80s, he was eventually tracked down in Paris by a private detective, whereupon he said that he had 'wanted a break'. Pink Floyd's Syd Barrett, edged out of the band after a spell of mental illness in 1968, vanished from public life and turned up two decades later, living with his mum in Cambridge. If to lose one member is unfortunate, then Fleetwood Mac must qualify as careless. Two Mac members disappeared in quick succession: enigmatic, inspirational leader Peter Green went AWOL in 1970 and did not resurface until the 90s; the following year guitarist Jeremy Spencer said he was 'just popping out to get some newspapers' on Sunset Boulevard and subsequently turned up in the Children of God religious cult.

Wire, then, tries to remain positive. 'Richey could be working in a sewage works in Barry, for all we know. Done a Reggie Perrin.' (*Author's note: there is no sewage works in Barry. They just pump it straight on to the beaches*.) 'Maybe he'll disappear for five years and come back with the greatest book ever written, a huge beard, and really happy.'

On other occasions, however, Wire appears to accept that Richey may be dead. In an *Esquire* interview, speaking about Kurt Cobain, he said, 'I just hope he [Cobain] is up there with Richey jamming a Fall song. Real spazzy fucking dodgy song. I just hope they're playing the most shite punk rock in the world. Screaming their fucking heads off.'

Epic MD Rob Stringer believes that Richey carefully orchestrated the whole thing. 'Richey is a very ritualistic person. He doesn't act arbitrarily. And the scary thing is, he's the most well-read person I've ever known – he would be able to tell you the last words of all the world's most famous suicides, he would know the contents of Kurt Cobain's suicide note off by heart and he would know twenty different ways to disappear completely. He will have planned it. He may be in Tibet for all I know . . .'

Nicky Wire goes along with the premeditation theory. 'The week before he disappeared, he was in the best spirits I'd seen him in since the first breakdown, and I thought he was getting better. Sometimes now I think that he was happy because he knew he was going to do something.'

One persistent rumour – denied vigorously, it must be said – has it that Rob Stringer had, in good faith, loaned a book on the perfect disappearance to a fascinated Richey. Some versions claim that Richey had read *dozens* of books on the subject.

Then again, he'd read plenty of books on suicide. When I interviewed Richey in late 1993, he told me about two books, one pro- and one anti-suicide, which he had been reading. The first was by Harold Brodkey. 'He's written articles on death,' Richey told me, 'and on the futility of life. His basic argument is that most people's lives never amount to much. People are more upset when a five-year-old dies than a fifty-year-old, but both their lives are equally worthless.' The second book was Jeffrey Eugenides's *The Virgin Suicides*, a novel about a family of sisters who all commit suicide. 'One thing it says,' Richey told me, 'is that 33 per cent of all jump suicides have severe torn muscles in their shoulders, which means they jump off the bridge, then grasp and cling: the instinct for survival. Even when they're that far down, there's a reflex reaction to stay alive.'

Then, of course, there were his suicidal icons. 'Joy Division were a big part of my adolescence,' he said, 'and wrote the most beautiful lyrics ever. Ian Curtis was the only musician whose death I have ever been saddened by. Basically, anyone else could drop dead tomorrow and I wouldn't give a fuck. I wouldn't shed a tear.' Plus, of course, Richey had already tried once . . .

On the other hand, more than one of his heroes staged their disappearances. 'One of the best things I've ever read is J.D. Salinger,' he told *EP* magazine in 1991. 'After his big success, *Catcher in the Rye*, he just locked himself away in a basement for twenty years. But he was still writing. He'd got stacks of manuscripts on his shelves, but no one's ever seen 'em.' The interviewer asked, 'Can you see yourself doing that?', to which Richey replied, 'I'd like to think so.' (Having said this, however, Nicky Wire was even more of a Salinger fan than Edwards, and *he's* never disappeared.)

The other obvious comparison was with Arthur Rimbaud, the French symbolist poet. At the age of nineteen, Rimbaud published his final work, *Un Saison en Enfer* (*A Season in Hell*), which deals with his struggle to make a break with his past. It was poorly received by critics and, in response, Rimbaud burnt all his manuscripts and staged his own disappearance. Although he was generally presumed dead, he was actually gun-running in Africa. In late 1994, Richey Edwards was wearing a white boiler suit covered in felt-tipped Rimbaud verse.

And so it goes, around and around, without definitive evidence either way. In a way, this debilitating cycle of doubt, of theory and counter-theory, is grimly fitting. As Taylor Parkes of *Melody Maker* once wrote: 'Nirvana were all about certainty . . . The Manics, on the other hand, are all about doubt on every level, even down to Richey's sexual ambiguity. Which is why it's so horribly appropriate that Kurt shot himself and Richey just went missing.' In a debate in the same publication, Ed from Manics-inspired neo-punks S*M*A*S*H made the same point in cruder terms: 'It's like a Ruth Rendell mystery, innit? He's not dead, he's not alive, he's just missing.'

Nicky Wire feels this way, too: 'You can go in his flat and look at every book, every thing. At the end of the day, you haven't got a clue,' he told *NME*. 'He was adept at dramatic symbolism,' said James Dean Bradfield. 'You would expect something, just a tiny little thing. But at the end of the day, no matter how many little lies were going around, there were no clues.'

But maybe there *were*. One book Richey definitely did read shortly before disappearing was *Novel with Cocaine*, written in the early 1930s by the pseudonymous 'M. Ageyev', whose identity remains a mystery to this day.

According to an article written in the *Independent* by Emma Forrest, a close personal friend of both Richey Edwards and James Dean Bradfield at the time, Richey met an unspecified female friend on the night before his disappearance and gave her a copy of *Novel with Cocaine*, instructing her to read the introduction. The contents of the novel itself are probably not significant (the memoirs of a Holden Caulfield-esque adolescent, addicted to cocaine, living a *belle epoque* high life against the background of revolutionary Russia). The introduction, however, sheds a little light on the mysterious 'M. Ageyev' and the circumstances surrounding the publication of his novel. A Russian exile living in Istanbul who had previously spent time in a mental asylum, 'Ageyev' sent the manuscript of his novel unsolicited to a Paris-based Russian *emigré* journal called *Numbers*. The story was an instant hit, and when published in novel form, became a word-of-mouth *succés de scandale*. With fame beckoning, 'Ageyev' was invited to Paris, but chose instead to shun stardom and vanished without trace. The comparisons are obvious, and it is surely not too fanciful to assume that in pointing his female friend towards this story, Richey was trying to tell her something.

Many of the other, more glaring 'clues' Richey left behind – the car abandoned at a 'notorious suicide spot', the passport left on the table, the desk he ordered but never paid for – could easily be construed as red herrings, carefully planted to encourage the idea that he had committed suicide, and throw investigators off the scent. And what better time to plan a disappearance than under the cover of another big journey (to America), when you have already packed bags, drawn out money, etc? And was his new haircut calculated to make himself less recognisable? (Probably not: if so, he would surely have shaved his head that night, not a fortnight earlier.)

And whether Richey decided to live or die, the question remains: why did he abscond in the first place? Rumours that he had rowed with the band and invented an 'ear infection' because he didn't want to go to America have been dismissed as total rubbish. Indeed, as Rob Stringer states: 'What worries people so much is the fact that there was no blow-up, no row in the band, nothing. When he was ill last time, everyone saw it coming, but this time there were no signs.' Could there have been a purely physiological explanation? It seems that Richey had not been taking his Prozac, leaving him vulnerable to mood-swings. But the drug has a long half-life (it remains in the system for around a week), so this alone would not explain his sudden departure. And if he had suddenly decided to kill himself, then – to be blunt – wouldn't he have just done so there and then in the Embassy Hotel?

Another vital point, of course, is that it isn't a simple either/or question. It is wrong to assume that he either threw himself off the Severn Bridge or he's still out there somewhere, alive and well. There are any number of feasible permutations. The awful truth is that he may well have survived in hiding for a while, then killed himself two years ago. Or three months ago. He may be doing it now. Or tomorrow.

It scarcely bears thinking about, but these are the possibilities that those close to him must ponder every single day.

Some theories surrounding Richey's vanishing are stranger than others. The suggestion that he may have joined a religious cult or entered a monastery, apparently favoured by the Edwards family, is relatively credible given Richey's supposed religious conversion/confusion. Rachel Edwards wrote to all the monasteries in the UK asking if Richey were staying there, but every reply from the monks said that they were duty-bound not to reveal the names of their residents.

Slightly less likely is the theory advanced by a certain Bob Whitmore of Palma, Mallorca, who, by tracing connections between Richey's lyrics and the works of Aleister Crowley, 'proved' that Richey was part of a satanic sect. One fan even advanced the fascinating possibility that the date of Richey's disappearance may have been significant: it was the fiftieth anniversary of the liberation of the Nazi concentration camps. (The fact that Sid Vicious had committed suicide on 2 February 1979 can almost certainly be dismissed as coincidental; Richey had never expressed any particular admiration for Vicious.)

Then there were the conspiracy theories. For instance, some of the Manics' more trainspotter-ish fans read more into the band's eventual decision to continue than was really there. In 1994, James Dean Bradfield had said: 'If Richey left, the band would probably be over. I can't imagine the Manics without him.' Surely, then, ran the literal-minded interpretation, they wouldn't consider carrying on unless they at least knew that he was OK – right? Wrong. Several people, most of whom should know better, continue to imply that the band know of Richey's whereabouts. 'What I normally suspect in cases like this,' says PC Michael Cole, 'is that there are a number of people within his immediate circle who know exactly where he is.' It must be stated, immediately, that this is inconceivable. The idea that the visible psychological toll that Richey's disappearance has taken on the band, and his family's relentless appeals for his return, comprise some sort of elaborate front is nothing less than insulting.

'I want to fly and run till it hurts . . .' – 'AUSTRALIA'

The Manics' return to the public eye with the *This Is My Truth Tell Me Yours* album brought with it another inevitable rash of 'Richey' sightings. One night in October 1998, British barmaid Tracey Jones was working at the Underground pub in Corralejo on the tiny Canary Island of Fuerteventura, when a drinker came in whom she thought was 'just like Richey'. A few moments later, another customer (according to one version, a policeman) is said to have started shouting 'You're Richey from the Manic Street Preachers!', at which point the Richey lookalike ran towards the door and fled, leaving his drink unfinished. The second customer gave chase, but 'Richey' had fled.

According to Karen Zudic of Canaries local paper *The Island Sun* (which broke the story and opened a hotline for further sightings), 'It's a bit of a Robinson Crusoe island. The people who live there tend not to have much contact with the outside world. Richey – if it was him – would have gone unrecognised by the locals. Maybe he realised that, and that was why he was there. And since there are six ferries a day to Lanzarote, it's very easy to leave in a hurry should the need arise.' The *South Wales Echo* relayed the story in the UK, and *Wales on Sunday* helpfully added that there had since been four more 'sightings' in Goa.

One wonders exactly how many Richey James Edwardses the papers think are at large. On Monday 30 November 1998, the morning that 'The Everlasting' was released, the *Western Mail* ran a story, based on just one anonymous phone call, to the effect that Richey was a patient in East Glamorgan Hospital's psychiatric ward in Church Village (near Pontypridd). A senior nurse refused to confirm or deny Edwards's presence: standard patient-confidentiality practice, from which the *Mail* seemed to infer some sort of cover-up (given its geographical location, the hospital probably contains *scores* of R. Edwardses at any given moment). The story hinged upon the remarkable sentence 'But she [the nurse] seemed unperturbed by the idea that the hospital could be home to one of the world's most elusive stars, asking "Who is this person? I'll have to write his name down."'

Just *one* anonymous phone call, and another few column inches are wrung from the Richey mystery (if I rang the *Western Mail* tomorrow and said, "Richey's been living in my wardrobe for the last four years," would they print that too?). For family and friends, the whole cycle of raised hopes and eventual disappointment takes yet another cruel turn. According to subsequent radio reports, Nicky Wire visited the hospital to check the sighting out, just in case; while Graham and Sherry Edwards, according to the *Mail on Sunday*, flew to Fuerteventura.

In April 1998, the badly decomposed body of a young man was washed up at Caldicot, downstream of the Severn Bridge on the Welsh side. Gwent Police investigated the possibility that it was Richey but, after checking dental records, this was quickly eliminated.

At the moment, as far as anyone knows, Richey Edwards is not dead. 'It's very hard to judge with something that is now quite an old case,' says PC Michael Cole. 'He could be anywhere. And he could be doing anything. Of course, we still get told that Jim Morrison is selling chips in Stockport. If something's *that* outlandish . . .'

Quite. As Ted Kessler of *NME* put it: 'When we read that Elvis is working in a burger bar in Hammersmith we can be fairly sure of the story's inaccuracy, but a sighting of Richey can never be fully discounted.'

For now, though, the case remains 'open and inactive'. According to Met spokeswoman Jackie Jones, this simply means that 'The case isn't shut. If any new information comes to light we will investigate it.' In the meantime, Richey's royalties, now estimated to be over £1 million, will be kept in a trust fund, awaiting his return. In February 2002 – barring any dramatic news in the interim – Richey Edwards will officially be declared dead.

National Missing Persons Helpline
Helpline: Freecall 0500-700700
'Message Home' (discretion assured): Freecall 0500-700740
Donations: National Missing Persons Helpline Charity, c/o Roebuck House, 284 Upper
   Richmond Road West, East Sheen, London SW14 7JE

The Samaritans
Linkline: 0345-909090 (24 hours)
E-mail: jo@samaritans.org
Donations: The Samaritans, 10 The Grove, Slough, Berkshire SO1 1QP

i) . . . To where?

(THE ABSENT PRESENCE OF RICHEY EDWARDS)

'the failing candle.still.casts.casts a shadow' – PATRICK JONES

THOSE WHO ABSCOND FROM FAME FASCINATE the popular imagination far more than those who stick around to watch it die. Celebrity is a gift usually bestowed quickly, then slowly allowed to atrophy, progressively eroding the dignity of its desperately clinging recipient as it does so. When someone chooses to cast it aside, however, the public is confused: 'What, don't you *want* our lovely present?!'

In *Dead Elvis* by Greil Marcus, the author assembles a stupefying array of posthumous Presley ephemera, artefacts and anecdotes, not in an attempt to prove anything as trite as 'The King Lives On', but to argue that *something else* does: a cultural spectre which manifests itself in random and chaotic ways, far beyond the control of such linear, traditional notions as 'legacy' or 'remembrance'.

In a way, the cultural afterlife of Richey James Edwards is analogous to that of Presley: tiny but anatomically similar, an intensified microcosm, a case study. There is only one fundamental difference: Elvis grew and grew until he just plain blew up; Richey shrank and shrank until he faded from view completely.

That this man for whom humility (a more polite term for self-hatred?) was second nature should become an icon is the ultimate irony. James Dean Bradfield, talking to *Q* magazine, accepted that Richey Edwards will for ever be a cipher for alienated youth: 'Richey's myth is up and running.' And the Manics, as junior pop dreamers, were suckers for *all that* too. 'I can understand it,' Nicky Wire told *Top*, 'because when I was young – it's a sad thing to say – I found the thought of Ian Curtis or Brian Jones intensely exciting. But in reality it was such an un-rock 'n' roll thing to do; he was driving a crappy Vauxhall Cavalier in the pissing down rain – it's hardly driving a Cadillac around Los Angeles or something.'

A Richey autograph recently fetched £140 (and this is a man who signed a *lot* of autographs). The moment when that crappy Vauxhall Cavalier was found at the Severn Bridge, Richey – although his demise is by no means a certainty – added his name to the Sudden-Death Cult: Bolan, Cobain, Curtis, Dean, Monroe, Vicious, and all those other 99p *They Died Too Young* pocket books you see piled on the bargain table in Woolworths. He's *one of them*.

The first manifestations of Richey's cultural impact were direct and literal. In the spring of 1994, six Nirvana fans had killed themselves in the wake of Kurt Cobain's suicide. In the spring of 1995, young Manics fans began running away from home. On 3 March, seventeen-year-old Sally Allen, a sixth-form A-Level student from Swinton, south Yorkshire, grief-stricken at Richey's absence, went missing. Sally had already shaved her head and stopped eating. She was thought to have gone to Wales. A rash of similar copycat disappearances followed, Even now, a new case occasionally arises. In October 1997 Christopher Goodall, another seventeen-year-old from Stockport, Greater Manchester, also went missing. He had apparently regarded Richey's disappearance as 'the coolest thing in the world'.

For others, Richey's vanishing acted as a catalyst (or, if one wishes to be sceptical, an excuse) for their own self-destructive behaviour. While it would take a callous beast to claim that all self-mutilating Manics fans are attention-seeking phoneys, it would take a fool to claim that none of them is.

For some, as *Melody Maker*'s Stud Brothers wrote: '. . . his appeal lay precisely in the fact that he seemed so utterly and selfishly doomed – part Narcissus, part Icarus'. These people, without doubt, were as misguided as the grateful peasants who camped out in St James Park after 31 August 1997, weeping tears for a parasite princess whose social class had condemned them to serfdom. Taylor Parkes, also writing in *Melody Maker*, perfectly described 'the nation of orphans wriggling in the wake of Richey's leaving . . . half in love with death, too drunk on the import of their misery to ever confront it . . . they refuse to question the crooked conviction that the day their lives take shape again is just the day that they become like everybody else. This was never the point of Manic Street Preachers. This was never the point of Richey James.'

It was sometimes difficult to tell the real from the fake. On 8 April 1995, the anniversary of Kurt Cobain's death, *Melody Maker*, in a joint Kurt/Richey cover entitled 'From Despair to Where?', canvassed distressed Manics fans for their reactions to Richey's disappearance. Jasmine of Sunderland: 'I cut Richey's name into my arm because I'm so depressed.' Elizabeth of Harrow: 'I almost died when I heard he was gone, and have thought about killing myself several times since. I have to hurt myself to stay calm.' Jane of Brighton: 'I feel my whole life's been ripped in two. I'm scared of what lengths I'll go to if the worst comes to the worst.'

Some cases seemed more genuine than others. Beeza Seed of *Young, Pretty & Fucked* fanzine once told me: 'Richey's disappearance was the trigger that started my breakdown . . . but it was also the first day of my recovery. My mum died when I was sixteen, and initially I hated her for leaving me. But when Richey disappeared – someone worth grieving over – all my true feelings for my mum flooded out. People do project their own feelings on to Richey.' Some fans resented Richey for leaving, as Beeza had done with her mother. Micky Lee of London: 'The lack of consideration shown to his family and friends is unbelievable. No matter how bad he felt, he must have known they cared about him and that all they want now is a postcard or phone call. Is that too much to ask?'

Of course, there are plenty of Richey wannabes with too strong a self-preservation instinct to imitate his self-abuse. They don't aspire towards living like Richey, just looking like him. In the main, they choose his Glory Years – leopardskin, eyeliner and ratted hair – rather than The Decline. There is a perfectly good reason for this: looking ill might get you mothered, but looking foxy gets you laid.

As Beeza Seed says, people do indeed project their own feelings on to Richey – as they might do on to a saint, a religious icon, or even Christ himself.

In Richey's favourite comic strip, *Bad Company*, the main character Kano is described (in Richey's words) as: 'Colonel Kurtz meets the Virgin Mary'. In certain ways, Richey himself has taken on religious qualities. After 'The Vanishing of Richey Manic' documentary, *Select*'s David Cavanagh pointed out that fans spoke of Richey in Christlike terms (e.g. 'When I first found Him . . .'). One fan, in a letter to me, once wrote: 'Richey shines like Madonna might in the eyes of a Catholic.' Another, recalling a backstage encounter, said: 'He was like Jesus and we were the twelve disciples.'

Like any religion, The Church of Richey has its fundamentalist sect, which first appeared *circa* his hospitalisation, when the music-press letters pages were filled with missives from fans who believed that they, and only they, could save Richey (a case of oh, we do like to be beside the suicide). As more details emerged, the idolatry stepped up a gear, beyond mere canonisation. Richey's cutting and bleeding became deeply symbolic, a perverse sacrament. He became a stigmata martyr: 'He Bled For Our Sins.'

No religion is complete without guilt, and every Manics fan, sooner or later, had to engage in a degree of soul-searching after Richey's disappearance. There had always been an element of ghoulish voyeurism to the Cult of Richey – we were all of us (would-be) Spectators of Suicide, hypocrites happy to live a 4-REAL life by proxy. 'Stay just fucked up enough to write all those cool songs,' we seemed to be asking, 'but not so fucked up that you aren't around any more.' As one letter pointed out, many cynics in the press had seemed to think that, because Richey was still alive, he could not possibly be '4 Real'. Could they look themselves in the mirror after 1 February 1995? *Who's responsible? We fucking are . . .*

Perverse and bizarre as it may seem, what I can only term The Christing of Richey Edwards is now a *fait accompli*. Nicky Wire must feel like John the Fucking Baptist.

To date, no hymns to Richey have been written, but there are already several records about him. The Beautiful People wrote one; so too did Carter USM, whose 'Born on the Fifth of November', released in August 1995, was apparently about 'people like Richey, people who are too good for this world'. The best song, perhaps inevitably, came from someone who actually knew what he was talking about. Gold Blade, led by John Robb, the ex-*Sounds* journalist who had given the Manics their first music-press front cover, wrote the unnervingly gothic '4 Real 4 Ever' (on the B-side of '16 Tons'), as a single-minded narrative from Richey's perspective: 'I'm getting in the car, I'm going to the bridge . . . I've got a load of cash, I'm gonna leave the country.'

The most controversial record appeared in April 1997. Ideal, an indie quintet from Cheltenham, released the single 'Richey is Dead', a frustrated love plea from singer Will Hutchinson to a girl who refuses to accept the possibility/likelihood of Richey's death. The sleeve bore the classic '4 REAL' shot, the band's name superimposed on Richey's forearm. There was a brief flurry of outrage at the song from fans and journalists (the Manics and their management left it at a strict 'no comment'). *Sky* magazine smashed up the single and sent it back to Ideal in pieces. The band dared to tout for a gig in Blackwood, but were turned down. They are apparently still going, but there is no real interest.

No true fan of the Manics – the band which spat in the face of reverence, the band which sang 'I laughed when Lennon got shot' – can feel affronted by the record. In many ways, 'Richey is Dead' was truer to the Manics' original spirit than were any of the coded epitaphs/'Richey come home' pleas which they have written themselves (of which, more elsewhere). Like 'Randy Scouse Git', The Monkees' barbed bitch at The Beatles, it should be viewed as a backhanded compliment. It was a shameless publicity stunt, but . . . where have we heard *that* phrase before? The only legitimate grounds for condemning 'Richey is Dead' are that it simply isn't a very good record.

Ideal was not alone in cynically exploiting Richey's image in order to shift units. On the third anniversary of his disappearance, *Melody Maker* ran a spurious Richey front cover, titillating readers with the strapline: 'On the third anniversary of rock's greatest mystery, we ask: what *really* happened?' Inside, of course, the question was not answered. In an article which could have been replaced with four simple words, 'buggered if we know', no new information was brought to light, no new theories advanced. Instead, the feature consisted of a recap of the basic story, and the 'expert' opinion of a psychologist who had never met Richey. The *Melody Maker* cash-in proved just one thing: Richey Edwards's face still sold music papers.

In Martin Davidson's enjoyably terrible but uncannily prophetic 1983 movie *Eddie and The Cruisers*, Eddie Wilson, an ultra-cool, working-class Rimbaud-obsessed rock star, drives his car off a bridge just as his band is approaching the threshold of success. His body is never found, causing journalists to speculate that he has faked his own disappearance, and to search the lyrics of his final album, *A Season in Hell*, for clues.

One day soon, there may be some kind of remake. In addition to his quasi-religious status, Richey Edwards is one of the few contemporary rock stars whose life can be thought of in terms of the cinematic. 'It's only a matter of time before some film-maker does the Richey biopic,' Nicky Wire told *Q* in 1998. 'An Agatha Christie-type mystery. John Hurt as Richey, Leonardo DiCaprio as Sean . . . no one tall enough to play me.' James Dean Bradfield, warming to the theme, continued: 'I'll be the simple diamond geezer. Richey'll be in the corner cutting himself and I'll be going: "Don't think too much, man. Let's just go and have a pint." And it'll end up in Goa. Sunset. And Richey busking, smiling, happy.'

Richey Edwards, in a diary written for *Select*, once wrote: 'I wish I could be a seed.' I think he was.

10. EVERYTHING MUST GO

'Freed from our memory, escape from our history . . .' – 'EVERYTHING MUST GO'

AFTER THE INITIAL CHAOS SURROUNDING the vanishing of Richey Edwards had settled, the three remaining Manics dealt with their confused feelings in differing ways.

Nicky Wire retreated into domestic privacy in Blackwood. Sean Moore tried to take his mind off things by getting into DIY and, with his girlfriend Rhian, built a new room in the attic of his Bristol home.

For James Dean Bradfield, however, much of the remainder of 1995 constituted one continuous bender. 'I was stunned for six months,' he later told *Sky*. 'I waited for something to happen, but nothing did and I definitely thought about giving up. I got pissed out of my head for a while.' He rented a room in Terri Hall's London home and, for several months, you could stake your grandmother's life on bumping into him at the opening of an envelope, smiling and joking as if nothing had happened, defying all comers to dare broach The Unmentionable.

One fan – either brave or particularly stupid – approached Bradfield and asked: 'How can you be out having a drink? If I was you I'd be in my room cutting myself up by proxy for Richey.' Such accusations of callousness upset James. 'What am I supposed to do?' he rhetorically asked *Dazed & Confused*. 'I can't sit in my room for ever with the curtains closed being a cold fish.'

What James was doing, of course, was using alcohol to selectively screen reality. At the time, he convinced himself he was living some kind of romanticised Rat Pack high life. 'I used to have that *Barfly* mentality,' he later told *NME*, 'having almost Zenlike insights by meeting a stranger at a bar and having a good old yap. For a while I thought I was imbued with mythical Richard Burton-esque qualities. I thought I was a *bon viveur* cavalier.' Before long, though, he became wary of the image he was exuding. 'I don't wanna come across as a New York film star,' he told BBC Radio One, 'sitting at a bar going: "Hey, what d'you think, Mr Barman?"'

The decision for the band to continue was made quickly, but not lightly. In April, after 'two months of waiting by the phone and feeling ill and exhausted', Nicky, James and Sean held protracted talks with Richey's parents. The Edwards family encouraged the band to put out a record as soon as possible, in the hope that this might flush Richey out of hiding. It was a logic to which the Manics would continue to cling; when their fourth album made it big, Nicky said hopefully: 'When Richey sees all his records, he'll have to come back.'

And if he did? This was the biggest 'What if?' of all. The band had complex and conflicting emotions about the possibility of Richey's return. James seemed the most resentful of the three. Once, in an unguarded moment, he told an interviewer that after the hurt Edwards had caused 'he could never be our friend again' (an unfortunate statement, perhaps, but the deluge of outraged letters it provoked came mostly from people who had never even met Richey).

The humane thing to hope was that Richey, for his own sake, *never* returned to the public eye. As James told *Dazed & Confused*: 'When you consider all that's happened, and what we and his family have been through, I don't think there's any question of him coming back and just carrying on like nothing's happened. After all, even if he did, the chances are that he'd just do the same thing all over again.'

Nicky expressed similar doubts. 'I'd have no qualms,' he told me, 'about inviting him in . . . to my house . . . for a cup of tea, and a chat, and watch telly, but I'd have serious qualms about saying, y'know, "Come on tour!" And a lot of fans find that really harsh. They say: "Why do you say such things?" But you've gotta actually be around those things to realise it was totally unhealthy for him, and us.' Speaking to *Top*, he added: 'If he turned up with a Telecaster under his arm, I don't know . . . Unless he's had a miracle cure and become a Nietzschean strongman, I can't imagine him wanting to go through all that again.' James, by now, had revised his view. 'If he turned up like Robert Johnson when he went off in the wilderness for a year and he became the most amazing guitarist in the world, we'd go: "Right! The next LP is all yours." That would be cool . . .'

In August 1995, word leaked out that Manic Street Preachers intended to continue without Edwards. Immediately, the more crazed citizens of the Nation of Richey saturated the music-press letters pages, damning the other three for daring to carry on. James had little patience for such views. 'Quite a lot of the fans think that we're completely disrespectful to the memory of their "best friend" but, at the end of the day, y'know, he was my best friend, not theirs!'

Although the band had started tentative rehearsals surprisingly soon, shortly after the meeting in April, James later admitted: 'I didn't really feel as if I was in a band for four months at least.' On Saturday 24 September, for the second time in their career, James Dean Bradfield, Nicky Wire and Sean Moore went into Cardiff's tiny Soundspace Studios (now renamed Big Noise) to record a charity cover version.

War Child, an organisation aiming to offer medical, food and social relief to victims of the conflict in the former Yugoslavia, had set up a benefit album, *Help*, with the assistance of the Go! Discs label. The concept was that the Britpop élite – Oasis, Blur, Suede and the two 'Heads (Radio and Portis) – should go into the studio on the same day, and deliver a finished track just 24 hours later.

The Manics chose to commit to tape their version of Burt Bacharach's much-recorded 'Raindrops Keep Falling on My Head' (which James had often performed during his 1994 solo spots), in a light, breezy, acoustic interpretation featuring, for the first time ever, a

Sean Moore trumpet solo. Given its unhappy personal context, the devil-may-care cheeriness of 'Raindrops' was astonishingly evocative, lacing the closing line – 'Because I'm free, nothing's bothering me . . .' – with a supreme irony.

Although it was not new material *per se*, 'Raindrops' was a coded message to the world: *we still exist*. For the first time, the Manics felt that they had a future. In the following week's music press, it was announced that the Manics would play a low-key comeback show at Wembley Arena on 29 December, supporting The Stone Roses, a popular Led Zeppelin tribute band from Manchester.

'Nothing could be worse than rock music turning into a career' – JAMES, 1991

The 'Raindrops' session, brief though it had been, was enough to convince the Manics that they could resume work on their abandoned fourth album.

Their first abortive attempt was at Peter Gabriel's Real World studios near Bath, with New Order/Pet Shop Boys producer Stephen Hague. It didn't work, not through any particular fault of Hague's – one of his productions, 'The Girl Who Wanted To Be God', survived on to the finished album – but because the band did not enjoy working in what they described as 'a sterile, pop-industry studio'.

Instead, the Manics decamped to Domfront in Normandy to work with Mike Hedges in his picturesque Château de la Rouge Motte. Hedges had a reputation as something of a latterday Phil Spector, specialising in big, epic sounds, and heavy on string arrangements. James Dean Bradfield had admired his work on Wah!'s 'Story of the Blues', as well as during Siouxsie and The Banshees' mid-career orchestral phase, with Everything But The Girl and The Beautiful South, and, most recently, on McAlmont and Butler's stunning 'Yes'. Hedges apparently clinched the Manics gig because, when he heard a demo of the proposed first single, 'A Design for Life', he said, 'I think it should sound like a jukebox record.' Augmented by a keyboardist (part-time Sleeperbloke John Green) and a full string sextet conducted by Martin Greene, and with the help of mixer Ian Grimble and the Manics' trusty side-kick Dave Eringa, they set about recording it.

The Château was the antithesis of the antiseptic modernity of Real World, eschewing state-of-the-art gear in favour of classic equipment, including the actual wooden Redd 17 mixing console used by The Beatles, which Hedges had rescued from Abbey Road. It was, said James, '. . . the only legendary studio we've ever been to. A bit of lineage. It's like a museum of rock 'n' roll. It's dusty, there are cobwebs everywhere, you've got to kick things to make them work.' However, as he explained to *Q*: 'Mike uses old gear, but we didn't go there for a full-on rustic valve experience. He's one of the last of the old school fellas who really knows what he's doing.'

There were unconfirmed rumours that James had actually started writing lyrics (titles like 'The Hairdresser's Chair' and 'Jackboot Johnny' were bandied about) but, if this is true, they never surfaced. Nor did any of the 60 + songs Richey had left behind. Only Edwards songs which had already been works-in-progress back in January were used (otherwise, the three other Manics said, they would always be worried that Richey might not approve of the music accompanying his words), along with seven new Nicky Wire compositions.

The fate of the leftover Richey lyrics – the ones which had not been works-in-progress – remained undecided. Nicky had considered publishing them in the form of a poetry book (which remains a possibility, one day). 'There's some spine-tingling stuff there,' he told *NME*. 'He's not drug-addled or drink-addled, he's very disciplined and clean.' (This, of course, contradicts Sean Moore's comment that: 'There wasn't a lot to pick out . . . Most of it was very fragmented and rambling.') 'I still think he's an amazing lyricist,' Wire continued. 'There's one line – "I feel like cutting the feet off a ballerina" – a classic Richey image. To be honest with you, they're no more horrific than *The Holy Bible*. You can't get any more low than that, can you, really?'

The band did not find working without Richey all that strange: he had barely been part of the recording process anyway. 'The time we'd notice it,' James told *Dazed & Confused*, 'was when we'd be in Nicky's room socialising, and suddenly there'd be a lull in the conversation and we'd all realise that that was the point when Richey would have come up with one of his Richey-isms. I missed walking into his room and he'd be doing a collage and we'd watch telly and just natter. That's what you miss, not the professional stuff.'

All three Manics hugely enjoyed the experience of being back in the studio again (James called it 'summer camp'). 'Making that first foray into the rehearsal rooms was the most difficult thing,' he said, 'but, after that initial upset, the studio became our refuge. Getting into the pattern of recording took our mind off a lot of things. I conned myself that making the album was just unfinished work, because we'd already written seven songs for the album and they'd been set to music before Richey went missing.'

By early January 1996, with a short break for Christmas, the fourth Manic Street Preachers album was complete.

On 29 December 1995, in that weird, empty, hungover hiatus between the gluttony of Christmas and the revelry of New Year, the Manics – irony of ironies – made their return to public life on the coat-tails of fellow Hall Or Nothing act The Stone Roses (themselves making a comeback after a long absence). In 1990 the Manics had been at war with The Roses, in 1996 they were presented as part of the same entertainment package.

The atmosphere at Wembley Arena was strange. Outside, open-mouthed crowds passed each other as if they were drugged. Inside, among the sports-casual masses, were small pockets of diehard Manics faithful, easily identifiable by their clothing, carefully imitating various periods of the band's career (DIY slogans, leopardskin and white denim, army

'Special Guests' indeed.

fatigues and make-up). For perhaps 5 per cent of the crowd, this was the most anticipated moment of the year. For the remainder, it was just that week's big indie event.

As James Dean Bradfield, Nicky Wire and Sean Moore walked out on stage, the reaction was silence – but for different reasons. The Adidas-clad baggy throwbacks sat on plastic seats, arms folded, their only noise a gurgling from the straw in their 'medium'-sized Coca-Cola. The hardcore held its breath, occasionally breaking into stifled emotional wails. 'Calm down,' grinned Wire, 'it's only us!'

For the Manics themselves, one could be forgiven for thinking it was just another gig. They simply got out there and *did their job*, as dispassionately as an abattoir worker slaughtering a pig. In a short set, they aired five new songs (a bombastic pomp-rock number called 'Elvis Impersonator: Blackpool Pier', the already astonishing 'A Design for Life', the Phil Spector-ish 'Everything Must Go' and a couple of uptempo numbers, 'Australia' and 'Enola/Alone'). At that time, the band had refused publicly to confirm which were Bradfield/Moore/Wire compositions and which had been co-written with Richey. It was immediately obvious, however, that there was a shift from the gothic intensity of *The Holy Bible* back towards the melodiousness of *Gold Against the Soul*. Indeed, the Manics didn't perform anything from *The Holy Bible* itself – their latest album, their finest, and the one most strongly associated with Richey – concentrating instead on the most consumer-friendly of their hits ('Motorcycle Emptiness', 'You Love Us') – the ones an impartial arena audience might recognise.

Music apart, the Manics – for the first time in their stage history – did not really *give* much. They had not created any new image to speak of: with James in his familiar white V-neck T-shirt, Nicky in his Cardiff Devils shirt and Sean in Bosnian mercenary attire, they looked as if they had grabbed the nearest thing in the wardrobe to nip out to the 24-hour garage, rather than to play the most important gig of their lives.

They were also all visibly carrying a few extra pounds, having clearly sought recourse from the traumas of 1995 in comfort eating/drinking: a case of I Hate Myself And I Want A Pie. 'At least a third of my body must have been alcohol at that point,' James confessed later to *NME*. 'You'd go home to see your mam and she'd go, "James! I never thought you'd have a weight problem! Look at your dad!" And my dad's there, 55 years old, smokes forty a day, drinks, and he's completely fit and hard. My auntie comes in and goes: "Oooh, you fat little blob!"' One of the funniest descriptions of the newly porcine Preachers came from Luan of *Suicidal Lemons* fanzine: 'With his thin body and pot belly, Nicky looked like one of those snakes that unhinges its jaws and swallows eggs.' Maybe this was why Wire, who had said 'It's just so obscene that fat people are allowed in bands' back in 91, was now draped in a tentlike ice-hockey top.

No make-up, no slogans, no lippy pronouncements from The Wire – the gig was more like watching a rehearsal than a public performance. James occupied Richey's traditional stage-right position, but the gaping abyss just shifted centre-stage instead. Given the band's reluctant, diffident onstage manner, vitriolic anthems such as 'Motown Junk' and 'You Love Us' sounded hollow and misplaced in the context of 1996. (Hearing the line 'I laughed when Lennon got shot', the newly reunited Beatles would have been perfectly justified in writing a song that went, 'I laughed when Richey fucked off.' Indeed, at some point over the following year, James eventually changed the lyrics to: 'I laughed when baby got shot.') As seventeen-year-old fan Steve Hallam had told *Melody Maker*: 'When they play the songs live, the *meaning* won't be the same without Richey there.' In fact, certain songs gained even *more* meaning, unbearably so for James.

Nobody was expecting a guitar stand with a wreath around it, nor some back-projected black-and-white photograph reading 'RICHEY JAMES EDWARDS 1967–?', nor for Bradders to milk the emotion as if it were a Freddie Mercury tribute ('This one's for you, Richey!'), but the threesome's absolute refusal to acknowledge the situation was uncomfortable, *as if nothing had happened*. At the time, it all felt deeply wrong. Any Manics comeback was going to feel like a wake whatever happened, so it should have been a cathartic, emotional one. Close friends and family. Two thousand of us, that is, but *us*. And what, at this stage in their career, were the Manics doing supporting *anyone*? 'We purposely supported bands,' Wire later explained to *NME*, 'because we wanted to be anonymous – to ease our way into it. The fact that our own fans might be there made me nervous. We didn't want to face them that early, the emotion of that.' James felt the same way. 'I didn't feel that I could give or receive anything – in an emotional outburst, or bond with an audience or anything. I didn't want to see people in the front row going [*makes weeping noise*].' Fair enough. But afterwards, those who cared about the Manics were left feeling strangely empty.

The more you thought about it in retrospect, however, the more you could understand the Manics not wanting to feel anything but empty just now. It had taken tremendous emotional strength and bravery to do this at all.

'The hero of yesterday becomes the tyrant of tomorrow, unless he crucifies himself today' – JOSEPH CAMPBELL, *THE HERO WITH A THOUSAND FACES*

The Manics' Wembley appearance raised more questions than it answered. And I had to ask those questions, as *Melody Maker* sent me to the gig to conduct a vox pop of MSP fans. Most thought the band should carry on – but these, of course, were the ones who had turned up (I knew others who had stayed away on principle). Some, touchingly, even thought Richey might show up on the night.

It was clear that the Manics *would* continue in some form – James's deeply ingrained work ethic demanded it, and it was hard to imagine the three of them doing anything other than making music – but the argument that 'they need to make a living' was not enough on its own. This was the *Manics*. They were far too important for such vulgar considerations.

Back in February, I had hoped for a neat and tidy finale: maybe a four-track EP with some of Richey's bequeathed lyrics, released on the anniversary *in memoriam*, before they bowed out with dignity. The worst-case scenario, unlikely as it was, would be the Preachers plodding around like a wounded, limping animal, like the sad rump of The Clash which hobbled on for a year or two after Mick Jones left; or like the farcical attempt to continue the Sex Pistols after Sid Vicious died.

Barely better was the prospect of the Manics as a moderately popular indie guitar trio, like Therapy? or The Foo Fighters, a possibility which Everett True, reviewing the Wembley show for *Melody Maker*, accepted: 'It does occur to me that the new Manic Street Preachers could well become to the old Manics what Dave Grohl's Foo Fighters are to Nirvana; a bouncy Prozac version, minus all that annoying attendant angst and whining.' When they finally split up, nobody would notice or care.

Maybe, armed with a back catalogue of catchy, melodic rock songs, they would become bigger than ever and pawn their souls against gold, while quietly shedding their original, devoted fanbase.

In some ways, either of these last two possibilities would have been an acceptable, fitting outcome: a certain defeatism had always been inherent in the Manics, as had a built-in Hypocrisy Clause which meant that any accusation you threw at them could be accepted and absorbed with a Nicky Wire shrug, a grin and a 'we always said we were sluts/liars'.

A more positive blueprint, however, was the way in which New Order had risen from the ashes of Joy Division and gone on to create even more magnificent music than its original incarnation. The presence of a keyboardist on stage with the Manics recalled New Order's introduction of Gillian Gilbert on synthesizer after Ian Curtis's death, but the similarities were more than superficial: even without Richey, the Manics remained an exceptional musical unit with an underrated lyricist. Furthermore, like New Order, the Manics were assimilating dance influences (albeit indirectly, through remixes). In this case, however, shouldn't they stop trading as Manic Street Preachers and rename themselves? (An option which Wire publicly denied, but privately admitted that they had considered.)

The suggestion that by losing Richey the Manics had lost their justification for existing was one to which the band were, and still are, sensitive. Even now, four years on, Nicky will – unprompted – list the ways in which the New Manics are true to the spirit of the Old Manics, and insist: 'It's all still there.'

In March, the Manics played a couple of shows supporting Oasis – in many senses the successors to The Stone Roses – in Dublin and Cardiff, where they were greeted by chants of: 'Where the fuck is Richey?' from hostile Oasis fans.

In fact, they went on to spend much of 1996 as Support Band By Royal Appointment To The Gallagher Brothers. It was a situation not without irony: a band whose forthcoming single would begin 'Libraries gave us power' on the same bill as a band whose major songwriter boasted that he never read books. Nicky Wire's wife and brother both worked in libraries; one suspected that Liam Gallagher would feel out of his depth if a woman told him she was a Libran, never mind a librarian. In fact, everything the Manics hated about Madchester was true of Oasis: anti-education, anti-intelligence, anti-femininity, anti-glamour, pro-getting-wasted. Oasis was a worst-case-scenario, lowest-common-denominator cliché of what the working classes can be, encouraged by a southern bourgeois media clearly aroused by a northern bit of rough.

If Nicky had accused the press of treating The Happy Mondays as their 'little working-class playthings', this was doubly true of Oasis. The Manics, by contrast, were (and still are) the only positive working-class role models in pop; the only band to understand that, when you have nothing, you have nothing to lose . . . and are, therefore, free to be *anything*. By appropriating art and literature, flirting with different identities (a middle-class preserve: the poor are expected to remain 'real' and 'authentic') and refusing to be amusingly stereotypical oiks or belligerent beer boys for the titillation of the press (whose members, as Wire once remarked, 'don't understand that working-class people can have sensitivity'), the Manics were the anti-Oasis.

And, initially, they had been *openly* anti-Oasis. Richey had spoken, with withering sarcasm, of his admiration for Noel Gallagher's 'ability to write such cheerful lyrics'. It is, of course, all too easy to hold up any Richey statement, carved in tablets of stone, to cast a shadow over the present-day Manics. Back in December 94, however, in an uncharacteristically Wirean piece of vitriol, James had dismissed Oasis thus: 'They're just soft boys who haven't had their ration of chips and gravy so they're a bit lairy. It's like housewives who haven't had their Valium.' The feeling appeared to be mutual; the Gallaghers had once, in an interview, threatened to beat the Manics up.

By 1996, though, something had changed. During the weeks following Richey's disappearance Nicky had found himself listening to Oasis's *Slide Away* and *Live Forever*. As he told *NME*: 'That melancholia with an uplifting nature was what I wanted to get across on our album, that there is a vague kind of hope through sadness.' And even Richey himself, speaking to *NME*'s Stuart Bailie, had admitted (apparently seriously) that 'I would like to be able to write: "I'm feeling supersonic, give me gin and tonic", but I just can't do it. The last time I felt supersonic was when I was about ten years old, I expect.'

Although Nicky never made any claims for the Gallaghers' lyrics, he did say: 'Musically, I do genuinely love Oasis. They're so natural, I think it's above criticism. They have something that hits you like an elemental force. In many ways Oasis are the band we wanted to be, but never could be.' Speaking to *Vox*, he went further still: 'It's obvious to me that Oasis are the best band in the world.' James had also come round to the Mancunian millionaires. 'I do think pop stars can be shining heroes,' he later told *Q*. 'Liam Gallagher wears a suit of armour as far as I'm concerned.'

Whether or not this constituted a U-turn, the decision to support Oasis made sound commercial sense. Oasis's record-shattering success had given a huge lift to guitar-based rock in general, and arguably added an extra fifty thousand to the album sales of every other medium/large Britpop act. And there was at least one direct Manics/Oasis similarity. Noel Gallagher had famously got into trouble for wishing AIDS on a rival musician (Damon Albarn). Sound familiar?

After the Oasis shows, the Manics finally felt ready to face their own fans (rather than attempting to hijack someone else's).

In February – during the anniversary week of Richey's disappearance – it had been announced that the Manics would make their first headlining appearance as a three-piece at the Leeds Town & Country Club as part of Radio One's Sound City week. The gig, on 8 April, was broadcast live, with support from Cast and The Wannadies. On the eve of the show Nicky Wire had spent a sleepless, nervous night, but disguised his bloodshot eyes behind a slash of eyeshadow, adding a smear of rouge and a lavender blouse with matching choker. Just like old times? The audience certainly was, with several proudly displaying 1992-vintage MSP T-shirts. It was an emotionally charged atmosphere – two Japanese girls were seen crying throughout the gig – but Wire was in no mood to take the bows and accept a hero's ovation, and actually told off the audience for being 'too accepting'.

There was, by now, a new addition to the Manics set-up. Keyboardist Nick Naysmith, originally of Barry, South Glamorgan, and previously a member of a failed 80s electro-sleaze act called Red Lipstique, had joined the band as a semi-permanent member, and was tucked away discreetly in the corner stage-right. The band played a fuller set than at the Roses/Oasis shows, including a two-song encore of 'Motorcycle Emptiness' and 'Motown Junk', their first since the Marquee in 1991. They appeared to be hating every minute of it, but the important thing was that that crucial first headline date was out of the way.

Although they did play 'Faster' and 'Yes', they still seemed reluctant to include too many songs from *The Holy Bible*, a trend which would continue throughout the year. As Nicky Wire told me: '"Yes", which is one of the band's favourite songs, it really is, James finds it impossible to sing live. It may be in the third person, about a prostitute, but it's so personal to Richey, sometimes he says: "I can't do that live, I don't care how much I love that song." It's weird being onstage when you've got these fucking . . . myriad emotions going through your mind, that's when I usually forget what I'm playing.' When Bradfield did play 'Yes', he found certain lines (such as 'I hurt myself to get pain out') impossible to sing. Speaking to *Select*, he explained: 'I really enjoyed how *The Holy Bible* confronts the audience. But that album confronts us too. You play it onstage and you can feel Damien round the corner. It feels like handling a cursed chalice. You can feel the lesions breaking out all over your body.'

'My father still reads the dictionary every day. He says your life depends on your power to master words' – ARTHUR SCARGILL

At the end of 1994, James Dean Bradfield had admitted: 'At the end of the day, we haven't written the song that the milkman can whistle.' He had now. At the start of 1996, after the Wembley Stone Roses gig, I had written: 'I pray – and I do have a certain faith – that they'll make a record of such undeniable excellence that all preconceptions are atomised (not least, my own).' 'A Design for Life', released on 15 April, was that record.

Its very existence was gratifying enough. As Tessa Norton of *Firecracker* fanzine put it: 'After the black hole that was 1995, there's a certain thrill about seeing the words "Manic Street Preachers" in print.' Some fans were surprised to see it happen. Martin Carr, of The Boo Radleys, says: 'If there was one band who'd lose a member and not carry on, it would be the Manics. You just know that if bands like Sleeper lose a member, of course they'll carry on. I think it helped them. I don't think they'd have sold so many records if Richey hadn't gone. But it was such a beautiful record to come back with.'

In mid-1995, Nicky Wire had written a two-page treatise in poem form on the working-class condition, and handed it to James. 'As soon as I got those words,' said Bradfield later, 'I thought: "I've got to write the best tune ever." This was one of the first times in a while when I'd read a lyric and it sent a tingle up my spine.' Two weeks later, Bradfield telephoned Wire to tell him he had come up with something 'a bit special', and played him what he called 'this death-march' down the phone.

'A bit special'? An understatement. 'A Design for Life' was one of those rare, exceptional records which forces even the artists' most zealous detractors to swallow hard and admit: 'This is magnificent.' Towering yet graceful, filmic yet impassioned, colossal yet dignified, opulent yet direct, timelessly instant and instantly timeless, it was, in James's words, 'a bit of Ennio Morricone, a bit of Tamla, a bit of Spector. Our only reservation was that it might be too epic'. Written in a 6/8 quasi-waltz time signature and gilded with dramatic, swooping strings, it sounded like nothing else around at the time, but still managed to strike a populist chord. If it had been any more anthemic, you would expect to see Colin Jackson climbing an Olympic podium.

In Frank Sinatra's 'Summer Wind', which James and Sean had adored since hearing it in a Mickey Rourke movie called *The Pope of Greenwich Village*, a lilting organ motif mimics the bobbing motion of the waves on the sea. 'A Design for Life' was built around just such a maritime motif from Bradfield's guitar. Given recent history, this made for queasy listening. It might have been an unfounded projection from the mind of an over-imaginative listener but, as Annie Nightingale, guest reviewer in *Select* put it: 'Whatever it's about – it could be about furniture – you can't help but associate it with Richey.'

In fact, the subject of 'A Design for Life' – the title was partly stolen from a contemporary Volkswagen advertisement and partly inspired by Joy Division's 'An Ideal for Living' – is the suspicious death of working-class values, and the spiritual degeneracy and enforced demoralisation of the underclass. As Wire later told MTV: 'It was the middle of Britpop, and people patronisingly assumed that being working class meant thick-ness, taking drugs, and no intellectualism whatsoever. We were taking working class-ness back from the media.' The opening line, 'Libraries gave us power', was inspired by a stone engraving reading: 'Knowledge is Power' which Wire had seen above the doors of Pillgwenlly Public Library in Temple Street, Newport. 'The thing I liked about reading back in history,' he explained to *Dazed & Confused*, 'was the fact that every Welsh town had an institute with a library and a swimming pool, which every miner had paid 50p a week specifically for.' Pillgwenlly Library was actually founded in 1888 by Victorian philanthropist Lord Tredegar, not by miners, but Wire's point remained valid. The inscription also chimed somehow with a phrase from Winston Smith's diary which had caught Wire's eye while watching the film version of *1984* with his wife: 'Hope lies with the proles.' The less-discussed second line, 'then work came and made us free', was also inspired by a motto above an entrance. The gates of the Nazi death camps had borne the murderously mendacious promise: 'Arbeit Macht Frei' ('Work Brings Freedom').

With the second verse, 'I wish I had a bottle/Right here in my dirty face/To wear the scars/To show from where I came', the lyrics swing from the tenuous optimism of the first verse towards self-destructive nihilism. The song reverses and then repeats this journey twice more, in an unintentional microcosm of the band's entire career. The most misunderstood part of the song is the chorus: 'We don't talk about love/We only wanna get drunk.' Some listeners – newcomers to the Manics, it is probably safe to say – took the second part literally, failing to see the vicious irony (Wire's point was that, *in the eyes of the middle-class media*, proles are only interested in getting pissed). And yet they were only partly mistaken. 'Part of that lyric has no irony in it at all,' James told *NME* two years later. 'For a start, as a person, I've been in many a situation where I know not what to say but I know what to do, where I'm not articulate enough to make myself understood and, yeah, sometimes I do just wanna fucking get drunk, definitely and utterly, sometimes the most base reaction is the only one I've got. And those were the working-class considerations in that song.' Wire, too, understood the inarticulate, and sometimes misdirected, anger of the underclass. 'I have a concept of a working-class rage which is in some people,' he told *Select*. 'It's in Liam. It's in Linford Christie and Nigel Benn. It's in Paul Gascoigne. The desire to prove yourself . . . The 50s generation had the trade unions, they had morals and dignity. Now we've got sloppy: they'll steal a car when they're not even poor.'

Alongside Pulp's 'Common People', 'A Design for Life' was nothing less than the most important political record of the 1990s. Nicky Wire didn't trust any of his peers, even Pulp, to get it right. 'I wanted to portray the working-class culture I grew up with,' he told *Sky*. 'With the likes of Blur and Pulp, we thought it was all very caricatured. So we were trying to put the record straight, tell it like it really is . . .' It was a subject that had been preying on the band's consciousness for some time. Back in 1994, James had told *Melody Maker*'s Taylor Parkes: 'It just fucking sickens me that people have been conned into believing that you can't think in terms of class any more. As soon as working-class people lose their sense of belonging, they lose all their humility, and you get a classless society in the worst possible sense.'

If Wire's lyrics had brought out the musical best in Bradfield, they also moved him so much, he told *Q*, that he 'actually felt part of where I came from for once'. In fact, he was so affected that he thought about moving back to Wales, and made enquiries about househunting in Cardiff, although – mostly for career reasons – he eventually decided to remain in London.

After the intimidatingly meaningful 'Design', the B-sides inevitably appeared trivial. The extra tracks, depending on which format you bought, were either Art Garfunkel's 'Bright Eyes' (recorded live in 1994), the Chemical Brothers' mix of 'Faster', a number of gorgeous instrumental mixes of 'Design' itself from Apollo 440's Howard Gray (under the pesudonym Stealth Sonic Orchestra), or a handful of new songs. The pastoral 'Dead Passive', which namechecked Adam Clayton and Naomi Campbell, Hugh Grant and Elizabeth Hurley, concerned the emotional poverty of modern relationships (Wire was said to be mourning the fact that 'nobody gets married nowadays'). The edgy, paranoid Motown *noir* of 'Dead Trees & Traffic Islands' was inspired by a newspaper story about a man who had wandered on to a traffic island, collapsed and died, and whose body lay unnoticed for several weeks; the title was originally intended for a script written by Nicky for the ITV drama series *Cracker*, about a murderer who dumped bodies on roundabouts. In the end Wire decided not to send the script to the producers (whether because it was too good for television, or because it was too bad, remains unclear). Most bizarre of all was 'Mr Carbohydrate', a semi-comedic description of Nicky's domesticated lifestyle (discussed in detail in 'Domestication Terrorist'). Possibly its most absurd line ran: 'Have you heard of Matthew Maynard?/He's my favourite cricketer/I'd rather watch him play than pick up my guitar . . .' Maynard is the sanction-busting Glamorgan villain who toured South Africa at the height of apartheid (a fact that Wire, who owns a signed Maynard bat, prefers to brush under the carpet). In fact, Nicky had originally wanted to eulogise Welsh golfer Ian Woosnam (he once said he would like to be Woosnam more than anyone in the world), but James put his foot down.

The design of 'Design', like its title, was a conscious echo of the Joy Division/New Order transition: a plain, metallic, embossed cardboard sleeve, it was almost identical to that of 'Ceremony'. Nicky confirmed that this was no accident. 'The artwork for this new single is very New Order and so is the title: clean, and minimal. There are a lot of reference points. Ian Curtis killed himself on the eve of an American tour . . . and, between the three of us, we can still be very sarcastic and pisstaking about the whole thing and ourselves, and that helps. It's the New Order school of thought: "Ian Curtis was a twat, 'cos he ruined our American tour."'

The video for 'A Design for Life' remains one of the most breathtaking examples of the artform. Along with the inevitable 'performance' footage (sadly demanded by most broadcasters, often to the detriment of the clip), the director had created a brutal juxtaposition of stunningly symmetrical images of class difference – the red roses on a blueblood's hat at Ascot and the trickle of blood on a Poll Tax protester's brow, polo-playing aristocrats swinging their mallets and mounted police crashing their batons down on rioters' heads – intercut with slogans, projected in *1984*-style block capitals, from writers like Orwell and designers like Le Corbusier and Gaudi: 'HOPE LIES IN THE PROLES', 'SENSE OF BELONGING', 'READ THE DICTIONARY EVERY DAY', 'MAN DOES NOT CREATE, HE DISCOVERS', 'A HOUSE IS A MACHINE FOR LIVING IN', 'USEFUL IS BEAUTIFUL', 'TOMORROW IS TOO LATE' and, most tellingly among all the class-war imagery, 'VIOLENCE FOR EQUALITY'.

Although all concerned were proud of the song, the Manics held no unrealistic expectations of chart success. 'I was confident that we'd get our nominal Singles of the Week in the press,' Nicky told *NME*, 'but beyond that I thought "eleven or twelve in the chart will do me. Or fifteen or nineteen."' As well as those nominal Singles of the Week, 'Design' actually received favourable reviews from some unlikely sources. 'It might be quite good,' said Professor Stephen Hawking of Caius College, Cambridge, 'if I could make out the words . . .'

In fact, the song sold 93,000 copies in the first week alone (for comparison, 'Motorcycle Emptiness' sold 100,000, but that took five years), and entered the charts at No. 2. Only 'Return of the Mack' could keep the return of the Manics off the top, but Mark Morrison's swingbeat classic outsold MSP by a mere 7,000 copies.

James celebrated in Gascoigne's, a Hammersmith bar, with the Hall Or Nothing crew, and then at Antonio's in Westbourne Grove. Enough drink was consumed to have Martin Hall doing the moonwalk. Sean, at home with his family, kept the champagne on ice, refusing to pop the corks unless 'Design' reached No. 1. Nicky listened to the chart rundown and smiled quietly to himself, then celebrated with tea at his mam's. After all, the Manics had their first band interview since 1994 in Cardiff the next morning, so he didn't want to overdo it.

'I knew it was a proper hit,' James told *Q*, 'because blokes in my Mam's betting shop kept whistling it.' Mike Hedges's initial assessment, 'I think it should be a jukebox song', was proving prophetic. It would eventually become a karaoke-machine favourite – the ultimate populist accolade. Suddenly, MSP was a successful band. A bittersweet pleasure, as Wire later admitted: 'I suppose it could be the halcyon days ahead, but getting to No. 2 doesn't seem like such an achievement. I can't help thinking: "Richey, if you could have held on a little longer, maybe then you could have had all these things you wanted. You might have been happy."'

'For the real who feel, for the tall who are small' – ORIGINAL DRAFT, 'NO ONE KNOWS WHAT IT'S LIKE TO BE ME'

On Friday 26 April, the Manics warmed up for two further Oasis gigs at Manchester City's Maine Road stadium with a low-key show at the downstairs bar of the Haçienda club. The Haçienda, set up by Factory's Anthony Wilson, was a regular haunt of the Manchester pop élite and, before the gig, New Order/Joy Division bassist Peter Hook approached Sean Moore to say: 'Sorry to hear about Richey . . . at least we had a body!' The gallows humour was warmly appreciated.

The Manics without Richey, by their own admission, had yet really to click as a live spectacle. 'Live, we haven't reached the height of excitement we had with Richey,' Nicky acknowledged. 'The sound and the playing are good, but in terms of us looking at one another and knowing we could take on the world, change people's lives . . . we haven't regained that and, without Richey, without the aura, perhaps we never will.' James, too, admitted that it didn't feel right. 'Occasionally, when you're playing live, you catch yourself thinking: "We shouldn't be doing this", but quickly you stop yourself.' Sometimes, they would forget, and expect to see him next to them onstage. 'It's looking over and not seeing Richey knocking back his ten vodkas,' said Wire.

The viewer's eye, too, was drawn magnetically to the void stage-right: Richey's iconic presence even more noticeable in its absence. The yawning emptiness would never be filled, save for a keyboardist tucked discreetly behind the speakers. To this day, James and Nicky rarely wander over to that side of the stage (except on one occasion when a television director made Nicky stand there, an experience the band found 'horrible'). They made it clear they had no intention of hiring a replacement guitarist, despite a ludicrous rumour on Teletext that The Stone Roses' recently departed John Squire was going to join the Manics. 'Mind you,' joked Wire, 'they wouldn't exactly be queuing up for that one, would they? "Guitar player required. Must mutilate himself onstage and carry impossible demands on his shoulders forever."'

The inside of the Haçienda was an emotional pressure cooker. 'There were a few heavily dramatised tears being shed down at the front,' Bradfield told *Select*. 'You could see the faces of all these people in the crowd,' he elaborated in *Dazed & Confused*, 'looking at us like they're trying to see the pain inside my head. I spend enough time getting over this whole thing in private. I don't need these people who hardly even knew Richey trying to bond with me about him.' The atmosphere was too much for Nicky, who spent most of the show hiding behind dark glasses, and who on two occasions needed to sit down.

Then James forgot himself again. 'In the old days,' he told *Select* afterwards, 'Wire would bump into me onstage, and I'd turn round and shoot Richey a look: "What is he like?" On Friday I looked over and there was no one there. I just thought: "What the fuck did I do that for?"' It was Wire's turn next. 'I remember the introduction to "From Despair to Where", looking over to where Richey would have been standing, swigging at a bottle of whisky, and *there was no one there*. And when we came offstage, I virtually had a breakdown. I was just crying hysterically for about three hours, like a twat.'

While Sean got away from it all with a night at the Bugged Out club, Nicky just sat and wept. Prior to 1 February 1995, there hadn't been a single day in five years when he and Richey hadn't spoken; since that day he had been keeping it all in. His flood of tears was only the second time since Richey's disappearance that he had actually cried. 'The next day,' he told *Dazed & Confused*, 'I thought: "Well, it was going to happen some time." And funnily enough, his mother had called me that night as well, and she'd been really upset. Must have been a bit of karma in the air.'

After the histrionics of the Haçienda, the Oasis gigs themselves were cold, passionless affairs. Tickets had long been sold out by the time the Manics were added to a bill which included the more conventionally Oasis-friendly likes of Cast, Ocean Colour Scene and The Bluetones. Inside Maine Road, the Manics fan-count was practically zero. Walking into a football stadium in leopardskin and make-up and seeing thirty thousand Mancunian heads turn and stare is a sobering experience (I pushed to the front, searching for Welsh flags and familiar faces, but found no one). The Manics' set was another disappointingly functional one (no mouthing off, no silly costumes), and by the end James's voice was reduced to a barely audible croak. At the Holiday Inn afterwards, Epic threw a party in the Manics' honour, which drew actresses from *Brookside*, footballers from Manchester United and, most surprisingly of all, that notorious hellraiser Nicky Wire.

'I saw the best minds of my generation destroyed by madness, starving, hysterical, naked' – ALLEN GINSBERG, *HOWL*

Nicky Wire's tears in Manchester were only the first outward sign of the psychological toll which Richey's disappearance had exacted on the remaining Manics.

On the recommendation of a Welsh doctor, Nicky was receiving bereavement counselling. He had been offered a course of the sedative Temazepam, but declined (perhaps conscious of the effects Prozac had had on his friend), and was being treated for stress-related illnesses. Previously, an expensive but useless Harley Street doctor, after a full examination, recommended that Nicky should wash the skins of fruit when travelling abroad. (Which, knowing him, he almost certainly does anyway.)

Perhaps the hardest thing Nicky has to deal with is that, without a body, he'll never be able to mourn Richey properly. His emotions will be forever on hold. 'At the end of the day, you can't feel grief because you don't know if he's dead. You feel anger, sympathy and sadness. The tragedy lies on a personal level. On a professional level, as a band, it doesn't really come into it. You don't think: "Oh, the band's fucked." We've known each other too long for that. It's the personal element which is the hardest to take.'

One such personal element was the gnawing worry that Richey's disappearance was a judgement on Nicky, James and Sean. 'That's what hurt as much as anything: the fact that perhaps he just didn't like us anymore.' Another was the permanent state of unrest in which they must henceforth live. As Nicky told BBC2's *Close Up*: 'He could turn up on the doorstep tomorrow.' This was a scenario which, at first, gave Wire terrifying dreams. To this day, whenever the phone rings and Nicky misses it, he dials 1471 to see who rang. If it's a number he doesn't recognise, he won't be able to sleep that night. 'If I get a phone call and it's a wrong number,' he told *Select*, 'or the person just puts the phone down, it can ruin your whole week.'

James Dean Bradfield has a more head-on way of dealing with things. By October 1996 he was reading Jeffrey Eugenides's *The Virgin Suicides* and a book on Yukio Mishima: both had been highly influential on Richey, both deal with the subject of suicide. James also has 'macabre and disturbing' dreams about Richey. 'They're really uncharacteristic – he was the most unintimidating, sweet person to be around, and all the dreams are very scary. I wouldn't want to go into the details. Very dark and very hard. Physically very intimidating. I wake up extremely unhappy.'

'Everything's for sale . . .' – 'YES'

Manic Street Preachers' fourth album was released on 20 May 1996. You only needed to glance at the cover of *Everything Must Go* to know that something had changed: this band had been *redesigned*. Printed in nice, calming Coventry City blue, Mark Farrow's sleeve was a masterpiece of neat, uncluttered modernism. For the first time, the band's faces – clean, scrubbed, *blank* – appeared on the front. Its only conscious statement seemed to be that there was no statement. Below the title stood a pair of wide-spaced parentheses, containing no text, just a yawning void (which spoke louder than words ever could).

The title came to Nicky after seeing a photo of his brother Patrick Jones's young son in front of a shop window that was displaying the sales banner 'EVERYTHING MUST GO!' (The album's original working title was *Sounds in the Grass*, after a Willem De Kooning painting). Patrick had written a play with the same title (due to open at Cardiff's Sherman Theatre on St David's Day 1999), and his brother borrowed it. *Everything Must Go* is, without question, the most listener-friendly record ever released by Manic Street Preachers: lush but not over-elaborate, tough but melodic, monumental while stopping just short of pomposity, and with Martin Greene's strings and Mike Hedges's production adding a classy Spector-esque sheen. For some, the new sound is too mature, the leap mainstream-wards from *The Holy Bible* too extreme (one reviewer, on its release, compared it to Foreigner's music). James Dean Bradfield himself wryly described it as Manic & The Mechanics (a case of 'From Revelations to Genesis'?). When one German interviewer overstepped the mark, asking, 'The lyrics are very powerful, but don't you think that the music often comes down on the wrong side of Bryan Adams?', Bradfield walked out.

Perhaps inevitably, *Everything Must Go* was also compared/contrasted to *Movement* – the album made by the remaining members of Joy Division after the death of Ian Curtis. However, James Dean Bradfield's sense of the anthemic, like Bernard Sumner's pop sensibility, prevented the Manics from making anything that sounded despondent. *EMG* possesses a different kind of strength: a melancholy positivism, a battle-scarred optimism. Stuart Bailie of *Vox* picked a fine Samuel Beckett quote to illustrate this conflict: 'I can't go on. But I will go on.' Nicky Wire described it as 'Faded optimism. I've always been a bit more like that than Richey. I've never ever . . . trawled the depths. We didn't want to make another manic-depressive album. We couldn't cope with going through the same misery again. But it's still a pretty dark album.' Even in its darkest moments, however, there are always shafts of light at the end of the tunnel. It is the sound of a band happy to be alive, happy to have survived. 'I'm glad I'm still here,' said Wire, 'and not in some institution somewhere.'

Indeed, Wire's outlook on life seemed to have changed beyond recognition. 'Where there's nature, or where there is breathing, there are true moments of joy. You've just got to recognise them. And not take them for granted. And that's what I try to do, have moments of elation in life, however small, five minutes a day, and be able to think: "Yeah, that'll do, that'll do me now."' Some critics accused the band of selling out, or of softening up (even James acknowledged that the judgemental intolerance of *The Holy Bible* had been replaced by a gentler humanitarianism). So . . . New Manics, New Danger?

Hardly. It was all too tempting to compare the moderate, make-up free, MOR Preachers to Tony Blair's smiley/slimy, media-friendly New Labour. However, *Everything Must Go* is dedicated to Tower Colliery, the Cynon Valley pit which, threatened with closure by the government, was taken over from the National Coal Board by a miners' collective and turned around a £4 million profit in its first year. Manic Street Preachers had parted with many things, but traditional socialist values were not among them. 'I don't think we're Old Labour,' Wire told *Q*, 'more Classic Labour. The outspoken sexiness of Bevan, Skinner and Livingstone. We're more John Prescott than Peter Mandelson. Libraries gave us power . . . not the Internet.'

One noticeable difference between New Manics and Old Manics was that the lyrics scan better, flowing *with* the music rather than chafing against it. This has a simple explanation: most of the lyrics were written by Nicky Wire. You could name the five Richey songs with your eyes closed: in style and content, they stuck out like rusty nails. Wire explained the decision to include Edwards's songs: 'We were thinking it might be better to put them out on an EP later, but somehow I think, if he's out there, he'd like to hear his songs . . .'

'I grow weary of the old tongues' – FRIEDRICH NIETZSCHE

The album's opening track, 'Elvis Impersonator: Blackpool Pier', went one step further than the mimetic, undulating riff of 'A Design for Life' by beginning with the *actual* sound of waves lapping on a shore, haunted by spectral back-masked voices. If Richey Edwards *had* drowned in the Severn, this was bleak irony indeed. The eerie soundscape gave way to a disquietingly unpredictable chord progression which made the listener still more uneasy, before the whole thing erupted into a big, bombastic rock monster. A rudimentary version of 'Elvis' had been demoed before Richey's disappearance, with an unfinished Edwards lyric which Wire later had to complete. Nicky subsequently admitted that he didn't fully understand what Richey had been getting at (except the broad subject of the Americanisation of Britain) and found it hard work, which may be why the final Wire/Edwards draft doesn't quite hang together. Although musically strong, 'Elvis' is weakened by its petty lyrical concerns: 'Limited face paint and dyed black quiff/Overweight and out of date.' It was a pointless attack on a harmless target: more Morrissey's 'Everyday Is Like Sunday' than Public Enemy's 'Fight the Power' ('Elvis was a hero to most/But he never meant shit to me'). The track ends with an almost inaudible James singing 'Dixie', from Presley's 'American Trilogy' (extracts from each part of the 'Trilogy' appear on subsequent Manics B-sides).

Then, after 'A Design for Life' itself came the first 100 per cent Richey song. 'Kevin Carter' is a harrowing requiem for the photographer who won the Pulitzer Prize with a shot of a vulture standing on a dead Rwandan baby (it was used as a *Time* magazine cover shot) and who then, unable to handle his guilt at the way he gained recognition, committed suicide. It was a topic only Richey would even think of turning into a song (he had read about the photographer in a book called *The Life and Death of Kevin Carter*), and one which could easily, like so many Richey lyrics, be read as a metaphor for his own life. Just as Edwards had been criticised for only writing about negativity and hate, Carter had been attacked for making his name with war pictures. To these attacks, his response was: 'What do you expect me to take pictures of – flowers?! I'm a *war* photographer.'

The imagery of the song is at once obscure yet highly effective: 'The elephant is so ugly/He sleeps his head, machetes his bed/Kevin Carter, kaffir lover forever . . .' (elephants, in Carter's memoirs, signified the nightmares he had about Rwanda). Bradfield stabbed the song along with abrasive, metallic guitar chops, like daggers to the spine, and Sean Moore added a great *Sweeney*-style trumpet break ('What a talented little boy,' said Sice of The Boo Radleys, guest singles reviewer in *Select*). Sadly, Moore would never play the 'Kevin Carter' solo onstage (someone called Tony stepped in instead).

'Enola/Alone' contained possibly the most crucial line on the whole record. 'All I want to do is live, no matter how miserable it is . . .' was Wire's considered response to the Nation of Richey doom-wallowers. Like its mother album, this song was about finding, against all odds, a desire for life. And like 'Stay Beautiful' and 'From Despair to Where' before it, 'Enola/Alone' was a gorgeous, bittersweet, paradoxical mix of dynamism and resignation. The palindromic title – a time-honoured MSP trick – is echoed by the lyric itself: 'From my birth a rellik, a killer . . .' *Select* speculated that 'Enola' was based on ideas lifted from Roland Barthes's *Camera Lucida*, but Wire said that it stemmed from 'me looking at my wedding photos and seeing two people standing right by me who are not around any more' (Philip Hall and Richey Edwards). Incredibly, it was never chosen as a single.

Kicking off with a classic 'Be My Baby' drumbeat, the title track of the album surged into an irresistibly Spector-esque wall of sound. Speaking to MTV, James offered a fascinating explanation of this song's everything-including-the-kitchen-sink maximalism: 'I wanted it to be extreme, almost shit. I like it when our music almost overheats.' The song acts both as an apology and as a fuck-you to the fans who thought the Manics should have packed it in: 'Freed from the memory/Escape from our history/And I just hope that you can forgive us . . . but everything must go.' (*Select* believed that the line 'Escape from our history' was inspired by Jean Baudrillard, the French semiologist who simultaneously castigated and celebrated the way in which the proliferation of media drowns meaning, and severs links between signs and their referents.) Since their comeback, the Manics had been carrying the weight of their own history in an ambivalent mood somewhere between 'he ain't heavy, he's my brother' and a funeral pall-bearer. 'Everything Must Go' was a goodbye to all that, a farewell to (scarred) arms. 'It does stand for getting rid of some of the baggage,' James confirmed, 'and learning that we have to break our own rules sometimes.'

'Small Black Flowers That Grow in the Sky' was another Edwards lyric – as if anyone needed telling. The title was almost a comic parody of a Richey songtitle, yet, once you had stifled your sniggers, you felt faintly seasick at the thought of how far the creator's mind must have drifted from normality even to have come up with such an image. A beautiful, acoustic set-piece for Welsh harp and guitar (James is accompanied by harpist Julie Aliss), 'Small Black Flowers' was as delicate and perfect as the finest cut glass. The lyric deals with the mental torture suffered by zoo animals. Richey and Nicky had both watched a BBC *QED* documentary on European zoos, and phoned each other immediately afterwards to discuss writing a song. It was inevitably (and I believe, correctly) seen as a thinly veiled allegory for Richey's own torment: 'Here chewing your tail is joy . . .' Wire, however, is sceptical about this tempting interpretation. 'Obviously, people will say Richey was gonna use this image to represent his "mental cage", but I dunno, maybe he just wrote it about the TV show.'

'The Girl Who Wanted to Be God', named after a biography of Sylvia Plath (who had once said: 'I'd like to be remembered as the girl who wanted to be God'), was the only song on *Everything Must Go* co-written by Edwards and Wire simultaneously, rather than in sequence. It quickly became popular with female fans, who were perhaps wishfully imagining themselves in the title role, but to my ears it is one of the album's weakest moments ('Motorcycle Emptiness' *lite*). Nicky, once again, admitted that he didn't have a clue what it was really about.

'Removables', which lamented the lack of permanence in modern culture, was *über-Richey*. A one-take, as-live recording, *Select* called it 'one of the coldest things they've done'. Richey's macabre shorthand was so compact it was almost abstract ('Killed God blood soiled skin dead again . . .'), and the references to the 'aimless rut of my own perception' seemed out of place amid the tentative optimism of the surrounding tracks (with good reason: the song was actually an out-take from *The Holy Bible*, written in early 1994 when Richey was hopelessly under the spell of Kurt Cobain). Then again, was the chorus – 'all removables, all transitory' – simply Richeyspeak for 'everything must go'? It certainly seemed to chime with the books in the river, the shaving of the hair, etc. With the couplet 'A bronze moth dies easily/Unknown to others, weak to me', 'Removables' also highlighted the Manics' strange fixation with moths (see also 'Little Baby Nothing'). Spiders and moths were a recurring Sylvia Plath theme, and Van Gogh had been fascinated by death's-head moths, but the Manics' interest began with a Tennessee Williams poem called 'Lament for Moths', about how the sensitive people, or 'moths', will always be crushed by the 'mammoths'. 'That really hit us,' said Wire, 'the sudden realisation that we were the moths of the world.'

'Australia', despite its themes of flight and escape, was not directly connected to Richey's disappearance, but actually about *Nicky's* desire to flee the horrors of 1995. Not that he'd ever actually gone there: 'I ended up going to Torquay, which is hardly Australia.' (How old-fashioned, how British, how Nicky Wire.) But it was a straightforward metaphor: Australia is as far away as you can get without leaving the planet altogether. Given its musical mood – 'Australia' was a brazenly upbeat rock-out with an exuberance comparable to *The Charge of the Light Brigade* – *Select* had half a point when they called it 'an existential Brooce Springsteen . . . more "Born to Die" than "Born to Run".' However, a more telling comparison, once again, was *Butch Cassidy and the Sundance Kid*: in their final bolt-hole, the two renegades talk about fleeing to Australia, all the while knowing they have zero chance of survival. 'Interiors (Song for Willem De Kooning)', a sketchy, choppy number built on a Northern Soul bassline reminiscent of Saint Etienne's 'Nothing Can Stop Us', is a curious little item. Willem De Kooning, born in Rotterdam in 1904, moved to the US in 1926 to become, alongside Jackson Pollock, the century's leading Abstract Expressionist. In later years he developed Alzheimer's Disease and could barely speak, but continued painting till the end, even though he had no memory of what he was depicting (doctors believed his art was actually reversing his illness). Nicky Wire wrote the song after seeing De Kooning's story on television. In the context of the album, 'Interiors' makes partial sense: it is another song about memory (Alzheimer's = an enforced escape from the recent past). Yet, to a certain extent, 'Interiors' highlights a minor problem with Wire's songwriting. Richey Edwards would trawl the world for subject matter; Nicky Wire would write about a documentary he happened to catch on BBC2. If he had been watching *Driving School* instead, would he have written 'Brakepads (Song for Maureen)'?

In 1991, the Manics had promised *Snub TV* that 'We'll never write a love song.' They had now. 'Further Away', written by Nicky in the depths of his homesickness on the 1994 Suede tour, is straightforward to the point of triteness – 'The happier I am when I'm with you/The harder it gets when I'm alone' – but likeable enough to carry it off. James had been opposed to recording it at first (for old-skool MSP party-line reasons), but eventually decided: 'It is healthy to be able to do whatever we like without having to think, "Wait a minute, we're the Manic Street Preachers."'

The elegant, stately, colossal closing track, 'No Surface, All Feeling', is another song which was inspired by Wire's disenchantment with life in a rock group. For all the world it appears to be about Wire's feelings regarding the missing Richey . . . but in fact it was demoed in Cardiff's Big Noise (formerly Soundspace) in January 1995, before Richey's disappearance: proof that anything/everything the Manics do now is haunted and tainted by context. Only the vocals and the ending (gargantuan drum rolls phasing from left to right) were re-recorded from the original demo. The song was actually about the Manics growing further away from each other. Wire himself didn't feel wedded to the band any more. 'It's about, for the first time in my life, "I don't want to be with you two,"' he told *Q*. 'Not "I hate you" but "it's not like it used to be". Everything's changed since Richey left. Apart from onstage and in the studio, although we're still best friends, we've got different lives.'

On 26 May, *Everything Must Go* rocketed into the album charts at No. 2. It was only held off the No. 1 spot because label-mate George Michael had decided to release his first album in six years on the same day. Normally, the sixty thousand that the album sold in the first week (eventual sales topped four hundred thousand) would have been more than enough. 'We're like The fucking Who, we are,' an exasperated Wire told *Sky*. 'We'll never have a No. 1.'

In one of his early letters to the press, Richey Edwards had written: 'We wanna be the biggest rock 'n' roll nightmare ever. We'll do whatever is required and give you the biggest posthumous record sales.' Some detractors, bewildered by the success of *Everything Must Go*, cynically suggested that he had unwittingly fulfilled his promise. One *NME* journalist actually described the Manics as 'a band that has thrived on the publicity surrounding the disappearance of Richey Edwards'. The Manics had undoubtedly scored a lot of points for the way in which they had conducted themselves since Richey's departure ('quiet dignity' was a phrase one would never have associated with Manic Street Preachers five years earlier). At the same time, however, it was all too easy to 'blame' – if that's the right word – the high sales of *Everything* on factors such as a critic's sympathy vote, or on the hype value of their missing member.

Yet this was to overlook the one simple, obvious, overwhelming cause: *Everything Must Go* was the most magnificent rock record of the year.

*   *   *

On 23 May the Manics took their *Everything Must Go* set on a tour of the UK's medium/large venues, supported by fellow Welsh rockers Gorky's Zygotic Mynci, starting at Glasgow Barrowlands. Compared to the Oasis supports, the band's first proper headlining tour since 1994 was far more akin to Manics shows of the past. They were even playing some of the ultra-macabre *Holy Bible* material (including, once in a sky-blue moon, 'P.C.P.'), something they had previously shied away from doing. At London's The Forum on 28 and 29 May, however, James announced that this would be the last time they would play 'Yes'. It was a lie, but one which, curiously, he would repeat intermittently throughout the year. Nicky, meanwhile, had finally hit his stride and was revelling in being onstage. After the London shows, for two nights running, I engaged him in a furious bar-room debate on social class and pop culture. Eyes twinkling, fangs flashing, Wire was back on form.

On the last day of May, the Manics played their first proper homecoming show since Richey's disappearance – not including the Oasis show in Cardiff – at the Newport Centre (in the VIP bar afterwards the entire combined populations of Blackwood and Pontllanfraith seemed to be present). The atmosphere, although highly emotional, verged on being celebratory. *Everything Must Go* had only been out a week, and already everyone knew every word.

A European tour, planned around the Euro 96 football championships (the band didn't want to miss a single game), brought them back down to earth. Europe had yet to fall under the Manics' spell, and they found themselves inside the sort of tiny venues they hadn't played since the pre-Sony days. In Germany, in particular, they played to waxwork-like, arms-folded indifference. Only James's love for *bratwurst* made the trip bearable.

Amazingly, there was no Nicky Wire medical calamity on any date, but there had been one directly prior to the tour. Before an appearance on BBC2's *Later with Jools Holland* Wire tore a shoulder ligament, and James was forced to rope in Pete Townshend's bassist as a last-minute replacement on 'A Design for Life', 'Everything Must Go' and 'Small Black Flowers That Grow in the Sky'. Wire was subsquently photographed with a bottle of pain-killing paracetamol in his hand, which was mistaken in some quarters for a cheap, sick stab at controversy.

Back in the UK in time for the festival season, the Manics played T in the Park near Glasgow – the site of their first festival appearance as a trio two years earlier – where guests at the Hilton beheld the unlikely sight of Nicky Wire swimming in the hotel pool at 9 a.m. Nicky wasn't the only Manic on a health kick. James, stung by being called 'a little fatty' by his auntie, had taken up morning runs again, around the streets of west London, 'because my chin was slapping around my thighs'. These days, though, he kept a more relaxed pace: 'I always swore I would never become a jogger. I was a runner, not a jogger. Now I have to admit I've become more of a jogger.' At the Phoenix Festival on 19 July, where the band suffered the ignominy of playing on a bill beneath country-rock dinosaur Neil Young, there was an even stranger sight to be seen in the VIP enclosure: Manic Street Preachers mixing, chatting and – gulp – socialising with other bands.

The choice of the next Manics single, on 29 July, was an easy one: the title track of *Everything Must Go*. A strange video showing the band bouncing on trampolines in front of a scarlet backdrop watched by bored-looking kids (and with a heavily symbolic cherry tree shedding its petals in a gale force wind) did not prevent it from reaching No. 5. Extra track 'Black Garden', with its driving Joy Division guitars and lines about frozen embryos and dead swallows, is basically Wire possessed by the spirit of Edwards, planting a carefully arranged bed of small black flowers. 'Hanging On' is non-specific melancholia set to a jangling Northern Soul chord progression, 'No one Knows What It's Like to Be Me', originally written on the 1994 Suede tour, represents Wire's self-pity shot in Widescreen. CD2 features a remix from the Chemical Brothers, in what was to be the Chemicals' last dealings with the Manics. Shortly afterwards, Nicky Wire was quoted as saying: 'Just because we've had the fucking Chemical Brothers remix our records doesn't mean we like dance music.' The ChemBros were not impressed. 'See you later, then,' Tom replied via *NME*. 'Had it with your pomp rock!'

The Manics were back in the pay of their aristocratic masters, Oasis, throughout August for a series of enormous outdoor mega-gigs. The first two dates, in Loch Lomond on Saturday 3 and Sunday 4 August, were overshadowed by the death of a roadie; he was crushed by a truck in front of Noel Gallagher, whose performance was seriously affected. The Manics' timeslot was 5.41 p.m., between Cast and Black Grape, and a bottle-throwing crowd added to the bad vibes.

On Saturday 10 and Sunday 11 August they rejoined the Gallaghers in the grounds of a stately home at Knebworth for what would be the biggest concerts in British history with a combined audience of over 250,000 people (one in twenty of the UK population applied for tickets). Taking the stage to a sea of Ocean Colour Scene wicketkeeper hats and Oasis T-shirts, the Manics, billed between OCS and The Prodigy, were the only support act to play both loch Lomond and Knebworth. By all accounts, they were terrible, failing to bridge the distance to the back of the field despite the giant Digiwall screen. James tried to lead a chant of 'Oggie Oggie Oggie! Oi Oi Oi!' before 'Everything Must Go', but to little response. After that, a bored-looking Bradders was just going through the motions.

James later compared Knebworth unfavourably to Maine Road. 'It just seemed like a bunch of southern tossers in comparison,' he told *Sky*. 'It made us think the whole of the south of England was just a fucking shithole. There was no magic to it.' Wire agreed. 'Loch Lomond was shit, too, although the loch was nice. I just felt the life was being sucked out of me during those summer gigs – there was just no spontaneity about them. They were just entertainment.'

To be brutally honest, they were barely even that. As *NME*'s Steven Wells noted: 'It was part of the original Manics game-plan to burn out and not fade away. But that burn-out looks likely to end with neither a bang nor a whimper – but with a long, workmanlike slog.' Many devotees were disappointed by the band's deliberately workmanlike attitude and blank stage presence. Between band and fans there was, regrettably, *nil communication*.

Over the four dates, the Manics had played to 340,000 people. Whereas once the band would have (ab)used such a platform to disgust, offend, wind up (and in some cases, hospitalise) everyone in sight, this time Nicky hid behind sunglasses while James merely barked the occasional 'Cheers' or 'This one's called "Faster"'. Wire said he no longer abused the audiences because 'You can't do that if you want them to go out and buy your records afterwards.' Making converts and selling CDs was the name of the game now, Nicky's justification being: 'We've been through Hell . . . now let's have success.' 'It's what people want, isn't it?' he told *NME*. 'They want well-played, good, sensibly dressed songs. So I've convinced myself that it's a tactic to get in a position where perhaps the bigger we get it might be easier to subvert. Maybe then we'll dress up again and I'll strip again like I did in Thailand. If I've still got the guts to do it.'

Which he probably didn't. As James admitted to *Sky*: 'Nick's idea of an ideal gig is him being linked by satellite from his front room. He could play bass and watch Sky Sports at the same time. Then, when the show was over, he'd be in his living-room.'

Joking, but only just.

Another aspect of the New Manics which certainly disappointed the diehards was the consciously dressed-down, no-frills image. At Knebworth, Nicky wore designer khakis and Sean wore expensive Tommy Hilfiger sailing gear. Glad rags were out, clobber was in. It was a look which Alan Partridge might have termed 'sports casual'. One headline-writer dubbed them 'Next Generation Terrorists', another writer considered them somewhat more downmarket, tagging them the 'Littlewood Manic Street Preachers'. Sean, who buys all his clothes from Paul Smith or Katherine Hamnett, was deeply offended – the nearest he gets to bargain shopping is buying Armani jeans in the Harvey Nics sale.

James, explaining the Manics' New Normality, told *Select*: 'We just wanted to diffuse the chance of anyone reading anything symbolic into the artwork or the way we looked.' Nicky rightly resisted any pressure to become a Richey substitute. 'I'm not going to crucify myself and stub cigarettes out on my arm and become an anorexic just to please people,' he told *The Face*. Fair enough – but the rumour that Nicky and James had been spotted in a *surf* shop, for fuck's sake, took some swallowing.

The Manics had always oscillated between genders, but this was their blokiest phase yet. It was not, however, the first time they had stopped wearing make-up. Nicky temporarily gave the slap a rest *circa Gold Against the Soul* because he felt 'a bit old to be doing all that at 24'.

This time, he told me, he felt 'too old at 27'.

By now, *Everything Must Go* had gone gold in the UK. On 30 September, a third single was lifted from the album: 'Kevin Carter' was an unexpected choice, but it still made No. 7. The video, riddled with high-speed images of cameras, guns and microphones, begins with the voice of an actor: 'The eye it cannot choose but see.'

Along with the now-obligatory remixes (having pissed off the Chemicals, it was down to Monkey Mafia and Stealth Sonic Orchestra to do the honours) were some intriguing extra tracks. 'Horses Under Starlight' was, give or take a few 'ba-ba-bas', the Manics' first-ever instrumental (not counting vocal-free mixes of existing tracks). A gorgeously evocative piece of easy-listening lounge music dignified by a Sean Moore trumpet melody, it is a homage to Burt Bacharach and Brian Wilson (James is a huge Beach Boys fan), and was something Bradfield had wanted to do for a long time. Nicky, explaining the title, reminisced: 'When we were all together, the four of us with Richey, and my brother Pat, we used to go up Pen-Y-Fan pond and we used to read the beat poets like

Kerouac, and there were all these wild horses opposite, and we used to do it in the dark. So we wanted a peaceful bit of music to go with that memory.'

'Sepia', a thinly veiled 'come home' plea in the disguise of a West Coast rock song, was the most explicit expression yet of Nicky's feelings about Richey. The title was presumed by some to be yet another reference to *Butch Cassidy and the Sundance Kid* (which ends, famously, with a sepia still). The remaining track, the angry, punky, politicised 'First Republic' ('our ode to republicanism') sounded more like 1991-vintage MSP than the 1996 version.

Throughout September, the Manics supported Oasis yet again, in America. This episode is described elsewhere, but suffice to say it was not a runaway success. Undaunted, however, the band flew back to Heathrow in the knowledge that their UK tour was a complete 40,000-ticket sell-out. Kicking off in Livingston Forum on 5 October, the support band for this jaunt was another Taffpop act, Catatonia. Everything (give or take a Hull gig cancelled due to a power failure) ran smoothly; it was a glorious, unforgettable tour.

Hitherto, the New Manics had still failed to put on anything you could call a show (illuminated gauze columns are pretty, but after ninety minutes they tend to pall). As Nicky Wire admitted: 'Without the visual, iconoclastic weight of Richey, it's just not right.' Now, at last, they had done something about it.

On its *Achtung Baby* and *Zooropa* tours, U2 – stealing techniques originally developed by conceptual artist Jenny Holzer – livened up its stage act with huge, projected slogans. On the *Everything Must Go* tour, Manic Street Preachers – developing techniques originally stolen by conceptual rock group U2 – livened up *their* stage act with huge, projected slogans. In addition to the mottoes already used in the 'A Design for Life' video, they used an entire Dylan Thomas poem, 'I See the Boys of Summer' (written in 1934 in a mood of depression and misanthropy), a mesmerising word-by-word run through the lyrics of 'Faster' (the word 'lizards', left hanging in the air for five seconds, was inexplicably chilling), a Japanese art-house movie chosen by James Dean Bradfield, idyllic footage of waterfalls and streams, and a wall of flame.

At the end of each gig, the Manics did in fact use the 'visual, iconoclastic weight of Richey' by screening the original Heavenly video to 'You Love Us'. The spectacle of the young Preachers in their glory days twenty feet high on the screen, while the tiny stick-men onstage performed the song live down below, was undeniably effective. It was arguably a supreme piece of emotional manipulation and, as such, it worked: when the lights came up, the room was filled with people sobbing and hugging one another. Or at least choking back the lumps in their throats. The band's original intention, however, had been to reclaim Richey as *theirs*. 'It was almost a matter of pride,' James told *NME*. 'This is how cool we used to be! It was "Hey, look at that, that's what we did." And also, it was taking it back from other people, just a tiny bit, y'know, as a band, bringing him back to us. Not in a nasty way, in a way we needed to.'

October 1996 was as revolutionary for the Manics as October 1917 had been for the Muscovites. For the first time, Nicky felt that they had truly been liberated from the shackles of history. 'It was only the first gig of this tour where I felt like we really had escaped our back catalogue of disaster,' he told *Select*. 'It just seemed we had a new audience, people who seemed ignorant of the subtext of what the Manics had been about.' In Leeds, one of those ignorant new fans was a young man called Lee Sharpe; even footballers came to see them these days. Everywhere, MSP traditions were being demolished. Mid-tour, on 16 October, James co-hosted Radio One's Evening Session – even Steve Lamacq was forgiven now. The only song on the set list drawn from the band's heaviest millstone, *The Holy Bible*, was 'Faster'. According to James: 'It epitomises something about Richey's lyrics in that there's not a lot of self-pity there. It's all about discipline, and there's still a certain positive energy in playing that song, whereas a lot of the songs on *The Holy Bible*, of course, just sound like an anthology of a self-fulfilling prophecy.'

To the delight of all true Manics fans, by the autumn tour The Wire had found enough self-assurance to slap on the warpaint again and to misbehave. Through fanzines such as *Black Velvet*, he had appealed for 'cat masks, tiaras, glitter and make-up' (most of Nicky's make-up is sent by fans), and needed little encouragement to use them. Even James was now unafraid to be effeminate. In Aberdeen, in a voice camper than Kenneth Williams, he asked the Scots crowd: 'I feel fat in this top, what do you think?' James denied this was any kind of exercise of bridge-building with the band's increasingly disenchanted long-term fans. 'If we wanted a bridge-building exercise,' he insisted in *Q*, 'we'd do a revue show. I'd come on with the white jeans, go off for a costume change, come back on with the rock 'n' roll hat and the glasses and Bruce Springsteen beard, then the sailor suit, then the nondescript Mr C & A garb.'

Just as their egos were threatening to run away with them, another pride-puncturing European tour came around. Little had changed since last time: in the Berlin Loft on 6 November, the pin-drop hush of 'Small Black Flowers' was violated by the sound of jovial Germans chatting in the bar. 'I can hear you, you fucking bastards,' raged James mid-song. 'SHUT UP!'

On 29 November, in a *Melody Maker* interview, I asked Nicky about his feelings, nearly two years on, about Richey's disappearance. An extract of that interview follows.

To get by from day to day, do you find it easier to assume you won't see him again?

'No. I honestly . . . especially after Chuck D and his "2Pac is alive" theory, I thought: "Fuck me, Richey's gonna be pissed off with that, 2Pac's outdone him!" I really did. I thought, "Oh dear, what's he gonna do next?!"'

He digresses into a discussion on the conspiracy theories surrounding the murder – or otherwise – of the rapper.

'It got me thinking when I was reading it, though, If 2Pac's done it, it's unbelievable! It's amazing the stuff Chuck was coming out with: 2Pac got cremated the next day, Las Vegas is a pay-off town, there's no homies out there in the desert, there's only one alleyway you can go down . . . Unless Chuck D's insane, I dunno. Maybe it's one conspiracy theory too far. I mean, 2Pac's mate got killed as well last week.'

I laugh, nervously.

'It's not a blind hope or anything. I genuinely kind of think that Richey's still out there . . .'

He mists over. At one point, it looks as if he's about to start crying. He still isn't used to this. I feel guilty for raising the subject, but then I remember: he raised it. Human decency overrides journalistic ruthlessness, and I desperately try to think of something else to talk about. But there isn't anything. We continue.

It must be difficult to remain realistic about percentage chances, when emotionally you are hoping for one outcome, but deep down you fear the worst . . .

'Doctors keep saying, "You've gotta accept it, he's dead," but I don't think anyone can accept someone's dead without a body.'

In a way, that would be equally unrealistic: just a trite psychological device to block it out, to put a full stop on things.

'Yeah. If I accepted he's dead, I don't think it'd make much difference to me. I mean, what happens? You say, "Oh, he's dead," and then what? And I don't see it in terms of blocking anything out or putting a full stop on anything. I see it as an ongoing situation that you've got to come to terms with. Which is really difficult. I mean, it's gonna be two years now, in February. Which is quite a long time. To be dangling. Dangling man . . . And it's a long time, if he's alive, to be out there as well, it really is.'

Nicky avoided watching Channel Four's *The Vanishing of Richey Manic* documentary, and tries to avoid reading magazine articles on the subject.

'I've really made a conscious effort to blank that out, to remember what I remember, rather than remember what I read. Every time I see something like that, I think of something I know, for definite. I think it's good that we've kept certain memories to ourselves, because that keeps that sort of bond there. It doesn't become a myth.'

His Rupert Bear pyjama case is being squeezed to within an inch of its life now.

'For us it's still . . . a bloke. I think it's really important that we keep hold of that.'

Some things you never get used to . . .

'1996 felt like hoovering around the edge of a black hole' – TESSA NORTON, *FIRECRACKER FANZINE*

On 9 December, something of a UK mini-tour began with a date, rescheduled from October, at the Humberside Ice Arena. The supporting cast this time featured not one but three Welsh acts: Super Furry Animals, Stereophonics and Catatonia. (Oh, and Tiger). Nicky Wire's facepaint was by now reaching uncontrollable levels. At the Manchester Apollo, he kept the faithful waiting for an impolite amount of time before evntually ambling on in a Santa hat. 'Sorry we're late,' he beamed, 'I was doing my make-up.'

The atmosphere inside the Cardiff International Arena on 12 December, in a 6,000 sell-out, was a hundred times more euphoric than on the Manics' previous prodigal return to Wales (in Newport back in May). With support from the Super Furries and Catatonia, it was a celebration of the revival of Welsh pop, a Christmas knees-up and a heroes' ticker-tape parade rolled into one. As well as Andy Williams's 'Can't Take My Eyes Off You', the adopted theme tune of the Welsh football team, James played the Welsh National Anthem as an overture to 'Motorcycle Emptiness'. (In Manchester, he had played the intro to The Stone Roses' 'Waterfall', a Mancunian National Anthem half a decade earlier). Nicky had now hit on an inspired marriage of sports-casual and glam-terrorist clothing: baggy jeans, silver puffa jacket and neon blue eyeshadow. He had also, gratifyingly, rediscovered his venom towards the Manics' musical peers. 'If any of you out there own any Ocean Colour Scene or Kula Shaker records,' he mischievously snarled, 'BURN THE FUCKERS!'

The band's three London dates, on 14, 15 and 16 December constituted a mini-tour of the capital, taking in the south (Brixton Academy), the west (Shepherd's Bush Empire) and the north (Kentish Town Forum) of the city. MSP's growing status was now high enough to attract celebrity guests, both on- and offstage. At the Empire, Spice Girl and Manics fan Mel B endured chants of 'Scary! Scary!' to watch the band. Midway through the set, a tiny, skeletal young woman took the stage. James Dean Bradfield proudly introduced 'Miss Kylie Minogue', and strummed the opening chords to 'Little Baby Nothing'. Certain sections of the crowd, mindful of Minogue's refusal to sing on the original recording, booed Kylie. It was certainly a fascinating and ironic reversal of fortunes. Who was doing whom the favour now? The Manics working with Kylie had once been a laughable idea, conceived in the absurdly optimistic hope that some of her pop glamour might rub off on them. Now it was they who were the big-name act, and she was copping the second-hand credibility. Kylie aside, it was a somewhat substandard show. Nicky Wire's only public edict, before 'Theme from M*A*S*H', was 'This is dedicated to Sunderland for murdering Chelsea', apparently in the mistaken belief that this would offend the west London audience (in fact, Shepherd's Bush is firmly inside QPR territory).

The following night at The Forum – the last Manics show of 1996 – was far superior. 'Yes' returned to the set for the first time since it had been used in the same venue back in the spring. Once again, James said it would be the last time ever (and once again he lied). Nicky pointedly dedicated the song to 'Our Richey'. He thought for a second, then reapproached the mike. 'I repeat, *our* Richey.'

All night, Liam Gallagher had been making a spectacle of himself by dancing on a table on the balcony. During 'Motown Junk' he wandered onstage and started kissing Nicky, then wandered off again, air-drumming as he went. Later, while James was doing his acoustic spot, Liam walked into the Manics' dressing-room and asked permission to come on later and 'do a bit of dancing'. Sure enough, during the 'You Love Us' encore – with its accompanying Richey footage, the emotional apex of the show – a clearly drunken Gallagher ran onstage, pulled a Jesus Christ pose, smashed a beer bottle on the floor, and wrestled a grinning Nicky Wire to the ground. ('Anyone can pull me to the ground,' Wire told *Select*. 'Kylie could have decked me the night before. I'm the softest person in rock.')

The crowd was split down the middle. Half the room cheered; the other half raised a two-finger salute. To the purists, the juxtaposition of the genius Edwards and the idiot Gallagher was an outrageous act of sacrilege. Earlier in the gig, Nicky

EPIC RECORDS INVITE YOU TO AN
AFTERSHOW PARTY

FOR THE
MANIC STREET PREACHERS

CELEBRATING THEIR SELL-OUT UK TOUR
MON 16 DEC–11PM TILL LATE

WINDY TUESDAY
2–3 GREENLAND PLACE, CAMDEN, NW1

ADMIT ONE. NOT TRANSFERABLE
RSVP JACKIE HYDE

had dedicated 'A Design for Life' to Dennis Potter, Dennis Skinner, Arthur Scargill and Antonio Gaudi, and now here he was, backslapping with this proudly illiterate apeman who had probably never made it to the end of an Enid Blyton. Nicky, though, couldn't see the problem. 'It was incredibly chaotic,' he told *Sky*, 'and I loved every second of it. He enjoyed it too – the last I saw of him that night was lying face-down on a kebab-shop floor.'

The debate raged on afterwards at a special party Sony had thrown for the band in a Camden wine bar. The party wasn't just to celebrate the end of the tour, nor to toast the festive season. By now, *Everything Must Go* had gone platinum.

James Dean Bradfield drove home for Christmas to see the folks, Sean Moore went to Bristol to open some fresh cardboard boxes, and Nicky Wire went back to Blackwood to enjoy a spot of tonsillitis.

It was a very good year.

j) Domestication terrorist

(NICKY WIRE – BORING FUCKHEAD?)

'They call me a boring fuckhead, they say I might as well work in a bank/I tell them I wish I was, they tell me I'm sick in the head' – 'MR CARBOHYDRATE'

O N 21 MARCH 1991, during Heavenly Records' package jaunt to Paris, Nicky Wire had been caught on his hands and knees in the tour bus, doing something perverse and unusual. But there was nothing Lewinsky-esque about the bassist's secret indulgence. In direct contravention of rock-star wildman tradition, Wire was not engaged in a sex act, nor was he trashing the vehicle in a fit of cathartic rage. He was tidying up.

(NB: In south Wales, the word 'tidy' is slang for 'good', 'great' or 'excellent'.)

'I'm a sensible lad, really' – NICKY

Amid the precipitation of rose petals and ticker tape which greeted the Manics' triumphant renaissance with 'A Design for Life', few noticed the quite extraordinary track on the B-side. A great song of self-justification, describing his new domesticated, sedentary lifestyle with a mixture of heavy pathos and pride, 'Mr Carbohydrate' was Nicky Wire's personal anthem as much as 'Yes' belonged to Richey Edwards. The title came from the nickname given to Wire by the remainder of the Manics camp, in recognition of his spectacular transition from the Twisted Wirestarter to Couch Potato. In 1999, Nicky Wire is the least rock 'n' roll man alive . . . and proud of it.

In the early days of the band's career, the media habitually failed to distinguish between Nicky Wire and Richey Edwards: the Glamour Twins, a two-headed Medusa spitting soundbite venom. A closer inspection, however, revealed Edwards to be the more thoughtful and contemplative of the two, whereas Wire was the genius of the wind-up, mouth almighty. Where Richey's lyrics grew increasingly introspective, Nicky's were outward-looking. The pair channelled their violence in opposite trajectories: Richey would slash at himself; Wire would lash out at others.

This is the man who prayed for the construction of a bypass over the Vale of Avalon, the man who wished AIDS death on Michael Stipe and called for the internment of New Age Travellers, the man who hospitalised a security guard at Reading and a cameraman at the Astoria. In the days when he would down a bottle of red wine before a gig and swig Babycham onstage, such 'shocking' antics could be accepted and digested – filed away in the Hall of Fame as the habits of just another pissed-up rock 'n' roll degenerate.

The unnerving truth is, however, that these were not the outbursts of some alcohol-addled, drug-crazed casualty, but the callous, vicious thoughts and actions of a sick, twisted but *completely sober* man. These days, apart from the odd relapse, celebratory binge or glass of *rouge* consumed now and then 'for the blood', Wire rarely touches a drop. Breathalyse him, take a blood test, look into his eyes: perfectly focused, and perfectly insane (amazingly, Wire was voted a mere 85th in *Kerrang!*'s '100 Maddest Rock Stars' poll). He is the clear-eyed berserker, the sober sociopath, the teetotal terrorist, the man who puts the 'temper' in temperance. Like a victim of Tourette's Syndrome, *he can't help himself*, alcohol or no alcohol. 'My brain's the only organ in my body that functions properly, and it's the one thing I've got that's an advantage over everyone I meet. Physically, I'd always lose in a fight. So I try to keep it in good working order. Like Davros on *Dr Who*. I'm a pickled brain in a wheelchair.' Nicky is also a notorious wuss when it comes to hangovers. 'Wire's a delicate petal and a drama queen,' says Caffy St Luce; or, as he himself told *NME*: 'Whenever Sean gets wrecked he makes a point of showing he's hard the next day. Whereas I'm lying in bed going, "Cancel everything!"'

Drugs, too, hold no fascination for Wire. 'I just find them incredibly boring, and I find the people that take them incredibly boring.' As James told *Q*: 'He could sit down like Bill Clinton and say that he never inhaled, and people would believe him.'

Nicky admits to just one addiction. Housework.

'A friendly Dyson, that is real decadence' – 'PROLOGUE TO HISTORY'

Nicky Wire is the Anti-Quentin Crisp. When Richey disappeared, James reacted by going on a drunken night out that lasted six months. Nicky locked himself away and, in the nascent spirit of everything must go, started spring-cleaning. 'I was dusting constantly and Hoovering,' he told *Vox*. 'Any bacteria had to be destroyed.' He set about turning his home into Le Corbusier's 'machine for living in', sanitising his environment with meticulous zeal.

Wire admits that he may actually suffer from OCD (Obsessive-Compulsive Disorder), a genuine form of mental illness. 'There's a definite Howard Hughes factor to my life, a Kleenex protocol.' As he told *Select*, it began way back in his teens. 'When I was fifteen or sixteen, I think I was really close to OCD. I had certain little traits like switching the lights off thirty or forty times to make sure they were off, and locking the door twenty or thirty times. It wasn't so much cleaning stuff then, it was more of a safety thing.'

His main behavioural 'tic' nowadays is Hoovering. If Wire were a Teletubby, he would be Noo Noo. He owns not one, not two, but *three* Dysons (the futuristic bag-less vacuum cleaners that bear a strange resemblance to R2D2 from *Star*

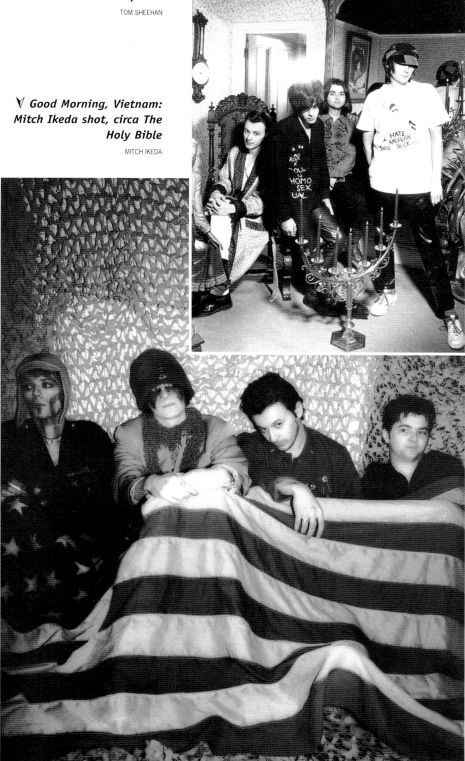

> *James Dean Bradfield's short-lived Noel Coward phase*

TOM SHEEHAN

∨ *Good Morning, Vietnam: Mitch Ikeda shot, circa The Holy Bible*

MITCH IKEDA

◄ *Richey and James getting matey, Glastonbury 1994*

STEPHEN SWEET

∨ *The writing's on the wall: French tour, 1994*

PAT POPE

🔺 **Richey's new tattoos, inspired by Dante... and Coppola**

ROY TEE

THE PRIORY HOSPITAL

HERE TO HELP

◄ **The Priory, Roehampton: "Here to help".**

I'VE SEEN THE
FUTURE
IT IS
MURDER

➤ *Richey's silver Vauxhall Cavalier, photographed by Police at Aust Services*

JOHN CHEVES

⋁ *The old Severn Bridge*

◄ *The library that inspired 'A Design For Life'*

ALISTAIR HEAP

Λ *Sean Moore prepares to smash the cistern*

TOM SHEEHAN

◄ *James Dean Bradfield, 1997: maybe older, maybe wiser...*

STEPHEN SWEET

Wars): one upstairs, one downstairs, one spare. If he comes home from tour and the house is un-vacuumed, 'I get a bit tetchy. When I come home and Rachel obviously hasn't Hoovered for the past four days – because she's not as into it as I am – I'm straight out with the Hoover. She goes out, takes the dog up the mountain, and I have a big clean.' Fans now send him as many Hoover bags as they do tiaras and make-up. One fan even despatched a bag filled with dirt for him to throw on his carpet so he could Hoover it up afterwards. 'I liked the idea of that,' Nicky told *NME*.

Another obsession is removing his dog Molly's hair from the upholstery. 'The dog sits on them,' he complains, 'so I use Sellotape to get the hairs off. It may sound odd, but last week I spent about an hour and a half doing that at twelve o'clock at night.' Every hotel room occupied by Wire also becomes a colonial outpost of his little empire. He once told *Select*, 'When we go to a hotel I remake the bed before I do anything . . . I just like everything tucked in and nice, just so when you get in you're completely . . . flat,' conjuring up alarming visions of the neurotic Monica Geller from *Friends*. He loves nothing better than 'drying a few clothes with the hairdryer, washing a few undies in the sink', and has been known to do this for *three hours* at a time. Before going to bed, he carefully packs the clothes into his suitcase, so he's ready for the morning.

The *Zeitgeist* of the mid-1990s was irony; Nicky Wire, typically perverse, got into ironing instead. 'Isn't ironing brilliant?' he enthused in *Select*. Metaphorically, ironing is the perfect Wire pastime: forcibly applying order and neatness to a disordered, messy world. He is the ideal househusband, tending to the shrubbery and mowing the lawn (until his back starts to ache and he has to have a sit down), while Mrs Wire goes to work at the library. When Wire went through a phase of appearing onstage in a woman's dress and headscarf, many assumed he was aiming for the classic film-star glamour of, say, Grace Kelly. But, as we have said, compare Wire in drag with a photograph of Hilda Ogden, the singing cleaning lady of *Coronation Street*, and make up your own mind.

> *'Sometimes I just stay in bed and think about the day when I can retire, forget everything'* – 'MR CARBOHYDRATE'

There is something of the crotchety old man about Wire, from his aching bones right down to his taste in casual golfing wear. As Sylvia Patterson wrote in *NME*, he looks 'like he's two thousand years old on the inside'. He is part xenophobic alternative Alf Garnett, part neophobic Young Fogey. Even his obsession with gambling is a giveaway. His roots in old-style Welsh working-class culture run deep: at heart, Wire is an elderly man in William Hill bookmakers on Blackwood's high street (although he would later intellectualise his gambling habit in rather more poetic terms: 'Compulsive gamblers may be viewed as money-lovers but, with the odds always against, I view them and myself as haters of money – logically we are likely to lose, we usually do, and nothing beats that feeling of giving all your money away for a useless thrill').

If Nicky were not Welsh, you would call him a Little Englander. His distrust of anything foreign is best exemplified by his somewhat traditional eating habits. In food terms, he is an arch conservative who is suspicious of 'strange foods, like avocados' and says: 'I'm really particular about Sunday dinner. I've got to have everything just the way I like it.' When he can be persuaded to fly (he has been terrified of planes ever since a near-miss between a jumbo jet and the Urals), he has to arrange a special in-flight diet: a tray of oven chips. 'If there was a Marks and Spencer in every city in the world,' he says, 'I'd be all right. Unless I see it being cooked right in front of me, I'm not very keen on food full-stop.' Wire, who failed to become a vegetarian 'because I don't like vegetables . . . you can't beat a lovely roast chicken or a leg of lamb', proudly states that his favourite food is chips ('I like everything fried'), his favourite drink is Ovaltine, and that he insists on full-cream milk ('skimmed is the lowest of the low') in his impossibly weak tea. Richey Edwards once ate a reindeer steak in Norway. Wire, meanwhile, had packed a bottle of vinegar to go with his chips. Whereas most bands on tour worry about where the next line of cocaine is coming from, Wire frets over whether there is a bottle of decent tomato ketchup on the rider. His dietary cautiousness sometimes spills over into outright paranoia. In 1996, during an interview in a hotel room, he handed me some Belgian chocolate from the minibar and asked me to translate the ingredients (printed in French) for him. When I told him it contained nuts, he wouldn't eat it. He was once seen nibbling the chocolate coating from a Snickers bar and throwing the peanut-filled core in the bin ('I'm so bloody paranoid about dying from eating the peanuts').

'People tell me I should get out more, but the TV is my best friend/Cynicism is the only thing that keeps me sane' – 'MR CARBOHYDRATE'

'He's a very Richard Briers person, very cardigan, pipe and slippers.'

When James Dean Bradfield said this he was referring to Richey, but the description fits Nicky more snugly. Nicky Wire is, in every sense, a domesticated man, a chronic sufferer from *hiraeth* (a peculiarly Welsh form of homesickness) who rings his mum every day on tour, lists his favourite journey as 'coming home over the Severn Bridge' and, when he gets there, visits his parents every day.

Wire's strongest natural instinct is hibernation. 'If I ever had loads of money, I think I'd just stay in my house,' he said in 1992. 'After J.D. Salinger wrote *Catcher in the Rye*, he just built a concrete bunker and lived on his own – that's the sort of thing I'd like to do.' Nicky's Blackwood bed is, to a great extent, the Manics' spiritual home. Beds, sleeping (and sleeplessness) are a recurring Manics theme: 'I just want to lay down in my bed', 'I write this alone in my bed', 'I feel like I'm missing pieces of sleep . . .'

Now, of course, Nicky does have loads of money. And, indeed: 'I spend half my life in silence,' he told *NME*. 'I think solitude and silence are probably the two most important things to keep me sane. I could be happy in these four walls for the rest of my life. I'd be happy if I never fucking left Wales again. It might seem like a prison to some people, but the prison I've put myself in makes me feel happy.'

When he isn't sleeping, gardening or Hoovering, he is watching television. There are countless references to TV in the Manics' (and specifically, one suspects, in Nicky Wire's) lyrics: 'Sunk deep in my TV/Maybe sucked the soul from within me'

('Another Invented Disease'), 'The statue of liberty/Looks so solemn on my TV' ('Enola/Alone'), 'For the first time ever/I don't understand my television' ('Sepia'). Whether following the golf on Sky or engrossed in the latest Jimmy McGovern, Wire spends the majority of his spare time sucking on a cathode-ray nipple for sustenance. If Richey Edwards obtained most of his information about the outside world from books, Nicky gets his from television: 'I've learnt more from TV than I ever did at university.' The lyric to 'Interiors (Song for Willem De Kooning),' for example, was inspired not by a visit to an art gallery, nor by even a skim through a biography, but by a documentary on BBC2. On the last night of the October 1996 tour, Nicky snubbed the end-of-tour party and rushed back to his hotel to catch the end of *Prime Suspect*.

'Be regular and ordinary in your life, like a bourgeois, that you may be violent and original in your work' – GUSTAVE FLAUBERT, QUOTED ON MANICS MERCHANDISE *CIRCA* 1997

Like the great surrealist painter René Magritte, Nicky Wire leads an almost defiantly normal life with his wife and dog in a small provincial town. For years, however, the fact that he was a fruit-juice-drinking, early-to-bed homebird was a secret – a music-business in-joke. In 1997, he came out of the (cleaning) closet in spectacular style.

'Mr Carbohydrate' was just the start. At the Brit Awards, Wire walked up to collect the Manics' two statuettes for Best Band and Best Album wearing a white, spraypainted T-shirt, in parody of his 1991 situationist wardrobe, bearing the slogan 'I [HEART] HOOVERING'. 'I do love Hoovering,' he explained, unrepentant. 'My wife bought me a new Hoover a few weeks ago.' It was a stroke of genius. This was more like it: if you are gonna be a home-loving recluse, be it pro-actively, *aggressively*. Nicky Wire, Domestication Terrorist! In part, at least, he had finally honoured the boast: 'We live in urban hell/We destroy rock 'n' roll' – he lives in a nice terraced house, and he has destroyed rock 'n' rollism – by becoming its polar opposite, its antithesis, its nemesis. Mr Carbohydrate = Mr Anti-Rock 'n' Roll.

In an age when clichéd 'bad boys' like Liam and Robbie and self-conscious decadents like Molko and Manson are giving predictable, time-honoured 'outrageousness', 'excess' and 'misbehaviour' one last spin for the titillation of the tabloids and the prurience of the press, Wire's ascetic, straightedge troublemaking is arguably the only true rebellious stance left (Wire's cocoon-like existence has even inspired a semi-serious thinkpiece in the *Guardian* to the effect that 'staying-in is the new going-out'). This cautious, slightly paranoid man, who checks the ingredients on chocolate bars, has never even had a drag on a cigarette ('must have been because my dad smoked 60 rolly-rolls a day'), laments the fact 'there's not enough darts on the telly nowadays', is scared of flying and has never learnt to drive because that scares him too, is the most subversive man in pop. This is a paradox, but not an oxymoron. Nicky Wire is both a keen gardener and a dangerous lunatic. Most people, when Wire flashes that famous smile, see a sweet, homely Cheshire Cat. I see a shark.

Last time I interviewed Nicky, I asked him what his plans were for the rest of the year. He answered: 'Nothing – TV, writing, cleaning.'

11. THIS IS MY TRUTH, TELL ME YOURS

'We're still in love with the idea of The Beatles kissing the tarmac at JFK. We're still in love with the word "million"' – JAMES, 1994

THE FOURTH SINGLE FROM *Everything Must Go* had been released on 2 December. 'Australia' was a disappointing choice (particularly when the anthemic 'Enola/Alone' and the moving 'No Surface, All Feeling' were left to rot as album tracks), the band's least satisfying release since 'Slash 'N' Burn'. Despite the reflective, melancholic lyrics, musically the song is simplistic, cheerful FM rock, all light, no shade.

Furthermore, the B-sides to 'Australia' hinted at a worrying lack of creative inspiration: along with Lionrock and Justin Robertson remixes and a Stealth Sonic Orchestra reworking of 'Motorcycle Emptiness', the Manics displayed their indie-kid roots with cover versions of two mid-80s cutie atrocities, Primal Scream's 'Velocity Girl' and Camper Van Beethoven's 'Take the Skinheads Bowling', plus Andy Williams's 'Can't Take My Eyes Off You'. Probably the best thing about the whole package was the inner sleeve, featuring a strangely amusing photo of a black sheep. You can take the band out of Wales . . .

Wire actually admitted that 'Australia' was merely a ploy to gain broadcast exposure: 'We just wanted to get it on the Sydney Olympics and make some money.' On this level, at least, it was a success: James's intro riff was used as the backing to countless television and radio sports round-ups. (One could almost picture Nicky, cocooned in his armchair, watching an FA Carling Premiership trailer on Sky Sports featuring Faustino Asprilla and Denis Bergkamp in fast-cut action to the sound of those familiar opening bars, and smiling with satisfaction at a job well done.) 'One of the best moments ever was when Australia beat England 76-0 at rugby,' Wire told *NME*. 'I was happy enough anyway, but when they played "Australia" afterwards . . .'

James, too, later admitted that this was no coincidence. 'When we recorded "Australia",' he told *NME*, 'we had problems getting it right, and we had to have it remixed in the end by Dave Eringa. I said to him the only way I could see it working was to make it as shiny as possible, make it like it's playing when they're showing the goals on television.'

Nicky Wire, by now, had mutated into Sporty Manic, the Mel C of the valleys. Alarmingly, his obsession with sport actually seemed to have outgrown his love of pop. 'There's two things I couldn't live without,' he confided to *NME*, 'and that's sport and chips. If there was a choice between music and never seeing the Olympics again or Wales play rugby again, I'd ditch the music.'

Sometimes, this seemed like a harmless eccentricity (taking the stage in a *Boxing News* T-shirt and shadow-boxing with the front row; coming over all starstruck when he met Chris Eubank at *Top of the Pops*). On other occasions, it manifested itself in some supremely sad behaviour. He admitted to Darren Broome of BBC Radio Wales: 'I pick my Welsh rugby and football team every week. I write it down.' He had sulked throughout the Phoenix Festival because he had missed the British Open for the first time since the age of five. He had actually ditched his beloved Tottenham Hotspur for Barcelona and Lazio on Eurosport (classic armchair-supporter conduct), then gave up football altogether for rugby, cricket, ice hockey, boxing, athletics and, probably, crown green bowling. On one occasion, he actually watched ten consecutive hours of women's golf.

For Nicky, sport is the only area of life where a natural meritocracy applies, where the best person always wins. Also, as he told Darren Broome: 'I think it can lift a nation, as much as arts or music can lift a nation. The Welsh rugby team should listen to us and Super Furry Animals before they go out on the pitch. They'd decimate the opposition.'

The Manics' new ubiquity was not restricted to sports coverage. 'To be universal,' said James in *Q*, 'you've got to stain the consciousness of the people.' 'Australia' plastered their ceilings and papered their walls.

Suddenly, and improbably, the Manics were part of the background noise of British life: piped over the speakers in Top Shop, playing in the Vic and the Caff on *EastEnders*, underscoring the emotional traumas on *This Life*, soundtracking trailers to *E.R.* Harry Enfield's Kevin the Teenager and *Brookside*'s Rachel Jordache had MSP posters in their bedrooms. A Manics question cropped up on *University Challenge*. 'Richey James?' came the answer. 'Sorry,' corrected Jeremy Paxman, 'it's Richey Edwards.' Before long, there was even a Manics tribute band (a highly reliable barometer of popularity) – the hugely entertaining Walsall-based Generation Preachers. Nicky's neighbours knew who he was now, and waved, calling: 'See you on *Top of the Pops*!' Your mum had heard of them. Your brother bought their last album, thinking it was their first. They were, literally, household names.

Somewhat worryingly, however, by early 1997 Nicky Wire seemed to be lapsing into small-c conservatism. He was even reading the *Daily Telegraph* (although he insisted that it was 'for the sport'), and it was starting to show. Asked by *NME* to name his Villain of the Year, he named Dunblane killer Thomas Hamilton (fine, but what about Slobodan Milosevic? Franjo Tudjman? Pol Pot?). It was a sensible, Middle-England kind of response. 'Guns petrify me. I've got no qualms about banning guns full-stop in Britain. I'm fucking sick of all these liberty groups saying their hobbies are gonna be taken away. Fucking hell, play darts, then.' An amusing answer, but something of a U-turn from 'fuck the Brady Bill'.

There was nothing wrong with the Manics becoming somewhat less *rock 'n' roll* in their old age: 'If the tabloids went for us,' James admitted in *Sky*, 'they'd get bored pretty quickly, we don't do anything.' That, of course, had never been the point: it didn't matter how the Manics walked it as long as they knew how to talk it. But Nicky's scattergun mouth appeared to be on a safety catch these days. 'I used to look forward to interviews,' he told *NME*, 'use them as an opportunity to make a point, but now they're an opportunity to fuck up.' He still swore at the mention of names like Radiohead but, a year later, he would eventually admit that he 'quite liked' them. Instead of attacking his rock peers, he was increasingly making fogey-ish remarks regarding boy bands, complaining about 'manufactured pop made by dodgy male models'. A safe and pointless target: the real enemy, Wire should have known, was NOT the openly trivial pop acts, but rock's false prophets who clothed themselves in the trappings of 'seriousness' without a message of any consequence to justify it. It was utterly disappointing to hear him making statements that anyone who slung a guitar around his or her neck for a living could smugly agree with.

One advantage of the thawing of the Cold War between the Manics and their peers was that it allowed them to work with other bands.

Richey's line on collaborators was roughly similar to that of the French Resistance (not that he was ever likely to be invited) and, in the past, Nicky had been in agreement. 'We're never gonna mix with other bands; we prefer to be isolated,' he had told Manchester's KFM in 1992 (admittedly, in the same interview he also said: 'We're the only band who reserve the right to contradict ourselves').

The first concrete example of the policy of making friends with auld enemies came on 27 January. Back in 1991, Graham Massey of Manchester techno pioneers 808 State had spoken disparagingly of the Manics: 'I worked as the soundman at this club [The Boardwalk] for a year, and I saw too many bands doing this (punk revivalism) for it to make any impression any more.' By 1997, Massey had clearly revised his opinion, inviting James Dean Bradfield as guest vocalist on 808's new single, 'Lopez' (this was becoming a definitively late 90s thing: Chemical Brothers with Noel Gallagher, Goldie with, er, Noel Gallagher). There was nothing technoid, however, about 'Lopez'. Tranquil and dreamlike, with bittersweet Wire lyrics in lines like 'Solitude bides time' and 'Joy gives me my last regret'; were it not for the nagging, jittery percussion and the Brian Eno/Propellerheads production, it could easily have been a Manics track. James also tried his hand as a producer with new Heavenly signings Northern Uproar, a teenage quartet of scally truants playing rough-edged Merseybeat. NU was possibly the least Manics-esque band imaginable, but James, defending the collaboration in *NME*, said, 'People who wouldn't give them credit were pussies probably picked on by their PE teachers at school.' (Spot on, actually, but disconcerting nonetheless to see the Manics siding with the bullies over the bullied.) James also gusted – sorry, *guested* – with The Beautiful South onstage and on *Later With Jools Holland* for a rendition of 'Old Red Eyes is Back', the band's wry tale of incipient alcoholism, and provided ambient guitar sounds at a Patrick Jones poetry recital in Blackwood. Not to be outdone, Wire, under the name 'Nicky Jones', wrote 'Waiting for Today to Happen', yet another lyric about bedridden paralysis and existential doubt, for the Lightning Seeds' *Dizzy Heights* album. Was nothing sacred?

Manic Street Preachers had ended 1996 among the year's biggest sellers, one of only three artists – and the only British act – to have scored four Top Ten hits, alongside Boyzone and Celine Dion. These were their peers now.

The British music industry loves nothing more than a home-grown success, and honoured the new, establishment-friendly Manics with enough awards and accolades for Nicky Wire to joke that his dad had had to reinforce the mantelpiece. In the pre- and post-Christmas period, just about the only gongs *Everything Must Go* did not win were a Smash Hits Award (although the Manics did perform at the Poll Winners' Party), or a Mercury Music Prize (although they were nominated). The Manics had already swept the board in the critics' and readers' polls in the rock press, topping the Best Album, Best Single and Best Band votes in *Melody Maker*, *NME* and *Select*. James won the Sex Symbol poll in *Melody Maker* (Nicky came seventh), and rated well in *Select*'s Most Shaggable poll. He was also heralded as fourth-best Britrock Guitarist by *Total Guitar* (an accolade which, one suspects, he enjoyed just as much as the others). James and Nicky came third and fourth respectively in *Melody Maker*'s Man of the Year category, and Wire, in *Select*, was chosen as one of the Most Important People of the Decade.

Many observers – even well-wishers – suspected that there was something of a sympathy vote at work here. Brett Anderson of Suede, variously the Manics' tour-mate/rival/kindred spirit, watched this about-face with just a hint of bitterness. 'It's like, suddenly everyone says they like the Manics: "Ooh, my favourite album of the year!" Two years ago, they wouldn't have dared.' Dickon Edwards of Orlando, which had itself attracted a modest but intense fanbase of disaffected Manics devotees, wrote in *Melody Maker*: 'The Culture of Despair has given way to The Culture of Sympathy. Hi, *Q* magazine, Hi, Brit Award . . . The same shallow scum who once threw stones are now falling over themselves to salute the band's valiant Carrying On in the Face of Loss. Permission to be sucessful in this country, it seems, can only be granted if the victories are Pyrrhic, the circumstances mitigating.'

Nicky, too, admitted that the band's New Acceptability was a weird situation to be in. 'It's ironic how it's finally OK to like us!' he told me. 'We always evenly divided critics in the past. Lately, a lot of them have admitted that they went through an American fetish of listening to shit like Sonic Youth, then they came out of it and realised that they liked us. Maybe we're just acceptable because we've been hanging around for five or six years now. I dunno, perhaps it's because we've actually made the best record. I think *The Holy Bible* and *Everything Must Go* are both perfect, but we wouldn't have expected as many people to like *The Holy Bible*. Of course, we were anticipating a certain sympathy vote this time. People don't like to rock the boat, and it's a tragic situation whichever way you look at it, so obviously we were gonna get a honeymoon period. But if we hadn't had a record like "A Design for Life" . . . I mean, if we'd brought out something like 'Of Walking Abortion' as our comeback single, I don't think it would've lasted so long.'

The first major ceremony of the 1997 season was the Brat Awards at the Camden Centre on 28 January. The *NME*-sponsored Brats, originally conceived as an alternative to the Brits, had now basically become a dry-run for the Brits themselves. The Manics left the building with a swag bag containing five Brats (a bronze hand with the middle finger raised), which put James's bemused face – he looked uncannily like a junior Stan Laurel – on the following week's *NME* cover, standing between Jarvis Cocker and Noel Gallagher. The first four awards – Best Album, Best Single, Best Live Act, Best Band – were a foregone conclusion (the Brats are based on the already published *NME* Readers' Poll). Wire dedicated the Brats haul to Arthur Scargill, '. . . but you probably haven't heard of him yet 'cos you're all London Tories'. Scargill, former president of the NUM during the Miners' Strike and now leader of the Socialist Labour Party, had been a hero to the teenage Wire (the Manics had once planned a miners' benefit, but for various reasons it had never happened). Wire had even given a donation to the SLP – so much for New Manics/New Labour – and Scargill returned the compliment by coming to see a Manics gig at Liverpool Royal Court (he traded political rants with the band backstage, and even had his photo taken with them, thumbs aloft). The fifth award was for a 'humorous' category called 'Best Song Including the Name Kevin'. James threw it at presenter Mark Radcliffe's head.

Socialist Labour Party
9 Victoria Road, Barnsley, South Yorkshire S70 2EB, tel/fax: 01226-770957

On 24 February, at Earls Court, it was time for the real thing. On a night otherwise memorable for Ginger Spice's famous Union Jack minidress (and for the sequinned basque she spilled out of), the Manics, who had never previously been nominated for any Brit Award, won two statuettes for Best Album and Best Band, equalling the two awards won by The Spice Girls in their breakthrough year. When James Dean Bradfield had his photo taken with Mel C, she was the one who looked starstruck.

Walking through the VIP tables to collect the first Brit, Nicky Wire, like Ginger Spice, was wrapped in a flag: the Welsh dragon (although, sadly, not in the form of a minidress). Under the flag, he was wearing a 1991-style DIY top, sent to him by two Swedish fans, bearing the awesome aerosol legend 'I [HEART] HOOVERING'. ('I used to have one that said, "I WILL KILL MYSELF ON VALENTINE'S DAY",' Wire said later, 'but I do love Hoovering. My wife bought me a new Hoover a few weeks ago.')

Sean Moore, first in line, was presented with the BPI statuette by Welsh hurdler Colin Jackson and 'Welsh' footballer Vinnie Jones. James was the first to speak. 'We've got to dedicate this to the wisdom of Mr Philip Hall and the coolness and intelligence of Mr Richey Edwards. And for once in our lives we have got to say "thankyou" to our fans and our mums and dads.' Then Nicky Wire took the podium. 'This is also for every comprehensive school in Britain which the government is trying to eradicate. They've produced everything – the best bands, the best art, the best everything. Oh, the best boxers too.' Sean said nothing.

A strangely slow, funereal rendition of 'A Design for Life' followed (although it was satisfying to see images of the Poll Tax riots and slogans like 'VIOLENCE FOR EQUALITY' broadcast to a television audience of millions. Then the madness commenced. At the post-Brits party, Nicky actually drank two glasses of wine, lost all his money on the VIP blackjack tables and ended up doing impressions of Jim Carrey. He eventually had to flee a lust-crazed Zoë Ball, who was trying to kiss him and wouldn't take no for an answer. 'The celebrations were very muted,' Wire told Radio One the following morning, 'but quite exaggerated for me. I was up till half past twelve. My latest night in five years, probably.'

Yet another trophy followed on 29 May. At the less-publicised but perhaps more prestigious Ivor Novello Awards, 'A Design for Life' was named Best Contemporary Song (joining previous winners such as Cliff Richard's 'Summer Holiday', Queen's 'Bohemian Rhapsody' and Take That's 'Pray'). The ceremony afforded James and Sean the chance to hang out with Led Zeppelin's Jimmy Page and Robert Plant; curiously, the next Page and Plant album sounded distinctly like the Manics.

In the tabloid press, the Manics' victories brought an inevitable upsurge of interest in the Richey story. The Edwards family, canvassed by the *Daily Mail*, said that, although they were 'pleased, delighted and thrilled for the band', they found such occasions painful because 'our son should have been there'. Richey's sister Rachel added: 'Funnily enough, I don't think their success will encourage Richey to make contact if he is alive. He didn't like being famous . . .'

'*It's all business now, isn't it? We're a business. Manic Street Preachers is a brand name, just like Pepsi*' – NICKY

Manic Street Preachers was suddenly, against all odds, respectable; a band of which mums and dads could now happily approve. 'We've had quite a few letters saying we're a band parents like,' Nicky told *Select*, 'because we're quite moral and quite intelligent.' Speaking to *Melody Maker*'s Taylor Parkes, he made a hugely ironic comparison between the Manics' apparent status, and Dadrock favourites R.E.M. Later, I asked him to explain himself. 'I meant more that we're being *perceived* like them,' he clarified. 'We're being accepted by *Q* magazine and MTV as the elder statesmen of British alternative rock. I didn't mean we were going to *become* them.'

One of the rules of success in Britain is that one must be seen to be humble and self-deprecating – however falsely. It was a lesson the Manics had finally learnt. 'Before,' James told *Select*, 'we were very gung-ho, and we made it clear that the scale in which the public bought us was very important to us. With this album, in the way we talked about it, we were the most timid we'd ever been. It was strange, because it was the most un-Manic we've been about an album, and then it was the most successful.'

Not that everyone was happy for them. As James later told *Q*: 'I felt as if we were the only band ever to win awards who could actually piss people off by winning. There was a feeling that by winning awards for our least Manic-esque performance we'd be alienating our old audience. We've never felt that when we've won awards our fans were very happy for us. They think, "You kissed ass."' James could, he admitted to Radio One, see the hardliners' point. 'It's strange, the things you feel the most gratifying are the most traditional. Like the Ivor Novello award made me, Nicky and Sean feel like such a solid band. I feel slightly ashamed that that means so much to me. Every trinket of success we got from *EMG*, deep down we knew it was everything we should spurn, but still we fluttered our eyelashes: "Thank you, thankyou." We failed on that level.'

Certainly, it was to the disappointment of many that Nicky failed to honour his promise in *Sky* magazine that: 'If we won a Brit Award, I'd get my dick out, piss on it and say: "This is what it means to me . . . you can shove it up my arse."' However, as he explained in the same magazine: 'If we'd got one when I was young, I probably would have done it. I felt so superhuman back then that nothing could hurt me. We were so strong and young and politicised that nothing mattered. Unfortunately, I don't feel like that now. If I did do it, I'd probably be thrown in prison and get done under the Obscenity Act, my mother would have a nervous breakdown and my wife would leave me.'

One happy side-effect of the Brits was that sales of the entire Manics back catalogue (not just *Everything Must Go*) rocketed. *Generation Terrorists* sold an extra 110,000 (bringing the total to 320,000), *Gold Against the Soul* 75,000 (250,000) and *The Holy Bible* 62,000

(150,000). *Everything Must Go* eventually totalled 1,125,000 (the 800,000 it sold in the UK gave it triple platinum status), and 'A Design for Life' a quarter of a million.

Why had it taken so long for the Manics' populist mission actually to work? 'There was no way "Motorcycle Emptiness" could be a hit in 1992,' Wire told *Select*. 'British culture was so divided: The Levellers, the arse end of Madchester, shoegazing, acid house . . . "Motorcycle", "La Tristesse Durera" and "A Design for Life" we thought could be big hits. "Tristesse" would be Top Ten now, piece of piss.' Maybe it's just as well. 'If we'd fulfilled the promise of the sixteen million albums and everything,' he continued, 'then I'd be running for the President of America by now.'

It was minor tragedy that the Manics' messianic drive to conquer the world had seeped away, just when they had made a record capable of doing it. 'With Richey going missing,' Nicky admitted to Radio One, 'our ambition is hugely dented. Staying alive is enough.' A few months later in his Langham Hilton hotel room, I put it to Nicky that, all things considered, the Manics' long-overdue success could not be easy to enjoy wholeheartedly. 'Yeah,' he said, 'It's not half as sweet as it would have been five years ago. It's gratifying, but it's not . . . well, I still get times when I just wanna fuck off home, however well things are going. The rigmarole that goes with the job . . . At least Richey's got a couple of Albums of the Year, for the first time! He might be alive, wishing on that . . .'

'Buy me, I'll change you. Culture is a chequebook. We are all bourgeois now' – RICHEY, 1992

The Manics had, technically, become a millionaire band in the spring of 96, when they signed a new £1 million publishing deal. Since then, the sales of *Everything Must Go* must have ensured that Nicky, James and Sean are each millionaires in their own right. Nevertheless, they are far from ostentatious when it comes to displaying their status as rock 'n' roll *nouveaux riches*. Some of the spoils of fame – free Adidas gear, unnecessarily spacious hotel rooms – are inevitable, but private jets and Rolls-Royces in swimming pools have never been the Manics' style. Nicky still lives in a modest £35,000 house and, after the band's show at the Royal Albert Hall, he and his wife went on holiday to Tenby, a quaint but determinedly unfashionable seaside town in west Wales. Wire's only real indulgence, not altogether unpredictably, involved multiple purchases of Dyson upright vacuum cleaners. Oh, and when he waters his plants nowadays, he uses Evian. 'It's hard mixing money and socialism,' he accepted, 'but to be honest all I do is the same things, but more. I buy more records, I buy more books. I still class myself as working class.' When James travels home to Gwent these days he is more likely to splash out on a chauffeur-driven hire car than to mix with the common herd on British Rail but, otherwise, a less outwardly flash rock icon you could not hope to meet. Only Sean, a self-confessed shopaholic, has occasionally fallen into an orgy of consumerism, spending much of his spare time attempting to buy an even bigger Nicam Stereo Home Cinema TV set than the one he bought the previous week. Sean has had a huge flight case custom-made to carry his electrical 'kit': DVD player, Playstation, stereo, the lot, all ready-wired and foam-cushioned. Just open the lid and switch it on. Indeed, Sean's excesses – a real case of 'From feudal serf to spender, this wonderful world of purchase power' – almost deserve a chapter of their own. The band's only other vaguely rock-star-like behaviour is the fact that, on tour, security man Steve accompanies them everywhere (although to be fair, he does so more as a mate than as a bouncer).

James, in 1993, had told Radio One: 'It's always been one of our ambitions to be surrounded by sycophants, because we've been treated as scum all our lives.' By 1997, he had realised that ambition. 'He has succumbed to those London ways,' Sean Moore told *The Face*. 'Everything – cleaners, gardeners, interior designers . . .' In rock 'n' roll, the richer you get, the less you actually do for yourself. When you get really wealthy, you don't even wipe your own arse any more. Wealth makes a child of you, turns back the clock: first you become a messy teenager whose mum tidies up after you; before long you are back in nappies.

James's drinking habits also took an alarming turn. Instead of visiting his beloved traditional pubs, he was now socialising with fellow VIPs and members of the Taffia (London's Welsh media mafia) in appalling celebrity hangouts like the Met Bar, Soho House (where he has membership) and even, on one occasion, the Groucho Club.

Nonetheless, the band deny having ascended to the Britrock Aristocracy alongside Damon, Liam and Jarvis, 'because we can still walk down the street without being recognised'. When Sean and James travel by train, they still get asked by suspicious train conductors if they realise they are in First Class. When James bought a luxurious bachelor pad in St John's Wood, he turned up in a scruffy 'Wales' T-shirt with four weeks' growth of beard. The builders looked him up and down, then asked: 'Have you come to do the doors, then?' The same day, he had been accused by a shopkeeper of mugging somebody in the street, and had had his credit card confiscated because he didn't look like the sort of person who ought to own one.

Social class is something you cannot rid yourself of, no matter how you try. It is inherent, inescapable. You can't buy yourself up a class any more than you can buy yourself down one (those who attempt the latter, like Blur, end up looking ridiculous: the Beverly Hillbillies in reverse). Manic Street Preachers are millionaires. And they are prole scum. No contradiction.

Nicky Wire had been a fan of The Boo Radleys since catching their set at Reading 1994. For several months, the Boos' classic *Giant Steps* LP was rarely off the Wire Walkman. The feeling was reciprocated: BR songwriter/guitarist Martin Carr lists *The Holy Bible* among his Top Three albums of all time, and the Boos played an acoustic cover of '4st 7lbs' on Radio One's Simon Mayo show. The bands had also met socially. Carr and Bradfield had hit it off at a Brats party in 1995, finding that they shared a love of obscure 80s indie bands like The Hoodoo Gurus and Pale Fountains, and one of James's first social outings after Richey's disappearance was to a Boo Radleys party at the former HQ of MI5. In 1996, when the Boo Radleys were supporting Suede in Europe, they went on their night off to see the Manics play Paris. There were just eighty people in the audience, and James, spotting the Boos in the crowd, changed the title of 'Small Black Flowers' to 'All The Leaves are Tim Brown' (after the Boos' bassist). After the show, the Manics were asked to support them on a tour of France, where the Boos can draw crowds of two thousand.

Instead, however, The Boo Radleys accepted the support slot on the Manics' UK tour. It was a delicious value-for-money double bill. Even by Manics standards, the pre-show hysteria on this tour was extraordinary. At the first date, at Blackpool Empress Ballroom on 2 April, people were fainting even before the *support* band had come on. In a poetic mirror image, Nicky Wire himself fell flat on his arse during 'Stay Beautiful', and still looked cool. The intensity of devotion the Manics inspired took the Boos by surprise. 'It's scary and cool as well,' says Carr. 'Since that tour I get lots of letters from Manics fans. They found out I was getting married, and I got loads of wedding cards.'

On 5 April, at Glasgow's SECC, even the seen-it-all, emotionally numb Manics were moved by the crowd reaction (MSP had, for some reason, always been especially fondly received in Scotland). 'It was the first time in my entire life where I had a lump in my throat,' James told *Q*, 'where I really felt that I'd bridged that gap between us and the audience. I felt corny as hell, like I had a big white flag flying out of my back pocket, the closest I've seen to Oasis's Maine Road experience – that tidal wave, the feeling that an audience wanted to almost claw the music into their mouths and their ears, to spoon-feed themselves with everything the band had to give.' James responded with some of his most kinetic performances for years, spinning and barking like a bull terrier high on tartrazine.

The Wire, having perfected his bizarre but inspired glam-casual look (sheepskin snorkel, eyeshadow, khakis, tiara, Vans, pink boa on the mike stand), wasn't just dressing up again but *acting* up: scaling the monitors, acting out the songs ('swallow! swallow!'), and seriously fucking up the basslines to 'Tristesse' and 'M*A*S*H' in the process. 'I never liked that pile-of-shit song,' he grinned, to cheers. In Doncaster his amp caught fire and in Plymouth he broke his toe, although it isn't exactly clear how he managed that.

The reason for this erratic behaviour soon leaked out: Wire was on the vino again. Having previously claimed to be a Ribena Light-only man, he later admitted: 'I've had a glass of red wine now and again, for the blood. I still don't enjoy it. I had a full one on the plane to Dublin recently and I was absolutely wild, like being fifteen again. Only for twenty minutes. It really went to my neck and I couldn't walk. Red wine always goes to my neck. It sort of flops down. Floppy-alcoholic-neck syndrome.'

Despite all distractions, the Richey-shaped hole stage-right still drew the eye of the older fan. Occasionally, guest trumpeter Tony would appear, glinting in the darkness like a ghost, but no one else ventured into the void. In Brighton, a 'Where's Richey?' heckle from the crowd prompted an unfortunate response from James: 'I'm afraid there are a few necrophiliacs in the crowd.' Later, when the implications dawned, he retracted. 'None of us think that Richey's dead anyway,' he told *Q*. Throughout the tour, Nicky sat a toy Snoopy on his amp (which could have been either hugely significant, or utterly coincidental). Wire, Bradfield and Moore seemed to be increasingly comfortable with the more Richey-centric parts of their back catalogue, as songs like 'This is Yesterday', 'Yes' and 'P.C.P.' ('from our triple-platinum-selling album *The Holy Bible*) made cameo appearances on the set list.

Despite the two bands' mutual appreciation, The Boo Radleys discovered, like Kinky Machine before them, that the Manics are not the most sociable of tour-mates. 'I couldn't believe the bodyguards and stuff,' says Martin Carr. 'It didn't seem necessary. It's not as if they're Oasis or something. Nicky had a guy taking him from the dressing-room to the stage.' Which was about as much as the two bands saw of each other. 'That's my only regret. Our dressing-room was always miles away. We hardly saw them. Apparently they don't like noisy bands, but it's not as if we're a chimps' tea party. They didn't even come up to say "hello".' Carr shouldn't take this reclusiveness personally, however, as even within the Manics camp there are divisions. While James deigns to mix with the noisy, boozy crew, Nicky and Sean dine together in a quiet, smoke-free room with cutlery and napkins arranged in obsessive symmetry.

Issued via
SJM Concerts

ROYAL ALBERT HALL

SJM Concerts present

MANIC STREET PREACHERS
+ Special Guests

Saturday, 12 April 1997
at   7:30 PM
Doors open at 6:30 PM

1997 SJMS01 Y

Door   6

Stalls L

Row   8

Seat   091

£ 0.00
COMP

The tour culminated on 12 April with the Manics' first ever appearance at the upturned flower bowl of the Royal Albert Hall. On the morning of the show, Allen Ginsberg, whose *Howl* had opened many an early Manics gig, died. The prestigious venue drew a larger than usual celeb-list (Boyzone, Julia Carling, actors from *EastEnders* and *Twin Town*), probably there for the after-show party where, in a particularly cheesy ceremony, the band was presented with three platinum discs.

Inside the Hall, the atmosphere was disappointingly muted (largely because standing tickets were limited, forcing most fans to sit politely on red velvet seats), although the clip of the Last Night of the Proms from the 'A Design for Life' video was pregnant with irony in the surroundings. The acoustics in the Albert Hall are poorly suited to rock music, and the show only took off twice: during 'Motown Junk', which featured a headscarf-wearing Wire standing on the speakers with his hands on his hips, and in the encore of 'You Love Us' with the original Heavenly/Iggy Pop ending (in the run-up to the general election, the chant 'Hey, passive electorate, die die die' was particularly barbed). As the song ended, Nicky Wire – followed by James and Sean – threw his mike to the floor; then the band's entire stage equipment – speakers, drums, the lot – came tumbling down. Not quite the Astoria in 94, but a touch more exciting than Elgar.

'Who's responsible? You fucking are' – 'OF WALKING ABORTION'

On 15 April 1989, 96 innocent people, aged between 10 and 67, turned up at Sheffield Wednesday's Hillsborough Stadium to watch a football match between Liverpool and Nottingham Forest, and went home in body bags. A decade on, the campaign to bring those responsible to justice through the Court of Appeal has yet to succeed. It was an event which engraved itself on the Manics' consciousness. As Nicky Wire told BBC Radio Wales: 'I remember me and Richey were watching *Grandstand*, and they flashed to the commentator who said: "Something's gone terribly wrong." I couldn't stop watching it all night. You can't help yourself, you tune in to see what the next body count is. It was horrific. It's stayed with me for a long time.'

On 10 May 1997, a benefit concert for the Hillsborough Justice Campaign and the families of the dead was held at Liverpool FC's Anfield Stadium. When it was first advertised, there had been no mention of the Manics on the bill, just a teasing 'PLUS *VERY* SPECIAL GUESTS' on a bill featuring The Lightning Seeds, The Beautiful South, Dodgy, Space and Stereophonics. Nicky had been moved by Jimmy McGovern's Granada TV movie about the disaster, screened the previous December. This was a charity which was beyond criticism: a cause which, *by definition*, could never be funded by the state.

It was a magical day. The Manics played a short mid-afternoon, hit-packed set to a rapturous, scarf-waving reception from the 35,000-strong crowd. Standing on the sacred turf of Anfield under a sunny sky and with an as-yet-undiscredited Labour Government, and hearing the opening bars of 'A Design for Life', ranks as one of the most perfect moments of this writer's life, for one. In the circumstances, many Manics lyrics were loaded with even more poignancy than usual ('What price now/For a shallow piece of dignity?'). Afterwards, James and Nicky admitted to feeling over-whelmed, even slightly choked up, by the wonderful atmosphere. Nobody believed Sean's typically contrary claim that it was 'just another gig' (he's a lifelong Liverpool supporter).

The concert climaxed with a massed choir of stars, led by Holly

> ## Manic Street Preachers
> ## Anfield Set List   10/5/97
>
> ### AUSTRALIA
> ### FROM DESPAIR
> ### KEVIN CARTER
> ### LA TRISTESSE DURERA
> ### ENOLA/ALONE
> ### EVERYTHING MUST GO
> ### MOTORCYCLE EMPTINESS
> ### NO SURFACE ALL FEELING
>
> **************************
> ### RAINDROPS
> **************************
>
> ### YOU LOVE US
> ### DESIGN FOR LIFE

Johnson, singing the tear-jerking Liverpool anthem 'You'll Never Walk Alone' while 35,000 voices chanted: 'Justice! Justice!' James Dean Bradfield skulked about in the background, allowing others to take centre-stage, while Nicky Wire and Sean Moore watched from the executive boxes. They knew that the day belonged to someone else.

The Manics' charitable impulses were strong enough to overcome the most deep-seated animosities, even towards their sometime Madchester foes. The Charlatans, said James back in the mad old, bad old days, '. . . just want to be a 60s pop band and they're good at it, but what does it mean? Personally I can't find anything in The Charlatans' music or lyrics.' Nicky had gone further, publicly banning Charlatans fans from MSP gigs on the grounds that 'they've all got moustaches'. On 17 May 1997, however, James played a solo spot supporting The Charlatans at 'Where Are You?', an all-night benefit for the National Missing Persons Helpline held at the Brixton Academy. Bradfield went onstage early in the evening, played three acoustic songs, then left without saying a word. He didn't need to.

Twelve feet high on Oxford Road, the capital letters on the gigantic advertising hoarding spelt out the words: 'MANIC ON THE STREETS OF MANCHESTER'.

Manic Street Preachers had been a *de facto* arena rock band (if not yet a stadium rock band) for some time. However, discounting a couple of leisure centres and an ice-hockey rink, they had yet actually to *play* one in anything other than a support capacity. On the Oasis tours, they had liked what they had seen, and decided to try it themselves. It was, Nicky explained, another way of liberating themselves from their past. 'At small venues we miss Richey more. If you're in a small club and facing the audience and they want to hear one of your old songs and you know Richey's not there . . . At big ones you can lose yourself. I don't like all that stuff about seeing the whites of the eyes. I'd seen that for fucking six years non-stop. I can lose myself much more in a big gig. I feel much freer. It might be better for a punter, but we're the ones doing it.'

On Saturday 2 March at 9.30 a.m. – the time had to be advertised precisely for the sake of the mentalists – tickets went on sale, at a price of £15, for what remains the Manics' biggest UK headlining show, due to take place at Manchester's fifteen-thousand-capacity Nynex Arena on Saturday 24 May.

It was what might be called throwing yourself in at the deep end. The Nynex, a brain-bogglingly immense indoor-basketball arena, resembles nothing so much as the Tunguska meteor crater with seats and a roof. Regardless of Nicky's reasons for preferring large venues, and despite the enormous video screens, one had to feel sorry for the fans stranded hundreds of yards back and Snowdon-high at the rear of the hall, who might as well have stayed at home and watched the gig on video (which, a few months later, they would actually be able to do).

After what seemed like an interminable support bill of Mansun (dull by their standards), Audioweb (a gruesomely inappropriate record-company buy-on) and Embrace (which Wire, appallingly, actually likes), the Manics came on to the Stealth Sonic Mix of 'A Design for Life' and chimed into a note-perfect 'Everything Must Go'. There were some slight signs of early nerves – James announced 'Faster' as 'Enola/Alone' and forgot the words to 'Motorcycle Emptiness' – but they soon found their stride. Nicky wound up the locals by dedicating 'Motorcycle Emptiness' to 'Albert Camus, not, I repeat, NOT for Peter Schmeichel' (Camus, of course, being a French-Algerian goalkeeper/philosopher; Schmeichel being a rednosed Danish-Mancunian goalkeeper), and climbed the biggest speaker stack of his career. Rumours that he needed oxygen afterwards were unconfirmed. Once again they played 'Yes', providing yet another stay of execution for that most troublesome of songs, and James touchingly dedicated 'This Is Yesterday' to the Edwards family. At the end of 'Motown Junk', he added the bizarre coda: 'We travel in the dangerous slipstream of Paco Rabanne and different kinds of aftershave every week.'

'I've met the man in the street, and he's a cunt' – SID VICIOUS

And the Nynex, as a matter of fact, did reek of aftershave.

Prior to 'A Design for Life', the Manics simply did not attract hotdog-munching, lighter-waving stadium-rock cattle. But their new million-selling, Brit-winning, arena-filling status had brought with it a new kind of Manic fan: displaced Oasis lads in Ben Shermans and Timberlands, clutching pints of Carlsberg and waiting for the hits. The 'new scum/new dumb' prophesied by the Manics on 'Soul Contamination' had arisen. At every show on the 1997 tour, beer-swilling Cast blokes (now the majority) and mascara-and-leopardskin kids (now a minority) eyed each other with suspicion. Rapidly, a full-scale Manic Civil War broke out between the 'New Fans' and 'Old Fans'. As Neil Kulkarni, reporting on the Blackpool gig for *Melody Maker*, noted: 'This isn't a gig, it's a *bona fide* style war.' The battle lines were drawn: Nation of Richey Edwards versus Nation of Ralph Lauren. In the main, the theatres of war were the letters pages of the rock press, but actual violence was not a rare occurrence. Helen and Adrian of Bolton, who had first-hand experience of this, took a militant Old Fan view: 'Every single new fan out there is a total wanker. I've had the shit kicked out of me about ten times by trendies, drunk footie lads and Cast fans.' At Reading, I saw a young teenage couple pushing their way towards the back of the hall in tears. They had been punched in the faces. And nor was the aggro confined to the moshpit: even The Boo Radleys were considered fair game. 'I've always hated all that élitist "I was into them before you" stuff,' says Martin Carr, 'but we did suffer from the *Everything Must Go* fans. Students on the pull. I've never had anything thrown at me, ever, except at Manics gigs.'

Some old skoolers – the 'nancy boys and anti-girls', as Kulkarni called them – took this phenomenon as a cue to leave the Manics altogether, many of them moving on to other eyeliner-friendly bands (Mansun, My Life Story, Kenickie); or to the proto-goth 'New Grave' movement (Marion, Placebo, Strangelove), which, ironically, the Manics were credited with starting. One deserter, J.S. of London, called the Manics 'The Genesis it's OK to like. James even looks like Phil Collins.' Another fan, called Sean, complained: 'Nowadays they look as if they're in control of their vehicles – they used to look as if they weren't in control of *anything*!' Another, Steven, said: 'No matter how much they deny it and protest, Richey WAS the backbone of the band. He gave these pathetic bastards the edge and necessary menace to become what they were.' Some detractors took their anger too far. At one show, when James stagedived into the crowd, a member of the Manics crew watched in horror as a male fan stood in the pit holding a knife aloft, hoping to gore the singer as he fell.

From the perspective of the Richey-ists, the Manics' tactic of entryism had actually been too successful: in passing themselves off as a straightforward, mainstream rock band, they had attracted hordes of straightforward, mainstream people. For some, this was all about snobbery, pure and simple. 'The Manics are out there now, in the public domain,' wrote Neil Kulkarni, 'and *that's* precisely what pisses off the old fans – the availability of the Manics now, the way you can walk in on them off the street, with no password, no invitation, without the Manics' *permission*.' The band themselves found such élitism frustrating. 'We're not giving out free cans of Hip Oil at the door' said James. 'We are an obvious white male experience with a hint of despairing young girls – that's our forte.' In fact, Nicky Wire seemed almost to enjoy the thug factor, telling *NME*: 'You get gigs like Manchester Nynex when the button-down shirt brigade turn up and there's a bit of pogoing and, yeah, a few elbows go in a few faces, but we would never want to do a gig *without* that physicality.'

'Organise your safe tribal war . . .' – 'MOTORCYCLE EMPTINESS'

There were many who suspected that the internecine dispute was nothing but a media fiction. According to Hall Or Nothing's Caffy St Luce: 'It all blew up because the press had nothing to write about that month. It's exaggerated. There's no apartheid. People move on, others join, others stay . . .' At the end of 1997, *Melody Maker* staged a debate/quiz/face-off between 'Old Fans' and 'New Fans', hoping for the fur to fly, only to find that they all liked each other really.

The explanation was simple: the whole argument was based on a false premise. It wasn't the *vintage* of the fan that mattered, but the *type*. A lot of the so-called 'Old Fans' were, in fact, much younger than The Lads, but had quickly made up for lost time, immersing themselves in the Manics' *oeuvre*, devouring the back catalogue, the old interviews, the recommended reading list. It was not the 'New Fans' *per se* that were the problem (many newcomers were just as intensely versed in the band's history as the veterans), but only an accident of birth – the teenagers had simply been too young back in 92 – which had prevented them from getting into the Manics sooner. And the more teenagers who discovered the Manics now, surely, the better. The group which really rankled was the *casual* fans; it was the late twenties/early thirtysomethings who had only just woken up to the Manics, and who had little interest in the band's messages or cultural significance, of whom one was suspicious. These people had no excuse: it wasn't as if the Manics had ever been some sort of underground cult act, or a best-kept secret. From 1991 onward they had always been a major-label concern, on ITV's *Chart Show*, on countless magazine front covers, on *Top of the Pops* with every single, on billboards on railway-station platforms, the lot. They were always a great band, and they were there for the taking. One had to ask – *where were you in 92*?!

That said, it was obviously marvellous that the Manics had finally won the audience that their songs merited. As John Robb of *Sounds* and Gold Blade points out: 'They're even more out of context now than ever: a politicised stadium rock band, surrounded by other stadium rock bands playing moaning ballads.' Wendy of Derbyshire, a fan at the Blackpool gig, represented the conciliatory stance when she said: 'I've liked the Manics since "Motown Junk", but I think it's great that everyone likes them now. I want them to be the most famous band in the world.' This mass market is *exactly* what the Preachers always craved, needed, deserved – but many wondered whether the masses would ever truly get the message. 'It's weird what's happened to them in the last year,' says Martin Carr of The Boo Radleys. 'You hope they can still put the same intelligence across as they used to, but you wonder when you look at the audience singing along to lyrics like "We don't talk about love, we only wanna get drunk" like it's a fucking drinking song or something.'

Nicky Wire remains more optimistic. 'People might say no one gets it,' he told Radio One, 'but at the end of the day, a million people have got that record ['A Design for Life'] in their homes, and the first line is "Libraries gave us power", so something must seep through.' These people are not all philistines. At Nynex, for instance, the merchandise-stall copies of Patrick Jones's *The Mute Communion* sold out. (When Patrick subsequently did a reading/signing at Cardiff's Virgin Megastore, Manics fans from as far away as the Home Counties turned up, proving the demand for anything Manics-related . . . literally.)

The day after the Manics have been in town, provincial shopping centres are full of townies with the words 'HELL IS OTHER PEOPLE' (Sartre) and 'I HAVE NOTHING TO OFFER THE WORLD EXCEPT MY OWN CONFUSION' (Kerouac) on their backs. *That* is power. *That,* the purists would do well to remember, is exactly what Richey wanted.

'Preach not because you have to say something, but because you have something to say' –
OSCAR WILDE

Now that Nicky Wire finally had the ear of the public, he seemed to be having difficulty knowing what to say to it. 'To be honest with you,' he told me in December 96, 'I'm finding it really, really hard to write any lyrics. Apart from B-sides like "Sepia", I've only written one proper song, in terms of anything we could use on the next album. I'm really struggling. I've got writer's block. In terms of content, I worry about us because . . . "Interiors" was about a fucking abstract painter, pretentious as fuck, but I've still got to keep doing it. I've never been in a position when things have gone relatively well, I've been successful financially, so I'm kind of . . . it's hard to know what to write about.'

Nothing to piss him off any more, I suggested? 'Yeah, there is, but not on the same magnitude.'

And he could hardly write a whole album about potatoes, art galleries and Ian Woosnam . . .

'So anyway, that's what I find quite scary at the moment, trying to come up with ten or twelve songs. I really like "Sepia", I think it's really beautiful lyrically, but I can't write songs about missing Richey for ever. I try to keep them to a minimum anyway.'

Whatever Nicky wrote, people would assume it was about Richey anyway. 'Yeah. Obviously there's gonna be some coming out, consciously or unconsciously. And that kind of worries me as well . . .'

On 22 August 1997, evidence appeared that Nicky had finally overcome his writer's block. At a warm-up gig for the Reading Festival at the Newport Centre, the now all-too-familiar *Everything Must Go* set was enlivened by two brand-new songs. 'Ready for Drowning' progressed from a gorgeous Stax-organ intro into handsome, elegiac MOR. Like 'Australia', this appeared to be another escape song ('I'd go to Patagonia, but it's harder there') and, as a drunken, bony-finger-jabbing Wire would explain to me subsequently, a deeply moral song (of which, more later). 'Born a Girl', a tranquil acoustic requiem to Wire's feminine side, spoke for itself.

The following night, for the first time ever, the Manics were headlining a major festival. There was no little irony in the fact that Reading, the Manics' erstwhile 'Cultural Chernobyl' and scene of Nicky's infamous bouncer-braining, was now being described by James as 'our spiritual home'. The on/off civil war within the Manics' fanbase had been simmering all weekend, with the tiara-and-glitter faithful (already there in their hordes for Suede, Kenickie and My Life Story) and the polo-shirted squaddies sneering at each other with equal venom.

The bizarrely anachronistic supporting bill – The Lemonheads, whose Evan Dando outraged Manics fans by asking, 'Where the fuck is Richey?', and the crushingly dull Orb – made it feel like 1991 again. The support bands could almost have been chosen as a deliberate context-setter, like the collage of headlines from outraged Tory tabloids used by the Sex Pistols for their reunion gigs. The Manics responded with one of their most exciting shows since those times – one of the ten best I have ever seen. As soon as Nicky Wire walked out in a lunchbox-revealing see-through blue camouflage dress – £10 in the Warehouse sale – you knew this would be something special. It was the first time he had worn a frock on stage since 1993. Apparently, I may have been partly responsible for this: in the afternoon, a Hall Or Nothing employee told me that Wire had heard about my own outfit (a huge gold-sequinned crown) and was determined to outdo me. Later, however, he revealed that transvestitism was a regular part of his domestic life (he tries on Rachel's dresses but they are too small for him), and he was only doing it in public because he had lost some weight. Embarrassingly for the music press, but amusingly for everyone else, *Melody Maker* and *NME* both featured near-identical live shots of the frocked-up Wire on their covers, obviously taken just a split-second apart and from exactly the same angle. The image clearly had a profound effect on the readers. Three weeks later, when *Melody Maker* conducted a 'Sexiest Lad in Rock' poll, Nicky received more votes than all the other candidates combined (although the published result was secretly fixed in favour of Placebo's Brian Molko).

Although the Manics had been touring for far too long, having spent a year and a half plugging *Everything Must Go* to death, with a set Sean had already been describing as 'old hat' back in April, the Saturday night at Reading was shot through with an near-unbearable level of poignancy. 'Yes' was almost too much for James. He still skipped that 'I hurt myself to get pain out' line, and could only manage 'Everyone I've loved or hated always seems to leave' by pulling a Popeye squint and screaming. Between songs, Wire and Bradfield provided light relief with a *Morecambe and Wise*-style double act (Wire: 'Aah, where's your bloody dress?'; Bradders: 'Just 'cos *you* wear a bloody dress, woooh!'). The closing 'You Love Us' was mind-blowing: gorgeous, gorgeous Edwards in white denim and black lace on the big screen, Wire down below, hands on hips, screaming incoherent fuck-you farewells. Brilliant.

The final show of the *EMG* era the following day, at Semple Stadium in Thurles, Co. Tipperary, was something of an anti-climax. A crowd mainly present for The Prodigy, Reef and Kula Shaker showed little interest in the Manics. For the first year in the band's history – including 95 – there would be no Christmas gig.

> 'I keep dreaming that you're in love with me, like I'm in love with you/But dreaming's all I do/If only they'd come true . . .' – KYLIE MINOGUE, 'I SHOULD BE SO LUCKY'

In September 1997 the Manics completed another collaboration – one of which they had dreamt for six years. Kylie Minogue (whom they had originally approached in 1991 to sing guest vocals on 'Little Baby Nothing') had finally joined the band for a live version of the song at the Shepherd's Bush Empire in December 1996.

A small section of the crowd that night had booed her, and there were even rumours of death threats in the post, which Kylie denied. 'No, I haven't got any hate mail,' she told me. 'I think a journalist posed the question "Oh, so you'll be getting hate mail now?", and so now everyone thinks I have. It's not beyond imagination that the music press have had letters, or the Manics have, probably written in blood, you know? Saying: "How could you work with *her*?!"'

Whether or not the Manics' Barmy Army bore hard feelings about Kylie's previous rejection of the band, Nicky, James and Sean didn't. 'We've always admired Kylie,' James told Radio One's *The Net*. 'We asked her to sing a song with us a long time ago and she said "No", but obviously things come round and I'm not one to hold a grudge.' There was even a rumour that a re-recorded a version of 'Little Baby Nothing', featuring Kylie, was in the pipeline, for eventual inclusion on a Greatest Hits compilation. Kylie cagily denied the rumours, although she did say, 'I'd love to do that again, actually, that song . . .'

For the record, I asked her what really went on back there in 91. 'I never knew about it,' she insisted. 'I don't even know if it reached management level. I just imagine the big front door at PWL, and these scruffy little Welsh guys in eyeliner, and the doorman saying: "Manic *Street* Preachers?!" It just would not have figured. I was the last to find out about a lot of things – things that I was doing, let alone things that I was in no way, shape or form going to do. So for me it's that much more thrilling that it's happening now, because I am some kind of fatalist, and to work with the Manics now is all the more potent because there is that invisible history.'

Minogue had been courting a more adult, indie audience for some time, collaborating with Nick Cave and appearing on magazine covers with Bobby Gillespie. At some point in early 1997, James Dean Bradfield was having a pint with Tom Tomlinson of Minogue's label DeConstruction, who mentioned that Kylie was working on a new album and, hey, how about trying to do something *this* time. A meeting was arranged. 'I met James at his place,' she remembered, 'and gave him some lyrics, and he played me a track – I can't remember what it was, something Tamla Motown-ish – and said, "What do you think about this vibe?" We just had a brief chat, a cup of tea, and off he went with my lyrics. He was busy, about to go on tour, and there was that Manics fever, so I didn't hold my breath or get too excited in case nothing happened, but . . .'

On 8 September 1997, a Kylie/Manics single, 'Some Kind of Bliss' (music: Bradfield/Moore; production: Eringa), was released. A dignified Stax pastiche, it inducted MSP into the hallowed company of Kylie conspirators including Jason Donovan, Nick Cave and, er, Keith Washington. James had actually taken two separate Kylie lyrics and combined them into a highly Preacher-esque treatise on culture, alienation, boredom and despair: 'Good to be here/Time to be alone/Find the space where I belong/Not succumb to fear . . .' Kylie's subsequent album, retitled from *Impossible Princess* to simply *Kylie Minogue* in the wake of the tragic death of the Queen of Hearts, contained another Manics collaboration. 'I Don't Need Anyone' (lyrics: Wire/Minogue; music: Bradfield; production: Eringa) was pure *EMG*-era Manics – basically MSP's 'Australia' with added flutes 'n' strings and a Motorcity backbeat. Both were considerably better than, say, Nicky Wire's work with The Lightning Seeds or Sean Moore's unreleased Tyrolean oompah project; both absolutely vindicated the Manics' previously unrequited desire to record with Kylie. However, Sean Moore, for one, didn't enjoy the experience of working outside the band context. 'When James and I wrote that little ditty,' he later admitted, 'it was four days of misery. It just seemed utterly pointless.' James, in retrospect, also expressed misgivings. He was dissatisfied with the single's sales: 'Some Kind of Bliss' barely dented the charts and, a year later, Kylie was dropped by DeConstruction. 'Seeing the commercial result,' he told *NME*, 'I probably failed her. That's the only thing I'm upset about . . . I'm embarrassed that I failed her.'

As well as the myriad collaborations, product-starved Manics fans had two new(ish) things on which to spend their money in the autumn of 97. On 1 September, the band's first six Sony singles – the ones lifted from *Generation Terrorists* – were re-released, with more or less the original artwork (although, for some reason, presumably copyright, 'Slash 'N' Burn' omitted its original B-side, 'Motown Junk'). The singles re-entered the chart at between Nos. 41 and 55. The singles were also available separately in a grey cheesecloth-covered box set which looked uncannily like a computer floppy-disk container. Another pointless consumer item.

The first commercially available Manics video, *Everything Live*, followed, on 29 September. Shot at Nynex in May, it makes disappointing viewing. With just one exception (a clever cut between rehearsal-room and live renditions of 'Elvis Impersonator'), the video is packed with every rock-video cliché in the book: boom swoops over the crowd, girls on their boyfriends' shoulders, 'the guys' larking about backstage. Also, inexplicably, the performance was edited, and 'Yes', 'Small Black Flowers', 'Stay Beautiful' and 'Raindrops Keep Falling on My Head' all landed on the cutting-room floor. The fan was left with just 63 minutes' worth, which included substandard documentary footage and a mind-bogglingly shallow interview ('What football team do you support?', 'Can you drive?', 'Have you been on the Beijing railway?'). *Everything Live* succeeded in its primary purpose – feeding demand for Manics products in the run-up to Christmas – but failed miserably to convey an accurate sense of what it was actually like to be there. Who was responsible? Manic Street Preachers were. The credits roll ended: 'Executive Producer: Nicky Wire'.

'We just want to clear everything away. Maybe, after us, music won't seem as important as actually changing the world' – RICHEY, 1992

The first time I saw James Dean Bradfield in 1998, at a Catatonia gig in London, he had a beard. 'You know how it is,' he smiled, 'personal vanity goes out of the window in the intensity of the studio . . .'

Rather more disturbing was the news that Nicky Wire – thus far the only Manic never to have experimented with facial hair – had also grown a beard. By several accounts, it was a somewhat pitiful attempt: wispy, with lots of gaps (fortunately, after just one unflattering promotional photo of Manic Beard Preachers was released, they all decided to have a shave).

James, Nicky and Sean may have looked as though they had been living off locusts and honey in the wilderness, but the truth was more prosaic. They had been making another album.

The process began in August 1997, when the band booked into Whitfield Street Studios in London's West End to demo a couple of tracks with Howard Gray of Apollo 440 (a.k.a.

Stealth Sonic Orchestra). This, Nicky Wire was at pains to stress, had nothing to do with any U2-style rock/dance interface. James Dean Bradfield had always wanted to make a record with the crystalline, spacious electronic sheen of Simple Minds *circa The American*, and Gray, who as a very young man had engineered the Minds' *Sparkle in the Rain*, was the man for the job. In the event, however, none of the Whitfield Street recordings made it on to the finished album, turning up as B-sides instead. Another recording from the London sessions which did not make the final edit was a duet with Sophie Ellis-Bextor, singer with Theaudience (also managed by Hall Or Nothing); the fate of the duet, at the time of going to press, remains uncertain.

Next stop, on 7 September, was Big Noise (formerly Soundspace) in Cardiff, where Sean laid down a few drum tracks with Greg Haver. Recording began in earnest when the Manics, together with Dave Eringa, flew to France to reunite with *Everything Must Go* producer Mike Hedges at his Château de la Rouge Motte in Domfront, Normandy, where they spent the remainder of September. After a short break, they recorded sixteen tracks – the bulk of the album, plus B-sides – either side of Christmas.

In January, a little time was spent in Wales's legendary Rockfield studios, working on more B-sides with Dave Eringa. Shortly afterwards, the band decamped to nearby Mono Valley, a residential Welsh farmhouse. By now, cabin fever had set in, and James regularly sneaked out to the local pub, prompting Nicky – like Flo in *Andy Capp* – to set strict drinking limits ('Two pints, then you're coming back, right?') and to check James's pupils for dilation to gauge whether he had been on the sauce.

Completing the circle, the band returned to London for final mixing and for what James calls 'a bit of tinkerage', first at Abbey Road and then at George Martin's Air Studios, a converted church in Hampstead. Air's only other tenants were the Arsenal football team, recording a single to celebrate their league/cup double.

The album was finally put to bed in mid-June. In total, the Manics had recorded in three separate countries and used seven different studios: Whitfield Street (England), Big Noise (Wales), Château de la Rouge Motte (France), Rockfield (Wales), Mono Valley (Wales), Abbey Road (England) and Air (England). Historically, few great albums have been made by such serial studio-hopping. Would the Manics be the exception that proved the rule?

'All you can do is leave clues throughout history towards something better. Towards progress' – NICKY

Nicky Wire had long been fascinated by the Spanish Civil War. In 1936, a revolutionary government with popular support was crushed by the right-wing General Franco, with the aid of Nazi Germany and Fascist Italy – a rehearsal for the Second World War itself.

Released on 24 August, the Manics' comeback single, 'If You Tolerate This Your Children Will Be Next', uses the Civil War as the pretext for 'a subtle rallying cry to stand against things you know are inherently wrong' and as a warning regarding present-day conflicts (such as that in Kosovo). As a general theme for a song, it is comparable to that of 'La Tristesse Durera (Scream to a Sigh)'. Nicky's specific interest in the Civil War had begun when he first heard The Clash's 'Spanish Bombs' and diligently started researching a song on the subject. In addition to The Clash's influence, 'If You Tolerate

This Your Children Will Be Next' was also inspired by *Homage to Catalonia*, George Orwell's diary of his spell as a foot soldier in the communist CNT, and by Nicky's own visits to Barcelona ('I've walked Las Ramblas, but not with real intent . . .'), a CNT stronghold during the war. James shared the fascination: years earlier, he had tracked down a single about the Spanish Civil War by anarcho-punk band The Ex, featuring a 36-page booklet of CNT rebel songs.

The line: 'If I can shoot rabbits, then I can shoot fascists' is a quote from a Welsh farmer who, like many idealistic Britons, went to fight for the International Brigade on the side of the communists (the line had previously been used as a T-shirt slogan on the Manics' 1997 tour). As a statement, it was only partially successful: the majority of the Manics' audience would *never* feel able to shoot a rabbit.

In a roundabout way, however, this was Wire's point, for the lyric speaks of his fear of becoming 'a gutless wonder'. 'If You Tolerate This' is a song of shame on behalf of his apathetic generation: 'Gravity keeps my head down . . . Or is it maybe shame?' It was basically another way, seven years after 'Repeat', of saying 'Useless Generation'. This time, though, the taunt is self-critical: 'It's directed at myself,' he told Darren Broome of BBC Radio Wales. 'I wouldn't have gone to Bosnia to help their side.' Sometimes, Wire's musings on the subject were not dissimilar to the familiar mantras of elderly British Legion veterans, disgusted by the fecklessness of youth ('God help us if there's a war', 'What we need is a really good war', 'People these days don't know they're born').

'People have a nervous breakdown about booking their fucking holiday, don't they, in this day and age?' Wire ranted to *NME*. 'Generations today are incredibly blasé about how lucky they are, they seem to have no understanding about how literally millions, seven million people or whatever, laid down their lives for us, just so we can be here now. There's no way people would go and fight for a cause today like the International Brigade fought fascism, something that you know is wrong, regardless of economics. The purity of that ideal I find incredibly powerful. People say: "Oh, George Orwell went there and didn't really get into the action", but he still got shot. I doubt whether Douglas Coupland would go . . .'

There comes a point in any highly successful band's career where it can take for granted the attention of its audience; where it can take liberties, and has the freedom to release absolutely *anything* in the knowledge that it will still go straight in at No. 1. The Manics had now reached that point. In contrast to the singles which had heralded their previous albums ('You Love Us', 'From Despair to Where', 'Faster', 'A Design for Life'), 'If You Tolerate This' didn't slap you *upside tha hedd* and force you to listen. Something of a grower, a slow-burner with its 'treated'guitar sounds and downbeat feel, it sounded more like an album track than the Big Comeback Single, and its gentle elegance seemed ill-suited to primetime radio rotation. Nicky described it as 'the most subtle thing we've ever done' (perhaps it was *too* subtle: some European journalists thought it was about the Belgian paedophile scandal).

The chorus, as several people noticed, bears an striking resemblance to The Stranglers' 1979 hit 'Duchess'. The Manics admitted that there was a similarity but insisted it was coincidental, adding that they didn't even own any Stranglers records. 'When we actually heard it,' said Sean, 'we thought, "Bloody hell, it does sound similar," but nothing was intentional.' The Stranglers' publishers threatened legal action, but the punk veterans themselves didn't seem bothered. 'We don't have it in for the Manics at all,' said bassist Jean-Jacques Burnel, mischievously adding: 'When we hold the launch party for our new CD, we'll be inviting the Manics along. That way, they can get first pickings, just in case there's anything they'd like to use.'

Remix duties this time were assigned to David Holmes and Massive Attack, whose moody, atmospheric reworking soon replaced the orchestral 'A Design for Life' as the Manics' walk-on music. (In a reciprocal gesture, James produced, played bass and sang backing vocals on Massive Attack's new single, 'Inertia Creeps'.) In addition, the single was accompanied by two new tracks. 'Prologue to History' is a fantastic clattering racket of a song, weirdly reminiscent of The Charlatans with their trademark Hammond organ replaced by a rickety piano, and with James hollering to make himself heard over the everything-turned-up-to-eleven production and the urgent post-baggy beat (the lyric namechecked 'Shaun William Ryder'). Although there was a thinly veiled reference to Richey ('my former friend who's now undercover'), 'Prologue' was basically a semi-ironic hymn to Nicky Wire's own virtues: 'Today a poet who can't play guitar . . . Next year the world's greatest politician . . . Yesterday the boy who once had a mission . . .' Nicky confessed to a sneaking desire to go into politics: 'Being Welsh Minister of Sport and Culture sounds perfect,' he told *NME*. For immediacy alone, 'Prologue to History' might have made a better single than its A-side. It was followed by the enigmatically titled 'Montana/Autumn/78', another indie-dance pastiche – this time weirdly reminiscent of Jesus Jones.

The cover, featuring an old blurred photograph of CNT soldiers, used the same font and layout to those of *Everything Must Go* and its spin-off singles. Yet, where those sleeves had been meaningfully mute, this time the idea just seemed devoid of meaning. All that it actually appeared to convey was: 'Yes, it's those Manic Street Preachers – the ones you bought all those records from last year.' If this tactic was intentional, it worked.

On Friday 28 August, while the gaze of the rock world was elsewhere (a field in Reading, to be precise), Manic Street Preachers made their return to live action after almost exactly a year's absence. If the Cork Opera House, a modern 1,200-capacity theatre, seemed a surprisingly large venue for a low-key warm-up, it was only an index of the scale on which the Manics were now working. Despite the remote location, the crowd was gratifyingly knowledgeable (some sections repeatedly chanted for 'Revol', a fans' favourite which the band now hates). The show itself was anything but low-key, mostly due to the antics of Nicky Wire, who drowned out James by screaming along to every word of 'You Love Us', swigging ostentatiously from a bottle of red wine. According to crew member Andy Gritton: 'It's because he's happy.'

The following night, supporting The Verve at Slane Castle outside Dublin ('It's an honour to be playing with them,' Nicky rather cringeingly told MTV), he was clearly even happier. He managed to hold it together long enough to meet Mo Mowlam, Secretary of State for Northern Ireland, who had requested an audience with the Manics before the show. 'She was really surprised when I actually talked politics with her,' Wire told *Select*. 'The first thing I said to her was: "What was it like in the H-blocks?" She seemed quite taken aback.' Onstage, however, it was a different matter. Apart from a lone obsessive

THIS IS MY TRUTH, TELL ME YOURS

who threw a copy of Sartre's *La Nausée* at the band ('That's the sort of present we get from our lovely fans,' grinned Wire), the Manics met with a lukewarm reception from an 8,000-strong crowd which, give or take a few Welsh flags a dozen rows back, consisted almost entirely of Verve fans. When 'A Design for Life' finally livened them up, James sarcastically commented: 'Oh, so at last it's one you know?' An obviously drunk Nicky didn't seem to notice: his comical conduct included wandering into a rambling and sentimental anecdote about how we should all love our mums, and falling on his arse from a crouching position. This time, 'Motown Junk' got the screamalong treatment.

The Manics had plenty of reasons for drinking that night. When they came offstage, news reached them from the mainland about the first-week sales of their new single. It had been a nervous week. On Monday, the day of release, Wire confesses to having paced around record shops looking wistfully at copies on the racks. Sixty thousand copies *left* the racks that day but, on the Tuesday, sales slowed up. By Wednesday, mid-week figures were not looking too good, suggesting that the single might enter the charts as low as No. 3. The Manics were fighting a fierce challenge from 'One For Sorrow' by line-dancing Eurodisco Abba-impersonators Steps. They weren't even helped by their own families: James's mother actually bought the Steps single. 'I said: "Mam, don't buy it, they might beat us!" but she bought it anyway . . .'

It was a close call. By the time record-shop tills shut on Saturday, the Manics had sold 176,000 copies, just 6,000 ahead of Steps. It was enough to give the Manics their first ever No. 1 single, knocking Ireland's own Boyzone off the top. Twenty-two years since the last No. 1 about the Spanish Civil War – 'Fernando' by Abba – the Manics had finally done it. This made them the first Welsh act to top the chart since Shakin' Stevens' 'Merry Christmas Everyone' in 1985, and created the longest-titled No. 1 since Scott McKenzie's 'San Francisco (Be Sure to Wear Flowers in Your Hair)' in 1967, before any of them were born.

The Manics and their entourage reacted to this historic triumph in different ways. James, still a little hungover from the night before, shrugged: 'Oh, we're Number One.' As he later explained to *Select*: 'I was just relieved – not to be a perennial bridesmaid any more. It's nice to be taken off the shelf.' Sean was equally cool, but Nicky cracked open the champagne and celebrated as if he had just scored a winning try against England. 'I wanted to phone everyone up and tell them we were No. 1,' he told Steve Lamacq of *NME*, 'but then I realised I didn't have any friends.' Martin Hall was in tears. After just four glasses of champagne, Nicky awoke in the morning with a splitting hangover. That night's show in Belfast, perhaps uncoincidentally, was a less-eventful performance; Wire, wearing a 'FOREVER DELAYED' T-shirt, barely spoke all night.

Eyeliner-and-tiara fans didn't have much to cheer about in Ireland, when all three Manics took to the stage in cream and white Gap-style gear. Nicky even wore a padded bodywarmer. The Manics' status as gurus of casual wear appeared intact (the T-shirts on the merchandise stall bore the label 'Valley Boy', prompting rumours of an imminent MSP fashion range). The sole concession to glamour was Sean's sparkly new silver drumkit. There were no projections to watch at any of these gigs, either – this time it was just about the music, man. And the music was just a little rusty. James regularly found himself forgetting the words. 'You ought to have heard him in Ireland,' Nicky laughed in *Melody Maker*. '"Doo da doo doo da doo, la tristesse . . ."' Johnny Dankworth and Cleo

Laine, he was. Mind you, I couldn't remember the bass parts, so I can't have a go at him.' Across the three gigs the Manics played six songs from the forthcoming album, but the number of songs from *The Holy Bible* – a reliable index of how comfortable the Manics are with their history at any given time – was just one: 'Faster', which they sang in Belfast (without balaclavas on this occasion, oddly).

The Manics' week-long reign at the top of the charts saw them all over our television screens on shows like *Top of the Pops* and *TFI Friday*. The much played video, directed by long-time collaborator Wiz, was apparently inspired by Mike Nichols's futuristic eugenics thriller *Gattaca*. The band, trapped in a space-age pod as part of some unspecified totalitarian scientific experiment, are forced to play the song over and over until it makes them sick (a handsome, helmet-wearing Wire vomits copiously). Meanwhile, in the room next door, a disturbing family of mannequins without eyes, mouths or ears acts as a mute embodiment of the song's 'see no evil, speak no evil, hear no evil' message.

By the time MSP made their first appearance in mainland Britain, in Wales on Sunday 13 September, they were no longer No. 1, having been displaced by fellow combat-wearing Brit winners All Saints. The Manics were late additions to the bill of an enormous free concert, organised by Radio One in Cooper's Field behind Cardiff Castle, which also starred Ash, The Divine Comedy, The Shirehorses, Embrace, Republica, Hurricane #1 and Robbie Williams (Williams, clearly affected by rubbing shoulders with the Manics, turned up on *Top of the Pops* the following week wearing a distinctly Wire-esque see-through frock).

The tent, said to be the largest ever erected on British soil, was crammed with ten thousand rabid Welsh pop kids. Taking the stage with military precision at exactly 8.47 p.m. to chants of 'Wales! Wales!', the Manics played just five songs: a radically slowed-down 'Australia', 'Everything Must Go', album tracks 'If You Tolerate This' and 'Tsunami' ('Tsunami' collapsed somewhat at the end: 'That's how we used to play in 1991') and the inevitable 'A Design for Life'. James renamed 'Everything Must Go' as 'Bobby Gould Must Go', a reference to the increasingly unhinged Welsh football coach, who responded with a truly surreal anti-Manics tirade on *Football Focus*: 'I tell you, I saw a documentary about those Manic Street Peaches [sic], and one of them disappeared and cut his arm up to get attention, and I don't think that's any example to set for our young people . . .' I probably wasn't the only one who fully expected to live out his threescore-and-ten without seeing live footage of 'Motown Junk' on *Grandstand* ('Australia', *perhaps*), but we were reckoning without the mono-browed managerial maniac.

The Cardiff concert was more than simply a philanthropic gesture from the Manics: it was a promotional exercise for the new album, which went on sale the next day. A nearby building was draped in a giant ad, with the record's title in Welsh (prompting a minor local furore when someone noticed that the translation was slightly inaccurate). At midnight, the Manics held a signing session in the nearby Virgin Megastore (which opened specially and hired in ninety extra security guards). The session drew five thousand fans, some of whom had been queuing for thirteen hours and had therefore missed the show. They weren't just 'New Fans', either – one brought a copy of 'Suicide Alley'.

The signing also saw the first public appearance of the Truth Box, a bizarre promotional stunt conceived by the Manics and their Sony product manager Angie. Based on Channel Four's touring Video Box, it was a mobile cubicle containing a camera, in which fans were requested to reveal a 'truth'. According to a spokeswoman: 'The kind of truths we are expecting are the unexpected, but they could be political, confessional, visual, verbal, comedy, romantic or illegal.' (After Cardiff, the Box went on to vist Megastores in Bristol, Leeds and London. The prize for the best entry was a trip to Barcelona with the Manics in October, the eventual winner being a girl whose presentation involved a collection of Manics dolls she had acquired from Japan. The fate of the 'truths' themselves was unclear, although it was suggested they would be screened on MTV at a later date.) The Greeting of the Five Thousand in Cardiff lasted until 3.30 a.m. The band chatted to everyone who waited; no one was sent away disappointed. This fan-friendly charm offensive continued in the press, where *NME* readers were invited to send the Manics their own interview questions. (Fan: 'What do you wear in bed?' James: 'Nothing.' Sean: 'Nothing.' Nicky: 'Calvins.')

This time, more than ever, the Manics were getting the hard sell. As well as the back cover of every music publication, their likenesses were plastered on giant illuminated billboards situated on major roads.

On a clear night, you could see them for miles.

'Too many of the artists of Wales spend too much time talking *about the position of the artist of Wales'* – DYLAN THOMAS

According to Alfred Du Masset, who is quoted on the sleeve of 'If You Tolerate This', 'Great artists have no country.'

And Nicky Wire has Wales. Manic Street Preachers' fifth, and most keenly anticipated, longplayer was heralded by Wire as 'the first true Welsh folk album', and not without justification. In contrast to the global politics of the *Generation Terrorists* era, this time Nicky began in his own front room, casting his sights at the Welsh Landscape outside his window, and rarely venturing beyond the border (the furthest away he went was Sheffield). 'If You Tolerate This', although ostensibly about the Spanish Civil War, takes a Welsh farmer as its departure point. Although Wire had recently stated, 'I don't want to become The Bard of the Working Classes,' he was well on the way to becoming unofficial Poet Laureate of the Valley-Folk.

Even the album's title has a peculiarly Welsh origin. Nicky, his wife Rachel and brother Patrick were standing halfway up a rain-lashed Tredegar mountain one night, attending an event to celebrate the life of formidable Welsh Labour politician Aneurin Bevan, on the fiftieth anniversary of his founding of the NHS. 'I remember thinking there's no way any member of another band would be doing this,' he laughed later. Suddenly, an old Bevan speech started playing over the crackly tannoy. When Nicky heard Bevan's voice, one line rang in his ears, capturing his imagination: 'This is my truth. Tell me yours.' The next Manic Street Preachers record had a name. It was a declarative, antagonistic, confrontational title, the sort Dexys Midnight Runners might have chosen. 'I was a bit scared to have a title like that. It would have been much easier to call it *Manic Street Preachers*, as a lot of bands do with their fifth album. It's quite an inclusive title. It's saying: I'm open to other ideas.'

The sleeve, too, bears plenty of Welsh elements. The cover photo – a distressingly pointless shot of the three Manics standing on a windy beach in their best Gap slacks (James looked like someone who has just realised he has locked his keys in the car) – was taken near Portmeirion in north Wales, on the same flat, white sands where Patrick McGoohan, as 'Number Six', was chased by a giant white balloon in *The Prisoner*. Inside is a 32-page booklet of Polaroids, one for each song, taken by Nicky Wire and Mitch Ikeda, and scratched artistically by Wire. (He had an esteemed forerunner: the last pop star to have released a book of arty Polaroids was Duran Duran's Nick Rhodes.) The package also contains an extract from 'Reflections' by R.S. Thomas, the fearsome poet of rural Wales (a devout cleric, a supporter of holiday-home arson and, perhaps significantly, a cornerstone of the South Wales Education Board's O-Level syllabus in the mid-1980s, although Nicky says that he only discovered Thomas through his librarian brother a couple of years ago). Wire even stole a line from the poem, 'there is no truce with my furies', for one of the songs.

While *This Is My Truth Tell Me Yours* was still a twinkle in the Wire eye, he speculated that: 'Musically, I think the next record will probably will be a bit more adventurous, a fusion of the polar opposites of *The Holy Bible* and *Everything Must Go*.' Mitch Ikeda, present at some of the sessions, hinted that it would be closer to *Gold Against the Soul*. In fact, it turned out to be nothing like any of them (and it certainly didn't sound like *Generation Terrorists*). With perhaps three exceptions, it was a move away from the epic, gung-ho sound of its predecessor. 'We wanted something pure and sonically beautiful,' the Manics explained. As they told *NME*, they had consciously cut back on 'the ubiquitous strings, which were getting out of hand'. They knew that *Everything Must Go* must *go*. The stadium-rock-with-violins formula was ditched, and unusual, un-rock instruments – sitars, Wurlitzers, omnichords, tampuras, melody horns, yang ch'ins (the Chinese traditional instruments most notably used in a pop context by the Wu-Tang Clan), accordions, mellotrons – were brought in, largely played by Nick Naysmith, whose role in the band had become more prominent and more permanent. These diverse elements are deployed in unconventional contexts, preventing the end result from sounding like some kind of World Music package tour. The traditional instruments are twisted and distorted into sometimes unrecognisable new sounds, an approach the band described as 'organic futurism'.

'With the last album,' said Wire, 'there was still a sense of euphoria – that we were still together and still actually making music – and you still got that real Manics rush. Which you get on this album, but it's more subtle.' He wasn't kidding. *This Is My Truth* is many things, but euphoric was not among them. In reviews, the descriptions 'resigned', 'insecure' and 'lacking confidence' regularly cropped up. *NME* wrote: 'If *This Is My Truth* . . . had a posture it would be shoulders hunched forward, head slumped, the body language of the vanquished.' *Melody Maker* said: 'It shares the pathos of *Everything Must Go*, but lacks its unstoppable sense of purpose.' A mood of downcast dejection permeated the album. 'If You Tolerate This' may have seemed a strangely muted choice for a single, but in the context of *This Is My Truth* it was practically 'Wake Me Up Before You Go Go'.

Was this an album about inertia . . . or simply an inert album? This was the crucial question. It was sometimes difficult to decide whether *This Is My Truth* is a conscious study of defeatism – a concept album *about* insecurity; or just an album made by a band itself in the midst of a confidence crisis – the involuntary *sound* of insecurity. It was, Wire told *Top*, 'more Fleetwood Mac's *Rumours* than Queen'. The mood is actually intentional, as he told BBC Radio Wales: 'On *Everything Must Go* we were euphoric just to be in a band, and that euphoria comes through. On this record we wanted to be more serene and less uplifting.' The songs were mainly written 'after ten at night, or when it was raining or dark. I'm not very good at writing lyrics in sunlight.' He also wrote a fair amount on aeroplanes, because 'it gives me really good pit of misery'.

Although the Manics stopped short of suggesting that Richey's absence was a blessing in disguise, they often hinted that it had certain tiny silver linings. 'It's become easier to have consensus,' James told *Q*. 'That would have been hard the way Richey was going.' It also allowed Wire to find his own lyrical voice. 'Nick has reached the level of wisdom and purity of the real poets,' said James, 'and I *will* use that word, where he can discard words, where everything is absolute and ultimate, somewhere I don't think Richey could've reached.' Yet, in a sense, Wire never writes alone: he always has Richey on his shoulder. 'Sometimes when I'm writing lyrics,' he told BBC Radio Wales, 'I can hear Richey's voice in me and I know he wouldn't like certain lines because they're too conservative. He would interject something much more dramatic, brutal and dark.'

Nevertheless, this was *his* album, as much as *The Holy Bible* was Richey's. Tellingly, the lyrics were credited not to 'Nicky Wire', but to 'Nick Jones'. 'Lyrically it's just my world,' he said, 'the world I exist in and the things that make me sad and make me happy, that make me get up in the morning and make me go to bed . . . There's such an undercurrent of what I watch, where I live and what I do.' Sean Moore sardonically told MTV that 'A lot of people have written, "Nicky Wire has taken on the burden of the lyrics," but I think it's the opposite: our lyrics have taken on the burden of Nicky Wire!'

Wire's stay-at-home reclusiveness made him vulnerable to accusations of insularity and parochialism. But, as James pointed out: 'He doesn't feel he has to experience everything directly in order to write about it. It's what I call "homestead lyricism". Nick sees his lyrics through existence, not experience, and I think that's a good way to write.' As Wire himself confirmed: 'I never feel the need to do a fucking bungee jump in the south of France or to drive a fast car just to prove "I'm alive!"' In this respect he is comparable to Philip Larkin: the reclusive misanthropist, watching from high windows as the world goes by, commentating with soured vitriol. Which, in its own way, could be a fascinating experience. Erika Sage of *Iconoclastic Glitter* fanzine said, 'I find this album more disconcerting than *The Holy Bible* ever was. It's a very, very personal album, like you're prying into something you're not supposed to look into.'

The difference was evident not only in the subject matter of Nicky's lyrics, but in their style. Even more than on *Everything Must Go*, his words possessed a clarity and a simplicity which would have been unimaginable from Richey. 'My writing style is so much more straightforward and literal,' Wire told *Top*. 'Richey's lyrics were so intellectualised, I didn't understand some of them myself.' Not that 'simple' necessarily equals 'banal'. 'The language is simpler,' Wire admitted, 'but the content is probably more complex. Each song has two or three themes.' For many listeners, lines such as 'The world is full of refugees/They're just like you and just like me' cross the line between simplicity and 'We Are The World' triteness – yet the new syntactic lucidity had its benefits. James said:

'It's made me want to *sing* more instead of shouting.' And he did. 'He sings like an angel on this record,' said a delighted Wire, 'which is incredible considering how much he drinks . . .'

'Oh, isn't life a terrible thing, thank God?' – DYLAN THOMAS, *UNDER MILK WOOD*

With its mood of faded triumphalism, opening track 'The Everlasting' was a direct descendant of *Everything Must Go*. Nicky had been looking for a songtitle along the lines of Blur's 'The Universal' or Joy Division's 'The Eternal'. Eventually, and not for the first time, he stole a title from one of his brother Patrick's poems ('everlasting' also happens to be one of Wire's favourite words, and was at one point considered as a title for the album itself). James apparently wanted it to sound like a traditional hymn such as 'The Old Ragged Cross'; Nicky described it as 'the "Motorcycle Emptiness" of this record'.

Over an obsolete, ancient synthi-drum, James, his voice at its most heartbreakingly plaintive, began: 'The gap that grows between our lives, the gap our parents never had . . .' ('People were happier forty years ago,' Nicky explained, 'less alienated from each other.' Where once the Manics' alienation was cause for perverse celebration, now it brought only regret.) Slowly, almost stealthily, the whole thing expanded and inflated from pocket-diary intimacy to widescreen universalism, with the anti-anthemic chorus: 'In the beginning/When we were winning/When our smiles were genuine/Now unforgiven/The everlasting . . .' From 'You Love Us' to 'Everything Must Go', Manic Street Preachers had never been shy of writing *about* Manic Street Preachers, and 'The Everlasting', gazing back on their early years, was a curious blend of 'those were the days' and 'good riddance' ('I don't believe in it any more/Pathetic acts for a worthless cause . . .').

After 'Tolerate', the Big Hit Single, came 'You Stole the Sun from My Heart', which begins with another old-fashioned computer beat (Sean had actually sampled it from the pinball machine at the Château), before booting boisterously into what Wire called 'one of those full-on Manics, jump-up-and-down-swigging-your-beer kind of songs, the nearest we've ever got to Nirvana'. Although the 'you' in the lyric was non-specific – it was about having to do something you hate – it emerged that Nicky had the Manics' touring schedule in mind. When a band's members start producing songs complaining petulantly about being in a band, it is difficult for them not to appear ungracious (although, admittedly, one of their greatest songs, 'Yes', partly falls into this category). After all, there are other ways to earn a living. No one is holding a gun to their heads . . .

The album didn't really take off until track four, 'Ready for Drowning' (a melancholic rock anthem in the style of Guns N'Roses' 'Don't Cry', U2's 'One' or Rod Stewart's 'First Cut is the Deepest'). One of the richest, most complex songs the Manics had ever written, it was a double/triple/quadruple metaphor encompassing the mythology of Richey Edwards, the insecurity of Wales as a nation, and the self-destructiveness of the Welsh as individuals.

The initial inspiration for the song came when Nicky took a taxi in Newport, very soon after Richey's disappearance, and the driver started talking about the local rock musician he had read about in the *South Wales Argus* who may or may not have jumped into the Severn. The story bore the headline 'JUMP OF DEATH' above a picture of the bridge. 'Ooh, what about that boy who's gone missing?' began the cabbie, failing to recognise his passenger, who told him he worked for Olympus Sports in Cardiff and didn't say another word.

This encounter was described in the first verse ('Drown that poor thing/Put it out of its misery'). As well as the Richey myth, the drowning theme had two other meanings. The first, as Nicky told *The Face*, concerned those who 'drowned' their sorrows with alcohol, 'the Welsh famous people who end up drinking themselves to death: Richard Burton, Dylan Thomas, Rachel Roberts [Welsh actress who committed suicide in 1980]'. The second meaning is the literal drowning of an entire Welsh community. In the mid-1960s, a village called Treweryn was evacuated and flooded to create a reservoir to supply Liverpool and Birmingham – a not uncommon scenario, which was presciently depicted in the moving 1948 film *The Last Days Of Dolwyn* (coincidentally featuring the first major screen role of a young Richard Burton). At low tide, Treweryn's church can sometimes be seen rising eerily above the water (an image which Nick Naysmith's chapel organ seemed consciously to evoke). 'When there's a drought now and you actually see the village come up,' said Nicky, 'it's a horrible sight.' Some locals say you can even hear the ghostly tolling of church bells carrying to the shore.

The enigmatic couplet 'I'd go to Patagonia, but it's harder there' also had its roots in Welsh history. In the nineteenth century, Welsh emigrants settled in Patagonia, the barren, windswept region of southern Argentina and Chile (to this day, a Welsh-speaking enclave exists there). It was a disastrous choice of new home: near-impossible to farm, and far more inhospitable than the country they had left behind. To Wire, this story spoke volumes about the Welsh psyche.

The album's second overtly Welsh story followed. Like 'Interiors' before it, 'Tsunami' resulted from a documentary Wire had seen on BBC2. Jean and Jennifer Gibbons, known as 'The Silent Twins', were two sisters from west Wales who gave up speech at the age of eight and communicated only with each other in a private language. In later life, after committing a number of relatively minor offences including petty arson, they found themselves imprisoned in Broadmoor, rubbing shoulders with Peter Sutcliffe and Dennis Nielsen at the Christmas party (hence the very Richey-esque line 'disco dancing with the rapists'). From their cell, the sisters wrote a volume of verse, *September Poems* (which Nicky sought out). When one sister died, the other began speaking, as if released from her silence. Hence the title: *tsunami* is Japanese for a tidal wave caused by an earthquake deep under the ocean; a sudden release, an outward reaction to a cataclysmic event buried deep inside. In this respect, The Silent Twins acted as an analogy for the Manics' own Glamour Twins. After Richey's disappearance, Nicky had found himself stepping out from the shadow of collective identity and having to address the outside world. The song itself, oddly uptempo given its topic, sounded like a football chant waiting to happen ('Toon Army, Toon Army . . .'), and featured James on electric sitar, phased and disguised to sound as little like Kula Shaker as possible (which did not prevent *NME* from cruelly comparing the song to something from The Mission).

'My Little Empire', a set-piece for cello and guitar recorded 'as live' (it was, Wire admitted, based directly on Nirvana's MTV Unplugged performance), dealt with addiction in general and with Nicky's obsessive-compulsive housework mania in particular. Despite those 'I [HEART] HOOVERING' T-shirts, Wire seemed more than a little ashamed of his own insularity, and of not caring about the world beyond his four walls. In many ways the downside of 'Mr Carbohydrate', the song implied that Wire's fastidious need for order and tidiness was as much an emotional crutch/psychological prison as any more obvious drug like heroin. Although Nicky told *NME*, 'I absolutely love the contentment that comes with boredom,' it appeared to be a bittersweet pleasure: 'I'm sick of being sick . . . I'm tired of being tired.' It was a definitive statement on the subject, and also, one hoped, a full-stop (Nicky's 'I like sport and Hoovering, me' interview patter, indulged and left unquestioned by too many sycophantic journalists, was starting to become a little tiresome by now).

'I'm Not Working', a sparse, snail-paced gothic *nocturne*, featured further sitar-work from James, plus Nick Naysmith on yang ch'i, the Chinese traditional instrument most notably used in a pop context by The Wu-Tang Clan. The possibly Radiohead-inspired lyric extrapolates Nicky's fear of flying into a metaphor for emotional emptiness/general uselessness.

The beautiful and understated 'You're Tender and You're Tired', which makes excellent use of John Lennon-style reverb on voice and piano, was another transparently Richey-related track: 'You're so fragile tonight/Been up hurting all night/It's not trivial like they think' (although Wire later intriguingly suggested that it was also connected with child abuse). It ends with a frankly bizarre outbreak of whistling *à la* Bacharach (for which the band actually hired a professional whistler). The last major rock record to have featured a whistling solo, it should be noted, was 'Wind of Change' by The Scorpions.

'Born a Girl', which dealt with Wire's longing to escape the prison of masculinity, is simple, unadorned, straightforward, obvious – and all the more heartbreaking for it. 'I wish I had been born a girl and not this mess of a man,' sang James over a rudimentary acoustic strum. Some women were offended by Nicky's apparent grass-is-greener assumption that females have it easy, but this was hardly his point. He was raging against 'the censorship of my skin' – against being born arbitrarily into the wrong body, into a gender for which he wasn't cut out. Considering the Manics' blokey new fanbase, this was an incredibly brave song for Nicky Wire to have written (and even braver for someone as manly as James Dean Bradfield to sing).

There was nothing much to say about 'Be Natural' – something of a dirge in which Nicky retreats from directness into obscure poetic abstractions ('No water tastes like lemonade/Slowly slowly it starts to fade') only he could understand.

'Black Dog on My Shoulder', which described Wire's private struggle to keep depression at bay ('My mouth is so dry/My eyes are shut tight'), had nothing to do with Led Zeppelin (whose 'Black Dog' is more concerned with arousal than anxiety), nor with Ian McEwan (whose *Black Dog* Nicky had never read). Astonishingly, it was actually inspired by miners' enemy Winston Churchill, who secretly suffered from manic depression but never sought treatment, and wrote in his diaries 'the black dog's on my shoulder again'. Considered at the time a possible future single, the song was, said Nicky 'not about rock-star depression, but [about] ordinary people, wracked by emotions but getting on with their lives'. Widely compared to that of country/pop songwriting genius Jimmy Webb, the accompaniment is incongruously breezy, planting the suspicion that the whole thing might be a secret piss-take of the portent always attached to MSP lyrics (Nicky Wire *owns* a black dog).

According to Nicky, 'Nobody Loved You' was the 'first song written directly for Richey'. In fact, by my reckoning, it was possibly the *eighth*, and there were plenty more where that came from. 'I've actually got an *album* of songs about Richey that we could do,' he revealed to *Select*. 'I've probably got fifteen lyrics I could give to James, but it just seems tacky.' The Manics could never write anything as plainly sentimental as 'Shine on You Crazy Diamond', which the remaining members of Pink Floyd wrote for troubled former singer Syd Barrett, but 'Nobody Loved You' came close. From any other lyricist, lines like: 'What would I give just for one of your smiles' and 'It's unreal now you're gone/But at least you belong' might have sounded corny but, given the context, they were deeply moving. One of the song's more enigmatic lines, 'Give me some of your carrier bags', carried a personal meaning. 'Me and Richey always used to turn up at each other's houses with carrier bags from Spillers Records in Cardiff,' Nicky told *Select*. 'I just always remember him with carrier bags.' A big, mid-tempo rock elegy in the same vein as 'No Surface, All Feeling', 'Nobody Loved You' has the slow but irresistible momentum of a glacier. And maybe this was where *This Is My Truth Tell Me Yours* should have ended. Probably the most talked-about song on the album when it was released was 'South Yorkshire Mass Murderer', inspired by Jimmy McGovern's television dramatisation of the Hillsborough tragedy, which pointed the blame squarely at the police. McGovern was heartened by the Manics' unequivocal endorsement of the Hillsborough Justice Campaign. 'I wish the British media had the balls of our singers,' he told *NME*, 'I'm impressed.' South Yorkshire's Assistant Chief Constable Ian Daines (not involved with policing Hillsborough on the day of the disaster) was less impressed. 'Judging solely from the title, it would appear to be in bad taste and is likely to cause offence to many people.'

The song was originally planned to include a speech made by 'Alby', a character in a McGovern-penned episode of *Cracker*, 'To Be a Somebody'. Alby believed that Hillsborough was the culmination of a full-scale assault on working-class culture and values which began with the Miners' Strike. In the end, however, it was decided that Nicky's lyrics carried sufficient political weight on their own. Unfortunately, the most political thing about 'South Yorkshire Mass Murderer' is its title: as James remarked in *NME*, 'Nick's the first commentator to brush away the words "manslaughter" or "Act of God" and replace them with "murder"' (*Who's responsible? The police fucking are*). But even that was abbreviated to the more harmless compromise 'S.Y.M.M.', perhaps because Nicky had heeded McGovern's concern that the Manics were exposing themselves to possible libel action. In subsequent interviews, Wire also appeared to be moderating his stance. 'It's not aimed at any particular person,' he told BBC Radio Wales, 'just the police and the authorities – the nebulous establishment. I don't want to prosecute anybody through this song or put anybody in prison. All it's saying is "Won't somebody please apologise?"'

The first eight lines were devoted to talking up the song's significance: 'The subtext of this song/I've thought about it for so long/But it's not really the sort of thing/That people want to hear us sing/The context of this song/Well I could go on and on/But it's still unfashionable/To believe in principles.' Such flimsy post-modern tail-chasing ruins the song: 75 per cent of 'S.Y.M.M.' was *about* 'S.Y.M.M.' It was as if Wire were saying 'Listen, everybody, I'm about to say something really important . . .' and then he didn't. 'S.Y.M.M.' didn't actually say much at all, beyond providing a namecheck for Jimmy McGovern and the refrain 'How can you sleep at night' (reminiscent of The Smiths' 'Suffer Little Children', which taunted Lancashire mass murderers Hindley and Brady with the refrain 'You might sleep, but you will never dream'). It was almost as if Wire had suffered an attack of stagefright at the gravity of his topic, and found himself lost for words. The final verse began, 'The ending for this song/Well, I haven't really thought of one . . .', to which the listener is perfectly entitled to reply: 'Well, sorry, mate, go away and come back to me when you *have* thought of one.'

'S.Y.M.M.' was a staggering piece of music and an incredible feat of studio-craft: a billowing six-minute rock opus, all backward drums and rippling waves of FX-pedal guitar. After so much fine evidence to the contrary, however, the song allowed the listener to leave the album with the false impression that Nicky Wire is a poor songwriter. Perhaps it should have been an instrumental.

The Manics reckoned that *This Is My Truth Tell Me Yours* was the best thing they had ever done (something which every band, by law, is required to claim for their latest record). It clearly wasn't, but, with repeated listening, it eases comfortably into third place. It is a flawed album – most reviews, on its release, gave it seven out of ten – but still a good one, containing enough evidence that Nicky Wire is a deeply underrated lyricist, and that the Manics can manipulate the canon of rock sonics with a versatility and grace unmatched among their peers.

The lukewarm reviews that the album received were perhaps inevitable – most journalists had only a couple of days in which to judge a compilation so subtle that it takes weeks to creep into the consciousness – but they were also symptomatic of the predictable anti-MSP backlash which had been brewing for some time. The extended honeymoon of the *Everything Must Go* era was over. *Melody Maker* had already cruelly described the comeback single as 'Everything I Do (I Do It For AntiFascism)'. Some long-term fans also took it as their cue finally to abandon the band (this was the first album with no direct Richey contribution). Leicester student Peter Cook, quoted in *Melody Maker*, said, 'The anger's gone from the previous album, and it's like: "Nicely, nicely, let's get to No. 1."' Which it did, effortlessly. Released on 14 September on LP, CD, cassette and, for the first time, Minidisc (the latter probably to keep Sean happy), *This Is My Truth Tell Me Yours* absolutely *flew* out of the shops from day one. Spokespersons for several Virgin Megastores described it as 'Definitely the biggest album of the year.' It rocketed to the top of the charts on Sunday 20 September, again holding off Steps at No. 2 (oh, how Steps must loathe the Manics).

On 15 September, the band returned to the concert conveyor-belt with a tour of unusual locations: small venues, often municipal leisure centres (some with as little as one-thousand capacity), in off-the-beaten-track towns the Manics had never previously played, including Bridlington, Hereford and Margate. The support act, Mogwai, was also an unusual choice: exactly the sort of avant-garde art-rock obscurantists the Manics had once raged against (Wire apparently thought Mogwai's album was 'nice Hoovering music').

The first show was at Kettering Arena, a leisure centre in rural Northants. After strolling on to the Massive Attack mix of 'If You Tolerate This' (the David Holmes version followed at lights-up), the Manics turned in a depressingly laborious performance. 'James . . . clocks on for the first night back at work,' wrote *NME*. Other reviews used words like 'stodgy' and 'dreary'. A sullen, silent Wire kept his Elvis shades on for most of the night and, when he took them off, his eyes were closed. During 'Faster' he actually *sat down*. Even the sight of a crowd-surfing wheelchair failed to shame him into action.

This was a problem. If Wire were not worth watching, there was nothing else to look at. The video screens of 1996/7 had been decommissioned, and the set itself was a pragmatic blend of crowd-pleasers from all eras ('Motown Junk', 'You Love Us', 'Stay Beautiful', an even-longer-than-usual 'Motorcycle Emptiness', 'La Tristesse Durera', 'Faster', 'Yes', 'A Design for Life', 'Everything Must Go', 'Kevin Carter', 'Australia'), along with new material ('If You Tolerate This', 'Nobody Loved You', 'The Everlasting', 'Tsunami' and an acoustic entitled 'My Little Empire'). There were no encores.

The following night, in Chester, Nicky appeared to have woken up. Dolled up in a tiara and a 'HOME IS WHERE THE HOOVER IS' T-shirt, and grinning broadly, he delivered a much more energetic show. By the time the Manics had crossed the border into Wales, they were firing on all cylinders at last. The gig on the 20th was at the Afan Lido, another leisure centre, perched on Aberavon Beach, Port Talbot.

On the afternoon before the show, Nicky Wire was due to be interviewed by Amy Raphael of *Esquire* magazine at the Marriott Hotel, fifteen miles down the M4 in Swansea. It later transpired that he had taken a cab into town and, in a startling exercise in emotional catharsis, visited the flat he had shared with Richey when they were students. He hadn't seen it for ten years. On the pavement outside, he broke down and cried. Back at the Marriott, he locked himself in his hotel room and drank a bottle of red wine. This time it wasn't because he was 'happy'.

When the night came round, the bottle of wine had clearly kicked in. The Port Talbot audience were strangely subdued, but the band, at least, were speaking to their public. Before 'Tsunami', Nicky – wearing what was variously described as an ice-hockey helmet or a red Spanish Civil War helmet, perhaps mindful of Singleton Park 1993 and anticipating another unwanted bottle of wine hurled at his head by hostile West Walians – recalled the band's teenage journeys to the town's Raffles nightclub. 'We all used to go there, then sleep out under the bridge with the tramps and the drunks. I hope they're still alive . . .' Later, in the preamble to 'Nobody Loved You', he reminisced about his college years in Swansea. 'This is for King Edward Road, this is for carrier bags, this is for Richey cooking me Fray Bentos pies . . .'

Later, in the dressing-room, where *Esquire* magazine finally caught up with him, he was pouring a whole bottle of champagne over his head, spitting food everywhere, and basically being Nicky Wire *circa* 1991. When he was introduced to Welsh parliamentary under-secretary of state Peter Hain, he made a somewhat less dignified impression than he had with Mo Mowlam in Dublin, by dribbling Jacobs Creek out of both corners of his mouth. Wire paid for his excesses the following night in Stoke, where he literally crawled onstage on his hands and knees, much in the manner of Manuel from *Fawlty Towers* ('I die here!'), just about made it through the set, and crawled off again.

Wire wasn't the only one in nostalgic mood. An unexpected result of the Manics' latest spurt of activity was that their original bassist, Flicker, a.k.a. Miles Woodward, came out of the woodwork, complaining that the band had turned their backs on him since becoming famous. He and a group of co-workers had been on strike from a factory in Oakdale over union recognition. 'I haven't seen them for three or four years,' he said. 'They just don't want to know. We started the band together, but they never come to see me. I don't know why it bothers me, but it does. Maybe they feel uncomfortable about how much success has changed them and how much our lives have changed. They used to be my mates, but they're not any more.' Woodward also made the bizarre claim that he had left the band back in 89 because it was turning 'more mainstream', making him perhaps the only person in Britain to claim that the Manics became crap when Richey Edwards *joined*.

Now that the Manics were a proper, grown-up band, they were finally accorded proper, grown-up analysis by the media. A number of high-profile documentaries accompanied the release of the album. Radio One broadcast a two-part history of the band's career; BBC Radio Wales interviewed Nicky Wire at great length; and MTV devoted a whole day to the Manics, including special interviews focusing on *Generation Terrorists* and *Everything Must Go*, and with the band choosing their favourite videos (Super Furry Animals, Madonna, Nirvana, The Clash and Public Enemy among them).

Best of all was Mike Connolly's BBC2 documentary, broadcast on 23 September as part of the channel's *Close-Up* arts series. The first terrestrial documentary made with the band's approval and co-operation, it thankfully laid the ghost of the abysmal 'Vanishing of Richey Manic' to rest. Managing to provide a bluffer's guide for newcomers and meaningful insight for old-timers was quite an achievement in just fifty minutes, as was capturing the humour and pathos so many observers (and indeed fans) fail to grasp. Enjoyable moments included a grown-up Richey Edwards playing on some swings (private camcorder footage donated by Nicky), James telling a cameraman onstage at Slane Castle to 'Get out of my fucking way', and the sight of the adult Manics huddled on the legendary Bradfield/Moore bunk bed, 'back home where they used to sit and yak and play'. The show cockily declared that *This Is My Truth Tell Me Yours* was a No. 1 album (it had been filmed before the album was even released). By turns touching and hilarious, it was a delight for the viewer. Nicky Wire, though, found it a draining experience. 'How much more of yourself can you give away,' he rhetorically asked *NME*, 'before you're left with fuck all?'

Meanwhile, a Christmas tour was announced, this time taking in the giant modern hangars befitting a band of its status (and with a more familiar support act: Catatonia). An incredible three extra nights at Cardiff International Arena had to be booked after the first two sold out within days, and at Wembley Arena, where the Manics would be headlining for the first time, they were obliged to add another date 'due to public demand'. It was quite possibly the first time the band had done *anything* 'due to public demand'.

The twentieth consecutive Manic Street Preachers Top 40 single was released on 30 November. Along with the inevitable remixes and a version of 'Small Black Flowers That Grow in the Sky' from the Nynex gig were two new songs. 'Valley Boy', despite a promising title, turned out to be a forgettable blast of MSP pomp-rock, in one ear and out the other. 'Blackholes for the Young', the long-awaited duet with Sophie Ellis-Baxter of Theaudience, was a strange piece of neo-psychedelia built on a church organ playing what sounded like Bach's *Toccata*, and yet another Manics anti-London song ('sipping cappuccino among the fumes . . .'). Without being unkind, one could see why it was omitted from the album.

'The Everlasting' sounded good as a single, improved, revitalised and ennobled somehow by being allowed to stand apart from its mother album, but despite another round of TV appearances (*TFI, TOTP, Friday Night's All Wright*) it entered the charts at a disappointing No. 11, and dropped out of the Top 20 the following week (admittedly, there was a lot of competition in the run-up to Christmas). The video, which featured the band and random members of the public spontaneously bursting into flames in London's Euston Station, might have received more screenings had it not arrived in the same week as the judicial enquiry into the death of musician Michael Menson, who was found burning alive on a London street.

As 1998 drew to a close, the now-familiar season of awards ceremonies began to crank into gear. At the impossibly lavish MTV Awards in Milan, at least two experiences were surreal and absurd enough to necessitate a quick arm-pinching reality check: finding themselves bundled into a tiny pre-stage holding room with none other than Madonna, and being required to climb into a limo at a hidden pick-up point at the back of the building just so they could be driven the few yards round to the front and make a carefully scheduled entrance for the sake of the paparazzi.

Back in London, the *Q* Awards gave the Manics the somewhat peculiar title 'Best Act in the World Today' (ironic considering that *Q* had only really discovered the Manics two years earlier). James Dean Bradfield, this time, didn't feel any shame or awkwardness at winning an award: 'I had a Ready Brek glow up there,' he confessed. At the bash afterwards, James came face to face with Nicky Wire's former nemesis: Michael Stipe. Wire was now apparently contrite: 'I just feel really embarrassed. We met Peter Buck in San Francisco on the last American tour and he was very nice. And the biggest irony of all is that I still consider R.E.M one of my favourite bands. When they were on *The Tube* doing "Driver 8" and Michael Stipe had purple eyeliner on, I thought "Fucking hell, that's fantastic." So anyway, I don't expect any of them ever to talk to me again.' Fortunately for a slightly embarrassed Bradfield, Stipe had decided to forgive and forget. 'Oh, I didn't know who they were so it didn't matter,' he said. 'It just seemed very dumb-headed. I mean, c'mon, I don't hold a grudge. About something like that, no. That's just stupidity.' James and the R.E.M singer shook hands and were photographed together (with Cerys from Catatonia) for the *Q* cover. *Heartwarming.*

The December 1998 tour was sponsored by Holsten Pils. Of course, the fact that a Manic Street Preachers tour had accepted corporate sponsorship at all was a Sign of the Times in itself, but the fact that it was a lager company seemed, if one were a pessimist, gruesomely apt. James Dean Bradfield, by now, looked like what he was, a thirty-year-old valleys man – three-day stubble failing to hide a spare chin – but Sean Moore had slimmed down and got himself a sexy new haircut, and Nicky Wire's zombie facepaint was at its most arresting for some time. The threesome did as good a job as could be expected of bridging the band/audience void that came with the vast Do It

All-style sheds the Manics were now playing – the slideshow was back, including R.S. Thomas's 'No Truce with the Furies' in its entirety, and Nicky Wire had taken to skipping over a rope, like a boxer in training, as his new party piece – but something, inevitably, was lost. Songs like 'Faster' were dropped, and the only song from *The Holy Bible* was 'She Is Suffering', presumably chosen in the mistaken belief that a ponderous power ballad would translate better in an arena setting. Wham!'s 'Last Christmas' was back, somewhat predictably, although James still hadn't learnt the words.

Signs were beginning to show that the anti-Manics backlash, and press criticism of their somewhat lethargic September tour, had stung the band. On the day of the first Wembley show, *Melody Maker* ran a feature which asked a variety of supposed MSP experts the rhetorical question 'Have the Manics sold out?' (Let the record state that my own views, which broadly speaking were 'Don't be silly, of course they haven't!', were skifully manipulated, paraphrased and mis-contextualised until they appeared to say 'Yes they have,' which earned me the sharp edge of The Wire's tongue, to put it mildly.) Between songs, James Dean Bradfield raged against '*Melody Maker* journalists who say "Ooh, the Manics just drink cups of tea on stage nowadays", while Wire launched a bizarre attack on the rash of bands who had recently been dropped by their labels (an epidemic which included the Manics' former tourmates Gorky's Zygotic Mynci and collaborator Kylie Minogue, although Wire seemed to have forgotten this), advising them to 'write some fucking tunes, you bastards'.

In Cardiff, the usual heroes' welcome (chants of 'Wales! Wales!' filling every silence) lifted the atmosphere somewhat, but was marred on the second night by violent running battles outside the International Arena between rival gangs of Welsh and English Manics fans. Maybe all that patriotic flag-waving was finally coming home to roost. On the last night – 22 December – James Dean Bradfield reminded us that the Manics will never completely escape from their history. 'Happy Birthday,' he said, 'to Richey James Edwards.'

'Do not go gentle into that good night/Old age should burn and rave at close of day/Rage, rage against the dying of the light' – DYLAN THOMAS

Sixteen million albums and Wembley Stadium? Maybe not, but three million albums and rising, and two nights at the Arena weren't bad. Nor were twenty consecutive Top Forty singles, a record unequalled in the 1990s.

By the time you are reading this, two of the three remaining Manics will have turned thirty (Richey Edwards would be 31). Two Manic Street Preachers' remarks on the subject of age: 'Thirty is a very desperate age . . . Rock music is being done by people in their thirties for teenagers' (Sean Moore); 'I hope we'll have the dignity to get out before we turn into wretches' (Nicky Wire).

Question One: Is it time, then, for these desperate wretches to call it a day?

Answer: At the end of the Belfast gig, a fan threw a home-made slogan T-shirt at Nicky's feet. He paused for a moment to read it, then held it up to the crowd. It read 'MSP WILL ALWAYS MATTER'.

Question Two: Sure, but will MSP always matter to Sean Moore, James Dean Bradfield and Nicky Wire?

Answers: 'No, not yet' and 'Yes, maybe . . . if they still want it to.' In the spring of 1998, James was asked by Stuart Maconie of *Q* whether the band was indestructible. 'Me and Nick have a sixth sense about things,' he replied. 'We'd know when it was over. Also, Nick has just shown me some new lyrics and, as ever, I'm shocked by how good they are. The end of the band simply does not compute.'

So – the future?

There will be at least one more album, which, says Nicky Wire, 'might be a *Nebraska*-esque, tender soft record, but I can't tell'. And one day there will be a Manic Street Preachers Greatest Hits album. It will be called *Forever Delayed* ('Forever' is another of Nicky's favourite words). It may contain anything up to 25 tracks. He may even write his own history of the Manics. Meanwhile, negotiations are already under way to release Richey's unpublished lyrics in book form.

And beyond that?

'We used to have these Stalin-esque five-year plans,' he says, 'but, since Richey disappeared, we have one-day plans. There's too much disaster lurking around the corner to look any further . . .'

And when it's all over? '. . . Nothing. I'm genuinely happy being sad and bored. I have no desire to do anything else. If I can survive, I'll be content walking the dog, living with my wife, seeing the family, watching the telly. It might change, but that's how I feel.'

One evening in the late 1990s, I was travelling through south London by train. Two office girls, in their mid-twenties, boarded the carriage and sat opposite me.

Girl A (apropos of nothing): 'D'you like those Manic Street Preachers?'

Girl B (glancing up from *TV Quick*): 'Who?'

Girl A: 'You know, they won two of those Brit Awards and one of them disappeared.'

Girl B: 'D'you reckon he's dead?'

Girl A (distractedly): 'Yeah, probably . . . Can I have a look at the TV pages?'

Manic Street Preachers: the group who 'won two of those Brit Awards and one of them disappeared'. There is, clearly, still some distance to be travelled before 'the intellectual working-class band who made a noisy racket' (James Brown, 1998) have indelibly scorched their world view into the popular consciousness. There is work to be done.

This is not the end.

'What's the point in always looking back . . . when all you see is more and more junk?'

DISCOGRAPHY

The commercially available works of Manic Street Preachers read as a testament to the obscenely exploitative nature of 1990s multi-format marketing (although the same could, of course, be said for just about any other major-label band). The techniques involved – making certain tracks available only on the cassette version, or remixes only available on the second CD – will always be controversial: is a band rewarding loyal fans by making juicy rarities available to them, or is it milking that very loyalty by forcing fans to buy the same single three or four times over? Either way, any attempt at completism is for mugs only – and/or for the very rich.

What follows is, to the best of my knowledge, the most thorough MSP discography in existence.

SINGLES

Suicide Alley/Tennessee (I Get Low) (SBS 002), 7-inch. 300 copies made, the first 200 with blue picture sleeve with photos of Nicky, Sean and James taken by Richey, the remainder with plain-white die-cut sleeve. A few came in hand-made sleeves, with press cuttings stuck on a plain cover.
August 1989. Chart position: n/a.

New Art Riot EP: New Art Riot/Strip It Down/Last Exit on Yesterday/Teenage 20/20 (Damaged Goods YUBB 4), 12-inch. Particularly collectable due to ever-changing sleeve and label colours. The first 1,000 came with black-and-white labels; the second 1,000 with yellow labels; later, red, orange and silver, and green were used. The first 500 came in a variety of sleeve colours: yellow, then blue, then pink (thereafter, back to blue).
22 June 1990. Chart position: No. 136.

Motown Junk/Sorrow 16/We Her Majesty's Prisoners (Heavenly HVN8 12), 12-inch.
Motown Junk/Sorrow 16/We Her Majesty's Prisoners (Heavenly HVN8 CD), CD.
21 January 1991. Chart position: No. 92.
You Love Us/Spectators of Suicide (Heavenly HVN10), 7-inch.

You Love Us (Radio Edit), one-sided 7-inch. Limited edition of 500.
You Love Us EP: You Love Us/Spectators of Suicide/Starlover/Strip It Down (Live) (Heavenly HVN10 12), 12-inch.
You Love Us/Spectators of Suicide/Starlover/Strip It Down (Live) (Heavenly HVN10 CD), CD.
7 May 1991. Chart position: No. 64.

Feminine Is Beautiful: New Art Riot/Repeat After Me (Caff CAFF 15), 7-inch. 500 copies made.
July 1991. Chart position: n/a.

Stay Beautiful/R.P. McMurphy (Columbia 657337 7), 7-inch.
Stay Beautiful/R.P. McMurphy/Soul Contamination (Columbia 657337 6), 12-inch.
Stay Beautiful/R.P. McMurphy/Soul Contamination (Columbia 657337 8), 12-inch. With stickered poster sleeve.
Stay Beautiful/R.P. McMurphy/Soul Contamination (Columbia 657337 2), CD.
29 July 1991. Chart position: No. 40.

Love's Sweet Exile/Repeat (Columbia 657582 7), 7-inch.
Repeat (UK)/Love's Sweet Exile/Democracy Coma (Columbia 657582 6), 12-inch.

Repeat/Democracy Coma/Love's Sweet Exile/Stay Beautiful (Live) (Columbia 657582 8), 12-inch.
   Limited-edition gatefold stickered sleeve.
Love's Sweet Exile/Repeat (UK)/Democracy Coma (Columbia 657582 2), CD.
28 October 1991. Chart position: No. 26.

You Love Us/A Vision of Dead Desire (Columbia 657724 7), 7-inch.
You Love Us/A Vision of Dead Desire/It's So Easy (Live) (Columbia 657724 6), 12-inch.
   Limited-edition gatefold sleeve.
You Love Us/A Vision of Dead Desire/We Her Majesty's Prisoners/It's So Easy (Live) (Columbia 657724
   2), CD.
16 January 1992. Chart position: No. 16.

Slash 'N' Burn/Motown Junk (Columbia 657873 7), 7-inch.
Slash 'N' Burn/Motown Junk/Ain't Going Down (Columbia 657873 6), 12-inch. Stickered sleeve, with
   free print.
Slash 'N' Burn/Motown Junk/Sorrow 16/Ain't Going Down (Columbia 657873 0), Digipak CD, gold disc.
Slash 'N' Burn/Motown Junk (Columbia 657873 4), Cassette.
16 March 1992. Chart position: No. 20.

Motorcycle Emptiness/Bored Out of My Mind (Columbia 658083 7), 7-inch.
Motorcycle Emptiness/Bored Out of My Mind (Columbia 658083 4), Cassette.
Motorcycle Emptiness/Bored Out of My Mind/Under My Wheels (Columbia 658083 8), 12-inch. Picture
   disc, stickered PVC sleeve.
Motorcycle Emptiness/Bored Out of My Mind/Crucifix Kiss (Live)/Under My Wheels (Live) (Columbia
   658083 2), Digipak CD.
1 June 1992. Chart position: No. 17.

Theme from M*A*S*H EP (Suicide Is Painless)/Fatima Mansions: Everything I Do (I Do It For You)
   (Columbia 658382 7), 7-inch.
Theme from M*A*S*H EP (Suicide Is Painless)/Fatima Mansions: Everything I Do (I Do It For
   You)/Sleeping with the NME (Columbia 658382 6), 12-inch.
Theme from M*A*S*H EP (Suicide Is Painless)/Fatima Mansions: Everything I Do (I Do It For
   You)/Sleeping with the NME (Columbia 658382 2), CD.
Theme from M*A*S*H EP (Suicide Is Painless)/Fatima Mansions: 'Everything I Do (I Do It For You)'
   (Columbia 658382 4), Cassette.
7 September 1992. Chart position: No. 7.

Little Baby Nothing (7-inch version)/Never Want Again/Suicide Alley (Columbia 658796 7), 7-inch.
Little Baby Nothing (7-inch version)/Never Want Again/Dead Yankee Drawl/Suicide Alley (Columbia
   658796 2), CD1.
Little Baby Nothing (7-inch version)/R.P. McMurphy (Live)/Tennessee (Live)/You Love Us (Live)
   (Columbia 658796 5), CD2 (released one week later).
Little Baby Nothing (7-inch version)/Never Want Again/Suicide Alley (Columbia 658796). Cassette.
15 November 1992. Chart position: No. 29.

From Despair to Where/Hibernation/Spectators of Suicide (Heavenly Version) (Columbia 659337 6),
   12-inch.
From Despair to Where/Hibernation/Spectators of Suicide (Heavenly Version)/Starlover (Heavenly
   Version) (Columbia 659337 2), CD.
From Despair to Where/Hibernation (Columbia 659337 4), Cassette.
7 June 1993. Chart position: No. 25.

La Tristesse Durera (Scream to a Sigh)/Patrick Bateman/Repeat (Live in Norwich)/Tennessee (Columbia 659477 6), 12-inch. Poster pack.

La Tristesse Durera (Scream to a Sigh)/Patrick Bateman/What's My Name (Live)/Slash 'N' Burn (Live) (Columbia 659477 2), CD.

La Tristesse Durera (Scream to a Sigh)/Patrick Bateman (Columbia 659477 4), Cassette.

26 July 1993. Chart position: No. 22.

Roses in the Hospital/Us Against You/Donkeys (Columbia 659727 7), 7-inch, pink vinyl.

Roses in the Hospital (OG Psychovocal Mix)/(OG Psychomental Mix)/(51 Funk Salute Mix)/Fillet-O-Gang Mix)/(ECG Mix)/(Album Version) (Columbia 659727 6), 12-inch.

Roses in the Hospital/Us Against You/Donkeys/Wrote For Luck (Columbia 659727 2), CD.

Roses in the Hospital/Us Against You/Donkeys (Columbia 659727 8), Cassette.

20 September 1993. Chart position: No. 15.

Life Becoming a Landslide/Comfort Comes/Are Mothers Saints (Columbia 660070 6), 12-inch.

Life Becoming a Landslide/Comfort Comes/Are Mothers Saints/Charles Windsor (Columbia 660070 2), CD.

Life Becoming a Landslide/Comfort Comes (Columbia 660070 4), Cassette.

7 February 1994. Chart position: No. 36.

P.C.P./Faster/Sculpture of Man (Columbia 660447 0), 10-inch.

Faster/P.C.P./Sculpture of Man/New Art Riot (in E Minor) (Columbia 660447 2), CD.

Faster/P.C.P. (Columbia 660447 4), Cassette.

6 June 1994. Chart position: No. 16.

Revol/Too Cold Here/You Love Us (Heavenly version)/Life Becoming a Landslide (Live in Bangkok) (Columbia 660686 0), 10-inch.

Revol/Too Cold Here/Love's Sweet Exile (Columbia 660686 2), CD1.

Revol/Drug Drug Druggy (Live at Glastonbury)/Roses in the Hospital (Live at Glastonbury)/You Love Us (Live at Glastonbury) (Columbia 660686 5), CD2 (released one week later).

Revol/Too Cold Here (Columbia 660686 4), Cassette.

1 August 1994. Chart position: No. 22.

She Is Suffering/The Drowners (Live)/Stay With Me (Live) (Columbia 660895 0), 10-inch.

She Is Suffering (7-inch Radio Edit)/She Is Suffering (Acoustic Version) (Columbia 660972 1), CD.

She Is Suffering/Love Torn Us Under/The Drowners (Live)/Stay With Me (Live) (Columbia 660895 2), CD1.

She Is Suffering (Radio Edit)/La Tristesse Durera (Scream to a Sigh) (Vocal Mix)/La Tristesse Durera (Scream to a Sigh) (Dub Mix)/Faster (Dub Mix) (Columbia 660895 5), CD2 (released one week later).

She Is Suffering (Radio Edit)/Love Torn Us Under (Columbia 660895 4), Cassette.

3 October 1994. Chart position: No. 25.

A Design for Life/Mr Carbohydrate/Dead Passive/Dead Trees & Traffic Islands (Columbia 663070 2), CD1.

A Design for Life (Stealth Sonic Orchestra Version)/(Stealth Sonic Orchestra Instrumental Version)/Faster (Vocal Mix) (Columbia 663070 5), CD2 (released one week later).

A Design for Life/Bright Eyes (Live) (Columbia 663070 4), Cassette.

15 April 1996. Chart position: No. 2.

Everything Must Go/Black Garden/Hanging On/No One Knows What It's Like To Be Me (Sony 663468 2), CD1.

Everything Must Go (Chemical Bros Remix)/(Stealth Sonic Orchestra Remix)/Stealth Sonic Orchestra Soundtrack) (Sony 663468 5), CD2 (released one week later).

Everything Must Go/Raindrops Keep Falling on My Head (Live Acoustic) (Sony 663468 4), Cassette. 29 July 1996. Chart position: No. 5.

Kevin Carter/Horses Under Starlight/Sepia/First Republic (Epic 663775 2), CD1.

Kevin Carter (Bust Loose)/(Stealth Sonic Orchestra Remix)/(Stealth Sonic Orchestra Soundtrack) (Epic 663775 5), CD2 (released one week later).

Kevin Carter/Everything Must Go (Acoustic) (Epic 663775 4), Cassette. 30 September 1996. Chart position: No. 7.

Australia (Radio Edit)/Velocity Girl/Take the Skinheads Bowling/Can't Take My Eyes Off You (Epic 664044 2), CD1.

Australia (Radio Edit)/(Lionrock Remix)/Motorcycle Emptiness (Stealth Sonic Orchestra Remix)/(Stealth Sonic Orchestra Soundtrack) (Epic 664044 5), CD2.

Australia/A Design for Life (Live City Hall Sheffield) (Epic 664044 4), Cassette. 2 December 1996. Chart position: No. 7.

If You Tolerate This Your Children Will Be Next/Prologue to History/Montana Autumn 78 (Epic 666345 2), CD1.

If You Tolerate This Your Children Will Be Next/If You Tolerate This Your Children Will Be Next (Massive Attack Remix)/If You Tolerate This Your Children Will Be Next (David Holmes Remix) (Epic 666345 5), CD2 (released one week later).

24 August 1998. Chart position: No. 1.

The Everlasting/Black Holes for the Young (with Sophie Ellis-Bextor)/Valley Boy (Epic 666686 2), CD1.

The Everlasting/The Everlasting (Deadly Avenger Mix)/The Everlasting (Stealth Sonic Orchestra Remix) (Epic 666686 5), CD2.

The Everlasting/Small Black Flowers That Grow in the Sky (live from Nynex, 1997) (Epic), Cassette. 30 November 1998. Chart position: No 11.

ALBUMS

Generation Terrorists (Columbia 471060 1), Double LP. Inner sleeve, stickered sleeve. Initial quantities gatefold. Some sold at HMV with free video.

Generation Terrorists (Columbia 471060 2), CD.

Generation Terrorists (Columbia 471060 1), Cassette.

Generation Terrorists (Columbia 471060 9), 2 picture-disc LPs. Clear plastic gatefold, 5,000 copies (released June 1992).

Generation Terrorists (Columbia 471060 0), Picture CD. 5,000 copies (released June 1992).

Tracks: Slash 'N' Burn, NatWest-Barclays-Midlands-Lloyds, Born to End, Motorcycle Emptiness, You Love Us, Love's Sweet Exile, Little Baby Nothing, Repeat (Stars and Stripes), Tennessee, Another Invented Disease, Stay Beautiful, So Dead, Repeat (UK), Spectators of Suicide, Damn Dog, Crucifix Kiss, Methadone Pretty, Condemned to Rock 'N' Roll.

10 February 1992. Chart position: No. 13.

Gold Against the Soul (Columbia 4740649), LP. Inner sleeve, some early copies in special yellow carrier bag.

Gold Against the Soul (Columbia 4740649 1), Picture disc. Clear plastic sleeve.

Gold Against the Soul (Columbia 4740649 2), CD.

Gold Against the Soul (Columbia 4740649), Cassette.

Tracks: Sleepflower, From Despair to Where, La Tristesse Durera (Scream to a Sigh), Yourself, Life Becoming a Landslide, Drug Drug Druggy, Roses in the Hospital, Nostalgic Pushead, Symphony of Tourette, Gold Against the Soul.
20 June 1993. Chart position: No. 8.

The Holy Bible (Epic 477421 1), LP. Inner sleeve.
The Holy Bible (Epic 477421 9), Picture disc. Clear plastic sleeve with insert.
The Holy Bible (Epic 477421 2), CD.
The Holy Bible (Epic 477421 1), Cassette.
Tracks: Yes, Ifwhiteamericatoldthetruthforonedayit'sworldwouldfallapart, Of Walking Abortion, She Is Suffering, Archives of Pain, Revol, 4st 7lbs, Mausoleum, Faster, This Is Yesterday, Die in the Summertime, The Intense Humming of Evil, P.C.P.
30 August 1994. Chart position: No. 6.

Everything Must Go (Sony 483930 1), LP.
Everything Must Go (Sony 483930 2), CD.
Everything Must Go (Sony 483930 1), Cassette.
Tracks: Elvis Impersonator: Blackpool Pier, A Design for Life, Kevin Carter, Enola/Alone, Everything Must Go, Small Black Flowers That Grow in the Sky, The Girl Who Wanted To Be God, Removables, Australia, Interiors (Song for Willem De Kooning), Further Away, No Surface, All Feeling.
20 May 1996. Chart position: No. 2.

This Is My Truth Tell Me Yours (Sony), LP.
This Is My Truth Tell Me Yours (Sony 491703 2), CD. Initial quantities with silver embossed title on box.
This Is My Truth Tell Me Yours (Sony), Cassette.
This Is My Trut, Tell Me Yours (Sony), Minidisc.
Tracks: The Everlasting, If You Tolerate This Your Children Will Be Next, You Stole the Sun from My Heart, Ready for Drowning, Tsunami, My Little Empire, I'm Not Working, You're Tender and You're Tired, Born a Girl, Be Natural, Black Dog on My Shoulder, Nobody Loved You, S.Y.M.M.
14 September 1998. Chart position: No. 1.

SINGLES REISSUES

New Art Riot EP: New Art Riot/Strip It Down/Last Exit on Yesterday/Teenage 20/20 (Damaged Goods YUBB 004P), 12-inch. Pink vinyl, 3,000 copies.
November 1991.
New Art Riot EP: New Art Riot/Strip It Down/Last Exit on Yesterday/Teenage 20/20 (Damaged Goods YUBB 4CD), Picture CD. 3,000 copies.
January 1992.

On 1 September 1997 the first six Columbia singles were reissued by Epic on CD in a limited edition of 12,000 each, mostly with the same track listing as the original release, and with identical or near-identical sleeve art:

Stay Beautiful/R.P. McMurphy/Soul Contamination (Epic MANIC1CD) Love's Sweet Exile/Repeat/Democracy Coma (Epic MANIC2CD).
You Love Us/A Vision of Dead Desire/We Her Majesty's Prisoners/It's So Easy (Live) (Epic MANIC3CD).
Slash 'N' Burn/Sorrow 16/Ain't Goin' Down (Epic MANIC4CD). The original also included Motown Junk.
Motorcycle Emptiness/Bored Out of My Mind/Under My Wheels/Crucifix Kiss (Live) (Epic MANIC5CD).
Little Baby Nothing/Dead Yankee Drawl/Suicide Alley/Never Want Again (Epic MANIC6CD).

They re-entered the charts on 13 September 1997 at positions between 41 and 55.

BOX SET

Six singles from *Generation Terrorists* (Epic) album; box set of 6 CDs. All six reissued Epic/Columbia singles (see above) were also made available as limited-edition box sets.
13 September 1997.

NOTABLE RADIO/PRESS PROMOS, ASSORTED RARITIES, ETC.

UK Channel Boredom/The Laurens: I Don't Know What the Trouble Is (Hopelessly Devoted 1), Flexidisc with picture sleeve. 1,000 copies given free with *Hopelessly Devoted* fanzine (cover price 50p). Later repressed or bootlegged. 1990.

New Art Riot (Damaged Goods YUBB 4), 12-inch single. White label, plain sleeves, stamped 'Made In Wales'. 100 copies. 1990.

You Love Us (Heavenly HVN10 P), 7-inch single. White label, picture sleeve, one-sided radio edit. 500 copies. 1991.

Stay Beautiful (Epic ESCA 5468), CD. Japanese promotional sampler, features Motown Junk, You Love Us (Heavenly version), Stay Beautiful, Sorrow 16, Starlover, R.P. McMurphy. 1991.

Stay Beautiful (Columbia 44K 74036), CD. American single, different sleeve (photo of band). Also features Motown Junk, Sorrow 16, R.P. McMurphy, Starlover. 1991.

5-Track CD Sampler (Columbia XPCD 171), CD. British promotional sampler for *Generation Terrorists* album, featuring Slash 'N' Burn, Motorcycle Emptiness, Another Invented Disease, Little Baby Nothing, Crucifix Kiss. 1992.

Stars and Stripes (Columbia), CD. American promotional sampler, features Slash 'N' Burn, Natwest-Barclays-Midlands-Lloyds, You Love Us (Columbia version), Democracy Coma, Crucifix Kiss, Little Baby Nothing, Repeat (UK). 1992

Stars and Stripes – Generation Terrorists US Mix (Columbia ESCA 5430), US version of album, also released in Japan. Born to End, Spectators of Suicide, So Dead, Damn Dog and Motorcycle Emptiness are omitted, as is inter-song dialogue; Democracy Coma is added. Slightly different sleeve, without literary quotes. 1992.

Slash 'N' Burn (Sony XPR 1752), 12-inch single. One-sided, picture sleeve. 1992.

Motorcycle Emptiness (Sony XPD 185), CD. 2-track radio edit. 1992.

Theme from M*A*S*H (Suicide Is Painless) (Sony APCD 7), CD. 3-track promo. 1992.

From Despair to Where (Sony XPCD 280), CD. One-track promo. 1993.

4 Tracks From *Gold Against the Soul* (Columbia XPCD 285), CD. British promotional sampler for *Gold Against the Soul* album, featuring From Despair to Where, La Tristesse Durera (Scream to a Sigh), Sleepflower and Life Becoming a Landslide.

La Tristesse Durera (Scream to a Sigh) (Sony 659477 7), 7-inch single. One-sided white-label test pressing. 1993.

La Tristesse Durera (Scream to a Sigh) (Sony XPCD 295), CD. One-track CD. 1993.

Roses in the Hospital (Sony XPCD 323), CD. 2-track CD: 7-inch version and OG Psychovocal Mix. 1993.

Done and Dusted (Columbia), 12-inch single. White label; includes Dust Brothers remixes of MSP tracks. 1993.

Symphony of Tourette (Columbia/Damont XPS 272-A), one-sided 7-inch. DJ-only promo, white label, unmarked sleeve. 1993.

Revol (Sony XPCD 469), CD. One-track promo. 1994.

Verses from The Holy Bible (MAN1C), Flexidisc. Given free with *NME*; features excerpts from She is Suffering, Yes, Archives of Pain and Ifwhiteamericatoldthetruthforonedayit'sworldwouldfallapart. 27 August 1994.

She Is Suffering (Sony XPCD 496), CD. One-track promo. 1994.

A Design for Life (Sony XPCD 2070), CD. One-track promo, plain grey embossed sleeve. 1996.

A Design for Life (Stealth Sonic Orchestra Version)/(Stealth Sonic Orchestra Instrumental

Version)/Faster (Vocal Mix) (ESCA 6445), CD. Japanese version of UK single, with picture sleeve. 1996.

Everything Must Go (Sony XPCD 2058), CD. One-track radio promo. 1996.

Kevin Carter (Sony XPCD 2081), CD. One-track promo. 1996.

Kevin Carter (Stealth Sonic Orchestra Remix) (Sony XPR 3049), 12-inch single. One-sided, white label, 30 copies in stickered card sleeve. 1996.

Further Away/Horses Under Starlight/Sepia/First Republic (ESCA 6578), CD. Japan-only single release, in place of Kevin Carter, with picture sleeve. 1996.

Australia (Lionrock Remix) (Sony XPR 3094), 12-inch single. One-sided, white label, 150 copies in stickered card sleeve. 1996.

Australia (Lionrock Remix)/Motorcycle Emptiness (Stealth Sonic Orchestra Remix)/Motorcycle Emptiness (Stealth Sonic Orchestra Soundtrack) (Sony XPR 3094), 12-inch single. Stickered card sleeve. 1996.

If You Tolerate This Your Children Will Be Next (Epic XPCD 2280), CD. One-track promo. 1998.

VIDEO

Everything Live (SMV 2007592), longform video. Edited version of Manchester Nynex show, 24 May 1997, plus documentary/interview footage. First 12,000 came with five Mitch Ikeda postcards. 29 September 1997.

VARIOUS ARTIST COMPILATIONS

Underground Rockers 2 (Street Link LCSCD 007), v/a LP. Includes Suicide Alley and Tennessee (I Get Low). 1989.

Indie Top Twenty Vol. 12 (Beechwood TT012CD), v/a CD. Includes You Love Us (Heavenly version). 1991.

Select Magazine Rather Generously Presents, v/a Cassette. Given free with *Select*. Includes Spectators of Suicide (Heavenly version). 1991.

Ruby Trax (Forty NME 40 CD), v/a Double CD. Includes Theme from M*A*S*H. 1993.

Phoenix 93 (*Melody Maker* MMMC 2), v/a cassette. Given free with *Melody Maker*. Includes From Despair to Where live at Phoenix Festival. October 1993.

Class of 94 (Vox GIVIT 9), v/a Cassette. Given free with *Vox* magazine. Includes Archives of Pain. 1994.

NME Xmas Dust-Up (*NME* XMAS 1994), v/a Cassette. Given free with *NME*. Includes Dust Brothers mix of La Tristesse Durera (Scream to a Sigh). 1994.

Evening Sessions Priority (*Circa* VTDCD 88CD), v/a CD. Includes Radio 1 Evening Session recording of Nirvana's Penny Royal Tea'. 1994.

Evening Sessions (*Melody Maker* MMMC 3), v/a Cassette. Given free with *Melody Maker*. Includes Radio 1 Evening Session version of From Despair to Where. 1994.

Volume 11 (VCD 11), v/a CD/magazine. Includes P.C.P. (Live at Glastonbury.) 1994.

Sharks Patrol These Waters (Volume BOVCD 2) v/a Double CD/magazine. Includes P.C.P. (Live at Glastonbury.) 1995.

Help (Go! Discs 828682 2), v/a CD (also on LP). Includes Raindrops Keep Falling on My Head. 4 September 1995.

Later Volume 1: Britbeat (Island 5242982), v/a CD. Includes live TV version of Small Black Flowers That Grow in the Sky. 1996.

Radio One Sound City (Harmless CTY CD 96), v/a CD. Includes live version of You Love Us from Leeds Town & Country Club. September 1996.

Phoenix: The Album (New Millennium PHNX CD 1), v/a CD. Includes live version of From Despair to Where from Phoenix Festival. 1997.

Your Generation (Sony SONYTV 25MC), v/a Double Cassette. Includes A Design for Life. 1997.

Twin Town: Original Soundtrack (A&M TOWNCD1), v/a CD. Includes Motown Junk.
11 April 1997.
Dial M For Merthyr (Fierce Panda NONGCD02/TIDY 003) CD/LP. Compilation of various Welsh bands; includes Strip It Down.
14 April 1997.
Total Guitar *Vol. 31* (TG 31 06 97), CD. Guitar instruction CD given free with *Total Guitar* magazine; includes excerpts and instrumental backing tracks from Motorcycle Emptiness, La Tristesse Durera (Scream to a Sigh), Australia and Kevin Carter.
June 1997.
The Hillsborough Justice Concert (V2 Records), v/a CD. Includes You Love Us and Raindrops Keep Falling on My Head live from Anfield.
3 June 1997.
The Lakes (BBC/Telstar/TTVCD2923), v/a CD. Soundtrack album from Jimmy McGovern's BBC2 drama series. Includes Kevin Carter. 1997.
House Of America: Original Soundtrack (EMI), v/a CD. Includes Motorcycle Emptiness. 1998.
Q 1998: Best (no label), v/a CD. Given free with January 1998 issue of *Q* magazine. Includes My Little Empire. December 1998.
The Manics have also appeared on any number of indie compilations (*Shine, Anthems, The Best . . . In The World Ever!* etc.) and also, perhaps bizarrely, on numerous AOR compilations with names like Drive, Drive Time and Drivin', available at all good petrol stations (their contribution is usually Motorcycle Emptiness or A Design for Life). Theme from M*A*S*H, long deleted as a single, can be found on something called *Greatest Hits 92*. Other unconfirmed sightings include Motown Junk on a benefit compilation for dolphins and on a Greenpeace album.

SELECTED BOOTLEGS
Lipstick Traces (KMA Records).
LP. Demos from winter 1990, 2 tracks from the Horse & Groom gig, and 1 acoustic recording from Radio 1. 1993, now deleted.
If You Want Blood . . . We've Got It!!!
Cassette. Full set from London Astoria, 1992.
Early Demos (Fierce Records).
CD. Demo tapes sent by band to label, which the label later unscrupulously bootlegged. 1992.
4 REAL (Cut Music Records, CD001)
CD. Full set from Bon Jovi show at Milton Keynes, 1993, 3 songs from Radio 1 Evening Session, 4 songs from *Top of the Pops*.
Interview 91 (Wax Records, MSP1CD)
Picture CD, semi-official (some 12-inch vinyl picture discs exist). Full interview from *Spiral Scratch* magazine with Alan Parker and Nina Antonia
Leeds 96/London 95
CD. Full set from Radio 1 Sound City gig at Leeds Town & Country Club 1996, full set from Stone Roses support gig at Wembley Arena 1995.
No Sunset, Just Silence (KTS Records, KTS 572)
CD. Edited set from Leeds Town & Country Club 1996, 4 tracks from Glastonbury 1994, 2 from Milton Keynes Bowl 1993.
The Return Of . . . Manic Street Preachers (Man records, MAN 1C)
CD. Full set from Amsterdam Melkweg 1996, 1 track from Glastonbury 1994.
Street Preaching (KTS Records KTS109)
CD. Full set from London Marquee, 1992, 2 songs from *Top of the Pops*, full set from Club Tikka (Japan 1992).

Tortured Genius (KMA Records KMACD006)

CD. The Horse & Groom full gig, 3 sets of demos, 3 tracks from Reading Festival 1994, 1 song from Clapham Grand charity show 1993, 1 song from Kilburn National 1992 (plus infamous Nicky Wire 'Stipe' remark), 1 song from Reading After Dark 1991 (plus legendary 'riot'), Feminine is Beautiful EP, UK Channel Boredom flexi.

Turning Rebellion Into Money (Dalmation Records, SPOT ONE)

CD. First 3 singles plus B-sides, 5 Sony B-sides, 6 demos from winter 1990, plus 1 acoustic recording from Radio 1. 1996.

Untitled (PFI 190769)

CD. Full sets from Phoenix Festival 1996 and Leeds Town & Country Club 1996.

Manic Street Preachers

Video. Full set from Fulham Hibernian Club, August 1991, Strip It Down promo, TV appearances from *Snub TV, Yamaha Band Explosion, Rapido, Vivid, Top of the Pops* and *Raw Power*, 25 minutes from London Astoria show May 1992 (MTV footage), 50-minute set from Frankfurt 1992 (German TV).

Manic Street Preachers

Video. Full set from Glastonbury 1994 (camcorder footage), full set from Clapham Grand 1994 (camcorder).

Live at the Astoria

Video. Two full sets from the London Astoria, 19/20 December 1995. Total running time 150 mins. 1996.

Newport Centre

Video. Full set from Newport Centre, 31 May 1996 (camcorder).

COLLABORATIONS AND GUEST APPEARANCES

Lightning Seeds: Waiting for Today to Happen, from album *Dizzy Heights* (Epic 486640 2). Written by Ian Broudie and 'Nicky Jones'. 1996.

Northern Uproar: Rollercoaster (Heavenly), single. Produced by James Dean Bradfield and Dave Eringa. 1996.

808 State and guest James Dean Bradfield: Lopez (Metaphorically) (ZTT ZANG87CD), CD single. Lyrics by Nicky Wire, vocals by Bradfield, music by 808 State, remixed by Brian Eno (original version also featured Don Solaris on the album). 27 January 1997.

Kylie Minogue: Some Kind of Bliss (deconstruction BM620), CD single. Lyrics by Kylie Minogue, music by James Dean Bradfield and Sean Moore, produced by Bradfield and Dave Eringa. 8 September 1997

Kylie Minogue: I Don't Need Anyone, from album *Impossible Princess* (deconstruction BM650). Lyrics by 'Nick Jones' and Kylie Minogue, music by James Dean Bradfield (drums by Sean Moore, keyboards by Nick Naysmith, string arrangements by Naysmith and Dave Eringa). Produced by Bradfield and Eringa. LP also includes Some Kind of Bliss. Originally scheduled for 22 September 1997, but postponed and retitled *Kylie Minogue* following the death of Princess Diana.

Massive Attack: Inertia Creeps (Circa/Virgin), CD single. Backing vocals, bass and production by James Dean Bradfield. 21 September 1998.

Patrick Jones: *Commemoration & Amnesia* (Big Noise), CD. Limited edition of 2,000. Poetry album with musical accompaniment, guitar on 2 tracks by James Dean Bradfield. Sleeve features 2 Nicky Wire Polaroids. November 1998.

Red Lipstique: Drac's Back/Drac's Back (dub) (Magnet MAG 221), 7-inch single. Early 80s synthpop novelty featuring Nick Naysmith. 1982.

WEBSITES AND OTHER INFORMATION

While there may be some veracity in the notion that every MSP fan is a fanzine editor, increasingly those with affluent parents are dropping their staplers and photocopier cards, and are taking the Preacher gospel to the information superhighway. The following list of MSP websites (with descriptions where available) is probably far from comprehensive, but it is the nearest thing to a complete directory that I could assemble at the time of going to press.

MANIC STREET PREACHERS OFFICIAL WEBSITE
http://www.manics.co.uk

MANIC STREET PREACHERS HOMEPAGE (UNOFFICIAL)
http://www.tmtm.com/manics/

ANOTHER INVENTED DISEASE
http://www.devt.demon.co.uk/manics/manics.html
Album lyrics, some articles and favourite song poll

ARCHIVES OF PAIN
http://www.frame.net/phase2/manic
Chat site for MSP fans

ASSORTED MANICS PRESS CUTTINGS
http://www.tmtm.com/manics/articles

DREAM MUSIC SEARCH ENGINE
http://www.dreammusic.com/artists/m/manic.htm

HOUSE OF MANIC STREET PREACHERS
http://www.geocities.com.sunset strip/9188/
Real audio clips of several tracks from each album

LORRAINE'S MANIC STREET PREACHERS PAGE
http://www.geocities.com/soho/5317/manics.html

MANICS LYRICS AND RELATED ITEMS
http://www1.tip.nl/-t892660/msp/msphome.htm

MANIC STREET PREACHING
http://www.erack.com/select/headliners/manic/manicsfront.htm
Manics history in Select On-Line (whatever that means)

MANICS WEB LINKS
http://www.pubcrawler.demon.co.uk/maniclnk.html

PATRICK JONES HOMEPAGE
http://freespace.virgin.net/r.coombes/p-main.htm

PHOTO GALLERY
http://www.nol.net/-dfx/manics.html
100 + photos (concerts, promo videos, TV etc.)

PICTURE OF NICKY HALF-NAKED
http://www.chat.ru/-cariad/manics.html

THE PUB CRAWLER'S DOMAIN
http://www.pubcrawler.demon.co.uk
Mainly, but not exclusively, Manics-related, with music and an image gallery

RICHEY BY RED
http://www.fringeware.com/hell/daly/richeybyred.html

SEAN FAN CLUB
http://www.geocities.com/sunsetstrip/lounge/9134/geobook.html

STU & DAN'S MANIC STREET PREACHERS PAGE
http://www.geocities.com/SunsetStrip/1597/msp.html
Useful links, plus news and a live review

TONY'S MANIC STREET PREACHERS PAGE
http://www.tmtm.com.manics/
Discography, lyrics, and many press articles

ULTIMATE BANDLIST – MANIC STREET PREACHERS
http://www.ubl.com.artists/002857.html
Artist update, clips/media, discography, biography, bulletin board, tour dates, photos, e-mail, lyrics, reviews

WE HER MAJESTY'S PRISONERS
http://www.win.or.jp/-sid10299/music/manics/whmp.html

Further MSP addresses (untitled):
http://www.westnet.com/consumable/1995/March27.1995/intmanic.html
http://www.tmtm.com/manics/articles/indecent.html
http://www.tmtm.com/manics/faq.txt

MANIC KARAOKE
Over the last decade, the Manics have performed more cover versions than the average cruise-liner showband. Here they are in full:
Bright Eyes – Art Garfunkel
Can't Take My Eyes Off You – Andy Williams
Charles Windsor – McCarthy
Damn Dog – Robin Johnson/The Sleez Sisters
The Drowners – Suede
God Save The Queen – Sex Pistols
It's So Easy – Guns N'Roses
Just Like Honey – The Jesus and Mary Chain
Last Christmas – Wham!
Penny Royaltea – Nirvana
Raindrops Keep Falling on My Head – Burt Bacharach
Stay With Me – The Faces

Take the Skinheads Bowling – Camper Van Beethoven
Teenage Kicks – The Undertones
Theme from M*A*S*H (Suicide is Painless) – Johnny Mandel/The Mash
Under My Wheels – Alice Cooper
Velocity Girl – Primal Scream
What's My Name – The Clash
Wrote for Luck – Happy Mondays

BITS AND PIECES . . .
Baby Love – The Supremes (James usually sings as intro to Motown Junk live).
Glory Glory Hallelujah – Elvis Presley (intro to Black Garden).
Hen Wlad Fy Nhadu – National Anthem, Wales (occasionally incorporated into Repeat live).
Lost in the Supermarket – The Clash (medley with Enola/Alone on Mark Radcliffe show, Radio 1).
Lust for Life – Iggy Pop (sampled as outro to Heavenly version of You Love Us, sometimes re-created by MSP live).
Safe European Home – The Clash (sometimes incorporated into ending of Enola/Alone live).
The Stars and Stripes – National Anthem, USA (intro to Patrick Bateman, occasionally incorporated into Repeat live).
Sweet Home Alabama – Lynyrd Skynyrd (incorporated into Motown Junk intro, December 1998 tour).
Waterfall – The Stone Roses (intro played before Motorcycle Emptiness, Manchester 1996).

. . . AND NEAR MISSES
Appetite for Destruction – Guns 'N' Roses (entire album practised by James Dean Bradfield in living-room).
Bye Bye Baby – Bay City Rollers (considered for Ruby Trax compilation).
Exile On Main Street – The Rolling Stones (entire album practised by James Dean Bradfield in living-room).
Fight the Power – Public Enemy (considered for *Generation Terrorists*).
Garageland – The Clash (busked by Bradfield and Wire in Cardiff arcades).
Geno – Dexys Midnight Runners (considered for Ruby Trax compilation).
Public Image – PiL (rehearsed for 1994 Therapy tour, but never actually performed).
School's Out – Alice Cooper (considered for Ruby Trax compilation).
Your Daughter is One – Robin Johnson (from the Times Square soundtrack, originally considered for *Generation Terrorists* but proved too difficult to learn. Dumped in favour of the simpler Damn Dog).

MISSING IN ACTION – Great Lost Manics Songs
Just about every song the Manics have ever written has eventually turned up somewhere or other, whether in demo form, on a bootleg, on a B-side, or with a different name. The following, though, remain AWOL – if they ever existed in the first place.

Anti-Social – vanished schoolboy number.

Colt 45 Rusty James – *Rumblefish*-inspired early track.

Doors Slowly Closing – the only publicly disclosed title of a lyric left behind by Richey in 1995 (described by Wire as 'total Ian Curtis').

Jackboot Johnny – James Dean Bradfield-penned anti-Nazi number from late 80s.

Third Time Love – sighting on European bootleg, Street Preaching, *circa* 1992, remains unconfirmed.

The Nazification of Happiness – Richey said that he had written this in 1992, but inexplicably it never surfaced.

The Hairdresser's Chair – another abortive attempt at lyric writing from James Dean Bradfield in the run-up to *Everything Must Go*.

Anniversary to Death – apparently a very morbid and apocalyptic Wire lyric which failed to make it on to *This Is My Truth Tell Me Yours*.

Alien Orders/Invisible Armies – inspired by a *Marvel* comic, started during summer of 1992 and intended for *Gold Against The Soul*, but never finished.

INDEX